"In a world become 'game-ified' aga provides the field manual for the or of history."

– McKenzie Wark, author of *The Beach Beneath*

CW00555524

"Richard Barbrook's approach to the Situationist International is so left field, he leaves virtually every other author addressing the subject looking like a dull academic plodder. Were he still alive, Barbrook's fellow iconoclast Guy Debord would heartily approve of such unacceptable theory."

– Stewart Home, avant-garde pornographer and Paul Hamlyn Foundation prize winner

"Richard Barbrook's book is a jubilant manifesto for ludic art and revolution – each in service of the other – for a participatory future. By bringing Situationist disciplines into a contemporary context, he shows how thinkers, gamers, artists, hackers and educators can resist assimilation, and their creative endeavours escape perversion, by the deadly, dominating forces of neoliberalism."

– Ruth Catlow, co-founder of Furtherfield and creator of *Rethinking Wargames*

"Like H.G. Wells, Guy Debord saw wargames as a valuable means of ludic subversion of established societal and military hierarchies. In this impressively eclectic and erudite book, Richard Barbrook explains with infectious enthusiasm how he and his group have striven to use ludic ideas to inspire and inform a new generation of radicals."

– Philip Sabin, Professor of Strategic Studies at King's College London and author of *Simulating War*

To Thiago
— the skilful general of
the 2009 battle of Rio!

CLASS
WARGAMES

LUDIC SUBVERSION AGAINST
SPECTACULAR CAPITALISM

Richard Barbrook

classwargames.net

Class Wargames: ludic subversion against spectacular capitalism
℗ Richard Barbrook

ISBN 978-1-57027-293-6

Designed by David S. and Anne L. Blanco
Cover image: *Toussaint L'Ouverture at Bedourete* © Kimathi Donkor (2004)
www.kimathidonkor.net

Released by Minor Compositions 2014
Wivenhoe / New York / Port Watson

Minor Compositions is a series of interventions & provocations drawing from
autonomous politics, avant-garde aesthetics, and the revolutions of everyday life.

Minor Compositions is an imprint of Autonomedia
www.minorcompositions.info | minorcompositions@gmail.com

Distributed by Autonomedia
PO Box 568 Williamsburgh Station
Brooklyn, NY 11211

www.autonomedia.org
info@autonomedia.org

DEDICATED TO

ELENA MIKHAILOVNA DUFFIELD
(NÉE VORONTSOVA)

1975–2012

COMRADE, CLASS WARGAMER & FRIEND

'While you live, shine
Don't suffer anything at all;
Life exists only a short while
And time demands its toll.'
– Seikilos

'Spectacular domination's first priority is to eradicate historical knowledge in general; beginning with just about all rational information and commentary about the most recent past. With consummate skill, the spectacle organises ignorance of what is about to happen and, immediately afterwards, the forgetting of what has nonetheless been understood. History's domain is the memorable, the totality of events whose consequences will be lastingly apparent. As thus, inseparably, history is knowledge that should endure and aid in understanding, at least in part, what is to come. In this way, history is the *measure* of genuine novelty.'

– Guy Debord
  Comments on the Society of the Spectacle

RESPECT DUE

Arty Barbrook-Black; Adeline Mannarini; Alan Freeman; Alastair Brotchie; Ale Freire; Alessandro Vincentelli; Alex Auld; Alex Galloway; Alexander Nikolic; Alexandra Poblinkowa; Alexei Blinov; Alexei Monroe; Alexei Tsvetcoff; Ali Tajvidi; Andriy Linik; Andy Cameron; Angelina Davydova; Anna Kolodziejska; Anne Blanco; Andrew Burgin; Anton Lukinskij; Armin Medosch; Ben Carmedy; Ben Vanovitch; Billy Cass; Brian Train; Bridget Cotter; Caterina Carta; Clare Solomon; Claus Voigtmann; Christian Nold; Clive Adams; Corrado Morgana; Dan Judelson; Daniel Hinchcliffe; Dave Douglass; Dave Green; David Blanco; David Bovill; Dibyesh Anand; Dick Pountain; Djahjah Bonorandi; Dmitry Golynko; Dominic Wells; Don Nicholson-Smith; Drica Veloso; Eva Pascoe; Farhang Morady; Frands Pedersen; Frank Boyd; Fred Turner; Fred Vermorel; Gill Woodward; Harry Pearson; Helen Barbrook; Henry Hyde; Hicham Khalidi; Hubert Czerepok; Ian Bone; Inke Arns; Isis Salvaterra; Jacqueline de Jong; James Moulding; Jane Pavitt; Joel Bauman; John Barker; John McDonnell; John Rees; John Wyver; Jonathan Duffield; Kateryna Onyiliogwu; Keith Franklin; Ken Wark; Kimathi Donkor; Lara Blazic; Lewis Sykes; Lisa Devaney; Lisa Vanovitch; Lyubov Bejkatskaya; Malcolm Hopkins; Malcolm Imrie; Marc Garrett; Marina Koldobskaya; Marta Kubik; Martin Housden; Mary Flanagan; Mel Franklin; Michael Kalivoda; Michèle Bernstein; Nik Gorecki; Niki Gomez; Olena Linik; Paolo Gerbaudo; Paul Gilroy; Pat McMath; Patrick Burke; Phil Sabin; Pil & Galia Kollectiv; Radhika Desai; Ray Holiday; Ricardo Blaug; Richard Parry; Richard Thomas; Rob Lucas; Rob McMaster; Robin Halpin; Russell King; Ruth Catlow; Sam Cooper; Simona Lodi; Sofia Korzova; Sophia Drakopoulou; Stevphen Shukaitis; Stewart Home; Suzy Robson; Tara Woodyer; Thiago Novaes; Tom Campbell; Tom Moore; Tom Vague; Tuesday Greenidge; Ursula Huws; Vladimir Rudykh; Wessel van Rensburg; Autonomedia; BOEM; *Chto Delat?*; Cybersalon; Cyland; *End Notes*; FleaPit; Firebox; Furtherfield Gallery; Housmans Bookshop; KCC & the Rocking Crew; LRC; Media Ecology Association; Midia Tática Brasil; NCCA; nettime; Pussy Riot; Raylab; Resonance FM; Theory & Practice; Toi-Toi; UCU; and *Weekly Worker*.

CONTENTS

ILLUSTRATIONS

Xenographs by Alex Veness

Inside Cover: María Mencía with Class Wargames at *Cold War Modern* in the Victoria & Albert Museum, London, England, on 31st October 2008.

Frontispiece: Richard Barbrook and Ilze Black playing *The Game of War* at Alex Veness' Bankside flat in London, England, on 28th October 2008.

Chapter 1: Richard Barbrook and Malcolm McLaren with Class Wargames at the *Wunderbar Festival* in the Baltic Centre for Contemporary Art, Gateshead, England, on 14th November 2009.

Chapter 2: Stefan Lutschinger and Danilo Mandic with Class Wargames at *What Is To Be Done? The Urgent Need to Struggle* in the ICA, London, England, on 13th October 2010.

Chapter 3: Ilze Black, Lucy Blake and Stefan Lutschinger with Class Wargames at *Cold War Modern* in the Victoria & Albert Museum, London, England, on 31st October 2008.

Bibliography: Fabian Tompsett, Mark Copplestone and Richard Barbrook with Class Wargames at *Cyberfest 2008* in the State Hermitage Museum, St. Petersburg, Russia, on 27th November 2008.

Index: Alex Veness with the Xenon-Eye scanner camera at Occupation Studios, London, England, on 14th March 2014.

Diagrams

XENON-EYE BY ALEX VENESS

Xenon-Eye is a hybrid camera constructed by Class Wargames co-founder, Alex Veness, combining a hacked digital scanner (to become a photographic plate) and a Victorian camera.

Xenon is a gas, rare in nature, but easily synthesised, whose name derives from ancient Greek, meaning 'strange' or 'peculiar'. Xenon gas creates brilliant, white light in all digital scanners' built-in lamps. In everyday use, these lamps light streams of documents placed on scanners' un-illuminated glass beds.

During its hack from document-reader to camera-plate, Alex Veness stripped a xenon lamp from an everyday scanner and re-named it *Xenon-Eye*. Fitted to a camera-back, *Xenon-Eye* can see lens-based images only because its bright xenon lamp is absent, otherwise it would blind its own scanner-head, instead of recording images projected by its camera's antique lens. Nevertheless, the scanner's lost xenon lamp lives on under the camera's new name.

Employing customised software to override the scanner's alarm at its severe hacking, and to make it a stable, functioning camera-plate, Alex Veness has used *Xenon-Eye* to document Class Wargames' public events since 2007, especially the playing of Guy Debord's *The Game of War* at national and international venues.

Xenon-Eye's lack of empathy, its predilection for representing humans as unnatural grotesques, can be understood as a parodic visual aesthetic for neoliberalism. As awareness grows of unchecked markets' indifference to human welfare, these images come to define the individual's true identity within the presiding system's logic: distorted, extruded and forced into unbearable forms. Far from showing people 'as they really are', *Xenon-Eye* shows them 'as they really exist': unwilling actors within the current socio-economic logic.

When the disillusioned majority finally throw off the shackles of spectacular capitalism, there will be no use for *Xenon-Eye*, and it will be ritually destroyed. Until that time, it will continue to record the colourless, painful distortions suffered by citizen-players, unwillingly forced to endure the intolerable indeterminacy of free markets and the distressing brutality of economic liberalism for the benefit of a tiny, super-wealthy elite; an increasingly despised bankocracy.

¡Hasta la victoria, siempre!

CLASS WARGAMES PLAYERS

Richard Barbrook – University of Westminster
Ilze Black – Queen Mary, University of London
Lucy Blake – Software Developer
Mark Copplestone – Copplestone Castings
Rod Dickinson – University of the West of England
Elena Vorontsova Duffield – WRN Broadcast
Stefan Lutschinger – Middlesex University
Fabian Tompsett – London Psychogeographical Association
Alex Veness – University of the Arts London

Class Wargames

- puts on participatory performances of Guy Debord's *The Game of War* and other subversive politico-military games;
- investigates gaming as a metaphor for social relations under repressive neoliberalism;
- celebrates the craft skills of gamers as artistic expression;
- creates a social space where lefties can meet & play with each other;
- re-enacts the proletarian struggles of the past in ludic form;
- trains the militants of the cybernetic communist revolution to come.

CLASS WARGAMES ON CAMPAIGN 2007–2013

Exhibitions

The Institute of Psychoplasmics, Pump House Gallery, Battersea Park, London, England, 9ᵗʰ April–26ᵗʰ May 2008.

Class Wargames – 'The Game of War', HTTP Gallery, London, England, 26ᵗʰ September–20ᵗʰ October 2009.

Class Wargames Presents Guy Debord's 'The Game of War', Institute of Contemporary Interactive Art, University of Bath, Bath, England, 19ᵗʰ January–26ᵗʰ February 2011.

Tomorrow Never Dies – European Cultural Congress, Design Gallery, Wroclaw, Poland, 8ᵗʰ–11ᵗʰ September 2011.

Games People Play, Centre for Contemporary Art and the Natural World, Haldon Forest Park, Exeter, England, 6ᵗʰ April–30ᵗʰ September 2012.

Invisible Forces, Furtherfield Gallery, McKenzie Pavilion, Finsbury Park, London, England, 16ᵗʰ June–11ᵗʰ August 2012.

Performances

23ʳᵈ October 2007 – *London Games Festival Fringe*, 01zero-one, London, England.

19ᵗʰ April 2008 – *Salute '08*, Excel Centre, London, England.

26ᵗʰ April 2008 – *The Institute of Psychoplasmics*, Pump House Gallery, London, England.

10ᵗʰ May 2008 – *1968 & All That*, Conway Hall, London, England.

31ˢᵗ October 2008 – *Cold War Modern*, Victoria & Albert Museum, London, England.

27th November 2008 – *Cyberfest 2008*, State Hermitage Museum, St. Petersburg, Russia.

20th April 2009 – *Guy Debord's 'The Game of War'*, Universidade Federal do Rio de Janeiro, Rio de Janeiro, Brazil.

29th April 2009 – *Guy Debord's 'The Game of War'*, Café com Letras, Belo Horizonte, Brazil.

25th July 2009 – *Guy Debord's 'The Game of War'*, Plan 9, Bristol, England.

26th–27th September 2009 – *Guy Debord's 'The Game of War'*, HTTP Gallery, London, England.

10th October 2009 – *Crash/Crush Festival 2009*, Bed Elze Gallery, The Hague, Netherlands.

27th October 2009 – *Guy Debord's 'The Game of War'*, Department of Media & Communications, University of Middlesex, London, England.

8th November 2009 – *Market Forces: Share International Festival of Arts and Digital Culture*, Turin, Italy.

14th November 2009 – *Wunderbar Festival*, Baltic Centre for Contemporary Art, Gateshead, England.

14th November 2009 – *Guy Debord's 'The Game of War'*, Estonian Academy of Arts, Tallinn, Estonia.

28th November 2009 – *Guy Debord's 'The Game of War'*, Yugoslav Workers' Club, Lokativ, Vienna, Austria.

19th December 2009 – *Resonance FM's Media Playground*, The Foundry, London, England.

27th January 2010 – *Guy Debord's 'The Game of War'*, Housmans Bookshop, London, England.

7th February 2010 – *Transmediale 10*, Haus der Kulturen der Welt, Berlin, Germany.

16th February 2010 – *Class Wargames Presents Guy Debord's 'The Game of War'*, Centre for the Study of Democracy, University of Westminster, London, England.

7th March 2010 – *Gender & Politics Free School*, London Free School, London, England.

21st March 2010 – *Skill Share Bazaars of Haringey*, Tottenham Chances, London, England.

14th May 2010 – *Birkbeck Debord Reading Group*, Birkbeck College, London, England.

30th July 2010 – *Parque del Sol 10*, St. Pölten, Austria.

18th September 2010 – *H.G. Wells Festival*, Folkestone, England.

13th October 2010 – *What Is To Be Done? The Urgent Need to Struggle*, ICA, London, England.

28th November 2010 – *The Futurological Congress*, Center for the History of East Central Europe, Lviv, Ukraine.

9th January 2011 – *Artists' Talk and 'The Game of War' Participatory Performance*, Institute of Contemporary Interactive Art, Bath, England.

26th February 2011 – *Participatory Re-performance of H.G. Wells' 'Little Wars'*, Institute of Contemporary Interactive Art, Bath, England.

19th June 2011 – *Virtual Futures 2.0*, University of Warwick, Coventry, England.

25th June 2011 – *Guy Debord's 'The Game of War' meets Vasily Chapayev*, Vse Svobodny Bookstore and Literary Club, St. Petersburg, Russia.

2nd July 2011 – *Guy Debord's 'The Game of War' meets Takako Saito's 'Liquor Chess'*, Tsiolkovsky Bookstore, State Polytechnical Museum, Moscow, Russia.

27th July 2011 – *Guy Debord's 'The Game of War' meets 'Chapayev and Void'*, Galereya Revolutsija, Irkutsk, Russia.

24th August 2011 – *Guy Debord's 'The Game of War' meets McKenzie Wark's 'Beach Beneath the Street'*, Housmans Bookshop, London, England.

2nd December 2011 – *Guy Debord's 'The Game of War' meets Takako Saito's 'Liquor Chess'*, Raylab, London, England.

8th–9th June 2012 – *Guy Debord's 'The Game of War'*, Live-Art-Festival: Postspectaculism, Hamburg, Germany.

23rd June 2012 – *Class Wargames Picnic & Subversion: Guy Debord's 'The Game of War'*, Furtherfield Gallery, London, England.

30th June 2012 – *Class Wargames Picnic & Subversion: 1791 Haitian Revolution version of Richard Borg's 'Commands & Colors: Napoleonics'*, Furtherfield Gallery, London, England.

18th August 2012 – *Guy Debord's 'The Game of War'*, Centre for Contemporary Art and the Natural World, Exeter, England.

19th August 2012 – *H.G. Wells' 'Little Wars'*, Centre for Contemporary Art and the Natural World, Exeter, England.

28th October 2012 – *Guy Debord's 'The Game of War'*, Housmans Bookshop, London, England.

31st October 2012 – *1791 Haitian Revolution version of Richard Borg's 'Commands & Colors: Napoleonics'*, Housmans Bookshop, London, England.

12th December 2012 – *Guy Debord's 'The Game of War'*, Housmans Bookshop, London, England.

24th March 2013 – *Guy Debord's 'The Game of War'*, Cowley Club, Brighton, England.

13th April 2013 – *The Life & Legacy of C.L.R. James*, WEA London Region, London, England.

23rd April 2013 – *Playgrounds of Insubordination*, Leipzig Centre for the History and Culture of East-Central Europe, University of Leipzig, Leipzig, Germany.

30th November 2013 – *Spielsalon 2013*, Kunsthalle Fredericianum, Kassel, Germany.

Class Wargames also hosted the *Ludic Science Club* at the FleaPit, London, England, in 2008–2009; and at Firebox, London, England, in 2013.

GAMES PLAYED ON CAMPAIGN 2007–2013

GUY DEBORD, THE GAME OF WAR (1977)

Historical Period
18th and 19th century Horse-and-Musket warfare.

Protagonists
The players are divided into two teams of North or South.

Pieces
The armies of North and South are both made up of the same number of pieces: 9 infantry, 4 cavalry, 1 foot artillery, 1 horse artillery, 1 marching general and 1 mounted general. Each unit occupies one square and no stacking is allowed.

Board
The board is a 20 by 25 grid of 500 squares divided down the middle along its longest side. The North and South halves of the board are distinguished by the asymmetrical locations of their common geographical features: 2 arsenals, 3 fortresses and a mountain range broken by a pass.

Movement
Taking alternative turns, the players of North and South can move up to 5 pieces of their armies on each go. Troops on horseback move two squares while those on foot move one square. Pieces can move both orthogonally and diagonally. Mountain squares are impassable.

Combat
Each side is allowed to initiate one combat per turn. Infantry and artillery units are stronger in defence than attack. Cavalry pieces can charge the enemy which makes them stronger in attack than defence. Fortresses and passes give extra strength to their defenders and prevent the enemy's cavalry charging. The outcome of combat is resolved by calculating the total points of the various units on both sides which can bring their combined strength to bear on the square under dispute.

If the defence is equal or stronger than the attack, this side wins. If the attack is one point stronger than the defence, the enemy unit has to retreat on its next turn or be eliminated. If it is two or more points stronger, then the defending piece is immediately removed from the board.

Other Factors

Infantry, cavalry and artillery pieces can only move and fight if they are in direct or indirect contact with at least one of the two arsenals on their side of the board. These lines of communications radiate outwards either orthogonally or diagonally from the arsenals. The two generals can provide relay links for the supply route connecting a piece to its arsenal. Any unit which is attacked while out of contact with an arsenal is automatically destroyed.

Victory Conditions

The progress of the game is focused upon the North and the South's attempts to outmanoeuvre each other's army with the aim of breaking its lines of communications to its two arsenals. When a player occupies an enemy arsenal, they can only destroy it with their one allotted combat in the next move. Final victory is secured when one side captures both of its opponent's arsenals.

Further Information

The full set of rules for *The Game of War* can be found in Alice Becker-Ho and Guy Debord's eponymous book and on the Class Wargames website.

CHRIS PEERS, REDS VERSUS REDS (2008)

Historical Period

1917–1921 Russian Civil War.

Protagonists

The players are divided into two teams of Bolsheviks or Social Democrats.

Pieces

Both sides' armies are made up of 28mm Russian Civil War figurines from Copplestone Castings' *Back of Beyond* series. The Bolshevik army consists of 40 Kronstadt sailors, 40 regular soldiers, 1 Lewis machine-gun team, 1 Maxim gun team, 2 commissars and Leon Trotsky. The Social Democratic army consists of 40 Czechoslovak Legionnaires, 40 peasant militiamen, 1 Maxim gun team, 1 field artillery piece and a general.

Board

The terrain is constructed out of 28mm scale buildings, walls and trees which represent a village and its outskirts on the approach to Kazan in Tatarstan, Russia.

Movement

The Bolsheviks and Social Democrats move one unit alternately until they both have completed this part of the turn. The two armies can activate as many as their units as they want on each go. Infantry figurines and the Lewis machine-gun team move two 1-to-6 dice throws x 6 inches (15 cm) in open terrain and one dice throw x 6 inches (15 cm) within the village. The Maxim gun team and the artillery piece move one dice throw x 6 inches (15 cm) in open terrain with penalties for moving within the village.

Combat

After all movement is completed, the two armies can engage in combat. Both ranged firing and hand-to-hand fighting are decided by throwing 1-to-6 dice. Infantry with rifles and machine guns get bonuses if the enemy figurines are in close order and penalties if they're at long range, stationary for that turn and/or behind cover. The Social Democrats' artillery piece is aimed by this player guessing the coordinates of the target on the terrain. Riflemen and the artillery piece throw one dice, the Lewis machine-gun team get three dice and the Maxim gun team has six dice. One enemy figurine is removed if the final score is 4, 5 or 6. Hand-to-hand fighting is resolved in a similar manner with the soldiers on each side throwing 1-to-6 dice with bonuses for overwhelming odds and/or penalties for attacking someone in cover. If the final score is two or more than the opponent's, the enemy figurine is killed and removed from the game.

Other Factors
Any unit which suffers significant casualties must test its morale. If it throws a 1-to-6 dice score less than its designated morale rating, the unit is routed and flees off the board. The Kronstadt sailors and the Czechoslovak Legionnaires have a higher morale rating than regular troops and peasant militiamen.

Bolshevik units can only move and fight if they are no further than 24 inches (60 cm) from Leon Trotsky.

Leon Trotsky and the Bolshevik commissars can prevent a unit on their side from routing by shooting one of its soldiers.

The Czechoslovak Legion will withdraw from the board if one or more Bolshevik units reach the middle of the village.

Victory Conditions
The Bolsheviks win the game if they drive all of the Social Democrat units out of the village. The Social Democrats win if they don't.

The Bolsheviks immediately lose the game if Leon Trotsky is killed.

Further Information
The full set of rules for *Reds versus Reds* is available on the Class Wargames website.

RICHARD BORG, COMMANDS & COLORS: NAPOLEONICS (2010)

Historical Period
1792–1815 Revolutionary and Napoleonic wars.

Protagonists
In our 1802 battle of Fort Bedourete scenario, the players are divided into two teams of Haitian Jacobins or French Bonapartists.

Pieces

The Haitian Jacobin army consists of 2 veteran infantry units, 5 regular infantry units, 3 militia units, 1 Parisian sans-culotte riflemen unit, 1 heavy cavalry unit, 2 light cavalry units, 1 foot artillery unit, Jean-Jacques Dessalines, Henri Christophe and Toussaint L'Ouverture. The French Bonapartist army consists of 2 French light infantry units, 5 French line infantry units, 3 colonial infantry units, 1 colonial cavalry unit, 2 French foot artillery units, 2 generals and Charles Leclerc. Each unit occupies one hex and no stacking is allowed except for generals.

Board

The board is a 13 by 9 grid of 97 hexes which represents Fort Bedourete and its immediate environs. The bastion is made up of 3 hexes on a hill in the centre of the board with a village hex to its west and a river running north to south to its east. There are wood and hill hexes along both sides of the river bank. There are also forest hexes scattered across the northern and southern edges of the board.

Movement

The two armies take alternate turns. Each side is dealt 6 command cards from the pack provided with the game which are used to activate their units on the board and/or implement special actions. When a card is played, a new one is picked up. Units can only fight and move when activated by a command card except for Toussaint and the unit accompanying him. Each of the different types of infantry, cavalry and artillery units is able to move in any direction up to the number of hexes designated in the game's army charts. Units must finish their move as soon as they enter a river, forest, fortification or village hex.

Combat

Both ranged fire and hand-to-hand combat are decided by throwing the special dice provided with the game. The number of dice thrown and their effects are determined by the type and quality of the units involved, firing range, the terrain of the hex and card bonuses. Depending upon the results of these dice throws, units can either lose one or more of their constituent blocks and/or be forced to retreat. Infantry can form squares to defend themselves against cavalry, but their side will temporarily be deprived of one command card until they come out of this formation. The presence of a general and/or nearby units will negate the effects of a dice throw forcing a retreat.

Other Factors
If in the same hex at any point during his move, Toussaint can activate one Haitian unit on every turn without needing a command card. This unit can only move when accompanied by Toussaint.

If Toussaint is in an adjacent hex to a French colonial militia unit, the Haitian player may throw one dice to persuade it to defect and join the cause of national liberation.

Victory Conditions
Each army needs 6 flags to win the game. One flag is gained for each destroyed enemy unit and for the sole occupation of the hexes which make up Fort Bedourete.

The Haitians immediately lose the game if Toussaint is either killed or captured.

Further Information
The full set of rules is contained in GMT Games' *Commands & Colors: Napoleonics*. The opening positions and special rules for the 1802 battle of Fort Bedourete scenario are available from the Class Wargames website.

H.G. WELLS, LITTLE WARS (1913)

Historical Period
Early-20th century industrialised warfare.

Protagonists
The players are divided into two sides representing armies of the major powers just before the outbreak of the First World War in 1914.

Pieces

Both sides' armies are made up of 54mm Britains' toy soldiers and cannon. Other manufacturers' products can be used if they look like they might have been owned by Wells' children. Each player's army consists of 50 infantry figurines, 25 cavalry figurines and 3 artillery pieces.

Board

The terrain is constructed out of wooden block buildings, twigs representing trees and square wooden boards of different sizes for the hills.

Movement

Taking turns, each side can activate all or some of its figurines on its go. Infantry can move up to 12 inches (30 cm) and cavalry can move up to 24 inches (60 cm). Artillery pieces can only move if they're accompanied by at least four figurines. Depending upon the type of their crew, they will move at either infantry or cavalry speed. Artillery pieces cannot move and fire on the same turn.

Combat

Hand-to-hand combat is decided by comparing the number of figurines on each side in the melee. If they are equal, all of the soldiers on both sides are killed. The superior side takes prisoners of the numerical difference between the two sides if its opponent's troops are too far away from the other soldiers of their army. The rest of this combat is resolved by removing equal numbers of figurines from both sides until the inferior side is eliminated.

As long as they're accompanied by four or more figurines, artillery pieces can fire up to four matchsticks on each move. If a matchstick directly or indirectly hits an enemy soldier, it is immediately removed from the game.

Other Factors

The length of each player's move is determined by the size of their army. They are allocated one minute for each group of 30 or less figurines and one minute for each artillery piece. As their army suffers casualties, the length of their move will diminish in proportion to its reduction in size. As soon as their allotted time is over, players must immediately stop moving their army, engaging in hand-to-hand combat or firing artillery pieces.

Victory Conditions

The winner of the game is the player who kills all of the toy soldiers in the other side's army first.

Further Information

The full set of rules for *Little Wars* is available in Wells' eponymous book and on the Class Wargames website.

1.0: THE ART OF WAR

'The [Situationist] game is the spontaneous way [that] everyday life enriches and develops itself; the game is the conscious form of the supersession of spectacular art and politics. It is participation, communication and self-realisation resurrected … It is the means and the end of total revolution.'

The English Section of the Situationist International, *The Revolution of Modern Art and the Art of Modern Revolution*, page 21.

1.1: PLAYING WITH PASSION

On Saturday 26th April 2008, in the Pump House gallery of London's Battersea Park, I found myself facing Fabian Tompsett across the board of Guy Debord's *The Game of War*. Agreeing that I would play South and he would be North, we began by secretly writing down the deployment of our pieces on this simulated battlefield. As shown in **Diagram 1** on page 110, the starting positions of these two rival armies diagonally mirrored each other. The South's troops were concentrated on the east of the board while the North's soldiers were grouped in front of its western arsenal. Winning the dice throw to decide who'd go first, Fabian made the opening move and I quickly responded with mine. For this match at the Pump House gallery, we'd both decided to adopt Napoléon Bonaparte's winning strategy in the 1797 Italian campaign. Our main force would keep the enemy's army pinned down in the centre while an outflanking cavalry attack – like that of the French raid led by Charles Dugua against the Austrian supply base at Trieste – would seize his undefended arsenal.[1] As turn followed turn, Fabian and I soon got into the familiar rhythm of Debord's game. We no longer had to consult the rules to know what we should be doing. We didn't need a timer to hasten our decisions. Thanks to our teenage obsession with wargames, we were both endowed with an instinctive ability to manoeuvre our miniature armies to the maximum advantage over the board.

Within a half-dozen moves, the South's western arsenal was no more and I was on the verge of taking the North's eastern bastion. The contest at this point must have seemed equally balanced to most of the audience at the Pump House gallery, yet I knew that I was already losing the game. Foolishly, like the Prussian generals fighting Bonaparte in 1806, I'd let my troops in the centre become separated from each other. After one of its infantry pieces was taken in a skirmish on the open terrain between the two mountain ranges, my army was soon in rapid retreat to a more secure position as I desperately tried to avoid a

---

[1]   See Emmanuel de Las Cases, *Mémorial de Sainte-Hélène*, pages 285–286; and David Chandler, *The Campaigns of Napoleon*, pages 122–125.

repetition of the Duke of Brunswick's humiliation at Jena-Auerstädt.[2] I'd lost the initiative on the battlefield and was fumbling for a response. Once again, Fabian had the psychological advantage over me. Only a week earlier at the *Salute '08* wargames convention, he had trounced me twice in quick succession. During the year that we'd been playing *The Game of War*, no one from our crew had been able to surpass him. Fabian was the master of the cunning attack and the impregnable defence. Above all, he understood how to intimidate his opponents into believing that they'd lost the game. For those in the know, the outcome of this match was preordained. At the Pump House gallery, I'd met my Waterloo.

Then, suddenly, the impossible happened: Fabian made the fatal error of leaving his mounted general unprotected. Seizing the moment, I inflicted the blow which would clinch the game by launching a cavalry charge to take this vital piece. As with Joachim Murat's division at the battle of Eylau in 1807, my brave warriors paid a high price for their audacity, but their sacrifice wasn't in vain.[3] Fabian had become Bonaparte in the 1812 Russian campaign. Deprived of the supply lines provided by its most mobile general, the strength of his army slowly dissipated with each move that it made towards the Moscow of my eastern arsenal.[4] For almost an hour, Fabian tried everything to retrieve the situation. Like Bonaparte facing the combined might of aristocratic Europe in 1814, he used all of his tactical cunning to delay the strategically inevitable.[5] But, at last, the decisive moment came: my infantry and artillery made an attack that succeeded in cutting Fabian's army into two. With his forces helpless, he ruefully conceded the game. The emperor had been forced to abdicate his throne. Still not quite able to believe what had just happened, I raised my arms in triumph and

---

[2]   See Carl von Clausewitz, *Notes sur la Prusse dans sa Grande Catastrophe 1806*, pages 81–135; and David Chandler, *The Campaigns of Napoleon*, pages 467–497.

[3]   See David Chandler, *The Campaigns of Napoleon*, pages 535–551.

[4]   See Carl von Clausewitz, *The Campaign of 1812 in Russia*, pages 94–100; and Michael Josselson & Diana Josselson, *The Commander: a life of Barclay de Tolly*, pages 91–165.

[5]   See Carl von Clausewitz, *Campagne de 1814*; and David Chandler, *The Campaigns of Napoleon*, pages 945–1004.

exclaimed: "I've won! I've won!! I've won!!!" After so many defeats at his hands, victory over Fabian was sweet.[6]

---

[6]   Photos of this game can be seen in the Events 2008 section of the Class Wargames website.

1.2: THE EXHIBITION PIECE

When Fabian and I fought our exciting match of *The Game of War* at the Pump House gallery in 2008, Class Wargames was still a regiment of raw recruits on this simulated battlefield. Founded in the previous year, all of our members had – in their different ways – been heavily influenced by the practical innovations and theoretical insights of the Situationist International. What had initially brought us together was our curiosity about the puzzling absence of any detailed discussion of Debord's *The Game of War* in the increasing number of laudatory journalistic and academic accounts of this New Left movement's impressive achievements. For these admirers, his ludic experiment was nothing more than a poetic metaphor for Debord's pugnacious attitude to life. Serious grown-ups would never waste their valuable time actually playing this frivolous diversion. However, in his 1989 autobiography, Debord had proudly insisted that *The Game of War* was his most important legacy to the future generations: a ludic meditation on the Situationists' many years of hard fighting against the class enemy.[7] But, when we read the contemporary hagiographies of the International, we would find only the briefest mention of the long hours that he'd dedicated to designing and refining this board game. For today's hipster artists, political dissidents and radical intellectuals, discovering that their Situationist hero was a nerdy male wargamer was an embarrassment which had to be passed over as quickly as possible.[8] Unconvinced by this dubious rewriting of history, we'd formed Class Wargames to investigate why Debord had been so convinced that his military simulation was the culmination of his life's work as a cultural and political revolutionary. Our vital task would be to promulgate a new subversive wisdom: playing *The Game of War* was the prerequisite for understanding how to apply the insights of Situationism in the early-21st century.

Our 2008 event at the Pump House gallery was only Class Wargames'

---

[7]   See Guy Debord, *Panegyric*, pages 63–64.

[8]   'Even among the inadequate milieu of hobbies, wargaming ranked very low. The non-believer regarded it – at best – as the province of socially inadequate geeks, at worst of gun-toting belligerents.' Harry Pearson, *Achtung Schweinehund!*, page 98.

third public performance of Debord's greatest creation. Crucially, despite having successfully mastered the mechanics of this military simulation, we then still didn't fully comprehend the cultural and political teachings embedded within *The Game of War*. Rereading his marvellous memoir, we'd discovered that Debord believed that he'd lived his own life according to the rules of his ludic masterpiece. For one of the more perceptive chroniclers of Situationism, this intimate revelation meant that *The Game of War* was undoubtedly his '… most autobiographical work'.[9] Over the next few years, Class Wargames would come to appreciate the profoundness of this smart analysis. When the contest at the Pump House gallery had taken place in 2008, we were at the beginning of a long campaign of ludic mischief which would span three continents across the globe. Little did we then realise, Class Wargames had embarked on our own idiosyncratic recapitulation of Debord's wonderful career. As exemplified by the Pump House match, the first phase of this campaign was focused upon promoting *The Game of War* as a Situationist leftfield artwork. As we gained experience by repeatedly playing Debord's simulation, the members of our collective would soon find themselves also following his personal trajectory from cultural sabotage into communist agitation. In this second stage of our campaign of ludic subversion, Class Wargames would increasingly celebrate *The Game of War* as Debord's masterpiece of Situationist political propaganda. Inspired by his love of toy soldiers, we would also reinforce this offensive manoeuvre by playing hobbyist wargames, such as Chris Peers' *Reds versus Reds*, Richard Borg's *Commands & Colors: Napoleonics* and H.G. Wells' *Little Wars*. Every deadly weapon must be mobilised for the revolutionary cause.

By becoming hardened veterans of mock combat, Class Wargames was eventually able to move into the third phase of this campaign of ludic subversion. At our 2008 event in the Pump House gallery, we'd distributed a leaflet which confidently described *The Game of War* as a 'Clausewitz simulator' without truly realising what we were

---

9   Vincent Kaufman, *Guy Debord*, page 267. Also see Guy Debord, *Panegyric*, pages 63–64.

saying.[10] It would take four years of playing and research before Class Wargames was ready to embrace the pedagogical possibilities of Debord's enthusiasm for refighting past conflicts. By moving their model armies across a miniature terrain, the participants at our public performances of *The Game of War, Reds versus Reds, Commands & Colors: Napoleonics* and *Little Wars* were learning the military theory which would be required to secure a decisive proletarian victory on the social battlefield. Our campaign had opened with an attack of aesthetic disruption which was next followed by an audacious assault of political proselytism. For this third stage of our ludic offensive, we would now devote our energies as members of Class Wargames to disseminating the skills of revolutionary leadership amongst the masses. Every worker had to know how to defeat the capitalist enemy.

Back in 2008, when the Pump House match was being played, we'd been far from possessing these key insights into Debord's insurgent ambitions for *The Game of War*. At this point in time, promoting Situationist political propaganda and military pedagogy were the – as yet undefined – goals of future phases of our campaign of ludic subversion. Instead, on that hot summer afternoon in Battersea Park, the opening stage of this offensive against spectacular domination was dedicated to advancing boldly on the front of heterodox art. Tellingly, as soon as the contest between Fabian and I was concluded, the members of Class Wargames couldn't celebrate the success of our event over a drink in the Battersea Park café until we'd carried out one last very important task. Before the Pump House gallery opened the next morning, our facsimile of *The Game of War* had to be returned to its allotted place in Pil and Galia Kollectiv's *The Institute of Psychoplasmics* exhibition. During the six weeks of their fabulous show, its gold-and-silver board and pieces were on display alongside paintings by Seth Coston, pottery by Francis Upritchard and a video installation by Amanda Beech in an upstairs room.[11] Discerning visitors to the gallery would have instantly recognised our contribution to this show from the striking black and

---

[10]   See Class Wargames, 'Communiqué #1'. The 1965 prototype of *The Game of War* was entitled *Kriegspiel Clausewitz-Debord*. See Emmanuel Guy, 'Où l'on Fait le Portrait de Guy Debord à Travers les Livres et son *Jeu de la Guerre*', page 178.

[11]   For more about these other participants in the exhibition, see Pil and Galia Kollectiv, *The Institute of Psychoplasmics*.

white photographs of Guy Debord and Alice Becker-Ho playing *The Game of War* in his valedictory 1978 film: *In Girum Imus Nocte et Consumimur Igni*.[12] Now, for the first time, they could appreciate his ludic experiment in all of its metallic glory. Thanks to a small grant from the *London Games Festival Fringe '07*, Class Wargames had been able to build a twice-sized replica of Debord's 1977 original design for *The Game of War*. In an intense burst of co-operative labour, we'd transformed 15 kilograms of pewter – along with some aluminium, wood and screws – into an exquisite artwork. Standing at waist height, our gold-and-silver recreation of *The Game of War* glistened seductively in the summer sun inside the whitewashed ambience of the Pump House gallery. Laid out in the opening positions in their book of the game, the pieces on the board commemorated the historical moment in the Auvergne when Debord and his partner began playing this exemplary contest.[13] All that was missing were these two Situationists moving abstract shapes across a stark grid in search of victory. Within the sanctified space of *The Institute of Psychoplasmics* exhibition, playing at war had become a beautiful artwork.

Opened in 1999 during a refurbishment of Battersea Park, the Pump House gallery was the beneficiary of an ambitious lottery-funded investment in cultural institutions undertaken by the British state.[14] For most of the 20th century, public subsidies for contemporary art had been justified on moral and aesthetic grounds. Culture was a respite from economics. But, by the time that Tony Blair was elected prime minister in 1997, his New Labour government had embraced a much more utilitarian concept of art. Under neoliberal globalisation, manufacturing was irreversibly shifting from the North to the South. Like other developed countries, Britain would have to earn its living from the expanding businesses of the information society: banking, consultancy, computing and the media. According to Blair's gurus, the building of new museums, galleries and concert venues acted as a catalyst for this post-Fordist restructuring of the

---

12   See Guy Debord, *In Girum Imus Nocte et Consumimur Igni*, pages 149–150, 177, 185–186, 194; and the cover band of Alice Becker-Ho and Guy Debord, *Le Jeu de la Guerre*.

13   See Alice Becker-Ho and Guy Debord, *A Game of War*, page 39.

14   See Pump House Gallery, 'About Us'.

national economy.[15] With London as second only to New York as a marketplace for contemporary art, high culture was itself a growing· sector of employment.[16] More importantly, cities across the world were now in competition to provide an attractive environment for a new generation of entrepreneurs and workers: the 'creative class'. Educated, tolerant and mobile, they congregated in those locations which nurtured their hipster lifestyles – and the companies which wanted to employ them would inevitably follow them there.[17] For New Labour, public subsidies for art institutions provided the urban infrastructure for these burgeoning creative industries. Culture was the cutting-edge of economics.[18]

Although the initial capital investment for the Pump House gallery came from a New Labour initiative, it was the local Conservative-controlled council that had covered the costs of *The Institute of Psychoplasmics* exhibition. In early-21st century England, even parsimonious Tories were willing to spend taxpayers' money on experimental art shows. For what had once been an affront to bourgeois good taste was now a pragmatic vote-winning policy. Contemporary artists like Damien Hirst and Tracey Emin were media celebrities. The Tate Modern had become the most popular tourist venue in London. Gallery openings were reported like the launches of new films, plays or albums. Multinational corporations and banks eagerly sponsored exhibitions and bought up innovative works for their own collections. Modern art had become mainstream in Blair's Britain.[19]

Paradoxically, the popularity of looking at unique or rare objects in a gallery space was boosted by the rapid spread of computing, the Net and mobile telephony across the world. With more and more time spent

---

[15]   See Stuart Hall and Martin Jacques, *New Times*; and Geoff Mulgan, *Connexity*.

[16]   See Chris Smith, *Creative Britain*; and GLA Economics, *Creativity*.

[17]   For the manifesto of this post-industrial economic strategy, see Richard Florida, *The Rise of the Creative Class*. The antecedents of this prophecy are traced in Richard Barbrook, *The Class of the New*.

[18]   Labour's arts minister calculated that the creative industries in 1998 contributed '... almost 4 per cent of [Britain's] GDP.' Chris Smith, *Creative Britain*, page 15.

[19]   See Julian Stallabrass, *Contemporary Art*, pages 50–100; and and GLA Economics, *Creativity*.

staring at screens, visiting exhibitions offered a visceral alternative for those immersed within the virtual environment. Like fans of live music and theatre, gallery audiences savoured the pleasures of a transient and physical experience. Crucially, whether from the classroom or the media, increasing numbers of people were now knowledgeable about contemporary art. When they went to a gallery, they were able to recognise and understand what they saw there.[20] Back in the 1990s, the YBAs had achieved celebrity status first in England and then globally by mixing and matching from iconic late-20th century art movements: Abstract Expressionism, Pop, Conceptualism and Minimalism.[21] Both these artists and their admirers were determined to appropriate the aesthetic genealogy of modern sensibility. Contemporary art was the heir of a long and hallowed tradition of insurrectionary cultural movements: *the avant-garde*.

Since the early-19th century, each generation had witnessed a small group of young artists declaring war upon the conventional tastes of their elders. By adopting the avant-garde moniker from the brave soldiers who scouted the way forward for the main body of an army on campaign, these radicals proclaimed themselves as the pioneers of the future in the present.[22] Across the decades, these cliques have opened their offensive against the old order by embracing the four leitmotifs of cultural subversion: innovative aesthetics, new technologies, bohemian lifestyles and radical politics. Although initially rebuffed with hostility or indifference, these avant-garde movements had eventually triumphed over the arbiters of good taste. Fortunately, as soon as one surge of artistic insurgency had become respectable, the next cohort of young dissidents would quickly emerge to challenge

---

[20] For the steady growth in art audiences, see Mayor of London, *Cultural Strategy*, pages 72–84.

[21] YBAs was the trendy acronym for Young British Artists such as Damien Hirst, Tracey Emin, Sarah Lucas and the Chapman brothers, see Julian Stallabrass, *High Art Lite*; and Brook Adams, Lisa Jardine, Martin Maloney, Norman Rosenthal and Richard Shone, *Sensation*.

[22] The most popular training manual of 19th warfare laid down that: 'The ... advanced guard should be composed of light troops of all arms, containing some of the *élite* troops of the army as a main body, a few dragoons prepared to fight on foot, some horse artillery, pontooniers, sappers, etc. ...' Antoine-Henri de Jomini, *The Art of War*, page 264. Emphasis in original.

this new stylistic orthodoxy.[23] When the Tate Modern opened in 2000, its curators had prominently displayed a timeline of the leading 20th century avant-garde groups and their most famous members across one wall of the third floor concourse of the gallery. For the mandarins of 'Cool Britannia', the grand narrative of modern art was a history of its rebellious artists.[24]

There could be no doubt that *The Institute of Psychoplasmics* exhibition at the Pump House gallery was showcasing the recreation of a lost classic of the 20th century's cultural upheavals. By adopting a minimal aesthetic, Debord had identified *The Game of War* with an illustrious avant-garde heritage. In their simplicity, its gold-and-silver board and pieces evoked Aleksandr Rodchenko's red-and-black *Chess* set for the USSR Workers' Club at the 1925 *Exposition Internationale des Arts Décoratifs* in Paris. Even more strikingly, the forts on the South side of the board closely resembled the castles in Marcel Duchamp's *Buenos Aires Chess Set 1918–19.*[25] For the hip audience of the Pump House gallery, Debord had chosen his historical references well. In exhibitions, books and lecture halls across the world, Rodchenko and Duchamp were lauded as heroic figures who'd helped to define the new aesthetic of the machine age: Modernism. Emerging from the turbulent times of the First World War and the 1917 Russian Revolution, it was their generation of radical artists that marked the final break with the cultural shibboleths of the 19th century art establishment. Symbolism and abstraction now superseded realism and ornamentation. During the 1920s, Rodchenko and Duchamp were at the forefront of the transformation of this new style into a fully-fledged multi-media phenomenon of paintings, sculptures, readymades, poetry, novels, plays, prints, posters, music, fashion, photography, films and – last but

---

[23] See Raymond Williams, *The Politics of Modernism*, pages 31–80; and Peter Bürger, *Theory of the Avant-Garde.*

[24] See Sara Fanelli, *Tate Artist Timeline.* In the late-1990s, Cool Britannia was a briefly fashionable phrase which identified the YBAs and Britpop bands with the reforming early years of the New Labour government, see Dick Pountain and David Robins, *Cool Rules*, pages 174–5: and John Harris, *The Last Party*, pages 242–3, 325–328, 355–360.

[25] See Margarita Tupitsyn, *Rodchenko & Popova*, page 119; and Larry List, 'Chess as Art', page 136.

not least – games.[26] For both artists, creating their *Chess* sets contributed to the democratisation of the Modernist aesthetic. Symbolism and abstraction mustn't be confined to the gallery within industrial society. When *Chess* sets became mass produced Modernist artworks, every pawn could dream of being a queen.

By sampling the iconography of Rodchenko and Duchamp for *The Game of War*, Debord was doing much more than showing respect to a couple of early-20th century style gurus. At the peak of their careers, both artists had been leading figures in the two celebrated avant-garde movements that today still epitomise the emancipatory potential of the creative imagination: Constructivism and Surrealism. Many of their illustrious peers had confined their ambitions to overturning the establishment's aesthetic orthodoxy. Modernism meant making innovative work with a contemporary sensibility. However, for Rodchenko and Duchamp, this cultural rebellion was only a means to an end. Enthusiastically identifying themselves with the utopian promises of the Bolshevik leadership of the 1917 Russian Revolution, they were members of avant-garde movements dedicated to inventing new forms of expression which could spark off an all-encompassing social transformation. On the one hand, the Constructivists – like their Bauhaus comrades in Germany – applied their aesthetic skills to designing the everyday objects that would make a better world for working people. On the other hand, the Surrealists created disturbing imagery which – by tapping into the unconscious – would liberate the minds of the masses. These two avant-garde movements had adopted different artistic strategies, but they both shared the same political aspiration. By overthrowing the stifling conventions of bourgeois taste, its members hoped to endow the proletariat with the intellectual confidence to join the revolutionary Left and begin the task of building a new world. In the Constructivists' and Surrealists' avant-

---

26   See Christina Lodder, *Russian Constructivism*; and Jacqueline Chénieux-Gendron, *Surrealism*, pages 29–110.

garde interpretation, Modernism meant making cutting-edge art with a Bolshevik sensibility.[27]

Fulfilling this imperative in their *Chess* sets, Rodchenko and Duchamp had done much more than transform a humble object into a thing of beauty. For them, these artworks contributed to furthering the collective liberation of humanity. Constructivist and Surrealist *Chess* sets proved that it was the exploited – not the exploiters – who now owned the imaginary future: the promise of better times to come in the present. Like political militants of the Bolshevik party, radical artists from these avant-garde movements were opening the way forward for the main forces of the proletarian offensive against monopoly capitalism. Their vital role involved not only leading the assault against the cultural dominance of the bourgeoisie, but also inspiring the working masses with visionary imagery. Avant-garde artists were Red Guards on the aesthetic front of the class war.[28]

It is not surprising that the strong influence of Duchamp's *Buenos Aires Chess Set* can be detected in Debord's design for *The Game of War*. For dissidents growing up in 1950s France, the Surrealists epitomised the revolutionary daring of the previous generation. Radicalised by the disaster of the First World War, Duchamp and his comrades had seen their aesthetic mission as breaking the hegemony of bourgeois ideology over the general public.[29] For these avant-garde provocateurs, the subversive power of their artworks was confirmed by rejection and hostility from the defenders of tradition. Each exhibition, film show, performance or publication was a guerrilla raid into enemy territory.[30] Imitating the fierce rhetoric and ideological intensity of a Bolshevik sect, this avant-garde movement had unashamedly identified its

---

[27] See Christina Lodder, *Russian Constructivism*; Éva Forgács, *The Bauhaus Idea and Bauhaus Politics*, pages 38–45, 182–193; and Helena Lewis, *Dada Turns Red*, pages 26–96.

[28] See Raymond Williams, *The Politics of Modernism*, pages 37–48; and Peter Bürger, *Theory of the Avant-Garde*, pages 47–59.

[29] See André Breton, 'Legitimate Defence'; and Helena Lewis, *Dada Turns Red*, pages 26–36.

[30] See Surrealist Group, 'Manifesto of the Surrealists Concerning *L'Age d'Or*'; and Helena Lewis, *Dada Turns Red*, pages 92–96.

impressive aesthetic and technical innovations with the Communist cause. The name of their magazine proudly affirmed their collective identity: *Surrealism In The Service Of The Revolution*. Leon Trotsky was the comrade general of these avant-garde artists – and they were aesthetic partisans of the Trotskyist Fourth International.[31]

In their movement's formative period, the Surrealists had enjoyed how the psychological serendipities of chance were revealed in the Victorian game of constructing random verbal or visual sequences: *Exquisite Corpse*. When played with insight, such childish pastimes were able to free the creative imagination from the confines of capitalist rationality.[32] Building upon this Surrealist insight, Duchamp had declared that *Chess* too was an artwork. Throughout his long career, its black-and-white chequered board and the Staunton pieces didn't just provide evocative political and sexual metaphors for his paintings, readymades, sculptures and films.[33] Duchamp argued that a revolutionary aesthetic experience could also be found within the patterns and rhythms of *Chess* itself. The 'mechanical dance' of Black and White moving their pieces across the board was a non-utilitarian activity which satisfyingly realised the anti-bourgeois ambitions of avant-garde art. By the 1930s, this enthusiastic amateur was not only a leading light of his local club, but also playing in international tournaments and writing match reports for the press. A decade earlier, André Breton – the pope of Surrealism – had teasingly predicted that his friend Duchamp was in danger of giving up art for *Chess*. However, the pioneer of readymades had an irrefutable response to this prognosis. Duchamp was an avant-garde artist – and he'd decided that playing *Chess* was making Modernist art.[34]

In the 1930s, Alberto Giacometti added his own quirky contribution to this Surrealist fascination with games by producing an unsettling series of ludic sculptures. While Duchamp had looked for artistic heterodoxy

---

[31] See André Breton, Diego Rivera and Leon Trotsky, 'Towards a Free Revolutionary Art'; and Helena Lewis, *Dada Turns Red*, pages 77–92, 140–160.

[32] See Alastair Brotchie and Mel Gooding, *Surrealist Games*, pages 10–12.

[33] Howard Staunton was the mid-19th century English *Chess* champion who appropriately lent his name to the ubiquitous set design of the industrial epoch, see Richard Eales, *Chess*, pages 137–138.

[34] See Francis Naumann and Bradley Bailey, *Marcel Duchamp: the art of Chess*.

in the movement of the *Chess* pieces, his comrade instead mocked the alienation of everyday life by ensuring that his creations were unplayable.[35] Ironically, by confounding their true purpose, Giacometti had also inadvertently revealed how games could be domesticated within the gallery system. By emphasising their purposelessness and uniqueness, his avant-garde artworks set themselves apart from the mass produced amusements of consumer capitalism. In contrast with Duchamp's *Chess* sets, Giacometti's sculptures excluded any participation by the audience in the creative process. His Surrealist games were games without players. The board and pieces had become objects of contemplation for visitors in a gallery.

When New York took over from Paris as the capital of Modernism in the late-1940s, its artistic stars and critics had initially shown little interest in Duchamp's and Giacometti's ludic experiments. Clement Greenberg and his acolytes were much more concerned with how Surrealism had anticipated the anti-realist aesthetics of Abstract Expressionism.[36] It was not until the early-1960s that the Fluxus group rediscovered the subversive possibilities of art games. Coordinated by George Maciunas, this avant-garde movement's performances, exhibitions and publications were dedicated to breaking down the barriers between its artists and their audiences.[37] In 1964, inspired by Duchamp's example, Fluxus began issuing a series of special *Chess* sets designed by Takako Saito. Instead of being identified by shape, their pieces were recognised through smell, sound or tactile sensation. Designed to befuddle its players, she famously created a set made out of glasses filled with coloured alcoholic drinks: *Liquor Chess*.[38] Contributing to this project, Yoko Ono in 1966 expressed her outrage at the American invasion of Vietnam by constructing the *Play It By Trust (All White Chess Set)* which wittily sabotaged the game's competitive mechanism by making all of the squares on the board and both sides' pieces in the colour that symbolised peace within Western culture. Inspired by Giacometti,

---

[35] See Mary Flanagan, *Critical Play*, pages 90–93.

[36] See Clement Greenberg, 'Avant-garde and Kitsch'; and T.J. Clark, 'Clement Greenberg's Theory of Art'.

[37] Macunias had been an inveterate wargamer since childhood, see Emmett Williams and Ann Noel, *Mr Fluxus*, pages 15–16.

[38] See Carolus Chess, 'Takako Saito'.

this New York avant-garde movement also began including rules for participatory games in its series of *Fluxboxes* along with the texts, scores and sculptures which so delighted the recipients of these miniature artworks. Like a DIY version of the group's live performances, these ludic experiments promised that everyone now had the opportunity to make Modernist art.[39] Unfortunately, as those who did try to follow their instructions soon discovered, the influence of Giacometti on these games wasn't entirely benign. Confounding their radical aspirations, the playability of the *Fluxboxes* was always secondary to their aesthetic impact.[40]

Living in the epicentre of Cold War Modernism, the best of New York's artists had by the 1960s learnt from Duchamp's readymades how to transform the imagery of consumer capitalism into Pop Art. Andy Warhol's Factory was the 1920s European vision of multi-media creativity in its improved and efficient American version: a cultural production line of paintings, prints, photography, films, publications and music.[41] But, for those with a more radical imagination in the 1960s, a revival of the revolutionary ambitions of the 1920s avant-garde movements promised much more. Another iteration of Modernism could only deliver stylistic and technical innovations. What was needed instead was a radical cultural shift that would catalyse a profound social transformation. Excited by this avant-garde prophecy, artists on both sides of the Atlantic began staging interactive performances and exhibitions in their search for new ways to express collective forms of creativity. By inviting the audience to participate in making their artworks, they weren't just ensuring that these happenings were spontaneous and ephemeral experiences which escaped the stultifying control of curators, collectors and critics.[42] Best of all, these new forms of Surrealist gaming did have multiple players. In his manifesto on the organisation of happenings, Michael Kirby proclaimed the ambitious goal of this new avant-garde: '... to "break

---

[39] See Celia Pearce, 'The Aesthetics of Play', pages 69–72; and Thomas Kellein, *Fluxus*.

[40] See Mary Flanagan, *Critical Play*, pages 112–113; and Thomas Kellein, *Fluxus*.

[41] See Marco Livingstone, *Pop Art*, pages 62–91, 114–139, 194–219; and Andy Warhol, *Popism*.

[42] See Michael Kirby, *Happenings*; and Mariellen Sandford, *Happenings and Other Acts*.

down" the "barrier" between presentation and spectator and to make the passive viewer [into] a more active participator.'[43]

On 27th May 1963, the Smolin gallery in New York hosted the one and only performance of *The First and Second Wilderness: a Civil War Game*. With Kirby as the master of ceremonies, a group of artists staged their recreation of this bloody confrontation in the 1861–5 American struggle to crush the slave owners' rebellion.[44] Four Union and Confederate generals in full uniform ordered infantry, cavalry and artillery pieces to be moved 1 or 2 squares across a gridded map laid out on the floor. As the game progressed, American football cheerleaders explained its rules, resolved combats with a spinner, updated the score board and kept up a running commentary on the action to the accompaniment of the taped noises of firing weapons and galloping cavalry. Watching on, the audience cheered or booed as the two sides won or lost pieces and territory in this theatrical contest. As its grand finale, the evening culminated in the burning of the Wilderness scenery along with a slideshow of death and destruction photographs from the original 1864 battlefield.[45] The New York avant-garde had won an interesting aesthetic victory on that evening. Building upon the achievements of the Constructivists and the Surrealists, they'd successfully transformed playing wargames into making art.

---

[43] Michael Kirby, 'The New Theatre', page 43. For the Surrealist antecedents of this imperative, see Peter Bürger, *Theory of the Avant-Garde*, page 53.

[44] The First and Second Wilderness battles took place between 5th–12th May 1864, see James McPherson, *Battle Cry of Freedom*, pages 718–734.

[45] See Michael Kirby, 'The First and Second Wilderness'.

1.3: HISTORY REPEATING ITSELF

By displaying our replica of *The Game of War* in the Pump House gallery, Class Wargames was making its contribution to the rediscovery of this forgotten icon of 20th century avant-garde art. In this first phase of our campaign of ludic subversion, our activities were devoted to upholding the Situationist banner of cultural rebellion. For the knowledgeable visitors to the show in Battersea Park, Debord's gold-and-silver board and pieces were clearly in the lineage of the earlier Modernist artworks of Rodchenko, Duchamp, Giacometti, Saito, Ono, Maciunas and Kirby. Yet, paradoxically, the inclusion of *The Game of War* within *The Institute of Psychoplasmics* exhibition had required the temporary prevention of its primary purpose: enabling two sides to engage in simulated combat against each other. Inside the gallery space, the pieces were laid out on the board in the starting positions for the match in Becker-Ho and Debord's eponymous book.[46] However, there were no chairs for North and South to sit at the table and begin playing the game. Should any curious visitor try to pick up the pieces, they would quickly discover that they were firmly stuck to the board with museum wax. If spotted, they risked the embarrassment of the curatorial staff scolding them for touching the exhibits. When placed inside the Pump House gallery, *The Game of War* became a museum object. As with one of Giacometti's ludic sculptures, there was no next move.

There was poignancy in this immobility. Back in 1977, Debord had set up a company with his publisher Gérard Lebovici to manufacture and distribute *The Game of War*: Les Jeux Stratégiques et Historiques. Like Duchamp marketing his *Chess* sets and Maciunas selling *Fluxboxes* by mail order, these two conspirators embarked on a publicity campaign to promote their first product. The four hand crafted metal sets which featured in the iconic photographs from *In Girum Imus Nocte* were commissioned. Debord and Becker-Ho wrote their book of the game. The rules were published in both French and English. Plans were made to manufacture cheap cardboard copies of *The Game of War*. Debord was convinced that his company had a potential best-seller on its hands

---

46   See Alice Becker-Ho and Guy Debord, *A Game of War*, page 39.

which would soon join *Chess*, *Draughts* and *Bridge* as a game played in the cafés, clubs and homes of the more proletarian and bohemian neighbourhoods. Everyone could be a player of *The Game of War*.[47] Then, on 5th March 1984, Lebovici was murdered in a Mafia-style hit by an unknown assassin in a Paris underground car park. Deprived of its generous patron, the promotional campaign for *The Game of War* went into terminal crisis. Debord even stopped showing his films in France and withdrew his books from publication in protest at the brutal murder of his friend.[48] On that fateful evening in 1984, *The Game of War* had lost its key player – and was almost forgotten for the next few decades. When Class Wargames' facsimile was put on show in the Pump House gallery, the frozen pieces of the 1977 gold-and-silver set became a disturbing memorial to those harsher times in which Debord's game had been invented.

In spring 2008, the gold-and-silver pieces of our replica were temporarily immobilised in *The Institute of Psychoplasmics* exhibition for a dialectical purpose: seducing the Pump House's audience into making the next move for themselves. Intrigued visitors could purchase the recently published English translation of Debord and Becker-Ho's book with its cardboard game in the gallery shop – or download RSG's unauthorised computer version.[49] Participation not contemplation should take precedence when appreciating this avant-garde artwork. A year earlier in spring 2007, Class Wargames' first attempts to play *The Game of War* had used a homebrew board and pieces made from my early-1970s teenage collection of 16th century Hapsburg and Ottoman toy soldiers. Inspired by the discovery of its rules in the back of Len Bracken's biography, we'd come together to find out whether this ludic experiment was worth investigating.[50] By carefully studying the moves of Debord's match with Becker-Ho in their book, we eventually worked out the formal structure of this ritualised combat. Much to our

[47] See Alice Becker-Ho and Guy Debord, *A Game of War*, page 7; and Alex Galloway, 'Debord's Nostalgic Algorithm'.

[48] See Guy Debord, *Considerations on the Assassination of Gérard Lebovici*.

[49] See Guy Debord and Alice Becker-Ho, *A Game of War*; and Radical Software Group, *Kriegspiel*.

[50] See Len Bracken, *Guy Debord – Revolutionary*, pages 240–251.

surprise and delight, the members of Class Wargames enjoyed playing *The Game of War*.[51]

In a serendipitous coincidence with the imperialist demonology of the 2000s, the recycled Hapsburg and Ottoman figurines of our home-made set mimicked the conflict between the Christian West and the Muslim East in the US government's War on Terror. Taking inspiration from this DIY version, we wondered whether the imminent 40th anniversary of the May '68 French Revolution could be celebrated by re-imagining Debord's game as a conflict between protesters and police on the streets of Paris. For the Left's pieces, infantry would be represented as workers, cavalry as students and artillery as rioters with Molotov cocktails. The mounted general had to be Guy Debord and, for the marching general, Daniel Cohn-Bendit – the instigator of the student protests at Nanterre University that had sparked off this uprising – would be a good choice. For the forces of reaction, the remix was also obvious: infantry as street cops, cavalry as riot police, artillery as tear gas grenadiers, the mounted general as French President Charles de Gaulle and the marching general as his prime minister Georges Pompidou. With the pieces sorted, the board's terrain features could easily be given a Paris 1968 makeover. The fortresses would be turned into street barricades, the mountains into apartment blocks, the passes into alleyways and the arsenals into television centres or newspaper headquarters. Enthused, we contacted Mark Copplestone – one of England's top figurine designers – to find out whether he'd be interested in making the pieces for this new set as a member of the Class Wargames collective.[52] The May '68 version of *The Game of War* would be the must-have souvenir of the 40th anniversary of the almost revolution of the baby boomer generation.

Fortunately, Rod Dickinson had a much better idea. Around the cover of the 2006 Gallimard edition of *Le Jeu de la Guerre* was a purple band with a vivid colour photograph of Debord's 1977 set design. He insisted in our group meetings that Class Wargames had to build its

---

[51]   In contrast, as a warning to all leftist games designers, the admirable politics of Bertell Ollman's *Class Struggle* didn't compensate for its dull play.

[52]   For examples of Mark's work, check out the Copplestone Castings website.

own replica of this iconic version of *The Game of War*. Rod had acquired international artistic recognition for his re-enactments of unsettling moments in recent history: the 1978 Jonestown mass suicide; the 1993 Waco massacre; and the 1961 Milgram experiment.[53] Respecting this experience, the rest of the collective was quickly convinced by his argument that making a May '68 remix of *The Game of War* would be a mistake. Class Wargames should instead focus its attention upon Debord and Becker-Ho playing their illustrative contest in the Auvergne. The artistic investigation of this special historical moment required the construction of a faithful facsimile of the 1977 set design. *The Game of War* was meant to be played with its original board and pieces.

By staging re-enactments, contemporary artists showed how much they'd learnt from the 1960s avant-garde's happenings and performances. Like Fluxus and Kirby, they also invited the audience to participate in the making of the artwork. Taking inspiration from the lively subculture of hobbyists who devoted their spare time to historical and fantasy role-playing, the goal of these avant-garde artists was to aestheticise – and subvert – this fascination with reliving the past.[54] By witnessing for themselves the actors in *The Milgram Experiment* inflicting apparently dangerous electric shocks on another human being, the audience at Rod Dickinson's 2002 recreation understood how they too might have succumbed to obeying immoral orders when bullied by authority figures. Empathy intensified not only the personal experience of the artwork, but also the political resonance of this 1960s American psychologist's research.[55]

A year earlier, on 17th June 2001, Jeremy Deller mobilised both veterans of the 1984–5 British miners' strike and members of re-enactment societies for a participatory performance of *The Battle of Orgreave*. By reliving together this decisive confrontation in the Tory government's

---

[53]   For more details on these projects, see Rod Dickinson's website.

[54]   See Inke Arns and Gabriele Horn, *History Will Repeat Itself*; and Sven Lütticken, *Life, Once More*.

[55]   See Rod Dickinson, 'The Milgram Re-enactment'; and Steve Rushton, *The Milgram Re-enactment*.

war against the organised working class, both its creators and onlookers affirmed that their own collective memory of these dramatic times was much more accurate than the media-promoted official accounts of this historical turning-point. In Deller's happening, those who'd been there at the original battle of Orgreave on the 18th June 1984 were joined in a common experience by those who'd taken part in its re-enactment 17 years later.[56] The avant-garde artwork now meant – most wonderfully – a public celebration of the Yorkshire coalfield communities' lost alternative to neoliberal globalisation: the live action role-playing game as the possibilities of the past challenging the limits of the present.[57]

With Rod Dickinson as a member, Class Wargames soon learnt how to make its own contribution to re-enactment art. The 2008 match at *The Institute of Psychoplasmics* exhibition was followed by further public performances of *The Game of War* in other gallery spaces, including the Victoria & Albert Museum in London and the State Hermitage Museum in St. Petersburg. Learning from these experiences, Class Wargames became determined to involve the audience more in our events. Equipped with travelling versions of its board and pieces, we began organising participatory contests of Debord's ludic invention during 2009 at art venues and educational institutions across Europe and in Brazil.[58] *The Game of War* had to be experienced as a DIY artwork. Built by Lucy Blake, our website also encouraged people to try playing Debord's game for themselves by providing its rules, board designs and other background information. Over the summer of 2009, with funding from the Arts Council of England, Class Wargames next completed a short film directed by Ilze Black explaining the origins and principles of *The Game of War*.[59] After its launch in September at Furtherfield's HTTP gallery in London, the collective's campaign to

56   See Jeremy Deller and Mike Figgis, *The Battle for Orgreave*; and Jeremy Deller, *The English Civil War Part II*. For eyewitness accounts of the vicious police repression against the striking miners, see Dave Douglass, *Ghost Dancers*; and Jim Coulter, Susan Miller and Martin Walker, *State of Siege*.

57   Revealingly, one of Deller's goals in staging *The Battle of Orgreave* performance was to politicise the usually apolitical hobby of historical re-enacting, see Matthew Higgs and Jeremy Deller, 'In Conversation', page 190.

58   For photographs of these performances, see the Events 2008 and Events 2009 sections of the Class Wargames website.

59   See Ilze Black, *Class Wargames Presents Guy Debord's The Game of War*.

promote Debord's game was reinvigorated. By combining screenings of the film with participatory contests, Class Wargames received a warm welcome on its 2009–11 European tour: *Crash-Crush* in Rotterdam, *Wunderbar* at the Baltic in Gateshead, *Transmediale 10* in Berlin, *The Futurological Congress* in Lviv and many other interesting venues.[60] During this first stage of our campaign of ludic mischief, our role at these events was to enable the members of the audience to turn Situationist theory into ludic practice. For a brief moment of time, the players of *The Game of War* were the makers of avant-garde art.

In these early years of the project, Class Wargames used performances, exhibitions, film, leaflets, xenographs, club nights, radio shows and social media to evangelise for the playing of *The Game of War* in its 1977 analogue design. The RSG digital version was a useful training tool, but this computerised contest lacked the tactile pleasures of the original version. Unlike in the 1990s, now that people were spending so much time looking at screens at work and in the home, there was no longer anything artistically adventurous about turning his physical invention into a virtual object. Best of all, by moving the gold-and-silver pieces across its board, the 21st century players of our twice-size facsimile were directly connected with the famous photos of Debord and Becker-Ho competing with each other over thirty years earlier. Like *The Milgram Experiment* and *The Battle of Orgreave*, Class Wargames' recreation of *The Game of War* was a public invitation for people to relive an evocative moment from the recent past for themselves. Debord and Becker-Ho had used this version of the board and pieces in their Auvergne hideaway. By playing with the 1977 analogue set, contemporary admirers of the Situationist International weren't just participating in the continuation of this transitory communal artwork. More importantly, as we would investigate more deeply in the next two phases of our campaign of ludic subversion, they were also taking their first lesson in the political and military teachings of *The Game of War*.

By touring with its replicas of the 1977 set, the members of Class Wargames had committed themselves to realising the most subversive ambition of re-enactment art: enabling the collective exploration of

---

60 For the photographs of these events, see the relevant years in the Events section of the Class Wargames website.

'... the relevance of what happened in the past for the here and now.'[61] In the early-21st century, *The Game of War* was a memory of the mid-20th century rebirth of the cultural avant-garde. More than fifty years on, Situationism still provided the tactical manual for today's leftfield artists: media outrages, appropriated material, urban interventions and user-generated content. In this first stage of Class Wargames' campaign of ludic subversion, the players of Debord's game were able to return to the times of the group's founders who combined these subversive cultural techniques together for the first time. By moving its pieces across the board, they briefly became Debord and Becker-Ho in the mid-1970s playing each other in their Auvergne cottage. During these matches, they could experience *The Game of War* as a transitory co-operative artwork which embodied these teachings of Situationism. In its public performances, Class Wargames' task was to help their participants to carry out this transformation of cultural theory into avant-garde practice for themselves. Everyone who played *The Game of War* was a Situationist.

As long as these ephemeral contests lasted, our ludic re-enactments became collective celebrations of Debord as the master tactician of leftfield art. In this first phase of our campaign of ludic subversion, our vital mission was to remind contemporary radicals of how much they were indebted to the very special moment in the late-1950s when the European avant-garde had redefined its identity. Moving analogue pieces across the board of *The Game of War* was an excellent method of understanding this original version of today's cultural dissidence. Players could discover for themselves how the expertise of the most advanced avant-garde art movement of the May '68 generation had been materialised in its simulated combat between North and South. Playing *The Game of War* was a DIY lesson in Situationist history. As Debord repeatedly emphasised, the perpetuation of spectacular domination depended upon the enforced loss of memory of what had already been experienced. Studying the history of the International's artistic adventures didn't just reveal the inspiration for *The Game of War*. More importantly, knowledge of what had taken place in this past moment in time explained why the avant-garde tactics of Situationism

---

[61]   Inke Arns, 'History Will Repeat Itself', page 43.

still hadn't lost all of their critical edge in the early-21st century. As the leitmotif of this first stage of our campaign of ludic subversion, Class Wargames' re-enactments of *The Game of War* paid homage to the unique moment when the codification of these techniques was the smartest response to the emerging Fordist methods of social control which still shaped the modern epoch of neoliberal globalisation. The lessons of history were there to be learnt on the game board.

1.4: THE NEW RADICALS

On 28th July 1957, Guy Debord was one of the eight representatives from the Lettrist International, the Movement for an Imaginist Bauhaus and the London Psychogeographical Association who came together at the Italian mountain village of Cosio d'Arroscia to form an organisation with the world-historical mission of resurrecting the European avant-garde: the Situationist International.[62] In this task, these leftfield artists were united in their certainty that the cultural upheavals of the early-20th century had run their course. Amongst the champions of Modernism, there'd always been an ambiguity about whether this new aesthetic had any wider social meaning. In the 1920s, the Constructivists and the Surrealists had argued that the primary purpose of making innovative art was advancing the worldwide proletarian revolution. Yet, for many of their contemporaries, the creative imagination had little to do with political commitment. Modernism only meant inventing new styles and types of art which distinguished them from their teachers and mentors. Unfortunately for these young artists, the forces of reaction weren't convinced by this confinement of cultural rebellion within the gallery system. In 1930s France, the ideologues of both the Catholic bourgeoisie and the Stalinist bureaucracy had denounced the degeneracy and worthlessness of Modernist art. Confirming the Surrealists' position, the flouting of aesthetic orthodoxies was seen in itself as a subversive act. Whether they liked it or not, all cutting-edge artists had to realise that they too were cultural revolutionaries. For the Surrealists like the Constructivists, Modernism was an insurrectionary call to arms against the philistine rulers of the planet.

At their inaugural 1957 congress, the founders of the Situationist International knew that their first task was explaining the strange fate of the 1920s avant-garde movements. Over in the Russian-occupied half of the continent, the totalitarian state had contemptuously crushed the small bands of dissident artists. By the time that Debord and his comrades met at Cosio d'Arroscia, the revolutionary dreams of Constructivism had long been forgotten and replaced by a kitsch

---

[62]   See Jean-Jacques Raspaud and Jean-Pierre Voyer, 'Situationist Data', page 176.

Stalinist version of 19th century academic taste: Socialist Realism.[63] But, at least, the radical artists in the East had preserved their integrity in defeat. For the Situationists, the real horror lay in the fate of the avant-garde movements in the capitalist West. On the American side of the 1945 Yalta Agreement's partition line, the cultural establishment had opted for a much more insidious – and effective – strategy for neutralising leftfield artists: fame and money. Once feared and ridiculed, the masterpieces of the avant-garde were now given pride of place in the top galleries, praised in textbooks and lauded in the academy. By the late-1950s, the utopian visions of Constructivism had become the hi-tech style of big government and big business. Surrealism's aesthetic and technical innovations were now an essential reference point for advertisers, film directors and designers. The term itself had even entered everyday speech as a synonym for bizarre.[64] Tellingly, for the progenitors of the Situationist International, the prerequisite for this official recognition of these 1920s avant-garde movements had been the disappearance of their revolutionary politics. Only by removing Bolshevism from Surrealism could its psychologically disturbing imagery be enjoyed without ever having to question the ideological conformity of the capitalist system. Seduced by celebrity status and hard cash, Breton, Duchamp and Giacometti had been made safe for mainstream audiences with their heretical opinions explained away as an artistic eccentricity. Worst of all, thanks to the Stalinists' censorship of experimentation and abstraction, the CIA-funded Congress of Cultural Freedom was able during the 1950s to co-opt other less principled avant-garde veterans as heroes of American tolerance and refinement. Far from inspiring the global insurrection of the exploited as had once been imagined, the aesthetic and technical innovations of Modernism were now strengthening the cultural hegemony of the ruling elites of the West.[65] Assembled in Cosio d'Arroscia, the progenitors of the Situationist International had a vituperative name

---

[63]   See October – Association of Artistic Labour, 'Declaration, 1928'; and Igor Golomstock, *Totalitarian Art*.

[64]   See Serge Guilbaut, *How New York Stole the Idea of Modern Art*; and Jane de Hart Mathews, 'Art and Politics in Cold War America'.

[65]   See Serge Guilbaut, *How New York Stole the Idea of Modern Art*; and Frances Stonor Saunders, *Who Paid the Piper?*.

for this corrupt domestication of the 1920s avant-garde movements: *recuperation.*[66]

The invitees to the 1957 conference were all seekers of a superior strategy for the Red fighters on the aesthetic front. More than anything else, they'd been brought together by a common commitment to devising innovative forms of art which couldn't be recuperated by secret police agents, rich collectors, bourgeois critics or cultural bureaucrats. Like their Modernist predecessors, these young artists applied their creativity to both the old and the new: industrial painting, altering 2nd hand pictures, experimental films, seditious graffiti, self-published journals and collaged books.[67] Crucially, these founders of Situationism were determined to avoid the fate of recuperation which had tarnished their Surrealist elders. The new avant-garde now realised that aesthetic and technical innovations were deadly weapons which could be turned against their inventors. Fortunately, by being self-critical about their own practice, these makers of radical art were able to resume the ideological assault against bourgeois hegemony. The Situationists were convinced that the tactical ploys of their new strategy were already battle-tested. By combining them together, the International would re-ignite the cultural revolution in the heartlands of the capitalist system. Artists were – once again – in the front line of the class war.[68]

In the early-1950s, Debord had first acquired a reputation within West European avant-garde circles for his experimental films. Turning Kazimir Malevich's Suprematist paintings into cinema, *Hurlements en Faveur de Sade* featured an alternating all-black or all-white screen with a soundtrack of mumbled voices and, for its final 24 minutes, complete silence except for the mechanical whirring of the celluloid projector. Unlike his contemporaries who would soon become the celebrated directors of the French New Wave, Debord wasn't interested in making

---

[66] See Guy Debord, 'Report on the Construction of Situations', pages 18–20; and Raoul Vaneigem, *A Cavalier History of Surrealism.*

[67] See Peter Wollen, 'Bitter Victory', pages 35–55; and Laurent Chollet, *L'Insurrection Situationniste*, pages 34–111.

[68] See Guy Debord, 'Report on the Construction of Situations'; and the Situationist International, 'The Adventure'.

Modernist versions of Hollywood blockbusters.[69] Instead, reviving the Surrealists' shock tactics, his film had been a premeditated affront to the expectations of the sophisticated audiences of alternative movies. Little did they realise, it was only when they began loudly protesting against the lack of any images let alone a plot in *Hurlements en Faveur de Sade* that Debord had succeeded in completing his subversive artwork: the spectators were now making their own cinematic experience.[70]

On 9th April 1950, Michel Mourre – a fellow member of the Lettrist International – had confirmed the potency of this avant-garde technique with a daring hoax perpetrated at Notre Dame cathedral in Paris. Dressed as a priest, he'd ascended into the main pulpit and given a sermon on the delights of atheism to the assembled worshippers and tourists until he was dragged away by the church's security guards. Most wonderfully, the outraged reaction of clerics, politicians and the media to this desecration of French Catholicism's principal shrine magnified this minor stunt into a major scandal.[71] The tactical lessons of this successful raid into enemy territory were clear. If they chose the correct target, a select band of artists could create political theatre that promulgated their revolutionary message to the masses. Best of all, whether they responded positively or negatively to these subversive interventions, their audiences inadvertently found themselves participating in the creation of a collective artwork. The new avant-garde had discovered its first retort to recuperation: *provocation*.

Inspired by the Surrealists' collages, the founders of Situationism began making subversive re-workings of the detritus of popular culture. By painting over pictures found in flea markets, Asger Jorn poked fun at the 1950s New York art establishment's horror of kitsch. Taking clips from mainstream movies provided big name actors, evocative dialogue and expensive sets for Debord's experimental films. When the speech bubbles in children's comics were replaced with the International's

---

[69] See Dorota Ostrowska, *Reading the French New Wave*, pages 1–96.

[70] See Guy Debord, *Hurlements en Faveur de Sade*; Anselm Jappe, *Guy Debord*, pages 48–50; and Thomas Levin, 'Dismantling the Spectacle', pages 78–85.

[71] See Guy Debord, *In Girum Imus Nocte et Consumimur Igni*, page 163; and Greil Marcus, *Lipstick Traces*, pages 279–284.

insights, superheroes became propagandists for libertarian communism, cowboys debated the best form of revolutionary organisation and porn stars analysed the theoretical weaknesses of the French Left.[72] More than anything else, these satirical remixes would come to define the distinctive look and feel of Situationism. By the 1950s, Bolshevik and Anarchist publications had become unimaginative not only in their content, but also in their design. Rejecting this po-faced militancy, the Situationists advocated stealing back what had been the Left's in the first place. Evoking the gift-giving festivals of the indigenous peoples of the Northwest Pacific, Debord and his comrades had already shown the effectiveness of this subversive tactic in the Lettrist International's free journal: *Potlatch*.[73] Learning from this experiment, politicised artists were now urged to reinsert the revolution back into Modernism through a wilful disregard for the copyright laws. Above all, they could enjoy mocking the idiocies of the mass media and the gallery system. Playful irony was the leftfield artists' antidote to advertising hype, bureaucratic dogmatism and cultural timidity. The new avant-garde had found its second tactical response to recuperation: *détournement*.[74]

Living on the margins of conventional society, the founders of Situationism treasured the inner city neighbourhoods with their dodgy bars, cheap restaurants and affordable accommodation which provided them with sanctuary. Because avant-garde artists in the 1820s admired the undisciplined lifestyles of gypsies, such quarters in Paris had long been identified with what the French had once believed to be the homeland of the Roma people: Bohemia.[75] As much a state of mind as a particular place, this distinct community of cultural dissidents had since then survived – and flourished – despite the constant threats of penury, censorship and eviction. Although the location within Paris

---

[72] See Asger Jorn, 'Detourned Painting'; René Viénet, 'The Situationists and the New Forms of Action against Politics and Art'; and Steef Davidson, *Political Comics*, pages 56–77.

[73] See *Potlatch 1954/1957*. The Situationists discovered this tribal gift economy in a 1923 classic of anthropology that had also inspired their Surrealist predecessors: Marcel Mauss, *The Gift*.

[74] See Guy Debord and Gil Wolman, 'Methods of Détournement'; and the Situationist International, 'Détournement as Negation and Prelude'.

[75] See Jerrold Seigel, *Bohemian Paris*, pages 23–25.

moved over time, the bohemian quarter was always the starting point of each new avant-garde movement in France: Romanticism, Realism, Impressionism, Cubism and Surrealism. During the late-1950s, like these illustrious predecessors, Debord and his fellow Lettrists had also met in bars, cafés and rented rooms to plot their aesthetic insurrection. Forging a common identity through intoxication, promiscuity and intense debates, young rebels once again sallied forth from their underground headquarters to overthrow the French art establishment. Coming from the first generation to grow up after the defeat of fascism, Debord's coterie revelled in their rediscovery of the subversive possibilities of the bohemian neighbourhood.[76] By forming the new avant-garde, they had become '... the alcoholic intellectuals of the non-working classes.'[77]

By the time that the Situationist International was inaugurated, their favourite inner city districts of Paris were already under siege by greedy developers and ambitious politicians. In the mid-19th century, the authoritarian regime of Louis Bonaparte had destroyed the medieval street system not only to enrich the property speculators amongst its supporters, but also to break up the proletarian quarters which were home to its bitterest opponents.[78] Thwarting this nefarious scheme, radical artists had kept faith with their bohemian community. When the rebuilding was over, the centre of cultural dissidence had shifted to the disreputable area of Montmarte with its cabarets, brothels and cheap flats.[79] As this area was gentrified in the 1890s and 1900s, the avant-garde next returned to its old haunts in the university district on the Left Bank. Half a century later, Debord had discovered his metier as a revolutionary artist in the bars, cafés, cinemas, theatres, lecture halls and bookshops of this bohemian neighbourhood.[80] Yet, ironically,

[76] See Guy Debord, *On the Passage of a Few Persons Through a Rather Brief Unity of Time*, pages 13–18; Jean-Michael Mension, *The Tribe*; and Greil Marcus, *Lipstick Traces*, pages 345–366.

[77] McKenzie Wark, *The Beach Beneath the Street*, page 17.

[78] See Henri Lefebvre, *Writings on Cities*, pages 75–77, 81; and Malcolm Easton, *Artists and Writers in Paris*, pages 57–146.

[79] See Jerrold Seigel, *Bohemian Paris*, pages 215–365.

[80] See Paul Webster and Nicholas Powell, *Saint-Germain-des-Prés*; and Jean-Michael Mension, *The Tribe*.

it was the influx of young rebels like him that began the process of gentrification in this quarter too. As in Montmartre at the end of the 19ᵗʰ century, their presence both alarmed and excited the monopolists of wealth and power. For the Right, the redevelopment of the inner city in Paris provided the opportunity not only to deprive the avant-garde enemy of its base of operations, but also to make money out of this newly fashionable area of town.[81]

The progenitors of Situationism knew that the first step in defending their bohemian quarter was dealing with the traitors in the Left's own ranks. Committed to improving the living standards of their core supporters, the leaderships of both the Social Democratic and Stalinist parties in France had convinced themselves of the political and social benefits of urban renewal. Enabling people to move from inner city slums to modern apartments in the suburbs was a vote winner. They knew that no self-respecting worker wanted to live like a dissolute artist. Countering this puritanical assumption, the Situationists emphasised the sociability and communality of their bohemian neighbourhood. Inspired by Thomas De Quincy's opium-fuelled wanderings around Victorian London and Charles Baudelaire's admiration for the dandy flâneurs of Second Empire Paris, members of the International mapped their emotional and intellectual responses to the urban environment while under the influence of alcohol and hashish. For those who knew how look beyond the glitter of consumerism, premonitions of the metropolis as a proletarian playground were everywhere.[82] Anticipating the great transformation to come, Situationist architects began planning the building of their libertarian communist city: the Haçienda. In this imaginary future, every worker would be able to live like a bohemian artist. The new avant-garde had developed its third tactical counter to recuperation: *psychogeography*.[83]

In its formative period, the Situationist International borrowed much of its theoretical analysis from the writings of a dissident Marxist

---

[81] See Henri Lefebvre, *Writings on Cities*, pages 77–85.

[82] See Guy Debord, 'Theory of the Dérive'; and Abdelhafid Khatib, 'Essai de Description Psychogéographique des Halles'.

[83] See Ivan Chtcheglov, 'Formulary for a New Urbanism'; Guy Debord and Constant, 'La Déclaration d'Amsterdam'; and Vincent Kaufman, *Guy Debord*, pages 137–145.

sociologist at Nanterre University: Henri Lefebvre. In a series of path-breaking books, he'd shown how the advent of Fordism had extended the dominance of capital beyond the factory and the office into everyday life. Far from being a peripheral issue, what happened in the streets and inside the home was now at the centre of the class struggle.[84] Proletarian strategy needed updating to deal with this new form of bourgeois order. Confounding the Left's expectations, the achievement of full employment and consumer plenty had led to greater loneliness and more alienation. Capitalism hadn't been weakened – it had become more insidious. In its 19th century liberal incarnation, poverty and repression had kept the proletariat in subordination. Now, with the arrival of Fordism, more sophisticated mechanisms of domination had taken their place. Architecture, shopping, advertising, fashion and, above all, the media were the guardians of this new epoch of capitalism: the bureaucratic society of controlled consumption.[85]

From Lefebvre's writings, the Situationists came to understand that the recuperation of the 1920s avant-garde movements was integral to this transition from liberalism to Fordism. When watching television occupied almost as much time as working and sleeping in most people's lives, the cultural question was now the essence of Left politics.[86] This meant that the new avant-garde must engage with the hopes and desires of the majority of the population. In the past, the only inhabitants of bohemia had been a tiny group of leftfield artists. But, with the arrival of the consumer society, increasing numbers of young people were joining this aesthetic insurgency against bourgeois conformity. In their fashions, music and sexuality, they flaunted their disdain for the conservative lifestyle of their parents' generation. Most wonderfully, this emergence of youth subcultures promised the democratisation of the libertarian mores of the avant-garde amongst the proletariat as a whole.[87] However, as Debord and his comrades also realised, the co-option of Constructivism and Surrealism had proved that aesthetic

---

[84]   See Henri Lefebvre, *Critique of Everyday Life Volume 1*; and *The Production of Space*.

[85]   See Henri Lefebvre, *Everyday Life in the Modern World*.

[86]   See Guy Debord, *The Society of the Spectacle*, pages 12–23, 112; Anselm Jappe, *Guy Debord*, pages 72–8; and Peter Wollen, 'Bitter Victory', pages 41–43.

[87]   See the Situationist International, 'Ideologies, Classes and the Domination of Nature', pages 106–108.

innovation by itself was no longer inherently revolutionary. Given time, the art establishment and the mass media could assimilate the most extreme avant-garde rebellion and, once depoliticised, make it into a weapon of bourgeois hegemony. The revolt into style failed by succeeding.

Fortunately, taking their cue from both the Surrealists and Lefebvre, the Situationists realised that the most effective response against recuperation could be found – in prototype – in the wild and joyful energy of protests, riots, strikes and festivals. During these outbursts of collective emotion, the market and the state temporarily lost their dominance over humanity. Détournement was much more than an artistic technique. In Budapest during the 1956 Hungarian Revolution and in Los Angeles during the 1965 Watts Uprising, the gift-giving potlatches of tribal communities had reappeared for a brief moment in a modern hi-tech form. When liberated from the alienating discipline of bureaucratic orders and capitalist commodities, people became playful, hedonistic and sharing. The Situationists were convinced that these spontaneous premonitions of libertarian communism revealed the winning tactic for victory on the cultural battlefield.[88] The early-20th century avant-garde movements had been recuperated because their members were only a small minority of society who could be easily bought off. Gratifyingly, it was impossible for the ruling elite of Fordism to welcome the massive crowds of carnival into its ranks without undermining its own exclusivity. The essence of revolutionary art had been revealed. It was not inventing a new aesthetic with new technologies that would liberate humanity, but providing the circumstances where everyone could freely express themselves. Inspired by this libertarian vision, Jorn proclaimed that making art collectively was a premonition of the communist future in the capitalist present. The avant-garde had forged its ultimate weapon against recuperation: *participatory creativity*.[89]

Equipped with these four tactics, the Situationist International

---

[88] See Guy Debord, 'Report on the Construction of Situations'; and the Situationist International, 'The Decline and Fall of the Spectacle-Commodity Economy'.

[89] See Asger Jorn, 'Critique of Economic Policy', pages 25–34; and Raoul Vaneigem, *The Revolution of Everyday Life*, pages 186–199.

was now ready to launch a new cultural revolution. Led by artists, insurrectionary politics became an avant-garde game. Like its Surrealist forebear, the International mimicked the ideological zeal and party fealty of the sectarian Left. There was a theoretical journal, manifestos, congresses, factions, expulsions and, in Debord, even a maximum leader.[90] Extremist Marxist rhetoric was proclaimed to outrage the custodians of bourgeois order. Revolutionary politics had become artistic détournement. Identifying participatory creativity as the premonition of social emancipation, the Situationists played this avant-garde game as an experiment in self-management. If artists could be militants, then the rest of the working class could also organise their own lives without the interference of managers, experts, enforcers and propagandists.[91] Capitalism was a competitive game with winners and losers. Egoism and conformity were the inevitable result. In its place, inspired by the writings of Johan Huizinga, the Situationist International would initiate a new co-operative game where everybody was a winner. Instead of passively consuming the media spectacle, its participants would be actively creating their own social life. For the Situationists, hedonistic play was the radical antithesis of alienated labour. Within its 'magic circle', intimacy and imagination could triumph over isolation and conformity.[92] Like Duchamp, Maciunas and Kirby, Debord and his comrades celebrated the collective playing of games as the epitome of non-utilitarian activity. Emancipated from both the market and the state by participating in these collective artworks, exploited workers would be reborn as avant-garde artists. In this Situationist revolution, libertarian communism was re-imagined as the potlatch game of human emancipation: '… born of the passion of playing … [where] … group activity facilitates the self-realisation of each individual.'[93]

---

[90] See Peter Wollen, 'Bitter Victory'; and McKenzie Wark, *The Beach Beneath the Street*, pages 61–66.

[91] See Guy Debord, 'Perspectives for the Conscious Alteration of Everyday Life'.

[92] See the Situationist International, 'Contribution à une Définition Situationniste du Jeu'; and Johan Huizinga, *Homo Ludens*, pages 1–27, 46–75.

[93] Raoul Vaneigem, *The Revolution of Everyday Life*, page 198.

1.5: THE ENGLISH SECTION OF THE SITUATIONIST INTERNATIONAL

During the first stage of our campaign of ludic subversion, the members of Class Wargames became enthusiastic practitioners of the four tactics of Situationist avant-garde art. Most wonderfully, we'd discovered that the intelligent application of their technique of provocation was still effective in the early-21st century. The public playing of military simulations was guaranteed to annoy the more moralistic activists of the pacifist Left. The tough Marxist terminology of our propaganda was an affront to the liberal sensibilities of the acolytes of Post-Modernism. Through our performances and publications, we were applying the Situationist tactic of détournement to politicise the apolitical hobbyist subculture of wargaming. We were also connoisseurs of the psychogeography of both the locations of our interventions and the terrain of Debord's miniature battlefield.[94] In this opening stage of our campaign, we'd proved ourselves to be diligent pupils of the avant-garde lessons embodied within *The Game of War*.

Above all, Class Wargames' interactive performances were putting the fourth – and most audacious – imperative of Situationist art theory into practice. Like the ludic experiments of Surrealism and Fluxus, Debord's *The Game of War* made possible a brief moment of participatory creativity within an alienated world. When moving the pieces across its board, the audience were no longer passive consumers of cultural commodities. Instead, by agreeing to observe a common set of rules, they could become artists making their own artwork. As Debord planned in the 1970s, these 21st century players of *The Game of War* experienced a fleeting premonition of the libertarian communist future in the present. Everyone was creative while taking part in this simulated combat. For Class Wargames, these collective performances of *The Game of War* were always – at least in part – re-enactments of the paradigmatic match between Debord and Becker-Ho in their

---

[94] 'The terrain does not merely constitute space, a formless mass of thinly spread squares. It is transmuted into psychogeography by the opposing armies which confront each other on the board, whose contestation determines the strategic pinch-points where the successful player uses their tactical advantage to ensure that they enjoy victory.' Richard Barbrook and Fabian Tompsett, *Class Wargames Presents Guy Debord's The Game of War*, page 15.

Auvergne hideaway. Looking back at this iconic moment in history enabled the players around its board to understand how Situationist ideas could decipher what was happening now.

As event followed event during this first phase of our campaign of ludic mischief, Class Wargames soon realised that its members were also engaged in another form of historical re-enactment. Most revealingly, our performances of *The Game of War* were becoming homages to the 1960s pioneers of English Situationism. It was their proselytising that had first interpreted the new avant-garde knowledge from the continent for the inhabitants of this off-shore island of Europe. It was their publications and actions that had introduced the English to the illicit pleasures of combining the four artistic tactics of Situationism: provocation, détournement, psychogeography and participatory creativity. Class Wargames was the grateful beneficiary of this missionary work. For over four decades, this English appropriation of Situationism had provided an instruction manual for radical avant-garde artists across the globe. Based in London, Class Wargames proudly identified itself with an illustrious lineage of DIY culture. Thanks to these 1960s trailblazers, English Situationism was now identified with the Sex Pistols, the Haçienda and Banksy. At Class Wargames' events, the collective playing of *The Game of War* was the ludic re-enactment of this aesthetic revolution. By activating its board and pieces, anyone could be a punk artist.

In 1974, Chris Gray published the first major English-language collection of Situationist writings which codified his generation's avant-garde interpretation of the International's programme: *Leaving the 20ᵗʰ Century*. Within its bright green covers, readers found – in whole or in excerpts – an exhilarating analysis of contemporary capitalism which was far superior to anything found in the sacred texts of the Bolshevik and Anarchist sects that then dominated New Left politics in England. *The Decline and Fall of the Spectacular Commodity Economy* took delight in praising the insurgent energy of rioting and looting. *The Revolution of Everyday Life* poured scorn upon the myth that new information technologies could liberate humanity from its woes. *The Society of Spectacle* condemned the overwhelming majority of the Left for succumbing to bourgeois recuperation – and looked forward to the imminent victory of the workers' councils over the

Fordist enemy. Moving beyond the tired slogans of Bolshevism and Anarchism, these impassioned critiques directed their fury against the new media-saturated consumer societies of Western capitalism. As Gray's book revealed, the Situationist International had developed the most advanced political theory for analysing the modern world. For its appreciative readers, *Leaving the 20ᵗʰ Century* would become the intelligent voice of 'the hard-but-hidden edge of student revolution in the late [nineteen] sixties.'[95]

In his introduction, Gray told the story of how the Situationist International had been formed to resurrect the rebel cause of avant-garde art. It was by searching for new forms of heterodox creativity that Debord and his comrades had come to understand the sophisticated methods of social control emerging within consumer capitalism. The recuperation of Constructivism and Surrealism had proved that the commodification of aesthetic and technical innovation could neutralise the ideological message of even the most radical of artworks. If it wanted to avoid this disgrace, the reborn avant-garde must adopt a more advanced strategy for disrupting the dull routines of everyday life under Fordism. In *Leaving the 20ᵗʰ Century*, Gray assembled a selection of articles, manifestos, reports and polemics which outlined the four Situationist tactics of pranks, remixing, urbanism and DIY culture. The theoretical writings of the International gave a smart political rationale to this practical handbook for aesthetic subversion. Gray explained that provocation, détournement, psychogeography and participatory creativity weren't just techniques for exposing the new mechanisms of Fordist domination. Above all, they provided the most effective stratagems for combating spectacular capitalism. Perceptive readers of *Leaving the 20ᵗʰ Century* could have no doubt. Situationism was avant-garde art in the service of revolutionary politics – and vice versa.[96]

By compiling *Leaving the 20ᵗʰ Century*, Chris Gray defined the English interpretation of this new subversive doctrine for his anglophone readership. As the next four decades would reveal, he'd published the

---

[95]   Tony Wilson, *24 Hour Party People*, page 118.

[96]   See Christopher Gray, *Leaving the 20ᵗʰ Century*, pages 1–6.

tactical manual that would make Situationist-style pranks, remixing, urbanism and DIY culture into the cutting-edge of this West European country's avant-garde art scene. *Leaving the 20ᵗʰ Century* was the original version of the Sex Pistols, the Haçienda and Banksy. The lasting impact of this book was Gray's reward for his pioneering work in promoting the ideas of the Situationist International in England. During the first decade of its existence, this new avant-garde movement had made slow progress in establishing an outpost on the other side of the channel. Ralph Rumney had attended the 1957 inaugural meeting at Cosio d'Arroscia and Alexander Trocchi was a valued member of the group. In 1960, the 4ᵗʰ conference of the Situationist International had been held in East London. Don Nicholson-Smith had worked with Debord and his comrades during the early-1960s while he was living in Paris. After his move to Copenhagen in 1961, Gordon Fazakerley had played a leading role in the International's breakaway Scandinavian Section.[97] Yet, despite these close connections, the overwhelming majority of English leftfield artists and activists had remained unaware of the new avant-garde teachings from mainland Europe. Instead, their attention was determinedly fixed on the exciting events taking place in the USA. Across the Atlantic, youthful radicals were already pioneering the heady mix of revolutionary politics and personal liberation which would come to epitomise the seditious spirit of the baby boomer generation.[98] Sharing a common language, English rebels had been heavily influenced by American alternative culture since the arrival of jazz music in the 1920s. Four decades on, young malcontents were eager to embrace the subversive ideals of the hippie movement. They too would overturn the established order by creating a New Left counter-culture in England: protest groups, rock bands, community media, arts spaces, housing co-ops and free festivals. On this West European island during the 1960s, the template for the youth insurrection against the American empire was made-in-the-USA.[99]

---

[97]　See Ralph Rumney, 'The *Vague* Interview'; Alexander Trocchi, 'Invisible Insurrection of a Million Minds'; Gill Woodward, 'Interview with the Author and Ilze Black'; and Gordon Fazakerley and Jacqueline de Jong, 'Drakabygget'.

[98]　See George Katsiaficas *The Imagination of the New Left*; and Carl Davidson, *The New Radicals in the Multiversity*.

[99]　See Richard Neville, *Playpower*; and George Melly, *Revolt into Style*.

It was at this key historical moment that Gray and Nicholson-Smith made their intervention which would fundamentally reshape the social imagination of England. In 1966, they'd both helped to produce the first issue of *Heatwave* which had been set up as the London offshoot of the Chicago Surrealist revivalists' *Rebel Worker*.[100] Like the American underground press, this new magazine also championed the New Left's seductive synthesis of political and cultural dissent.[101] *Heatwave* became one of the first publications in England which could happily place a revolutionary call to arms next to beat poetry, artistic illustrations and autobiographical accounts of drug-taking within its pages. In comparison, the Bolshevik or Anarchist publications of the time seemed very staid.[102] More than anything else, what would mark out *Heatwave* from its rivals on the traditional Left was its enthusiasm for the nation's multifarious youth subcultures. Adding Paris Situationism into the mix alongside Chicago Surrealism, Charles Radcliffe praised their exuberant defiance of bourgeois conformity as a spontaneous form of proletarian rebellion. With the advent of Fordism, the bohemian lifestyle of the avant-garde was being democratised. Every alienated worker now had the opportunity to become a hedonistic artist in their leisure time. While acknowledging the ever-present danger of capitalist recuperation, Radcliffe concluded by emphasising that: 'The youth revolt … has … made its first stumbling political gestures with an immediacy that revolutionaries should not deny, but envy.'[103]

This first revelation of the teachings of Situationism in the pages of *Heatwave* marked the culmination of two decades of searching for the avant-garde theory that could ignite a cultural insurrection in England. From the late-1940s onwards, as the country slowly recovered from its wartime sacrifices, official approval and funding of Modernist art had encouraged a burst of aesthetic and technical experimentation. In quick succession, young English artists recapitulated the stylistic achievements of their early-20th century predecessors who'd applied the principles of

---

[100]   See Charles Radcliffe, 'Two Fiery Flying Rolls', pages 327–329, 346–351.

[101]   For the history of these US publications, see David Armstrong, *A Trumpet to Arms*; and Mitchell Goodman, *The Movement Towards a New America*, pages 359–432.

[102]   See *Heatwave #1* and *#2* in Franklin Rosemont and Charles Radcliffe, *Dancin' In the Streets*, pages 381–486.

[103]   Charles Radcliffe, 'The Seeds of Social Destruction', page 400.

symbolism and abstraction to painting, sculpture, photography, film, fashion, graphic design and theatre. For most of them, Modernism only meant making innovative art with a contemporary sensibility. Aesthetic rebellion had been stripped of its revolutionary politics. Yet, despite this recuperation, the British establishment's toleration of cultural heterodoxy did begin to change the wider society. By the beginning of the 1960s, there was a flourishing bohemian scene of alternative galleries, cinemas, theatres, clubs and college venues across the country.[104] Eduardo Paolozzi, Richard Hamilton and Peter Blake had already created the first distinctively English contribution to Modernism: Pop Art.[105] Inspired by the avant-garde intransigence of the Constructivists and the Surrealists, radical artists now began organising happenings which subverted the commercial logic of the gallery system. During the mid-1960s, John Latham's *Skoob Tower* ceremonies and Adrian Mitchell's *Collage-Events* were admired as transient moments of participatory creativity that couldn't be packaged and sold to connoisseurs, curators or collectors.[106] When hydrochloric· acid was eating away Gustav Metzger's nylon-and-metal sculptures, the museum object had definitely met its aesthetic nemesis: Auto-Destructive Art.[107] Most wonderfully, these avant-garde interventions heralded the early stirrings of a hedonistic transformation of stuffy English society as a whole. On 11th June 1965, Trocchi had acted as the master of ceremonies at the *International Poetry Incarnation* in London's Albert Hall. Bringing together the literary stars of the beat generation, this happening became the first mass gathering of the English hippie subculture. As the Situationists had argued, avant-garde art would become truly subversive when it began remaking everyday life in its own image.[108]

What the editors of *Heatwave* had found in Paris was a dedicated group of intellectuals who were at the forefront of the New Left's

---

[104] See Jeff Nuttall, *Bomb Culture*, pages 11–103; and Simon Frith and Howard Horne, *Art into Pop*, pages 27–70.

[105] See Marco Livingstone, *Pop Art*, pages 32–45, 92–113.

[106] See Jeff Nuttall, *Bomb Culture*, pages 114–125.

[107] See Gustav Metzger, *Damaged Nature, Auto-Destructive Art*, pages 25–63.

[108] For eye-witness accounts of this event, see Jonathon Green, *Days in the Life*, pages 64–74.

melding of political and aesthetic rebellion. In contrast with the worthy publications of the Bolshevik and Anarchist sects, each issue of *Internationale Situationniste* – with its metal cover, gloss paper pages, minimalist layout and ironic illustrations – was a beautiful artwork. In this journal, Debord and his comrades had long championed the DIY ethos which was now driving the hippie generation's direct action campaigns.[109] Since the late-1950s, they'd been arguing that the new youth subcultures were latest iteration of the avant-garde insurrection. For the *Heatwave* group, what emphatically distinguished the Situationists from their American peers was their theoretical rigour. The writers of *Rebel Worker* and other underground papers in the USA also enthusiastically promoted a mix of participatory politics and leftfield culture. However, it was only the Situationist International that had formulated a detailed and penetrating analysis which could explain the new forms of class struggle emerging within Fordist abundance.

Most impressively, in *The Decline and Fall of the Spectacular Commodity Society*, they'd provided a lucid analysis of the world-historical significance of the 1965 Watts Uprising which had eluded the Bolsheviks and Anarchists. Far from deploring the looting of shops by the rioters like other Left groups, the Situationists had extolled this 'potlatch of destruction' as the revolutionary moment when the African-American youth of Los Angeles had broken the tyranny of consumer capitalism over everyday life by taking what they needed by force. Just like avant-garde artists, disenfranchised inner-city proletarians wanted to do things for themselves. In 1966, determined to forge a formal alliance with the instigators of this new wisdom, a delegation from *Heatwave* made a pilgrimage to Paris. After an intense meeting in Debord's flat, Gray, Nicholson-Smith and Radcliffe – along with Tim Clark – were inducted into full membership of the Situationist International.[110] Returning to London, these four friends set to work on producing translations of the key texts from the French – and applying their theoretical insights to what was taking place at home. For the first time, Situationism had acquired an English accent. Thanks to its four newest

---

109 See Laurent Chollet, *L'Insurrection Situationniste*, pages 21–111; and Günter Berghaus, 'Happenings in Europe'.

110 See Charles Radcliffe, 'Two Fiery Flying Rolls', pages 357–366.

recruits, the locals now had a clever interpretor of the new avant-garde teachings from the continent.

The founders of the English Section were fervently convinced that the 1960s youth rebellion was the harbinger of a fully-fledged proletarian revolution. During its short period of agitation, this group would never grow beyond a dozen or so supporters.[111] Yet, despite these limited resources, they took upon themselves the difficult task of popularising the Situationists' sophisticated interpretation of this New Left prophecy amongst the nation's political and aesthetic dissidents. To realise their ambition, the English Section would first have to overcome the old Left orthodoxy that Modernist art and popular culture were implacable enemies. In his 1957 classic *The Uses of Literacy*, Richard Hoggart had mourned the corruption of the children of the English working class by American-style consumerism. Dancing mindlessly to Top 40 hits in coffee bars wearing the latest fashions was a betrayal of everything that their valiant socialist forebears had fought and suffered for.[112] Growing up during the post-war boom, the militants of the English Section instinctively knew the fallacy of this old school Left argument. What Hoggart and his acolytes couldn't comprehend was the subversive potential of the new forms of popular culture. Aided by the recent arrival of immigrants from the Caribbean and the presence of African-American military personnel in the country, young people in England were learning how to shed their parents' imperialist prejudices and appreciate the pleasures of jazz, blues, rock 'n' roll, ska and soul music. Better contraception and more tolerant sexual attitudes were removing their fear of the puritan patriarch. Pot, speed and acid were helping them to lose their British stiffness and inhibitions.[113] Every concert, publication, party, screening, performance, demonstration, happening and exhibition was liberating social space from the grasp of the philistine establishment.[114] For the members of the English Section in the mid-1960s, Situationism was the subversive doctrine that explained

---

[111]   See Gill Woodward, 'Interview with the Author and Ilze Black'.

[112]   See Richard Hoggart, *The Uses of Literacy*, pages 205–272.

[113]   See George Melly, *Revolt into Style*, pages 3–124; and Mick Farren, *Give the Anarchist a Cigarette*, pages 5–114.

[114]   See Charles Radcliffe, 'The Seeds of Social Destruction'.

why this loosening of controls over everyday life had transformed what it meant to be a political revolutionary. Under Fordism, the Left required a theoretical analysis which was focused upon '... bringing the subjective and objective together.'[115]

During the late-1950s, the Campaign for Nuclear Disarmament had been the first mass movement in Western Europe since the early-20th century that had combined direct action protests and bohemian lifestyles into one rebellious movement. Crucially, these English pioneers of the New Left had no problems in making a clear distinction between their hatred for American atomic weapons and their admiration for American musicians, writers and painters.[116] As in other developed countries of the period, the rapid growth of youth subcultures gave confidence to those who were looking for more militant forms of political involvement than traditional parliamentary, trade union or student politics. Instead of delegating leadership to elected officials, these activists organised demonstrations, occupations and wildcat strikes that enabled them to take power into their own hands. It was this vehement rejection of the old Left's bureaucratic hierarchies that would create the New Left's distinctive identity.[117] Like avant-garde artists, its youthful activists also dreamt of a participatory future. As the most advanced current of this new working class, the English Section would provide the intelligent theory which illuminated the proletariat's arduous path from spectacular capitalism to libertarian communism.

Much to their delight, Gray and his comrades had discovered a prototype of the New Left insurgency close to home. In 1965, the Provo movement in Amsterdam had successfully mobilised a motley coalition of young workers, students and drop-outs in protest against the apathy and conservatism of Dutch society.[118] In both issues of *Heatwave*, they published enthusiastic reports calling for the lessons of this uprising to be studied – and applied – in England. If the New

---

[115] Gill Woodward, 'Interview with the Author and Ilze Black'.

[116] See Jeff Nuttall, *Bomb Culture*, pages 44–52; and Jonathon Green, *Days in the Life*, pages 5–7, 23–25.

[117] See David Widgery, *The Left in Britain 1956–1968*; and George Katsiaficas, *The Imagination of the New Left*.

[118] See Richard Kempton, *Provo*; and Richard Neville, *Playpower*, pages 21–24.

Left could shake up sleepy Amsterdam, just imagine what could be achieved in Europe's capital city of youth subcultures: London.[119] Yet, to their dismay, the founders of English Situationism found their Dutch comrades' attempts at theorising the 1960s generation's turn towards participatory politics unconvincing. Like *Rebel Worker* claiming descent from the US branch of Surrealism, the Provos had traced their lineage back to Anarchism. Both of these New Left groups were trying to understand what was now with what was past. Fortunately, by joining the Situationist International, the English Section had avoided making the same mistake. The modern world could only be understood with its most up-to-date theory.

In 1967, English Section published a pamphlet containing one of the most notorious Situationist texts: Mustapha Khayati's *On the Poverty of Student Life*. A year earlier, sympathisers of the International at Strasbourg University in France had taken control of its student union. Diverting funds from their intended purposes, they'd paid for the printing and distribution of free copies of Khayati's blistering attack on the multiple failings of the French higher education system. When these young militants were subsequently prosecuted for misappropriating the student union's money, the shock and outrage expressed by reactionary politicians, professors, judges and media commentators during the court case created invaluable publicity for the pamphlet's arguments amongst its intended audience.[120] Showing their admiration for this successful application of the Situationist tactic of provocation in Strasbourg, the English Section updated the title of John Reed's famous book on the 1917 Russian Revolution for its translation of Khayati's pamphlet: *Ten Days That Shook The University*. The target of this détournement was well chosen. With student militancy on the rise, the Bolshevik sects were already fantasising about establishing Red Bases in the nation's campuses which would ignite the 'Coming British Revolution'.[121] However, any unsuspecting reader who – from the pamphlet's title – thought that the English Situationists might share

---

[119] See Charles Radcliffe, 'Two Fiery Flying Rolls', pages 351–355.

[120] See the Situationist International, 'Nos Buts et Nos Méthodes dans le Scandale de Strasbourg'; and Vincent Kaufman, *Guy Debord*, pages 178–82.

[121] See Alexander Cockburn and Robin Blackburn, *Student Power*; and Tariq Ali, *The Coming British Revolution*.

this illusion would have been quickly disappointed. Far from praising students as the new political vanguard, Khayati's diatribe castigated them for their passivity and timidity. Most of these trainee intellectuals didn't even have the courage to protest against the ideological stupidities of the university curriculum. The only good thing about studying in higher education was that living off a student grant was easier than working in a boring job.[122] By publishing this polemic, the English Section had delineated itself against the dominant orthodoxy within the New Left. No minority – especially not a minority of radical students – could substitute itself for the working class as a whole. The proletarian revolution was poetry made by all.

Not surprisingly, traditionalists amongst the 1960s British Left were also highly suspicious of the student protest movement. Dedicated to Labour party and trade union politics, they '… saw the new [youth pop] culture as a distraction from the real issues.'[123] What made Khayati's pamphlet stand out was its contempt for this anachronistic attitude without making the opposite error of uncritically enthusing about campus militancy. Crucially, this Situationist theorist argued that the bohemian lifestyles of artists, hooligans and students were a premonition of the communist future in the capitalist present.[124] In their appendix to *Ten Days That Shook The University*, the English Section provided its own interpretation of this compelling prophecy. Through their hedonistic and spontaneous lifestyles, avant-garde art movements and youth subcultures were prefiguring the shape of things to come. In both the West and the East, experts were predicting that – with the greater economic productivity brought about by through the convergence of computing, telecommunications and media into the Net – people would soon no longer need to devote most of their waking hours to boring work in factories and offices.[125] Vaneigem's scepticism about technological utopianism was temporarily forgotten. In their appendix to Khayati's pamphlet, the English Section proclaimed that

---

[122] See Mustapha Khayati, 'On the Poverty of Student Life', pages 319–326.

[123] Michael Crick, *Militant*, page 56.

[124] See Mustapha Khayati, 'On the Poverty of Student Life', pages 326–337.

[125] See Marshall McLuhan, *Understanding Media*, pages 346–359; and Triple Revolution Committee, 'The Triple Revolution'.

the total emancipation of humanity was imminent. Within a decade or so, when the imaginary future of the information society arrived, alienated workers would be reborn as artist-intellectuals – and everyday life would become spontaneous, creative and playful. Cybernetic communism was a Situationist game where everyone is a winner.[126] The title of English Section's appendix said it all: *The Revolution of Modern Art and the Art of Modern Revolution.*

---

[126] The English Section was echoing the radicals in the East who argued that the invention of the Net would realise the disappointed promises of participatory democracy and economic self-management of the 1917 Russian Revolution, see Radovan Richta, *Civilisation at the Crossroads*; Aksel Berg, 'Cybernetics and Education'; and Richard Barbrook, *Imaginary Futures*, pages 136–161.

1.6: POWER TO THE PEOPLE!

The 1967 translation of Khayati's pamphlet with its long afterword turned out to be the one and only official publication of the English Section of the Situationist International. As a test of loyalty, the Paris headquarters ordered its London outpost to sever all contacts with a fiery New York magazine: *Up Against the Wall Motherfucker*. Debord had always been suspicious about the English Section's susceptibility to the psychedelic romanticism of the American hippie subculture. Now they would have to choose which side were they on. Not surprisingly, when this request from Paris was politely refused, its three remaining members were summarily expelled from the International.[127] Undaunted by this break with the mainland, the founders of English Situationism began 1968 by launching their own magazine: *King Mob Echo*. Reinforced by fresh recruits, they were now ready to launch their assault against the British establishment. Announcing its licentious ambitions, this New Left journal was named after a graffiti celebrating the insurgent multitude – 'His Majesty King Mob' – who'd burnt down Newgate jail during the 1780 Gordon Riots in London.[128] Although lacking the production values of *Internationale Situationniste*, its pages provided a similarly idiosyncratic melange of political diatribes and cultural polemics. Freed from French supervision, the writers of *King Mob Echo* could now happily mash up the insights of Debord, Jorn, Vaniegem and Khayati with those of William Blake, Karl Marx, Wilhelm Reich, Antonin Artaud and Ben Morea. Adapting to local conditions, English Situationism was finding its own voice.[129]

Then, in May 1968, the long-dreamt-of-revolution unexpectedly took place in France. A few months earlier, inspired by the scandalous

---

[127] See the Situationist International, 'The Latest Exclusions'; and David Wise, 'A Hidden History of King Mob'. For the story of these American comrades, see Black Mask & Up Against The Wall Motherfucker, *The Incomplete Works*.

[128] See David Wise, 'A Hidden History of King Mob'. For the 18th century 'political riots' that inspired this name, see George Rudé, *Hanoverian London*, pages 205–227.

[129] See the 6 issues of this magazine in the English Section of the Situationist International, *King Mob Echo*, pages 71–129.

activities of the Strasbourg Situationists, a small group of activists at Nanterre University had decided that they too would provoke the academic establishment and – when it predictably overreacted – their more hesitant peers would be swept up into their campaign of direct action.[130] Over the weeks that followed, the wildest hopes of these New Left agitators were fulfilled. Their localised confrontation with the university authorities in Nanterre quickly spread to other campuses across France. By the beginning of May, students and police were fighting each other in the streets of Paris. As the barricades went up and the Sorbonne was declared a liberated zone, the Stalinist and Social Democratic trade unions called for a general strike in solidarity with this youthful protest movement. For a brief moment, France appeared to be on the brink of a fundamental societal transformation. Massive demonstrations filled the streets of Paris and other major cities. Ten million people were out on strike. Workers were taking over the factories. Students were occupying the universities. Peasants were supplying free food to the protesters. Doctors and nurses were running the hospitals. Footballers declared that from now on they'd manage the football teams. On the walls of Paris, a revolutionary slogan proclaimed this new dispensation: 'Be realistic, demand the impossible!'[131]

Across the channel, the members of King Mob were mesmerised by the social upheaval that was shaking France. For those who understood, the Situationists were the occult theorists behind the May '68 French Revolution. Most gratifyingly for their English admirers, it was the International's searing attacks on consumer society which had inspired the striking posters and evocative slogans that would come to symbolise these dramatic events.[132] In Paris and other cities, the insurgent crowds were realising the International's libertarian vision of the proletarian revolution as a playful outburst of festive street

---

[130] See Daniel Cohn-Bendit and Gabriel Cohn-Bendit, *Obsolete Communism*, pages 25–28.

[131] See the instant journalist histories of May '68: Allan Priaulx and Sanford Ungar, *The Almost Revolution*; and Patrick Seale and Maureen McConville, *French Revolution 1968*.

[132] See Vladimir Fisera, *Writing on the Wall*; and Mésa, *Mai 68 – Les Affiches de l'Atelier Populaire*.

theatre.[133] Above all, the Situationists had kept faith with their most important strategic principle: 'We shall not lead, we will only detonate!' As the revolutionary crisis of May '68 reached its climax, Debord and his comrades joined up with the most radical elements amongst the Nanterre students and the libertarian communist sects to form the Committee for the Maintenance of the Occupations. Convinced that the moment of victory was near, these Situationists urged the striking workers to administer the death blow against the society of the spectacle by seizing control of the institutions of political, economic and ideological domination. Now more than ever, the old adage was true that any revolution that is made half-way was doomed to failure. The wage increases promised by the French bosses were meaningless when the abolition of the wage system was in sight. The leadership of Social Democratic and Bolshevik parties was obsolete when people were taking control over their own lives. Cybernetic communism would soon make everyone into players in a ludic celebration of mutual desire and collective creativity. There could be no compromises with the old system.[134]

When the strikers reluctantly went back to work and order was eventually restored in France over the summer of 1968, the Situationists could take pride in the uncompromising political positions which they'd championed during these revolutionary events. If nothing else, the International had proved that it was possible for the New Left to resist the temptations of bourgeois recuperation. Emboldened by the inspiring example of insurrectionary France, King Mob now set to work on applying the lessons of May '68 at home. Only a few months earlier, these young agitators had had no hesitation in placing themselves in the front line of the violent confrontation

---

[133] '[Jean-Jacques] Lebel regarded his participation in the burning down of the Paris Stock Exchange on 24th May 1968 as the pinnacle of his career as a happenings artist.' Günter Berghaus, 'Happenings in Europe', page 375.

[134] For the International's analysis of its involvement in the May '68 Revolution, see the Situationist International, 'Beginning of an Era'; and René Viénet, *Enragés and Situationists in the Occupation Movement*.

with the police outside the US embassy in London at the end of a massive demonstration against the American invasion of Vietnam.[135] Over the next two years, the growing circle of militants influenced by King Mob became heavily involved in two direct action campaigns in West London: the Claimants' Union which mobilised the recipients of state benefits and Up Against the Law which protested against police harassment of hippies and immigrants.[136] These activists threw themselves into Notting Hill's thriving underground arts scene. They took part in the liberation of a privately owned garden to provide a community playground for the deprived inhabitants of this bohemian neighbourhood.[137] As innovators of graffiti art, they defiantly expressed their disdain for the affluent society by daubing a slogan in large white letters on a nearby motorway intersection: 'Same thing day after day – tube – work – dinner – work – tube – armchair – TV – sleep – tube – work – how much more can you take? – one in ten go mad – one in five cracks up.' In a celebrated action on 21st December 1968, members of King Mob – including one dressed up as Father Christmas – went to a central London department store where they gave away the toys on the shelves to the children who were there with their parents. In the ensuing pandemonium, as the TV news and the press gleefully reported, security staff had to seize back the shop's property from crying kids while the police tried to arrest these Situationist subverters of the holy season of mass consumption.[138] The lessons of the Notre Dame and Strasbourg scandals had been well learnt in London. The spectacle could be turned against itself.

---

[135] See David Wise, 'A Hidden History of King Mob'; and, for eye-witness accounts of this protest, Jonathon Green, *Days in the Life*, pages 240–246.

[136] Living amongst Afro-Caribbeans, these white radicals were able to learn from the Black Power movement's strategy of self-reliance, see John Williams, *Michael X*, pages 81–93; and Jonathon Green, *Days in the Life*, pages 343–353.

[137] See David Wise, 'A Hidden History of King Mob'; and John Barker, 'Interview with the Author and Ilze Black'. For an overview of these late-1960s New Left protest movements in West London, see Jan O'Malley, *The Politics of Community Action*.

[138] See David Wise, 'A Hidden History of King Mob'; the English Section of the Situationist International, *King Mob Echo*, pages 92–101; and Gill Woodward, 'Interview with the Author and Ilze Black'.

In 1970, a handful of English activists formed the world's first – and only – Situationist terrorist group: the Angry Brigade.[139] Over the next two years, their feats of revolutionary daring would repeatedly grab the lead item on the TV news bulletins and the front page headlines in the newspapers. Blowing up the homes of smug Tory ministers and bullying Ford factory managers cheered up disgruntled workers who were forced to consume the tendentious monologue of the media spectacle. Bomb attacks against the Miss Word beauty contest and the Biba fashion boutique sabotaged the relentless sexist commercialisation of women's lives.[140] As John Barker emphasised, in stark contrast with other early-1970s New Left terrorist groups like the Weather Underground in the USA, the Angry Brigade never showed any interest in launching a direct assault on the security apparatuses of the bourgeois state. Instead, its revolutionary actions were carefully targeted on disrupting the consensual complacency of the mass media.[141] After much effort, the British police eventually identified the likely perpetrators of the Angry Brigade's campaign of violent protest. At the end of 1971, a house was raided in East London, incriminating evidence was somehow found and – after a famous trial at the country's top court – four New Left activists were sentenced to long terms in jail. Not surprisingly, the mass media was jubilant at this victory of law 'n' order over the young defendants in the dock. The spectacle had had its revenge on the defilers of the spectacle.[142]

Paradoxically, the demise of the Angry Brigade confirmed the arrival of Situationism as a distinct political current within the English New Left. Back in 1968, the small band of activists who'd published *King Mob Echo* had been almost alone in their enthusiasm for the theoretical insights of the International. At this historical moment,

---

[139] In contrast, the International's headquarters was contemptuous of the New Left's fascination with urban guerrilla warfare, see Gianfranco Sanguinetti, *On Terrorism and the State*.

[140] See the group's communiques in Jean Weir, *The Angry Brigade*, pages 23–39.

[141] See John Barker, 'The Weatherman Meets the Angry Brigade'; and 'Interview with the Author and Ilze Black'. John Barker was one of the four people sentenced to 10 years in jail for the Angry Brigade's campaign. For the story of the Weather Underground, see Dan Berger, *Outlaws of America*.

[142] See Gordon Carr, *The Angry Brigade*; Stuart Christie, *Edward Heath Made Me Angry*; and John Barker, 'Review Article: *Anarchy in the UK*'.

the overwhelming majority of the New Left in England still hadn't moved beyond the rigid ideological dividing lines of the 1917 Russian Revolution. Amongst this milieu, Situationism was too libertarian for its Bolsheviks and too Marxist for its Anarchists – and much too arty for both of them. Worst of all, this new avant-garde paradigm from the continent flouted the sociological shibboleths of early-20th century Left politics. King Mob was wasting its time trying to organise hippie drop-outs, petty criminals and welfare claimants in inner city London. Factory workers were the only section of the proletariat which could overthrow the capitalist system. For this iteration of the New Left, reviving the revolutionary past was the sole path to the socialist future.

Yet, by the time that the first issue of *King Mob Echo* appeared in 1968, the post-Fordist remaking of the working class was already underway within England's deprived urban neighbourhoods. In contrast with the majority of the New Left, the activists of this magazine had realised that – when the local population wasn't directly employed in manufacturing – community activism and cultural subversion were now the most effective forms of collective resistance. As its extreme manifestation, the armed actions of the Angry Brigade had expressed the ferocity of this growing youth revolt against the society of the spectacle.[143] A generation had been radicalised and was looking for a intelligent political theory to explain their deep hatred of consumer conformism. During the early-1970s, in the pages of *OZ, iT* and other English alternative publications, this more advanced Situationist interpretation of New Left theory was now given extensive coverage.[144] Their readers welcomed its brilliant intellectual confirmation that the libertarian mores of the hippie subculture prefigured the destruction of the entire rotten capitalist system. For them, the writings of Situationism provided the tactical manual for an intoxicating fusion of activism and art into the all-transforming revolution of everyday life. As the editor of the English underground newspaper *Friends* later recollected, the brightest minds of his generation now possessed: '... [the] rational explanation for our irresponsible behaviour and urges

---

[143] See John Barker, 'Interview with the Author and Ilze Black'.

[144] See Angelo Quattrocchi, 'The Situationists are Coming'; and Nigel Fountain, *Underground*, pages 58–59.

... [the theory] to see everything, absolutely everything, in terms of political activity.'[145]

1.7: THE LAST GANG IN TOWN

In 1969, Martin Housden and his Situationist friends in West London decided to launch an assault against the media spectacle by setting up their own rock band: Thanatos. With their celebrity status, country mansions and aristocratic friends, the rich and pampered pop stars who dominated the nation's airwaves were the epitome of the recuperation of the new youth subcultures by the entertainment industry. Learned in the avant-garde tactics of Situationism, Thanatos sought to subvert the fans who worshipped these false idols. Combining provocation and détournement, its planned repertoire included songs with lyrics taken from Jack the Ripper's letter taunting the police and William Blake's *Tyger, Tyger* poem. The messages in Thanatos' tunes would never fit comfortably into the Top 40 playlist. Above all, these songs were devised as communal scratch renditions. Everyone was going to be a star at their performances. By breaking down the barriers between the fans in the auditorium and the musicians on the stage, Thanatos would prove that the masses could make their own media.[146]

Unfortunately, the ambitions of this methedrine-inspired Notting Hill fantasy were never fulfilled at the time. Yet, in this thought experiment, these admirers of King Mob had anticipated the winning strategy which would soon become the leitmotif of English Situationism. During their short-lived association in the late-1960s, what had distinguished this island outpost of the International from the mainland headquarters was its close involvement with London's youth subcultures.[147] Despite their enthusiasm for teenage hooligans, Watts rioters and Strasbourg students, Debord and his comrades had always stayed aloof from the 1960s' new manifestations of bohemianism. Above all, they'd kept faith with the industrial proletariat as the revolutionary subject of history. During May '68, it was only when workers began occupying their factories and offices that the dominance of capital had been seriously threatened. In contrast, the activists of King Mob were convinced that the members of youth subcultures now made the best soldiers for anti-spectacular warfare. Mods, bikers, beatniks and hippies were the true

---

[146] See Martin Housden, 'Interview with the Author and Ilze Black'.

[147] See Charles Radcliffe, 'Two Fiery Flying Rolls', pages 374–375.

revolutionaries of everyday life.[148] Given its geographical location, this ideological divergence of the English Section from its French mentor was almost inevitable. Speaking the same language as the Americans and situated on the same continent as the Europeans, London was a sweet point of the emerging global youth counter-culture. Having lost an empire, the English had discovered a new role: turning on the world. Paris might have had the May '68 Revolution, but London had the Rolling Stones, the Kinks and the Who.[149] Not surprisingly, like *Up Against The Wall Motherfucker* and the Yippies in America, the militants around *King Mob Echo* dreamt of transforming this late-1960s cultural rebellion into a fully-fledged social revolution.[150] The Paris headquarters just didn't get it. Youth movements were the new revolutionary subject of history. The English Situationists had learnt to speak in the local dialect.

In 1974, Gray published *Leaving the 20th Century* to codify these insights. This founder of King Mob had been horrified by the bombings and shootings of the Angry Brigade. His book would provide English malcontents with a more subtle interpretation of the Situationists' strategy for New Left insurgency.[151] In its introduction, Gray explained that his compilation was deliberately selective. It was no accident that most of the texts in *Leaving the 20th Century* came from the '... initial, predominantly 'artistic', period of Situationist activity.'[152] During this formative stage, the International had formulated its cutting-edge combination of four avant-garde tactics: provocation, détournement, psychogeography and participatory creativity. With great skill, Gray devised *Leaving the 20th Century* as an instruction manual of cultural mischief for English Situationists. The armed actions of the Angry Brigade had ended in defeat. Learning from this reverse, the next

---

[148] See Charles Radcliffe, 'The Seeds of Social Destruction'; and the English Section of the Situationist International, *The Revolution of Modern Art and the Modern Art of Revolution*, pages 22–24.

[149] See George Melly, *Revolt into Style*; and Simon Frith and Howard Horne, *Art into Pop*, pages 71–93.

[150] For the manifestos of these US New Left media pranksters, see Black Mask & Up Against The Wall Motherfucker, *The Incomplete Works*; and Jerry Rubin, *Do It!*.

[151] See David Wise, 'A Hidden History of King Mob'; and Richard Parry, 'Preface'.

[152] Chris Gray, *Leaving the 20th Century*, page 6.

iteration of English Situationism must rediscover the delights of radicalising the nation's disaffected youth subcultures. By carefully studying the texts in *Leaving the 20th Century*, its readers could learn the intricacies of the International's four stratagems for fighting the media spectacle. Best of all, when they were successfully put into practice, everyone could become a Situationist.

By publishing *Leaving the 20th Century*, Gray became a proselytiser for the democratisation of avant-garde art in England. Across the world, visitors to galleries and exhibitions were drawn from the most privileged and educated sections of society. Amongst this minority, it was only a select few who were capable of understanding – and appreciating – how avant-garde artists were subverting aesthetic orthodoxy.[153] Yet, back in the 1920s, the Surrealists and Constructivists had briefly broken out of this cultural ghetto by identifying themselves with the Bolshevik cause. Radicals knew that it was possible to create the seemingly impossible: avant-garde art with mass appeal. With Surrealism and Constructivism having been largely recuperated, *Leaving the 20th Century* was a primer in the new subversive teachings from the continent which promised to revive this heady moment of aesthetic rebellion for the hippie generation. By studying Gray's book, English activists could learn how to apply the four tactics of Situationism to disrupt the turgid monologue of the media spectacle. In bohemian neighbourhoods across the country, there was already a thriving scene of rock bands, underground newspapers, head shops, communal squats, night clubs and free festivals. In his book, Gray had provided its denizens with battle-tested stratagems for radicalising this youth subculture. The insights of the avant-garde would no longer be confined within the gallery system. The most revolutionary art was going to be made out in the streets.

While compiling *Leaving the 20th Century*, Gray linked up with a new generation of cultural subversives. In 1970, from their safe base at Croydon Art School, a group of friends led by Jamie Reid had started a leftfield magazine: *Suburban Press*. Learning from their King Mob predecessors, these young activists soon became adepts of the

---

[153] See Pierre Bourdieu, *Distinction*; and Pierre Bourdieu and Alain Darbel, *The Love of Art*.

International's four tactics of aesthetic insubordination. Over the next few years, this English Situationist journal published thoughtful articles on the alienated spaces of modern life and the social impact of teenage disaffection. Even better, its readers were provided with the artistic means to put theory into practice inside the covers of *Suburban Press*. The more daring among them could stick up the magazine's flyers announcing a free shopping day at their local supermarket and plaster its official-looking posters denouncing the lies of the media monopolists around their neighbourhoods.[154] Endowing this revival of the avant-garde interpretation of Situationism with his prestige as a founder of King Mob, Gray asked Reid to design the layout of *Leaving the 20ᵗʰ Century*. Bombs and guns had proved their ineffectiveness in the anti-spectacular struggle. In its new iteration, English Situationism must instead focus upon the International's four techniques of artistic subversion. As would soon become apparent, Gray's message did successfully reach its intended audience. *Leaving the 20ᵗʰ Century* was about to become the tactical manual for the next upsurge of youth rebellion.

What – in the authoritative accounts – has given such historical importance to *Suburban Press* was its role as the harbinger of the punk movement in England. During the late-1960s, Reid had met Malcolm McLaren and Vivienne Westwood when they were all art students. Together, they'd discovered the ideas of Situationism by hanging around the periphery of the King Mob scene.[155] By 1971, Reid's two colleagues had teamed up to open a clothes shop at the cheaper end of London's Kings Road. For McLaren and Westwood, alternative fashion was much more than applied art. In their store, the ideas of *Suburban Press* would become tools of aesthetic dissent. Like the writers of *King Mob Echo*, they too were convinced that drop-outs, students and petty criminals were now the most rebellious elements within English society. Having studied *Leaving the 20ᵗʰ Century*, they set to work on applying its four Situationist tactics of artistic subversion to mobilise these disaffected young people for the revolutionary cause. Unfortunately, McLaren and Westwood's initial attempts to radicalise Teddy Boys and

---

154 See Jamie Reid and Jon Savage, *Up They Rise*, pages 17–46.

155 See Fred Vermorel, 'At The End, They Even Stole His Death', pages 206–208.

bikers floundered on the nostalgic rigidity of these outsider subcultures. In their shop's next makeover, sexual fetishists eagerly bought its new line of S&M clothing, but they too proved to be politically timid. Innovating and appropriating, McLaren and Westwood eventually found a group of eager recruits for their Situationist media uprising: the punks.[156] It was these devotees of their clothes shop that quickly became the catalysts of a radical transformation of the styles and attitudes which defined London's bohemian scene. Punk defiance not hippie pacifism was now the order of the day. As the Clash eulogised in their stirring song, this youth subculture took pride in being the London Trained Bands of the new English Civil War.[157]

By 1976, the *Suburban Press* posse was in command of the burgeoning punk movement. With a mixture of guile and chutzpah, McLaren was presiding over the rise of its seminal rock group: the Sex Pistols. Westwood devised the outrageous fashions that shocked both suit-and-tie commuters and denim-clad hippies. Reid's cut-and-paste designs for the Pistols' flyers, posters, record covers and adverts marked this new youth subculture's aesthetic break with the psychedelic 1960s. Bernie Rhodes – another *Suburban Press* contributor – was managing the Clash with its heady combination of amphetamine-powered tunes, tough political slogans and paint-splattered clothes. Fred Vermorel – a co-conspirator of McLaren's from his student days – was the learned chronicler of the punk movement. With *Leaving the 20ᵗʰ Century* as their tactical manual, these art school alumni were applying the four Situationist techniques of aesthetic dissidence to foment a new youth subcultural insurrection. Denouncing the hippie pop stars for selling-out labelled them as 'boring old farts'. Mixing and matching the fashions of Teds, bikers, Mods, S&M enthusiasts, glam stars and rent boys became the unique punk look. Swearing on a family TV programme set off a media storm that made the Sex Pistols into headline news. Banned from playing in venues across the country turned this band into the must-see live act of the moment. Being dropped by one multinational record label quickly led to a bidding war between its

---

[156]   See Fred and Judy Vermorel, *Sex Pistols*, pages 214–225; and Jon Savage, *England's Dreaming*, pages 27–129.

[157]   See The Clash, *Give 'Em Enough Rope*. For the decisive role of the London Trained Bands in the 1642 English Revolution, see Wilfrid Emberton, *Skippon's Brave Boys*.

rivals to sign the Sex Pistols. Confirming the analysis of *Leaving the 20ᵗʰ Century*, big business was as eager as ever to make money out of artistic subversion. Armed with this knowledge, the English Situationists were able to turn this process of recuperation against itself. Having secured a new contract with a music company, they now had the means to disseminate their insurrectionary message to the masses. In the summer of 1977, while the British establishment smugly commemorated the 25ᵗʰ anniversary of Elizabeth Windsor's accession to the throne, the Sex Pistols released a killer tune lambasting this celebration of hypocrisy and deference: *God Save The Queen*. When this record became the best-selling single of Jubilee week, the powers-that-be fixed the pop charts to prevent an anti-monarchist diatribe taking the Number One spot.[158] Most wonderfully, through this shocking Situationist détournement of the national anthem, buying a punk commodity had become a scream of proletarian defiance: 'We're the flowers in the dustbin, we're the poison in your human machine, we're the future, your future!'[159]

In its late-1970s iteration, English Situationism had won a notable victory over the spectacular enemy. Sabotaging the Queen's Jubilee was the fulfilment of the revolutionary ambitions of King Mob and *Suburban Press* – and much more. The turgid protests of the Bolshevik and Anarchist sects against this monarchist humbug had no resonance outside the usual suspects. In contrast, the intelligent application of Situationist tactics had succeeded in shattering the carefully constructed media image of the British people united in subservience to their bourgeois sovereign. What Thanatos had dreamt in 1969, the Sex Pistols realised in 1977. It was possible to release a Number One single that was unplayable on the Top 40 countdown show. In 1978, with money from the band's best-selling records, McLaren began making a film with Julien Temple that told the fabulous tale of how the Sex Pistols had battle-tested the International's tactics for subverting the media spectacle: *The Great Rock 'n' Roll Swindle*. The infamous provocations, clever détournements, psychogeographic evocations and communal celebrations of the glory days of punk were

---

158   See Fred and Judy Vermorel, *Sex Pistols*, pages 10–93; and Jon Savage, *England's Dreaming*, pages 107–367.

159   Sex Pistols, *God Save The Queen*.

all lovingly remembered in its melange of music videos, documentary footage, cartoon sequences and fictionalised re-enactments. Despite these genuflections to the genre, McLaren and Temple's film was no hagiographic rock documentary. Like *Leaving the 20ᵗʰ Century*, this movie provided a tactical manual for sabotaging the society of the spectacle.

Not surprisingly, writing his own history, McLaren cast himself as the Situationist mastermind behind the rise and fall of the Sex Pistols. Paying respect to King Mob, the film opened with a riotous crowd running with torches through the city streets of late-18ᵗʰ century London. Arriving at a gallows, these ne'er-do-wells started stringing up effigies of the Sex Pistols and then setting them on fire. No one – especially not the members of this iconic punk band – could escape retribution for elevating themselves above the mutinous multitude. Towards the end of the film, McLaren hammered home this anti-recuperation message. A young punk pretended to be the submissive fan of a decadent hippie rock star, but – as soon as they were alone – she revealed herself as his ruthless assassin. In the film's opening sequence, McLaren proclaimed his Situationist antidote for the corrupting powers of the music industry. Having lost their charismatic front man, the members of the band were holding auditions for a new lead singer. The title of this talent show said it all: 'Anyone Can Be A Sex Pistol'.[160] The film was a mess and the group was falling apart, but McLaren could still take satisfaction in the greatest achievement of the punk movement: the upsurge in participatory creativity across England. Over the course of *The Great Rock 'n' Roll Swindle*, McLaren helpfully summarised the tactical lessons of his adventures with the Sex Pistols into 10 commandments of cultural subversion for young dissidents.[161] In cinemas and video stores across the world, the revolutionary teachings of English Situationism were now available to one and all.

When, as a 19-year-old student in spring 1976, I went to see Patti Smith, Talking Heads and the Ramones at their first gigs in London,

---

[160]   See Julien Temple, *The Great Rock 'n' Roll Swindle*; Jon Savage, *England's Dreaming*, pages 497–541; and Joel McIver, *The Making of the Great Rock 'n' Roll Swindle*.

[161]   See Jamie Reid and Jon Savage, *Up They Rise*, pages 86–87.

there was no doubt that punk meant New York. This American city had defined the lo-fi sound and ripped-and-torn style of our new generation of cultural rebels. Even the name itself came from there.[162] Yet, before the year was out, it was London that was the undisputed global centre of the punk movement. The Sex Pistols and the Clash were now the leaders of the pack – and the pioneering New York bands had become their imitators. Once again, London had benefited from its unique linguistic and geographical position. Living in the capital of anglophone Europe, avant-garde innovators could take influences from both continents and then combine them into something superior. The initiators of punk in New York may have broken with the tunes and fashions of the hippie counter-culture, but they'd been unable to devise a hard-edged political strategy for preventing a repetition of its sad story of sold-out stars and broken promises. Fortunately, thanks to their proximity to Paris, their peers in London did have an effective response to recuperation by the music industry. In *Leaving the 20th Century*, they'd found a persuasive explanation for why the 1960s rock 'n' roll rebels had capitulated to the class enemy. Just like Modernist artists in earlier times, these hippie radicals had underestimated the seductive power of the cultural mandarins. Money and celebrity were the bourgeoisie's most dangerous weapons in the spectacular phase of capitalist domination. Exemplifying this recuperative process, underground musicians had been turned into pop stars whose privileged lifestyle negated their radical image. Playing an electric guitar might offend the older generation, but it was no more inherently revolutionary than making an abstract painting. Even if the message in the music was still sometimes subversive, rock 'n' roll had sold out to sleazy entrepreneurs obsessed with selling records, concert tickets and merchandising. Worst of all, the DIY ethos of the hippie movement had long been forgotten. The audiences at rock concerts were relegated to worshipping the lucky few who – through talent or hype – had made it on to the stage. Fortunately, by adopting the avant-garde tactics described in *Leaving the 20th Century*, English punks in the late-1970s now knew how to foment an aesthetic revolution that couldn't be recuperated by the corporate enforcers of spectacular capitalism. They would not suffer the same shameful fate as their

---

[162] See NME, *Punk 1975–1979*, pages 18–35; and Mike Evans, *N.Y.C. Rock*, pages 103–131.

hippie predecessors. When they were art school students, McLaren and his co-conspirators had come to understand that 'culture was a game' under Fordism.[163] For a decade, they'd gained experience in the anti-spectacular struggle. Now, under guidance of these *Suburban Press* veterans, the punks would become the best players of the culture game. Equipped with the four avant-garde tactics of Situationism, this late-1970s youth rebellion now had the skills to beat the class enemy. This time, the Left would win.

In his 1993 autobiography, Johnny Rotten – the lead singer of the Sex Pistols – contemptuously dismissed the claim that Situationist theory had inspired the punk movement as 'bollocks' and 'nonsense'.[164] Yet, for me, the opposite is true. It was at a Sex Pistols gig in summer 1976 that a Saint Martins College of Art student first told me about the insights of Situationism. Like many others from my generation, I would soon be absorbing the teachings of the International at second-hand through punk records, fanzines, posters and leaflets. In its English avant-garde version, Situationism made sense because its theoretical insights described what we were already doing. Inside the 100 Club, the punters on the dance floor were as much the stars of the show as the members of the Sex Pistols on the stage. As the pogoing crowds at these concerts instinctively understood, rejecting the media spectacle meant making your own media. Whether they knew it or not, every punk was a Situationist.[165]

When the *God Save The Queen* scandal was at its height, Debord phoned McLaren to thank him '… for getting my record to Number One!' As this veteran of *Suburban Press* later proudly recollected: 'I agree[d] with him. It was his idea, yes!'[166] London had to show maximum respect to Paris. It was the Situationists' tactics of provocation, détournement, psychogeography and participatory creativity that had recruited a turbulent multitude to the punk subculture. During their brief career

---

163 Fred Vermorel, 'At The End, They Even Stole His Death', page 207.

164 John Lydon, *Rotten*, page 4. Also see Stewart Home, *Cranked Up Really High*, pages 24–28.

165 See Jon Savage, *England's Dreaming*, page 351–358.

166 Malcolm McLaren in Joel McIver, *The Making of the Great Rock 'n' Roll Swindle*, page 61.

in the late-1970s, the Sex Pistols didn't just change the way that young people in England dressed and the music that they listened to. More importantly, this band's records and concerts acted as a call to arms for the excluded across the country. Adopting the punk attitude meant embracing the DIY ethos.[167] If anyone could be a Sex Pistol, then they too could become a musician, set up a record label, organise a club night, publish a fanzine, be a fashion designer or make a film. Within a year of the 100 Club gigs, almost every city and town in Britain had its own alternative punk scene which operated outside the constraints of the corporate entertainment industry. The bohemian avant-garde was being democratised across the whole country. The December 1976 issue of the *Sideburns* fanzine summarised this new DIY wisdom: 'This is a chord. This is another. This is a third. Now form a band.'[168]

In 1982, Factory Records opened a nightclub in Manchester named after the Situationist vision of the libertarian communist city of the future: the Haçienda. This moniker was no whim. Having discovered *Leaving the 20ᵗʰ Century* in the early-1970s as a student, Tony Wilson – the father figure of Factory Records – was a long-standing admirer of the avant-garde teachings of Situationism. When he signed a new band to this label, he'd always give them a copy of Gray's book for guidance. Through its releases, Factory promoted the punk subculture's DIY style of music-making. Like his peers in London, Wilson saw himself as devotee of the English Section's artistic interpretation of Situationism.[169] The building of the Haçienda was the next stage in Factory's multi-media campaign of leftfield records, concerts, posters, badges and publications. With its name taken from the pages of *Leaving the 20ᵗʰ Century*, this Manchester venue was founded to provide a transient space for participatory creativity. By the late-1980s, at the Haçienda as elsewhere across England, banging house tunes and good Es were helping young people divided by gender, income, ethnicity, sexuality and education to find a communal identity on the dance

---

167 Three decades later, the lead singer of the Buzzcocks remembered with pride that: '... punk was about being an active participant not a passive consumer.' Pete Shelley in Sam Bridger, *Punk Britannia*.

168 *Sideburns* in Jon Savage, *England's Dreaming*, page 280.

169 See Tony Wilson, *24 Hour Party People*, pages 50–51, 117–118; and Simon Reynolds, *Rip It Up and Start Again*, pages 92–97, 173–197.

floor. Echoing the moral panic over punk a decade earlier, politicians, experts and the media poured scorn on the irresponsibility, criminality and hedonism of this rave subculture. Determined to restore social discipline, the Tory government passed legislation clamping down on unauthorised parties where DJs were dropping the new underground sound.[170] No wonder that these British defenders of bourgeois morality felt threatened. Within the confines of clubs like the Haçienda, the dance floor really was a proletarian playground. As the Situationists had predicted, the democratisation of avant-garde art was the remaking of everyday life.

Both McLaren and Wilson were excellent students of *Leaving the 20th Century*. From Gray's book, they'd learnt the new avant-garde wisdom from the continent – and then successfully applied its four tactics of cultural subversion to ferment dissent amongst the nation's youth. In the late-1960s, King Mob had only a dozen members. Two decades later, as exemplified by the iconic status of the Sex Pistols and the Haçienda, English Situationism had become a mass phenomenon. Although most of them had never read *Leaving the 20th Century*, young people across the country were enthusiastically putting its avant-garde theory into practice. Their fanzines, indie labels, pirate radios and DJ parties ensured that participatory creativity was now the leitmotif of leftfield culture. Ironically, in this aesthetic victory, McLaren and Wilson had also opened the way for the recuperation of English Situationism. As the 1980s progressed, their imitators began occluding the subversive politics that had inspired the four tactics of subcultural rebellion championed by *Leaving the 20th Century*. In Tory Britain, as the Left suffered defeat after defeat, the Situationists' advocacy of the seizure of power by workers' councils increasingly seemed like a chimera. There was no alternative to neoliberal globalisation.

Reviving the less confrontational interpretations of Modernism, the 1980s boosters of Post-Modernism had provided the intellectual justification for this forgetting of the revolutionary mission of avant-

---

[170] See Mathew Collin, *Altered State*, pages 138–236; and Sheryl Garratt, *Adventures in Wonderland*, pages 160–195.

garde art. Aesthetic innovation was once again an end in itself.[171] Under this Post-Modernist dispensation, the four tactics of Situationism now became the cutting-edge template for promoting new bands, new TV programmes, new fashions, new movies or new publications. The Haçienda was nothing more than the name of a Manchester nightclub. In *The Great Rock 'n' Roll Swindle*, McLaren had set himself the task of discrediting the first – and favoured – enemy of the punk rebellion: the music industry. Brilliantly, he'd formulated the 10 lessons of pop subversion for his youthful audience of Situationist warriors. But, by the time that the film was released in 1980, it was the swindler who'd been swindled. Richard Branson's Virgin Music – the English exemplar of hippie capitalism – now owned the Sex Pistols brand. McLaren and his punk protégés were locked into a bitter lawsuit over the money spent on making the film.[172] For those of a cynical disposition, *The Great Rock 'n' Roll Swindle* could be interpreted in a very different way than it was originally intended. Far from being a searing critique of spectacular capitalism, this film was a business manual for entrepreneurial success within the rapidly expanding creative industries. As the Sex Pistols and the Haçienda had both proved, outrage, remixing, urbanism and DIY culture were clever techniques for attracting the attention of the fickle youth market. For the busy executive, McLaren had even helpfully summarised his Situationist strategy into 10 easy-to-remember sound bites: '...giving [media] capitalists a 'radical' rationale for what they ought to do in their own interest anyway.'[173] The class enemy had learnt how to play and win the avant-garde cultural game.

In its original 1957 French meaning, such recuperation was the contemptible mark of failure. However, two decades later, the English punks had begun the process of turning this negative into a positive. By creating their rock 'n' roll classics in the late-1970s, the Sex Pistols had been able to exert a subversive influence on youth subcultures across the world. Making a Top 40 record was now the most radical expression

---

[171] See Frederic Jameson, *Postmodernism*; and Neville Wakefield, *Post-Modernism*.

[172] See Joel McIver, *The Making of the Great Rock 'n' Roll Swindle*, pages 127–162; and Jon Savage, *England's Dreaming*, pages 522–541.

[173] David Widgery, *Beating Time*, page 64.

of avant-garde artistry.[174] Thanks to this pop incarnation, provocation, détournement, psychogeography and participatory creativity became increasingly identified as the aesthetic legacy of the English punk subculture. In 1989, Greil Marcus published a book which would come to define this Sex Pistols version of Situationism: *Lipstick Traces*. More than a decade after the band's demise, this American music journalist fascinated his readers with exciting revelations about the French origins of the English punk movement. Behind Johnny Rotten was Malcolm McLaren – and behind him stood Guy Debord. Curiously, in this influential narrative, a strange slippage in time took place. For most of the book, his account focused on the Situationists' adventures as a bohemian community of avant-garde artists in the decade before the International's greatest moment: the May '68 French Revolution. Excited more by London than Paris, Marcus emphasised that what was truly important about Debord's writings was their artistic influence on McLaren and – through him – on the Sex Pistols. In *Lipstick Traces*, Situationism meant punk outrages, appropriations, psychogeography and DIY media. Tellingly, Marcus overlooked that these cultural tactics were supposed to be combined into a political strategy which could deliver a proletarian victory in the class war. In his admiring codification of English Situationism, this American acolyte had inadvertently exposed its recuperative failings. Like its Modernist and hippie predecessors, the punk movement had also been systematically assimilated into the cultural establishment. Their aesthetic innovations might have transformed the tastes and styles of an entire generation, but the institutions of spectacular capitalism had survived and were now more powerful than ever. As Marcus' book revealed, the English Situationists had forgotten that the International was founded not just to create a new aesthetic. More than anything else, its driving ambition had been to catalyse the revolutionary transition into the next stage of human civilisation: libertarian communism. Leftfield art was in the service of Left politics.

A year before the publication of *Lipstick Traces*, Stewart Home issued his own manifesto of avant-garde experimentation: *The Assault on Culture*. By locating the International within the history of late-20th century

---

[174] See Simon Reynolds, *Rip It Up and Start Again*, pages 361–382 403–417, 491–515.

Modernism, this London-based novelist explained how the Situationists' four tactics of aesthetic insurgency had emerged out of a much wider milieu of artistic dissidence in Cold War Europe. In complete contrast with Marcus, Home strongly repudiated the growing cult of Debord as the prophet of punk rock rebellion. Instead, most of the credit for inventing the subversive techniques of English Situationism should be attributed to Jorn, Fazakerley and their colleagues in the Scandinavian Section of the International. When the International split in 1962, it was Debord's faction which had insisted that art must be subservient to politics. Rejecting this old Left attitude, the Scandinavian Situationists had instead emphasised that cultural rebellion was now the most subversive strategy for sabotaging spectacular capitalism.[175] Yet, despite his very different reading of the same history, Home's central argument in *The Assault on Culture* complemented that of Marcus in *Lipstick Traces*: punk rock was avant-garde art. Crucially, both authors emphasised the subversive power of this burst of aesthetic innovation. King Mob's dream that youth subcultures were the harbinger of the all-transforming proletarian revolution might not have been realised. But, despite this disappointment, the punk movement had succeeded in undermining the deferential and puritanical attitudes imposed upon their parents' generation. Thanks to these two opinionated books, English Situationism could now take pride in its own radical history and local roots. As this West European nation prepared to leave 20th century, leftfield writers, journalists and film-makers popularised a compelling narrative of four decades of cultural deviancy in London. The fans of punk could now make sense of this inspirational outburst of youth rebellion. In his 1992 *The West Eleven Days of My Life* publication, Tom Vague celebrated the bohemian psychogeography of Notting Hill which had nurtured both King Mob and the Clash. In his 1997 *Anarchy in the UK* book, he traced the hidden lineage that connected the Angry Brigade with the Sex Pistols. Reversing the Situationist position, libertarian communism was now placed in the service of avant-garde art. The primary importance of his heroes' revolutionary politics was endowing their cultural dissidence with a radical edge. The precise language of Marxist theory was transformed

---

[175] See Stewart Home, *The Assault on Culture*, pages 31–49; and Fabian Tompsett, 'Preface', pages 3–15. For the adventures of the Scandinavian Situationists, see Mikkel Bolt Rasmussen and Jakob Jakobsen, *Expect Anything Fear Nothing*.

into wild verbal provocations against the ideological conformity of bourgeois society. By mixing Chris Gray and Malcolm McLaren with Greil Marcus and Stewart Home, Tom Vague had perfected the English translation of the International's ideas: Pop Situationism.

1.8: THE WRITING ON THE WALL

On 26th–27th September 2009, Class Wargames hosted its *Game of War Weekend* at Furtherfield's HTTP gallery in London.[176] Taking pride of place in the front room stood our twice size replica of Debord's 1977 gold-and-silver metallic set. Around the surrounding walls, Alex Veness had hung his eerie xenographs of people playing *The Game of War*. Taken with a scanner-camera, these pictures created '… a visual aesthetic that describes contemporary experience: liquid, ephemeral and uncertain.'[177] In the back room, a new film was on continuous loop: *Class Wargames Presents Guy Debord's The Game of War*. With financial help from the Arts Council of England, we'd been able to make a Situationist video primer for this Situationist game. Like its inventor's later films, *Class Wargames Presents Guy Debord's The Game of War* was driven by the analytic wisdom provided by its voiceover and telling quotations. Imitating our mentor, the script was suffused with the provocative phraseology of Marxist theory. Following Debord's advice, this movie's imagery was carefully chosen to resonate with the audience's deep immersion within the media spectacle. Interspersed with clips of Class Wargames' performances, Ilze Black – its director – had constructed a visual détournement of the 21st century's vast store of fictional and documentary representations of the dramatic political and military conflicts of human history. Thirty years on, Debord's plagiarist techniques of film-making were still at the cutting-edge of avant-garde cinema.[178]

In our 'Communiqué #7' distributed to those attending the *Game of War Weekend*, Class Wargames proselytised for the Situationist possibilities of the new information technologies. Remixing films was expensive and difficult in the 1970s when Debord had made *The Society of the Spectacle* and *In Girum Imus Nocte* with celluloid stock in an editing room. Three decades later, Ilze was cutting and pasting a movie from our collection of videos and DVDs with Final Cut on a

---

[176] For more details about this event and its accompanying exhibition, see Furtherfield, 'Class Wargames – Game of War'.

[177] Alex Veness, *Xenon-Eye*, on page 10 above.

[178] See Guy Debord, 'On *The Society of the Spectacle*'; and 'The Use of Stolen Films'.

Mac laptop. Ironically, just like its open source rivals, such commercial software and hardware were now also potent weapons against the copyright monopolists of the creative industries. In the early-21st century, the avant-garde artistic tactic of détournement had become firmly embedded within everyday life. Above all, our multi-media show at the HTTP gallery celebrated *The Game of War* as the formative expression of Situationist ludic science. During those hot afternoons of that autumn weekend, Class Wargames laid out its resin copy of Debord's 1977 set in the courtyard outside the exhibition. By moving the pieces across the board at these two participatory performances, visitors to Furtherfield's space were completing the making of this collective artwork for themselves. As the teams of North and South battled for supremacy, they were learning to engage with the avant-garde tactic of participatory creativity. Everyone could become a Pop Situationist.

Three years before these two Class Wargames performances at Furtherfield's HTTP gallery, Gary Genosko – a Canadian academic – had tartly observed that the devotees of Debord should be thankful that: 'At least, [*The Game of War*] ... has not become a popular parlour game.'[179] Like one of Giacometti's sculptures, his ludic experiment was an unplayable avant-garde artwork. Since its formation in 2007, Class Wargames' had been determined to overturn this flawed assumption. During the first phase of our campaign of ludic subversion, we'd shown how people who played *The Game of War* with Debord's 1977 set could return to the special times when the four heretical tactics of Situationist cultural sabotage had been devised – and then think about how they could be re-imagined for the 21st century. Most gratifyingly, Ruth Catlow – Furtherfield's co-founder – had enthusiastically participated in our materialisation of Debord's collective ludic artwork at the *Game of War Weekend*. When formulating the strategy for the first stage of our campaign of aesthetic subversion, we'd been inspired by her pioneering contributions to this new type of creative expression. Back in 2003, evoking Saito's and Ono's Fluxus sets, Catlow had modified a computer *Chess* game to mark her outrage at the American invasion of Iraq: *Rethinking Wargames*. In this 3-sided version, while

179   Gary Genosko, '[Review of] Vincent Kaufman', page 3.

Black and White attacked each other with the back row pieces, a third player manoeuvred both sides' pawns in an effort to block this confrontation. The anti-imperialist message of this avant-garde piece of software was unambiguous. As peace was established on the board, its checkered squares of combat slowly turned into a lush green field. In this Situationist détournement of *Chess*, the pawns could thwart the queen.[180]

From 2003 onwards, Catlow and Marc Garrett – her Furtherfield co-conspirator – had been stalwarts of London's computer art games scene. In their exhibitions and publications, they'd lauded the avant-garde possibilities of this modern form of aesthetic imagination. Myfanwy Ashmore's 2000 *Mario Battle No.1* and Jodi's 2004 *Max Payne Cheats Only* challenged the competitive and hierarchical logic of the commercial gaming industry. Tiltfactor's 2009 *Layoff* and Jeremy Bailey's 2009 *Warmail* delivered a strong political message in ludic form.[181] In Catlow and Garrett's influential *Artists Re:thinking Games* book written with Corrado Morgana, the Situationist tactic of détournement was praised for giving theoretical clarity to what these artists were already doing.[182] Fifty years on, the insights of the International were flourishing within this new avant-garde paradigm. In its 2001 *Can You See Me Now?* and 2003 *Uncle Roy All Around* locative media games, Blast Theory had combined playing on-line and on the city streets.[183] In 2006, Ilze Black from Class Wargames had helped to create the *Porta2030* wireless network in East London which demonstrated how a local neighbourhood could be playfully remapped by its own inhabitants.[184] With the aid of new digital technologies,

180   See Ruth Catlow, *Rethinking Wargames*; and Mary Flanagan, *Critical Play*, pages 113–116.

181   See Furtherfield, *Zero Gamer*; and Ruth Catlow, Marc Garrett and Corrado Morgana, *Artists Re:thinking Games*.

182   See Corrado Morgana, 'Introduction *Artists Re:thinking Games*'.

183   See Blast Theory, *Blast Theory*; and Anne-Marie Schleiner, 'Dissolving the Magical Circle of Play', pages 7–8.

184   See Porta2030, *You Are the Net, You Are Porta-Porter*; and Ruth Catlow, 'Let's Do Lunch [2005]'.

anyone could – if only for a brief moment – put the Situationist tactic of psychogeography into practice.[185]

Earlier in that year, on 25th July 2009, Class Wargames had attracted a small and enthusiastic audience for its performance at Plan 9's *Summer of Dissent* festival in Bristol. Most appropriately, this collective playing of *The Game of War* coincided with a major exhibition by the local artist who'd become the nation's most skilled practitioner of Pop Situationism: *Banksy vs Bristol Museum*.[186] The long queues outside the City Gallery were confirmation of King Mob's insistence that the members of dissident youth subcultures made the best recruits for anti-spectacular warfare. Banksy had come out of the skateboard and DJ party scenes in early-1990s Bristol. Thanks to punk, the avant-garde teachings of English Situationism were now learnt on the streets as the leftfield tactics of media subversion.[187] Not surprisingly, when Banksy had started stencilling his striking designs around the city, the municipal authorities hadn't appreciated the artistic importance of his trip-hop graffiti. Delightfully, two decades later, these images were now being officially honoured as the local roots of Banksy's rise to international stardom. Inside the Bristol City Gallery, the ironic style and anti-authoritarian attitudes honed in illegal graffiti had expanded to include prints, paintings, statues, installations and animatronics. Most wonderfully, a multi-media happening had been allowed to take over the municipal museum for three months – and the entrance was free. Combining outlaw anonymity with celebrity status, Banksy had carefully negotiated the many temptations of recuperation which can ensnare successful avant-garde artists. As the large crowds from very diverse backgrounds at the Bristol City Gallery proved, Pop Situationism now had a mass public.[188]

---

[185] See Marc Tuters, 'The Locative Commons'.

[186] See Banksy, *Wall and Piece*. Tellingly, seven years earlier, Banksy had collaborated with Jamie Reid on The Centre of Attention's 2002 anti-Jubilee exhibition: *Vive la République!*

[187] See Steve Wright, *Home Sweet Home*; and Gil Gillespie, *The Naked Guide to Bristol*, pages 74–107.

[188] See the Bristol Evening Post, 'Banksy Comes Home For Bristol Show'; and Tim Adams, 'The Graffitist Goes Straight'.

The 2009 Banksy exhibition was a public celebration of the rebellious spirit of avant-garde art. Within the hallowed space of a municipal museum, the idiocies and crimes of big government and big business were being mocked to popular acclaim. For the few months of the show, the recuperators had been recuperated at the Bristol City Gallery. Elsewhere in the world, the four tactics of Pop Situationism had produced equally impressive results on the cultural battlefield. In 1990s New York, Critical Art Ensemble, RTMark and the Yes Men utilised provocation and détournement to launch daring media sabotage operations against corporate malefactors.[189] At the peak of that decade's dotcom boom, Etoy corporation – an Austrian net.art project – had played the winning move of participatory creativity in the cultural game by mobilising its many fans in a virtual *Toywar* to disrupt the shopping website of eToys – an American on-line retailer which wanted to steal its name.[190] The avant-garde techniques of Pop Situationism were now in sync with the historical moment.[191] From the mid-1990s onwards, the most utopian hopes of the International seemed to be becoming an everyday reality through the rapid spread and increasing power of computer networks. Soon, for the first time, the whole population would be able to make their own media. The pleasurable task of alter-globalisation agitators, leftfield artists and community groups was to lead the way into this digital future. At conferences like the Next 5 Minutes, Ars Electronica, Transmediale and ISEA or on mailing lists like nettime, Rhizome and Syndicate, the four aesthetic tactics of Pop Situationism were updated into 'The ABC of Tactical Media'.[192] Like punks and ravers before them, the activists of radical websites, alternative publications, independent labels, pirate radios, video collectives, squatted buildings, techno parties and free festivals were creating 'temporary autonomous zones' outside of the

---

189   See Critical Art Ensemble, *The Electronic Disturbance*; Julian Stallabrass, *Internet Art*, pages 91–95; and the Yes Men, *The Yes Men*.

190   See Etoy, 'The ToyWar-Story'; and Julian Stallabrass, *Internet Art*, pages 96–102.

191   See Mark Dery, 'Culture Jamming'; and Richard Barbrook, 'The Hi-Tech Gift Economy'.

192   See David Garcia and Geert Lovink, 'The ABC of Tactical Media'; and Adilkno, *Media Archive*.

cultural establishment's controls.[193] Living in the late-1990s boom years of neoliberal globalisation, these youthful dissidents conceded that the International's dream of the workers' councils overthrowing spectacular capitalism was an impossibility. Fortunately, this defunct revolutionary political strategy had also inspired four avant-garde art tactics which had never been more relevant. Above all, for these new media enthusiasts, the Situationist technique of détournement was the premonition of the dissolution of intellectual property within the Net's 'hi-tech gift economy'. Much to the horror of the music and film industries, their copyright commodities were metamorphosing into virtual potlatches. Although no sensible person could any longer believe in hardware communism, everyone was now a practitioner of software communism. In this iteration of Pop Situationism, political revolution had been superseded by cultural rebellion. As the 21st century arrived, the Haçienda could only be built in cyberspace.[194]

In 1992, Sadie Plant – an English academic – published the intellectual rationale for the Post-Modernist codification of Pop Situationism: *The Most Radical Gesture*. Like Marcus, Home and Vague, her narrative focused upon the subversive influence of the avant-garde artistry of the International. Crucially, by emphasising his penetrating analysis of media domination, Plant began the process of welcoming Debord into the pantheon of French master-thinkers who fascinated the ideological imagination of late-20th century Euro-American Cultural Studies: Louis Althusser, Roland Barthes, Jacques Derrida, Julia Kristeva, Jean-François Lyotard, Jean Baudrillard, Michel Foucault, Gilles Deleuze and Félix Guattari.[195] Back in the 1960s and 1970s, the founders of this new academic discipline in England had determinedly ignored the theoretical insights of Situationism. They'd known that King Mob had been not only a pioneer of the critical analysis of youth subcultures, but also the inspiration for their most radical manifestation: the punk

---

[193] See Hakim Bey, *T.A.Z.*; and George McKay, 'DiY Culture'. For a critique of this techno-utopian moment, see Richard Barbrook, 'The Holy Fools'.

[194] See Richard Barbrook, 'The Hi-Tech Gift Economy'; and 'Cyber-communism'.

[195] See David Harris, *From Class Struggle to the Politics of Pleasure;* and Alan Sokal and Jean Bricmont, *Fashionable Nonsense*.

movement. However, as adherents of the Bolshevik tradition, Stuart Hall and his colleagues at the Birmingham Centre for Contemporary Cultural Studies were repelled by the revolutionary ambitions of the Situationist International. Instead, in their writings, they argued that the updated Stalinist socio-linguistic theory promoted by Louis Althusser and his post-structuralist acolytes was the only credible method for understanding the new youth subcultures.[196] Befuddled by bourgeois hegemony, the masses could only be liberated by the small group of illuminated intellectuals who understood this esoteric doctrine. Not surprisingly, as intransigent opponents of libertarian communism, Hall and his fellow post-structuralists anathematised the anti-spectacular analysis of their Situationist rivals as a 'terrorist ideology'.[197] For them, it was unthinkable that there could be a smarter alternative to their revamped version of Stalinist socio-linguistics. Most notoriously, when *Subculture: the meaning of style* appeared in 1979, Dick Hebdige from the Birmingham Centre systematically airbrushed the English Situationists out of his account of the punk movement that had been fermented by them. Like the Bolshevik tyrant who'd ordered the 'linguistic turn' in social theory, these British disciples of Althusser were determined to purge their opponents on the Left from the history books.

By the early-1990s, even amongst the teachers of Cultural Studies, Hebdige's academic falsification had lost all credibility. Thanks to the writings of Marcus, Home and Vague, the punk movement was now widely recognised as the epitome of Pop Situationism. For those in the know, Debord not Althusser was the most intelligent critic of the media-saturated societies of contemporary capitalism. It was at this moment of ideological crisis that Plant's book came to the rescue of the beleaguered theoretical paradigm of Euro-American Cultural Studies. In an impressive feat of intellectual legerdemain, she attempted to

---

[196] See Centre for Contemporary Cultural Studies, *On Ideology*; and Stuart Hall and Tony Jefferson, *Resistance through Rituals*. For the original version of this mandarin analysis, see Joseph Stalin, *Marxism and Problems of Linguistics*; and Ethan Pollock, *Stalin and the Soviet Science Wars*, pages 104–135.

[197] When I was a post-graduate Politics student at Essex University in 1978–9, this was the phrase used by Chantel Mouffe to explain why we were banned from quoting Debord in our essays!

reconcile the irreconcilable. *The Society of the Spectacle* now became a brilliant anticipation of this academic discipline's elitist theories of sign systems, ideological state apparatuses, discursive practices, hyper-reality, bio-power and semiotic war-machines. Most gratifyingly, this meant that the masses who were making DIY media couldn't dispense with the leadership of the illuminated few. In her remix, the Situationist International's avant-garde art tactics had become completely divorced from its revolutionary political strategy. Ironically, by refusing to subsume his identity within a New Left sect, Debord had allowed himself to be recuperated as an eccentric individualist. The hardline Marxist language of his theoretical writings was now cherished as a punk provocation against bourgeois discourse. His devotion to libertarian communism had become nothing more than a romantic pose. For these 1990s adepts of Post-Modernism, Debord's political intransigence was instead admired because it had endowed him with those most elusive qualities within neoliberal capitalism: authenticity and integrity. Unlike so many of his New Left peers, he'd scornfully refused the rewards of a counter-cultural career like lucrative jobs, newspaper interviews, lecture tours, TV appearances, celebrity friends and public honours. Never succumbing to recuperation, the commander-in-chief of the Situationist International had always kept steadfast to his implacable beliefs: '... the hipster's Che Guevara.'[198]

After the defeat of the May '68 Revolution, Debord – with Becker-Ho – had gone into internal exile in the Auvergne countryside where – as he later confessed – he drank too much and wrote too little.[199] Paradoxically, in the Post-Modernist version of Pop Situationism, this artist-theorist's unflinching political commitment to libertarian communism became transmuted into unimpeachable proof of his moral incorruptibility. For his many admirers in academia and the art world, Debord's greatest creation was his heroic role in 1970s and 1980s as the lone bohemian prophet standing firm against the tawdry temptations of fame and money. Pop Situationism could now be re-interpreted as an avant-garde philosophy for aesthetic self-realisation.

---

[198] McKenzie Wark, *The Spectacle of Disintegration*, page 14. Also see Anselm Jappe, *Guy Debord*, pages 45–124; and Vincent Kaufman, *Guy Debord*, pages 209–269.

[199] See Guy Debord, *Panegyric*, pages 33–34.

In 2001, one of his English biographers was moved to proclaim: 'The power which [Debord] ... leaves us with today is the power to say No: to look the negative in the face and live with it forever.'[200]

When the Tate Modern in London opened in 2000, a timeline of the leading 20th century avant-garde movements was prominently displayed across one wall of its third floor concourse. Placed between Pop Art and Fluxus, the Situationist International was given due respect for its impressive aesthetic and cultural innovations between the 1950s and 1970s. Ironically, despite being responsible for the 1962 expulsion of the artists from the movement, Debord and Vaneigem were the only two of its members whose names appeared in this timeline.[201] Decades after they were first published, Situationist texts still provided a provocative analysis of the mutating manifestations of avant-garde art. Appropriated by Iain Sinclair, Peter Ackroyd and Will Self for their urban musings, psychogeography had already entered the English language during the 1990s as a fashionable phrase for the hipster appreciation of inner city neighbourhoods.[202] With the help of Marcus, Home, Vague and Plant, the Situationist techniques of provocation, détournement, urbanism and participatory creativity had taken their rightful place within the gallery system. Not surprisingly, this recognition of the International's achievements had been accompanied by their recuperation. During the 1990s, the YBAs achieved fame and fortune by stripping the four Situationist tactics of their radical proletarian politics. Once the 21st century was reached, innovative curators were championing art spaces as the privileged site of participatory creativity. Incorporated into the grand narrative of avant-garde art, Situationism had become another exotic oddity for the delectation of people visiting galleries as a leisure activity.[203] By the time that the *Game of War Weekend* was held at Furtherfield in 2009, totemic items from Jamie Reid and Vivenne Westwood were to be found in the permanent collections of the Tate

---

[200] Andy Merrifield, *Guy Debord*, page 149. Also see Stewart Home, 'The Self-Mythologisation of the Situationist International'.

[201] See Sara Fanelli, *Tate Artist Timeline*.

[202] See Merlin Coverley, *Psychogeography*, pages 111–137.

[203] See Julian Stallabrass, *High Art Lite*, pages 67–68; and Nicholas Bourriaud, *Relational Aesthetics*, pages 79–104. Also see Dick Pountain and David Robins, *Cool Rules*, pages 126–128.

Modern and the Victoria & Albert museum. Thirty three years after the banning of *God Save The Queen*, Pop Situationism had become a Post-Modernist national treasure.

When Class Wargames had opened the first phase of our campaign of ludic subversion, we knew that its members were fighting on an artistic terrain shaped by this counter-cultural defeat-in-victory. Fortunately, the four avant-garde tactics laid down in *Leaving the 20th Century* could still be applied with great effectiveness within the early-21st century's information society. By focusing its players' attention on military competition, our performances of *The Game of War* were a punk provocation against American-led imperialist expeditions to Iraq and Afghanistan. With its gridded terrain and abstract pieces, Debord's ludic invention was a sly détournement not only of *Chess* and *Draughts*, but also of family board games like *Risk* and *Stratego*. When the collective playing of *The Game of War* took place at the launch of the Brazilian edition of my *Imaginary Futures* book at the Café com Letras in Belo Horizonte on 29th April 2009 or as part of (C)hor 29 Novembar's 40th anniversary celebrations for the founding of the Yugoslav Workers' Club at the Lokativ in Vienna on 28th November 2009, the Situationist tactic of psychogeography was being successfully implemented at a unique moment in a special place. Above all, as Class Wargames' 'Communiqué #5' emphasised, these transitory experiences of participatory creativity with *The Game of War* had revolutionary cultural implications: 'Competition on a board is a prophecy of co-operation in everyday life.'

When Malcolm McLaren attended our 2009 performance at the Baltic Centre for Contemporary Art in Gateshead, the founding father of the punk movement immediately grasped the avant-garde ambitions of our artistic project. Everyone must be given the opportunity to learn how to become a Pop Situationist.During this first phase of our campaign of ludic subversion, Class Wargames' primary task was to facilitate those brief passages of time which realised the most utopian hopes of the 20th century's avant-garde movements: the aestheticisation of social existence. By playing *The Game of War*, passive spectators were transformed into active creators. Like Kirby's *The First and Second Wilderness* or Blast Theory's *Uncle Roy All Around*, Debord's ludic invention was an interactive collective artwork. Anticipating the DIY ethos of the Net, *The Game of War* transformed its players into artists. At Class Wargames' performances, the stars of the show were the members of the audience who decided where the pieces would move on the board. In this iteration of Pop Situationism, our communal re-enactments of *The Game of War* were a 21st century invocation of the original version of the Sex Pistols, the Haçienda and Banksy. We were diligent pupils of the English Section of the International.

In 2008, Anne-Marie Schleiner revealed her ultimate ambition for Situationist gaming: the abolition of all rules. Like the Surrealists and Fluxus, this American artist-academic had discovered the aesthetic pleasures of unplayable games. Mesmerised by the Post-Modernist master-thinkers of Cultural Studies, the limit of her ambition was to foster an ideological revolt against the dominant semiotic codes.[204] Curiously, in this remix of Pop Situationism, Schleiner never discussed *The Game of War*. Seen as a geeky oddity within Debord's oeuvre, his ludic experiment was too easily overlooked by his contemporary admirers. In its performances and propaganda for the first phase of our campaign, Class Wargames deployed the techniques of re-enactment art to combat the Post-Modernists' lamentable loss of historical memory. According to his admiring biographers, *The Game of War* was invented at a crucial point in the legend of Guy Debord. Having detonated the May '68 French Revolution, he'd been forced to retreat to an Auvergne village. Like the memoirs of Bonaparte dictated during his 1815–21 exile at St Helena, *The Game of War* was Debord's summation of a lifetime of world-historical struggles.[205] As we stressed at our performances, playing with its analogue 1977 board and pieces meant returning to this special moment when the four cultural tactics of Pop Situationism were combined together in ludic form for the first time. When North and South engaged in simulated combat, the audacious goal of the International was fully revealed: '… history is made mobile again, in an irreversible time where strategy can reverse the course of events.'[206] Under Class Wargames' guidance, the avant-garde art of *The*

---

[204] See Anne-Marie Schleiner, 'Dissolving the Magical Circle of Play', pages 12–16.

[205] See Vincent Kaufman, *Guy Debord*, page 267.

[206] McKenzie Wark, *50 Years of Recuperation*, page 30.

Game of War was once again in the service of revolutionary politics. Understanding the past was the precondition of defining the future.

Over that sultry September weekend in 2009, the players at the Furtherfield gallery collectively agreed to obey the strict rules of Debord's game. In making this collective artwork, they were enjoying participating within the transient space of ludic sociability designed by the maximum leader of the Situationist International. Through activating the gold-and-silver board and pieces of our replica of the 1977 analogue set, these participants in *The Game of War* were learning the tactical and strategic lessons of proletarian dissidence that Debord had embedded within its instruction manual. The radical message of this ludic détournement could only be understood by personally experiencing the ebb-and-flow of its ritualised combat. Like the 12 issues of *Internationale Situationniste*, *The Game of War* was created as a beautiful artwork. Crucially, by promoting the 1977 set as a lost classic of the late-20th century avant-garde, Class Wargames had manipulated the aesthetic allure of its gold-and-silver board and pieces to trash the Post-Modernist recuperation of English Situationism. Now that the name of Debord was written on the wall of the Tate Modern, every intelligent person must try playing *The Game of War* at least once. They weren't educated if they hadn't. Once seduced into obeying its rules, these players would momentarily find themselves living a 21st century simulation of the Situationist cultural revolution. By taking command of North and South, they were putting the International's four avant-garde tactics into practice. As the first stage of our campaign of ludic subversion reached its climax on that September 2009 weekend at Furtherfield's HTTP gallery, we could take pride in our hard-won mastery of the English Section's punk strategy of Pop Situationism. In these two participatory performances of *The Game of War*, avant-garde art and revolutionary politics were combined in dialectical unity. Class Wargames had issued the orders of combat to the assembled masses: Play-It-Yourself!

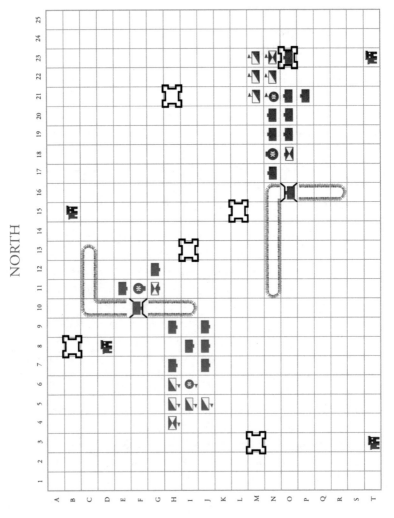

DIAGRAM 1

Pump House opening positions for Guy Debord's *The Game of War*

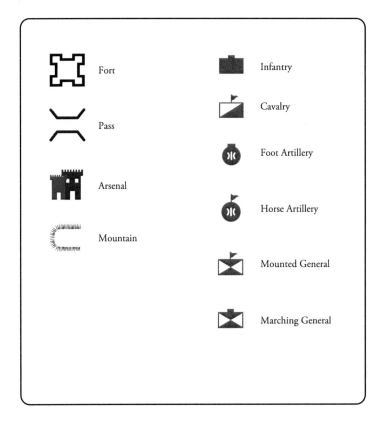

Fort

Pass

Arsenal

Mountain

Infantry

Cavalry

Foot Artillery

Horse Artillery

Mounted General

Marching General

2.0: THE SKILFUL GENERAL

'In actual fact, all the changes that happen in the world only take place because of ... highly sensitive scoundrels. Because, in reality, they do not anticipate the future at all, but shape it, by creeping across to occupy the quarter from which they think that the wind will blow. Following which, the wind has no option but to blow from that very quarter.'

Victor Pelevin, *Chapayev and Void*, page 36.

2.1: THE TEST OF BATTLE

It was in the early evening of 14th October 2010 and the members of Class Wargames were getting ready to make their contribution to *What Is To Be Done? The Urgent Need To Struggle* season curated by *Chto Delat?* at the ICA in London. During a six weeks residency for the gallery that autumn, this Russian avant-garde movement was publishing an issue of its eponymous magazine, putting on an exhibition of multi-media artworks and – which is where we came in – also hosting a series of talks, screenings and performances. By adopting *Chto Delat?* as their name, the members of the group emphasised their rejection of aesthetic experimentation for its own sake. In late-19th century Russia, this phrase had first achieved fame as the title of Nikolai Chernyshevsky's science fiction novel: *What Is To Be Done?* Inside its pages, the author had popularised the inspiring ideal of a self-sacrificing intellectual dedicated to liberating the masses from oppression and exploitation.[1] Paying homage to this guru of the Russian Left, V.I. Lenin borrowed its title for his 1902 Bolshevik manifesto on revolutionary organisation. Updating Chernyshevsky's vision, he'd argued that radical intellectuals should band together to provide a unified leadership for the plethora of political, social and national movements opposed to monarchical rule: *the vanguard party.*[2] Like its appropriation for the artistic avant-garde, this military metaphor of the detachment which opened the way forward for the main army was used to eulogise the audacious role of the enlightened minority who were proselyting for the future in the present.

According to Lenin, the primary task of the vanguard party was publishing a national newspaper which would spread its incendiary ideas amongst the increasingly disaffected inhabitants of the Tsar's territories.[3] When the Bolsheviks eventually seized power during the

---

1   For the importance of this novel for Russian opponents of the Tsar, see Franco Venturi, *Roots of Revolution*, pages xxii–xxv, 129–186.

2   See V.I. Lenin, *What Is To Be Done?*, pages 96–188; and Lars Lih, *Lenin*, pages 64–72.

3   See V.I. Lenin, *What Is To Be Done?*, pages 189–220; and Lars Lih, *Lenin*, pages 73–83.

1917 Russian Revolution, this political strategy was vindicated by victory. Ideological unity in opposition had prefigured the Left's firm leadership over the workers and peasants which delivered a decisive triumph over the monarchist enemy. Inspired by this heroic example, disaffected intellectuals throughout the 20th century tried to imitate this Bolshevik model of revolutionary organisation with more or less success. They too would form a vanguard party that could mobilise the masses to sweep away the established order. By harking back to Chernyshevsky's novel and Lenin's pamphlet, the activists of *Chto Delat?* had committed themselves to reviving this revolutionary project which had been discredited in its birthplace by the 1991 implosion of the Soviet Union. On the ICA's website, they explained that their group had been founded in 2003 as a '... self-organising platform for cultural workers ... [dedicated to] ... merging political theory, art and activism.'[4] Seven years later, these Russian dissidents had seized the opportunity – for the short period of *The Urgent Need To Struggle* show – to fulfil this insurgent ambition in London. The radical manifesto of the Eastern vanguard would be proclaimed inside the temple of Western Modernism: 'Art should exist not for museums and dealers, but in order to develop and articulate a new mode of emancipated sensuality. It should become an instrument for seeing and knowing the world in the totality of its contradictions.'[5]

With both personal and professional links to the Russian homeland of *Chto Delat?*, Class Wargames was honoured to be asked to participate in their programme of cultural mischief. During the three years of the first phase of our campaign of ludic subversion, we'd acquired plenty of experience in organising successful avant-garde art events. On that October evening in 2010, as the ICA bar filled up with expectant punters, Ilze Black waited for the correct moment and then clicked play on the DVD of *Class Wargames Presents Guy Debord's The Game of War*. Like the *Chto Delat?* exhibition next door, this movie also took pleasure in detourning the ambiguous iconography of the 1917 Russian Revolution. It was no accident that our audiovisual celebration

---

4   ICA, 'Chto delat? (What is to be done?) – The Urgent Need to Struggle'.

5   *Chto Delat?*, 'A Declaration on Politics, Knowledge and Art'. Most notably, the ICA was where Pop Art was invented in 1950s England, see Marco Livingstone, *Pop Art*, page 33.

of Debord's military simulation began with the Orchestra of the USSR Defence Ministry performing *The Internationale* over the opening credits. During the early-20th century, the Bolsheviks had transformed this inspiring anthem of workers' liberation into a marching song of Russian imperialism. But, by sampling their martial version in our film, Class Wargames was able to thwart these despicable recuperators. Evoking both military discipline and proletarian rebellion, this Stalinist remix of *The Internationale* now provided a very appropriate soundtrack for the opening section of our 21st century exposition of *The Game of War*. The Left had stolen back what was its in the first place.

After the screening of the Class Wargames film was over, the audience was then given its chance to put Situationist theory into practice. Divided into two teams, they took their places on either side of the board and pieces laid out on a table in the ICA bar. It was quickly decided that Fabian Tompsett would mentor the players of the South while Russell King – a veteran wargamer – was placed in charge of those who'd taken the role of the North. After a short explanation of the rules, the making of the communal artwork of *The Game of War* got underway. As they manoeuvred and fought with their miniature armies, the players of North and South were soon caught up in the intense drama of this simulated battlefield. Through their moves and counter-moves, these rival teams led by Fabian and Russell had become joined together in their mutual implementation of the Situationists' avant-garde tactic of participatory creativity. They were both competing and collaborating with each other. The discussions about *The Game of War* around the table were as important as the action on the board. Inside the convivial atmosphere of the ICA bar on that autumn evening in 2010, Class Wargames was realising one of its primary goals as an avant-garde art group: '… creating moments in time and space where the fate of an arsenal is experienced at an intense emotional, creative and intellectual level.'[6]

As in the 2008 Pump House scenario shown in **Diagram 1** on page 110, Debord and Becker-Ho had both chosen an initial deployment

---

6   Richard Barbrook and Fabian Tompsett, *Class Wargames Presents Guy Debord's The Game of War*, page 20.

that grouped their pieces together into one large block for the exemplary game in their book.[7] However, as we played match after match during the first phase of our campaign of ludic subversion, Class Wargames became increasingly dissatisfied with this concentrated placement and instead honed a new opening set-up which scattered the forces of North and South across the length of the board. For those trying out *The Game of War* for the first time, this layout of the two sides' pieces was much more entertaining because it favoured an aggressive playing style. When we'd begun with Debord and Becker-Ho's starting positions, unfamiliarity with the rules meant that newbies were reluctant to make any moves that endangered their armies' defensive security. If we hadn't intervened as umpires, these games would have taken far too long to get a result. Fortunately, by breaking up each side's initial deployment into two or three brigades of mixed infantry, cavalry and artillery units to create the initial deployment in **Diagram 2** on page 224, we could ensure that first time players were forced to go over onto the attack. As the facilitators of *The Game of War*, our job now became encouraging them to risk everything on this Situationist battlefield. Courage not caution would be the key to victory. On 20th April 2009 at the UFRJ in Rio de Janeiro, I was the master of ceremonies when both North and South had thrillingly found themselves within one move of taking each other's last arsenal after 90 minutes of hard fought combat. Djahjah Bonorandi and Thiago Novaes – the generals of the two sides – had never played *The Game of War* before that balmy summer evening in this university's café. It was the South that beat the North with a nifty cavalry move – and both of them who would be winners of this symbolic confrontation.[8] By creating a memorable contest with our new initial deployment for *The Game of War*, these Brazilian comrades had proved themselves to be adepts of the English strategy of Pop Situationism. Best of all, they now knew that putting Debord's cultural theory into ludic practice was a most enjoyable experience. From then onwards, the dispersed opening positions laid down in **Diagram 2** on page 224 would be named the Rio de Janeiro scenario in their honour.

---

[7]   See Alice Becker-Ho and Guy Debord, *A Game of War*, page 39.

[8]   See the photographs in the Events 2009 section of the Class Wargames website.

When planning our event for *The Urgent Need To Struggle* festival at the ICA, the members of Class Wargames decided that the time had arrived to experiment with a new initial layout for *The Game of War*. Rather than scattering the pieces across the board to optimise playability as before, we instead placed the contesting sides in a deployment which would let us re-enact one of the most famous confrontations in military history: the 1800 Marengo campaign.[9] In retrospect, the creation of this new scenario for *The Game of War* marked the definitive shift from the first to the second stage of our campaign of ludic subversion. The celebration of Situationist avant-garde art was turning into the advocacy of Situationist political propaganda. But, at the time, our attention was focused on a much more prosaic problem. For any traditional wargamer, the abstract structure of Debord's ludic invention would be the major obstacle to fulfilling our ambitious goal of recreating the Marengo campaign with any credibility. Unlike the Avalon Hill and SPI simulations which were so popular with American hobbyists around the same time that it was first published, *The Game of War* hadn't been designed as a '... paper time machine ... [the] object of which is to enable the player to recreate a specific event ...'[10] In 1980, Mark McLaughlin's *War and Peace* had utilised more than 1,000 counters and a 44cm x 120cm board for its 10 'historically accurate' scenarios which modelled the military campaigns between 1805 and 1815 that had decided the fate of Bonaparte's empire. As the inventors of Avalon Hill and SPI games were only too well aware, it was this obsessive attention to detail that shifted products to their nerdy male customers. However, Debord had contemptuously dismissed his American peers' obsession with faithfully simulating military history. In its explanatory book, he insisted that *The Game of War* was '... not the latest in the long line of simplified recreations of battles past ...'[11] Taken literally, this meant that it was impossible to re-enact the Marengo campaign with his 1977 ludic masterpiece. The pieces of *The Game of War* didn't represent the French and Austrian regiments that had fought in the 1798–1802 War of the Second Coalition. Its

---

9   See James Arnold, *Marengo & Hohenlinden*; David Chandler, *The Campaigns of Napoleon*, pages 264–304; and Reginald Burton, *Napoleon's Campaigns in Italy*, pages 103–133.

10   Jim Dunnigan, *The Complete Wargames Handbook*, page 13.

11   Alice Becker-Ho and Guy Debord, *A Game of War*, page 9.

board wasn't a stylised map of the different provinces of Europe during that period.[12] For our contribution to the *Chto Delat?* season at the ICA, the first task of Class Wargames would be explaining how the abstract construct of *The Game of War* could be applied to the historical circumstances of the 1800 Marengo campaign.

In the introduction to his and Becker-Ho's book, Debord provided an insight into his motivations for devoting so much time to this ludic project by quoting the opening line of a 16th century poem about *Chess*: 'What we play is a representation of war.'[13] The games produced by Avalon Hill, SPI and their imitators were flawed not just because trying to simulate a particular battle or campaign restricted the choices of armchair generals to what had happened during those particular historical circumstances. More seriously, so their customers could fight conflicts from many different epochs without difficulty, American designers adopted a common format for most of their publications: hex maps, cardboard counters, terrain penalty charts, zones of control and combat results tables. Not surprisingly, the experience of playing Henry Plantagenet at Agincourt in 1415 became very similar to that of taking on the role of Georgy Zhukov at Stalingrad in 1942.[14] As in a 1950s range of Ford motor cars, each Avalon Hill or SPI game had the same engine underneath its distinctive chrome.[15] Through this insight, Class Wargames now knew how to adapt Debord's creation for our own purposes. When analysed in its formal mechanics, *The Game of War* was no more abstract than the rigidly themed simulations of its US rivals. In his introductory notes, Debord explained that '... the aim has been, with the minimum workable territorial, force-level and temporal limitations, to incorporate all of the main difficulties and means encountered universally in the conduct of war.'[16] This meant

---

[12] This literalist approach was espoused by a 1983 game: Joseph Angiolillo, *Napoleon's Italian Campaigns.*

[13] Alice Becker-Ho and Guy Debord, *A Game of War*, page 9.

[14] This can be seen in two celebrated SPI and Avalon Hill games: Jim Dunnigan, *Agincourt*; and Lindsley Schutz and Thomas Shaw, *Stalingrad.*

[15] In 1986, Debord castigated the American game designers who'd been using '... the same colourful simulation for an infinity of historically specific battles over the last two decades.' Guy Debord, 'Letter to Floriana Lebovici', page 388.

[16] Alice Becker-Ho and Guy Debord, *A Game of War*, page 9.

that – like the Avalon Hill and SPI system – *The Game of War* could also provide a universal engine for simulating armed combat. All that Class Wargames needed to do was add the identifying chrome for its intervention in the *Chto Delat?* festival at the ICA.

Following this revelation, we were able to embed the historical specificity of the 1800 Marengo campaign within the formal structure of *The Game of War*. Comprising of infantry, cavalry and artillery units, its pieces could easily represent the French and Austrian armies in this conflict. Best of all, when the South became the West and the North was the East, the board could be imagined as the Central European lands over which these two nations had fought so bitterly.[17] The mountains and passes reproduced the terrain obstacles of not only the Alps and the Apennines, but also the Rhine, Danube and Po rivers. The South's line of forts were the frontier cities of Strasbourg, Geneva and Genoa while those of the North became the garrison towns of Mantua, Zurich and Bratislava. For the French player, their left arsenal symbolised Paris and the right one was Marseille. Their Austrian opponent's left arsenal became Trieste and the right one was Vienna. Enthused by this psychogeographical interpretation of Debord's board, Class Wargames set to work on devising the starting positions for the two sides in *The Game of War* shown in **Diagram 3** on page 226 which would enable us to recreate the Marengo campaign. Taking on the role of the Austrians, the North's army was divided into two strong contingents simultaneously pushing forward at the front of both flanks. As the French, the South's army consisted of a line of weak outposts with the bulk of its forces held back in the centre of the board. Like the rival commanders who'd clashed in 1800, the players of both sides could only win by making the most of these very different opening positions. The Austrians would have to break through their enemy's defensive line before the French were able to mobilise the concentrated power of their reserve corps.[18] It was the players that could master time and

---

17   See Maps 35–39 in Vincent Esposito and John Elting, *A Military History and Atlas of the Napoleonic Wars*; and the Marengo campaign map in David Chandler, *The Campaigns of Napoleon*, pages 272–273.

18   For a military analysis of the French and Austrian strategies, see David Chandler, *The Campaigns of Napoleon*, pages 264–304; and Reginald Burton, *Napoleon's Campaigns in Italy*, pages 103–134.

space who would be the winners of this ritualised combat. In the ICA bar on that October night, the rival teams of North and South weren't just building a collective avant-garde artwork together. By choosing this Marengo deployment for *The Game of War*, Class Wargames had turned this tabletop battlefield into an exacting test in military leadership. In this second stage of our Situationist campaign of ludic subversion, every proletarian must learn about the decisive role of the skilful general in the key moments of revolutionary history.

When the game at the *Chto Delat?* festival began, the North appeared to be in a very strong position. Like the Austrians in 1800, Russell's forces were already threatening to outflank their opponent on both sides. Most temptingly, there was only one infantry piece in a fort between his army and the South's eastern arsenal. Taking command, Russell persuaded his team of players that North's should seize the initiative by launching an attack on its left. Two cavalry pieces started moving forward towards their target while the accompanying infantry and artillery were swung into the centre to cover this advance. With some deft manoeuvring, the South's fort would be cut off from supply, the infantry piece guarding it taken and then, lacking any defence, the enemy's eastern arsenal was doomed. With Marseille gone, the road to Paris would be wide open. As an experienced player of both figurine and board games, Russell was confident that he chosen the strategy that made the most of the Austrian army's initial deployment. His side was already determining the pace of the game with its aggressive opening moves. As long as they kept the initiative on the battlefield, the players of the North would prevail.

Sitting next to Russell, Billy Cass didn't share the optimism of his commander-in-chief. Having participated in our performances of *The Game of War* on previous occasions, he well understood the dangers of the North's opening position. Far from being an advantage, the division of its army into two outflanking forces had weakened both of them. Crucially, neither contingent was capable of resisting the combined power of the South's reserve corps. Instead of widening the gap between its two flanks by advancing further on the left, the North had to concentrate all of its forces in the centre. Over the next hour-and-a-half, Fabian's team would confirm the wisdom of this strategic analysis. Like the French position in 1800, the South's initial deployment was much stronger than it looked. Although most of its pieces were placed far from the action at the back of the board, they benefited from being grouped together in the centre. The task of the South's outposts was to slow down the enemy's advance until this numerical superiority could be brought to bear on one of the two flanks of the North's divided army. In the 1800 Marengo campaign, Bonaparte had committed his reserves to a French offensive against the Austrians in Italy rather than in Germany.[19] On that 2010 evening in the ICA bar, Fabian and his comrades chose the alternative option. As move followed move, the South's massed cavalry, infantry and artillery pieces steadily advanced towards the North's right flank. Having problems in seizing the fort covering their opponent's eastern arsenal, the attention of Russell's team was at first occupied elsewhere. Like André Masséna's troops stubbornly defending Genoa in 1800, this lone infantry unit was buying valuable time for the South in this game of the Marengo scenario at the ICA bar.[20]

Much too late, Russell finally realised that his side had made the wrong opening moves. He should have listened to Billy's warnings. The North's right flank was too weak to resist the overwhelming strength of the South's reserve army which was now bearing down on it. Advised by Fabian, Elena Vorontsova Duffield – our new Leningrad-born member of Class Wargames – launched a series of devastating attacks that took piece after piece from the opposition. In response, Russell called off the attack on the South's eastern arsenal, but his army couldn't be concentrated in time to prevent the total annihilation of its right flank. Even the North's marching general had to be sacrificed in this debacle. As the South's forces began advancing into the centre between the two mountain ranges, Rod Dickinson intervened to help the North in organising a last minute counter-attack which succeeded in taking an enemy cavalry unit. However, it was obvious to all that this brief triumph couldn't reverse the inevitable outcome of the game. Bringing the rest of their forces into action, Elena and

---

[19]   For Bonaparte's strategic options in 1800, see David Chandler, *The Campaigns of Napoleon*, pages 264–270; and Reginald Burton, *Napoleon's Campaigns in Italy*, pages 103–110.

[20]   For an account of the siege of Genoa in 1800, see James Arnold, *Marengo & Hohenlinden*, pages 67–78.

Fabian were quickly able to overwhelm the North's remaining defences. With their army reduced to a handful of pieces, Russell's team was forced into a humiliating surrender.[21] Once again, the French had trounced the Austrians in this key confrontation in the 1798–1802 War of the Second Coalition. As we packed up the board and pieces, the members of Class Wargames could take pride that we'd completed our mission for *The Urgent Need To Struggle* festival. Our avant-garde art group hadn't only created a transitory moment of participatory creativity inside the ICA bar. Above all, in our re-enactment of the 1800 Marengo campaign, we'd also shown how *The Game of War* was an excellent tool for teaching about the vital role of military leadership within revolutionary struggles. We were now ready to move into the second phase of our campaign of ludic mischief. Taking our cue from the name of *Chto Delat?*, what needed to done by Class Wargames was to popularise the collective playing of *The Game of War* so that today's Left activists could learn the Situationist political precepts materialised within the ebb-and-flow of its ritualised combat.

---

[21] For the photos of this game, see the Events 2010 section of the Class Wargames website.

2.2: THE STORMING OF THE WINTER PALACE

Two years before the Marengo scenario game was fought during the *Chto Delat?* season at the ICA in London, Class Wargames had sent its own expeditionary force out to the wild East. On 27th November 2008, we'd had the pleasure of hosting an evening of ludic subversion for *Cyberfest 2008* at the Youth Educational Centre of the State Hermitage Museum in St. Petersburg.[22] Having recently joined our ranks, Stefan Lutschinger – a Viennese philosopher who was working as a curator-in-residence at the National Center for Contemporary Art – had shown his mettle by securing the invitation to participate in this wonderful exhibition. By arranging our performance at the Winter Palace, his goal was to promote Debord's teachings to the activists, artists and academics of the Russian Left. In the 2000s, Situationism was still esoteric knowledge in the East. Many of the key texts weren't available in translation and its four tactics of cultural subversion had been mainly learnt from second-hand sources.[23] Stefan was determined to help remedy this deficiency. As in many other countries, nearly two decades after the breaching of the Berlin Wall, Russian radicals had only partially liberated themselves from the ideological legacy of the Stalinist past. During the Cold War, the propagandists of both East and West had agreed that the Soviet Union was a non-capitalist society: 'really existing socialism'. Even for most of its opponents on the Left, the Russian system was the flawed precursor of the communist future while its American rival was defending a dying system.[24] Back in the 1960s, what had marked out the Situationists was their fierce rejection of this geopolitical mystification. Crucially, they'd insisted that the Soviet Union wasn't any variety of socialism. Instead, it was a backward form of capitalism. When the Bolsheviks had seized power in 1917, Russia was an overwhelmingly peasant country. Needing to mobilise

---

[22]   For its programme of events, see Cyland MediaLab, 'Cyberfest 2008 in Saint Petersburg'.

[23]   In 2008, the publication of the first Russian edition of *The Society of the Spectacle* was only a decade old.

[24]   For a New Left overview of this theoretical confusion, see Paul Thompson and Guy Lewis, *The Revolution Unfinished?*

the impoverished population behind its industrialisation drive, the new ruling elite had imposed its ideological monopoly upon Soviet society: the 'concentrated spectacle'. The promises of communist equality were now transformed into justifications of bureaucratic privilege. Terrorised by state violence, everyone had to submit to the 'absolute celebrity' at the apex of the totalitarian pyramid of power: Joseph Stalin.[25]

By identifying the Soviet Union as state capitalist, the Situationists had foretold its inevitable demise. In the West, the socio-economic system was much more evolved than in the East. Under Fordism, capitalism had become a consumer society providing a dazzling array of both commodities and ideologies: the 'diffuse spectacle'. The advertising agency was a more sophisticated – and much more effective – method of social control than the secret police. For the Situationists, the bitter geopolitical rivalry between the two superpowers hid their common purpose of dominating humanity.[26] Unlike most of the Left, Debord and his comrades were neither surprised nor dismayed by the eventual outcome of the Cold War. During the 1990s, the once distinct Russian and American versions of capitalism had finally fused into a single global regime of class domination: the 'integrated spectacle'. With the profusion of information technologies, the centralisation of power could now be combined with a cornucopia of choice. As the mutant offspring of Stalinist propagandists and Fordist publicists, the rulers of neoliberalism had become adept at hiding their hegemonic ambitions beneath ideological stupefactions. Above all, one of their favourite political tropes was forgetting the unsettling moments of recent history when the rebellious proletariat had asserted its desire for collective emancipation. The integrated spectacle was a perpetual present where no radical social change was – or ever had been – possible.[27] When Stefan arranged our invite to *Cyberfest 2008*, Class Wargames had been given the task of promulgating the Situationist antidote to this intellectual chicanery: remembering the tumultuous events of the past century in ludic form. Our duty was to re-enact the revolution.

---

[25]   See Guy Debord, *The Society of the Spectacle*, pages 41–42, 70–84.

[26]   See Guy Debord, *The Society of the Spectacle*, pages 25–34, 42–46.

[27]   See Guy Debord, *Comments on the Society of the Spectacle*, pages 5–23.

The location within the Hermitage for Class Wargames' first engagement in Russia was very appropriate. We were playing Situationist games in what had once been the offices of the General Staff of the Imperial Army. Our audience had to climb the same staircase to the top-floor as the Bolshevik troops who seize the Winter Palace at the climax of Sergei Eisenstein's *October* film.[28] Inspired by this evocative setting, Class Wargames was determined that its intervention at *Cyberfest 2008* must offend the ideological pieties of the 21st century Russian elite. Under Vladimir Putin's regime, a revitalised nationalist hegemony was being constructed by eclectically sampling from the contradictory iconography of the country's recent turbulent history. Two decades after the collapse of the Stalinist system, Leningrad had regressed to St Petersburg and the Hermitage was being repainted in gaudy monarchist colours. At the same time, the Russian victory over Nazi Germany and the achievements of Soviet cosmonauts were still symbols of patriotic pride. Seeking legitimacy for its corrupt hold on power, the ruling oligarchy had promiscuously appropriated the symbolism of both the Tsarist and Bolshevik past for its Post-Modernist version of the integrated spectacle.[29]

Echoing Debord, *Chto Delat?* emphasised in its writings that what was absent from this patriotic melange was any memory of the libertarian dreams of the 1917 Russian Revolution.[30] For a brief moment, the common people of this country had pioneered new ways of conducting politics, making art, organising the economy and fighting wars that promised to deliver the whole of humanity from oppression, ignorance and poverty. For its intervention at *Cyberfest 2008*, Class Wargames wanted to invoke these disappointed hopes of the early-20th century Left in its own idiosyncratic style. Back in 1963, as the concluding contribution to the Situationists' *Destruction of RSG-6* exhibition in

---

28 This was a key scene in the fifth and final act of this historical drama, see Murray Sperber, 'Eisenstein's October', page 24.

29 See Andrew Jack, *Inside Putin's Russia*, pages 14–27; and Chrystia Freeland, *Sale of the Century*, pages 345–351.

30 For their theoretical analysis of how Boris Yeltsin's neoliberal presidency blocked the revival of participatory democracy in early-1990s Russia, see Artemy Magun, 'The Post-Communist Revolution in Russia and the Genesis of Representative Democracy', pages 64–68, 73–74.

Odense, Michèle Bernstein had created tableaus of model soldiers to rewrite the course of proletarian history in our favour: *Victory of the Paris Commune*; *Victory of the Spanish Republicans*; and *Victory of the Workers' Councils of Budapest*.[31] Four decades before Deller's artistic celebrations of hobbyist subcultures, this founding member of the International was already detourning figurine wargaming for the avant-garde cause. Living with Debord at the time, she'd witnessed her co-conspirator's lifelong enthusiasm for miniature replicas of fighting men.[32] Most wonderfully, like the kitsch paintings that Jorn found in flea markets, these metal warriors were an aesthetic affront to the mandarins of the art world. Unlike the Surrealist and Fluxus games with their minimalist sensibility, toy soldiers were valued for the precise historical accuracy of their poses, uniforms and equipment. By placing her Situationist dioramas of detourned military figurines inside this Danish gallery in 1963, Bernstein wasn't only politicising the apolitical hobby of wargaming, but also undermining the cultural hierarchies of bourgeois society. Visitors to the *Destruction of RSG-6* exhibition didn't need an expensive arts education to appreciate the political message of her avant-garde intervention. Many years later, when I'd told her that we'd started playing *The Game of War* with my teenage collection of 28mm Hapsburg and Ottoman figurines, Bernstein laughed and said: 'Guy would have approved. I used to buy toy soldiers for him – boys will be boys!'[33] For the Situationists, fighting battles with realistic miniatures was making avant-garde art.

Taking our cue from Bernstein's visionary tableaus for the *Destruction of RSG-6* exhibition, Class Wargames was determined to play at revolutionary politics with toy soldiers in the Hermitage. Mark Copplestone was already designing and selling figurines for re-fighting the epic struggles of the 1917–1921 Russian Civil War.[34] With him as

---

31 See Mikkel Bolt Rasmussen, 'To Act In Culture While Being Against All Culture', pages 102–104.

32 A few figurines from his extensive collection were featured in the 2013 exhibition about Debord's life at the Bibliotèque Nationale in Paris, see Emmanuel Guy, 'Où l'on Fait le Portrait de Guy Debord à Travers les Livres et son *Jeu de la Guerre*', page 174.

33 Michèle Bernstein, 'Conversation with Author'.

34 See the *Back of Beyond* section of the Copplestone Castings website.

a member, Class Wargames could make a punk provocation against the simplification of this conflict into the choice between rival forms of authoritarian rule: the Tsarist Whites and the Bolshevik Reds. Challenging this historical orthodoxy, we deployed opposing armies of toy soldiers on a miniature terrain inside the Winter Palace to re-enact a key battle that had helped to decide which faction of the Russian Left would monopolise the revolutionary cause. Between 5th–10th September 1918 around Kazan, two types of Reds – Bolsheviks and Social Democrats – had fought against each other for their own interpretation of radical democracy: the Congress of Soviets or the Constituent Assembly.[35] By emerging as the victor in this Volga campaign, Lenin's vanguard party had defined what it meant to be a revolutionary for rest of the 20th century and beyond.

For Debord, the polarisation of the whole world into Eastern and Western social systems during the Cold War had been the culmination of this violent split between rival Left factions in the Russian Civil War. On one side, the disciples of Bolshevism championed the Soviet Union and the concentrated spectacle. On the other, the adepts of Social Democracy supported the USA and the diffuse spectacle. In both cases, the revolutionary parties of the working class had been recuperated as bulwarks of the capitalist system. Far from the Left seizing state power, it was the bourgeois state that had taken over the Left. Confounding Marx's hopes, the Marxist leaders of the oppressed had become the new oppressors. According to Debord, this double betrayal in the 1910s and 1920s marked the moment when spectacular domination had consolidated its hold over modern society. Prevented from collectively determining their own destiny in the workers' councils, the masses were relegated to passively observing the machinations of their managerial masters.[36] The fierce rivalry between the private and public owners of capitalist property was just a factional squabble within the same

---

[35] See Ewan Mawdsley, *The Russian Civil War*, pages 76–95; and Geoffrey Swain, *Russia's Civil War*, pages 43–58. With the exception of those who'd rallied to the Bolsheviks, the Socialist Revolutionaries – the Left's peasant party which had won a majority of seats in the 1917 elections for the Constituent Assembly – supported the Social Democrats in this confrontation.

[36] See Guy Debord, *The Society of the Spectacle*, pages 66–67, 82–85; *Comments on the Society of the Spectacle*, pages 5–7.

ruling class. In both the East and the West, the 'order-givers' ruled over the 'order-takers'.[37] When we were preparing for our performance for *Cyberfest 2008*, the members of Class Wargames were well aware that – despite the ending of the Cold War many years previously – the Left in Russia as elsewhere still didn't fully grasp the seditious message of this Situationist refutation of the early-20th century split between Social Democracy and Bolshevism. In the perpetual present of the integrated spectacle, the complexities of the past could only conceived as simplified myths of good guys against bad guys. Countering this Post-Modernist axiom, the careful study of history had now become a proletarian virtue. Understanding exactly what had happened was the precondition of knowing how to build a better future. If we wanted to exorcise the lingering ideological malfeasance of the Cold War, Class Wargames knew that our performance for *Cyberfest 2008* had to encapsulate the formative tragedy of 1917 in microcosm. Like Constructivism preceding Situationism, Chris Peers' *Reds versus Reds* would be played before Guy Debord's *The Game of War*.[38]

With the snow falling outside, we prepared our two toy soldier armies for their tabletop battle at the Winter Palace. Mark would command the Social Democratic forces of the Constituent Assembly who were defending a village which blocked the road to Kazan in the Tatarstan region of Russia. Most of his team's troops were peasant militia of doubtful quality, but they were backed up by a contingent of hardened veterans from the Czechoslovak Legion. I would take charge of the Bolshevik fighters for Soviet rule whose mission was to take this village on the Volga. Our army not only had more and better soldiers in its ranks, but also included an elite regiment of Kronstadt sailors.[39] Best of all, my role as commander-in-chief would be represented by a 28mm model of the Bolsheviks' most charismatic leader: Leon Trotsky.[40] Having placed the figurines on the terrain in the opening

[37]   See Paul Cardan, *Modern Capitalism and Revolution*, pages 1–26.

[38]   See the explanations of this game's scenario in Class Wargames, 'Communiqué #5'; and Mark Copplestone, 'Not Just A Game of Toy Soldiers'.

[39]   The army lists for this *Reds versus Reds* game are on page 22 above.

[40]   For his own account of how he led the Bolsheviks to victory in the Kazan operation, see Leon Trotsky, *My Life*, pages 411–426.

positions shown in **Diagram 4** on page 228, everything was now ready for Class Wargames' initial contribution to *Cyberfest 2008*. As soon as the audience arrived and settled down, the *Reds versus Reds* game commenced. Having the initiative, my band of Bolsheviks decided to launch an attack on the village with the large group of regular troops on our right flank. In response, Mark's Social Democratic forces opened up with rifles, machine guns and artillery to check our advance, but their firepower fortunately proved to be ineffective. Within a couple of moves, our right flank forces were engaged in fierce hand-to-hand fighting with the defenders of the village. In this combat, we had the advantage of not only pitting tough regulars against raw recruits, but also having a Bolshevik commissar standing behind them who would shoot anyone who might be tempted to run away from the fray. While Mark and his comrades were preoccupied with preventing the disintegration of their left flank, my side next sent our shock troops of Kronstadt sailors into the centre of the village to confront the Czechoslovak Legion with some of their comrades moving forward to distract the Social Democrats' right flank. Then, as the game was reaching its deciding moment, Mark's conscripts on the other side of the village broke and ran after suffering heavy casualties in their melee with our regular troops. Facing the combined might of the whole Bolshevik army, the Czechoslovak Legion was soon also forced to withdraw. Realising that their position was now hopeless, Mark's team gracefully accepted defeat in this game of *Reds versus Reds*. As in September 1918, the Soviet forces had once again achieved their objective. Having taken this village on the Volga river, they could now advance unopposed to the gates of Kazan. Above all, the Bolsheviks had secured their monopoly control over the Red side in the Russian Civil War.[41]

While waiting for our event to begin, the chic audience of *Cyberfest 2008* had carefully checked out the two games on display which we were about to play. Despite its cultural and intellectual kudos, it wasn't Debord's Modernist ludic artwork that had caught their attention. Instead, like the audience for Bernstein's dioramas in Odense, the

---

[41] Photographs of this game are in the Events 2008 section of the Class Wargames website.

crowd at the Hermitage was fascinated by the intricate details of the toy soldiers and scenery which Mark had skilfully made for the *Reds versus Reds* game. The uniforms and weaponry of his beautifully painted Russian Civil War figurines were as historically accurate as possible. The miniature buildings of his exquisitely constructed Volga village were in the appropriate style of the period. When he'd designed its minimalist board and pieces, Debord had endowed *The Game of War* with an avant-garde aesthetic. In contrast, the creative inspiration for Mark's *Reds versus Reds* soldiers and terrain came from outside high culture. He was an artisan who made his living within the hobbyist subculture of figurine wargaming. Like the fans of Avalon Hill and SPI simulations, these toy soldier enthusiasts were military history buffs who wanted to re-fight the battles of the past. However, they were not satisfied by moving cardboard pieces across a hex board. Instead, their desire for historical authenticity could only be satisfied by commanding large armies of figurines in the correct uniforms confronting each other across convincing looking terrain.

Unfortunately, this form of simulation also had its drawbacks. Focused on the joys of collecting toy soldiers and constructing scenery, these hobbyists had ensured that '… most realistic wargames are not much more than moving dioramas.'[42] They'd been trapped by the dilemma of trying to combine fidelity to the past in both the appearance of the battlefield and the experience of combat. At *Cyberfest 2008*, Class Wargames didn't make the same mistake. In his explanatory notes, Mark pointed out that the toy soldiers and terrain in our re-enactment of the 1918 Kazan operation were only '… representing in symbols (which in this case are paradoxically almost-realistic models) elements of historical reality, perceptions of Russia and, as the game progresses, the passing of time.'[43] Reinforcing his argument, he'd placed an interactive version of a Malevich painting on the edge of the board which tracked this confrontation between the two opposing Red forces. When mapped as abstract shapes, the movement of our figurine armies became a dynamic Constructivist design. In this opening move

---

[42]   Peter Tanner, 'Games Without Commanders?', page 38.

[43]   Mark Copplestone, 'Not Just A Game of Toy Soldiers'. Also see Stefan Lutschinger, *Malevich: A Suprematist board game.*

of our contribution to *Cyberfest 2008*, we'd successfully revealed the avant-garde art hidden inside the hobbyist subculture of toy soldier wargaming.

When playing *Reds versus Reds* at the Hermitage, I'd intuitively known what to do. Like Mark and Fabian, I'd also been an enthusiastic figurine wargamer during my teenage years. Growing up in the 1970s, we'd all read the classic texts of H.G. Wells, Donald Featherstone, Peter Young and Charles Grant.[44] These pioneers of the hobby had claimed that they'd devised sets of rules which created '… the greatest possible realism, to permit the tactics and practices with model soldiers that conform to those used in real warfare of the period …'[45] However, for our generation, their techniques for simulating combat were far too simplistic. The publications of the Wargames Research Group had offered a much more historically rigorous system for re-fighting the conflicts of the past. In their wake, as the decades past and the rule books grew ever longer, all types of warriors, weaponry and topography were given their own dice modifiers. Unfortunately, in this drive for accuracy, playing wargames became hard work.[46] Eventually, the wisdom of this hobby's pioneers was rediscovered. Simplicity was a virtue not a vice. Reflecting this 21st century trend, the *Reds versus Reds* rules that Chris Peers had devised for our intervention at *Cyberfest 2008* were definitely old school wargaming. They only covered a limited variety of troops, armaments and terrain features. Movement, combat and morale were all decided by dice throws.[47] They included jokey rules like allowing Bolshevik commissars to rally a retreating Soviet regiment by shooting one of its number for cowardice. While *The Game of War* provided a cerebral duel of wills in ludic form, *Reds versus Reds* was an amusing diversion for grown-up boys.[48] Inspired by Bernstein's

---

44   See H.G. Wells, *Little Wars*; Donald Featherstone, *War Games*; Peter Young and J.P. Lawford, *Charge!*; and Charles Grant, *The War Game*.

45   Donald Featherstone, *War Games*, page 23.

46   See Sue Laflin-Barker, 'History of Wargames Research Group'; and Harry Pearson, *Achtung Schweinehund!*, pages 113–135.

47   This old school feel was enhanced by having the movements and firing ranges of the different figurines designated in obsolete imperial measurements.

48   Chris Peers' *Reds versus Reds* rules were a shortened and adapted version of his popular *Contemptible Little Armies* set.

Situationist dioramas, Class Wargames' performance for *Cyberfest 2008* was dedicated to detourning this hobbyist method of fighting with figurines for its own seditious purposes. On that November evening inside the Winter Palace, I'd had great fun pretending to be the 28mm model of Leon Trotsky leading the Bolshevik army in its assault on Kazan. But, if this simulated battle was to have any wider resonance, Class Wargames would carefully have to explain the radical message embedded within its toy soldier playtime to the shrewd audience of *Cyberfest 2008*. Although still engaged in the first phase of our campaign of ludic subversion, we were already moving into its next stage of propagating Situationist revolutionary politics.

While the *Reds versus Reds* match was taking place at the Hermitage, Fabian kept up a running commentary on what was happening on the tabletop battlefield. In between elucidating the ebbs and flows of this simulated combat, he slowly revealed the iconoclastic reasoning that had inspired our détournement of figurine wargaming. By re-fighting the 1918 Kazan operation in miniature, Class Wargames was breaking with the Left's tired ways of thinking about the world-historical significance of the 1917 Russian Revolution. As Debord and Bernstein had realised, playing with toy soldiers was debating proletarian politics by other means.[49] It was no accident that we were hosting *Reds versus Reds* in the iconic building that had provided the spectacular stage set for the rousing final scenes of Eisenstein's *October*: the Winter Palace. For decades, this film has provided documentary imagery of the dramatic events that'd taken place in Russia during 1917.[50] Thanks to Eisenstein's skills as a movie director, generations of viewers have been convinced that Lenin's vanguard party came to power in a popular insurrection that culminated in the seizure of the Winter Palace which was then the headquarters of the national government. However, as Fabian now explained to the attendees of *Cyberfest 2008*, they'd mistaken a sectarian myth for historical reality. Far from being contemporary news reporting, Eisenstein's movie was an avant-garde artwork made a whole decade after the political upheavals that were portrayed in its narrative. During the intervening period, the Soviet

49   See Class Wargames, 'Communiqué #5'.

50   See David Bordwell, *The Cinema of Eisenstein*, pages 95–96.

state had been holding annual celebrations to mark its triumph over the Social Democratic supporters of the Constituent Assembly in Russia's former capital city.[51] Through these artistic re-enactments, the historical memory of 1917 was systematically rewritten to justify the Bolshevik regime's monopolisation of the Red cause. Tragically, the bureaucratic spectacle had supplanted proletarian democracy.[52]

As Fabian emphasised in his commentary during our *Reds versus Reds* game, Eisenstein's depiction of the storming of the Winter Palace in *October* was a cinematic fantasy. By the time that this iconic event occurred, the fate of Russia had already been decided. Under Trotsky's leadership, 'small armed detachments ... [of party activists, skilled engineers and military personnel] ... guided from a single centre' had successfully carried out a coup d'état during the previous two days by commandeering the barracks, utilities and communication hubs of the capital city.[53] The fall of the Winter Palace was then inevitable. In October 1917, the urban masses had carried on with their personal affairs while this transfer of state power between the rival Red factions had taken place without their direct participation.[54] Not surprisingly, the new Bolshevik regime felt threatened by its lack of democratic legitimacy. Holding annual re-enactments of the ousting of the advocates of the Constituent Assembly from national government would become its avant-garde artistic solution to this political conundrum. For the 1920 third anniversary celebrations in Petrograd, Nikolai Yevreinov directed 10,000 amateur actors in a mass performance of *Storming the Winter Palace* on a Constructivist stage set placed in front of the building itself. In this theatrical production, the

---

51   For a description of these festivities, see Vladimir Tolstoy, Irina Bibikova and Catherine Cooke, *Street Art of the Revolution*, pages 55–67, 87–120, 137–139, 140–143, 146–147, 150, 162–163, 171–189.

52   See Guy Debord, *The Society of the Spectacle*, pages 41–42.

53   Leon Trotsky, *History of the Russian Revolution*, page 272. Also see Curzio Malaparte, *Technique du Coup d'État*, pages 33–65; and Earl Ziemke, *The Red Army*, pages 11–14.

54   The famous memoir that inspired the script for *October* admitted that: '... a few blocks away [from the Winter Palace] we could see the trams, the crowds, the lighted shop-windows and the electric signs of the moving-picture shows – life going on as usual ... all the theatres were open ...' John Reed, *Ten Days That Shook The World*, page 95. Also see Leon Trotsky, *History of the Russian Revolution*, page 249.

Bolshevik coup d'état was re-imagined as a workers' uprising. This time around, the city's population did participate in the daring assault on the Social Democratic government's headquarters.[55] Seven years later, when Eisenstein was commissioned to make *October*, he created the avant-garde movie version of this ideological fabrication. Since '… the historical storming [of the Winter Palace] was something of a letdown … [his film] improved on it, focused it, and, for many contemporaries, made it seem more truthful than before.'[56] The vanguard party's re-enactments of this historical event had successfully smothered what had really happened in Petrograd a decade earlier. Far from being an eyewitness documentary, Eisenstein's *October* was the 1927 film of the Bolshevik dictatorship's live action role-playing game of the 1917 Russian Revolution.

On that November evening in the Hermitage, the 28mm figurine of Trotsky commanding the Soviet forces in *Reds versus Reds* symbolised our utter contempt for the vanguard party's spectacular recuperation of proletarian democracy. Producing *October* after this revolutionary leader's fall from power, Eisenstein had been forced to minimise his decisive role in the dramatic events of 1917. Yet, despite the pressures of official censorship, Trotsky was still the hidden star of the 10th anniversary cinematic commemoration of the founding of the Bolshevik state. A few fleeting glimpses were enough to hint at what'd been edited out of the film.[57] Like Lenin, Trotsky had become the role model for leftist intellectuals who wanted to reinvent themselves as hard men of action. He was the radical agitator that had not only successfully organised the October 1917 coup d'état, but also led the Red Army to a stunning victory in the 1917–1921 Russian Civil War. Here was the impoverished journalist from the provinces who'd transformed himself into the charismatic general in a white leather uniform on a

---

[55] See Vladimir Tolstoy, Irina Bibikova and Catherine Cooke, *Street Art of the Revolution*, pages 137–138; and David Bordwell, *The Cinema of Eisenstein*, page 82.

[56] James von Geldern, *Bolshevik Festivals*, page 2. Also see Susan Buck-Morss, *Dreamworld and Catastrophe*, pages 147–163.

[57] An explanatory title was even added to the film which falsely claimed that Trotsky had opposed the Bolsheviks' seizure of power! For the Stalinist rewriting of the *October* script, see David Bordwell, *The Cinema of Eisenstein*, pages 13, 80; and Murray Sperber, 'Eisenstein's October', page 10.

thoroughbred horse.[58] Most tellingly, Stalin – Trotsky's bitterest rival – had also adopted a military style of dress when he took over as the maximum leader of Bolshevism. In the decades that followed October 1917, this exhilarating vision of the 'prophet armed' would inspire revolutionary leaders in developing countries across the world: Mao Zedong, Võ Nguyên Giáp, Josip Tito, Che Guevara, Samora Machel and Yasser Arafat.[59] Even though they'd paid formal homage to Stalin's pragmatic cunning, these warrior intellectuals always remained in debt to Trotsky's heroic image. They too believed that the man in a uniform was the epitome of socialist rectitude: 'political power grows out of a barrel of a gun.'[60]

---

[58]   See the admiring account of his rise to power in Isaac Deutscher, *The Prophet Armed*.

[59]   See Robert Taber, *The War of the Flea*; and Geoffrey Fairbairn, *Revolutionary Guerrilla Warfare*.

[60]   Mao Zedong, 'Problems of War and Strategy', page 224.

2.3: THE ARMED STRUGGLE

When we hosted the performance of *Reds versus Reds* for the *Cyberfest 2008* festival, Class Wargames was still engaged in the first phase of our campaign of ludic subversion. As adepts of Pop Situationism, we were committed to implementing the International's four tactics of cultural sabotage to counter the recuperation of avant-garde art. This détournement of hobbyist wargames within the psychogeographically resonant space of the Hermitage wasn't just a provocation against aesthetic snobbery and pacifist moralism. More importantly, our collective playing of Chris Peers' military simulation constituted one of those transitory moments of participatory creativity which were so treasured by the English Situationists. Having achieved this decisive breakthrough on the cultural front, Class Wargames was now able to initiate the second stage of our campaign of ludic mischief. Paralleling Debord's own trajectory, the making of avant-garde art would become the propagation of libertarian communist politics. By playing *Reds versus Reds* inside the Winter Palace, Class Wargames was attacking the Bolshevik mythology of Eisenstein's *October* which still haunted the imagination of the 21st century Left. Far from championing proletarian emancipation, the two toy soldier armies on the replica Kazan battlefield were fighting for rival forms of capitalist domination: the concentrated spectacle or the diffuse spectacle. On this 2008 evening at the Hermitage, the amusing pastime of figurine wargaming had acquired a serious political purpose. Under the integrated spectacle, what passed for historical analysis was suffused with tired movie cliches. But, when the Bolshevik and Social Democrat teams moved Mark's 28mm miniatures into ludic combat, this passive contemplation of the past was transformed into active engagement with the dramatic events that have defined what it meant to be on the Left since the 1917 storming of the Winter Palace. Crucially, by placing the outcome of the Russian Civil War in doubt once again, Class Wargames was exorcising the malign influence of its ideological certainties over the present. There was nothing inevitable about the victory of the Bolsheviks. With some clever moves and luckier dice throws, the Social Democrats might instead have become the new masters of the Russian empire. There was everything to play for in our *Reds versus Reds* game at the Hermitage.

In his commentary, Fabian explained that our toy soldier simulation at *Cyberfest 2008* was re-enacting the militarised recuperation of the democratic hopes of the 1917 Russian Revolution. During the opening years of the First World War, the absolute monarchy had proved itself incapable of fulfilling the primary duty of any state: defending the national territory from foreign invasion. Discredited on the battlefield, the once-all-powerful despotism of the Tsars was swept away in February 1917 by a spontaneous outbreak of street demonstrations led by women workers in the country's patriotically renamed capital city: Petrograd.[61] Over the next few months, the disintegration of Russian state accelerated under the combined impact of military defeats at the front and social rebellion at home. As the chaos spread, rival Red sects fiercely quarrelled over which of them should determine the new political settlement. What would give the edge to Lenin's vanguard party in this faction fight was its growing support amongst the disaffected rank-and-file members of the Russian armed forces.[62] In October 1917, having secured the loyalty of the city's garrison, the Bolsheviks took over the national government by seizing control of Petrograd in the name of the forthcoming 2nd Congress of Workers' and Soldiers' Soviets. Appearing on its platform just after the fall of the Winter Palace, Lenin and Trotsky announced that the downtrodden masses were the new masters of Russia: 'Comrade toilers, remember that you *yourselves* are now governing the state ... Your Soviets are now the organs of state power with full competence to decide all questions.'[63]

Three months later, on 19th January 1918, the new government in Petrograd sent a contingent of Kronstadt sailors to dissolve the Constituent Assembly which – despite the voters having given an overwhelming mandate to the parties of the Left – inconveniently only contained a minority of Bolshevik deputies.[64] Breaking with the

---

[61]   The historical experts all agree that: 'There was no central leadership [at the beginning of the Russian Revolution] from any [political] party or well-known figure.' Oskar Anweiler, *The Soviets*, page 101.

[62]   See Isaac Deutscher, *The Prophet Armed*, pages 249–324; and Mark von Hagen, *Soldiers in the Proletarian Dictatorship*, pages 13–21.

[63]   V.I. Lenin, 'To the Population', page 419. Emphasis in the original. Also see Leon Trotsky, *History of the Russian Revolution*, pages 281–318.

[64]   See Evan Mawdsley, *The Russian Civil War*, pages 5–8.

political strategy of Marx and Engels, Lenin and Trotsky insisted that the dictatorship of the proletariat could no longer be realised through securing a socialist majority in a bourgeois parliament.[65] Polemicising against their Red opponents, these Bolshevik leaders declared that the direct democracy of the Congress of Soviets had now superseded the representative democracy of the Constituent Assembly. As if to confirm this analysis, the Social Democrats who dominated the Left in the German parliament would – before the year was out – be collaborating with the most reactionary elements of the old ruling class to block any radical change in the aftermath of their nation's defeat in the First World War.[66] In 1919, at the 1st Congress of the Communist International in Moscow, the Russian Bolsheviks proclaimed themselves as the champions of the new libertarian politics of Soviet democracy – and that the task of revolutionaries across the world was to apply these lessons of October 1917 in their own nations.[67] For rest of the 20th century, the warrior intellectuals of the Leninist vanguard party became the living embodiment of a militarised version of socialism. The Russian Civil War had proved that the possessors of property would brutally resist any diminution of their social power. As Trotsky argued, the Left must understand that: '... [the] question as to who is to rule the country ... will be decided ... not by references to the paragraphs of the constitution, but by the employment of violence.'[68] The Reds could only prevail in the class struggle by becoming better soldiers than their White enemies. Paradoxically, if they wanted to run their own lives through workers' councils, the masses would first have to learn how to obey the orders of their Bolshevik officers without question. Military discipline had become the precondition of radical democracy.

---

[65] In what would become an ideological leitmotif of the Bolshevik regime, Lenin's *State and Revolution* justified this dramatic reversal in position by selectively quoting from Marx and Engels' own writings! For the orthodox Marxist critique of this intellectual trickery, see Karl Kautsky, *The Dictatorship of the Proletariat*.

[66] See Franz Neumann, *Behemoth*, pages 3–29.

[67] See V.I. Lenin and Yukko Rakhia, 'Theses and Report on Bourgeois Democracy and the Dictatorship of the Proletariat'; and Leon Trotsky, 'Manifesto of the Communist International to the Workers of the World'.

[68] Leon Trotsky, *Terrorism and Communism*, page 75.

In his commentary for the *Reds versus Reds* game at *Cyberfest 2008*, Fabian took delight in pointing out that our toy soldier armies were re-enacting the historical moment that had fixed this authoritarian perversion of Left politics. With a grin on his face, he pointed towards the 28mm models of Leon Trotsky and the two Bolshevik commissars. The decisive role of these figurines in our *Reds versus Reds* game was a ludic metaphor of Situationist enlightenment. At the turning point of this contest at the Winter Palace, my team had ordered one of our commissars to execute a member of the wavering regular unit on our right flank which had prevented a potentially disastrous retreat. From then onwards, the Bolsheviks' victory in this rerun of the 1918 Kazan operation was assured. As Fabian now revealed, the players of *Reds versus Reds* in the Hermitage had just experienced the recuperation of Soviet democracy by the Leninist leadership of the concentrated spectacle for themselves. If the Bolshevik side wanted to prevail in this Russian Civil War game, dissent in the ranks must be dealt with harshly. In Chris Peers' rules, there was no provision for simulating the fighters of the Red Army assembling in a Workers' and Soldiers' Soviet to decide how to fight the enemy collectively. Trotsky and his commissars were the sole order-givers for the Bolshevik forces on the Kazan battlefield.

When planning our contribution to *Cyberfest 2008*, Class Wargames envisaged this match of *Reds versus Reds* as our ludic refutation of not only the historical fabrications of Eisenstein's *October* movie, but also the contemporary hucksters of vanguard politics. For almost two decades, the intellectual apologists of the integrated spectacle had loudly proclaimed that the collapse of the Soviet Union proved there was no alternative to neoliberal globalisation. Whoever the voters elected into power, the government must implement social and economic policies favouring big business and big banks.[69] Thanks to the magic of the free market, the rapid spread and increasing capabilities of network technologies were creating a 'new paradigm' where anyone with entrepreneurial zeal had the opportunity to be both rich and

---

[69]   Most notoriously, the victorious American empire was identified as the philosophical apogee of human civilisation in Francis Fukuyama, *The End of History and the Last Man*.

hip.[70] But, by the time that we'd arrived in St Petersburg for *Cyberfest 2008*, this neoliberal dogma was already past its sell-by date. Only a month earlier, the bankruptcy of Lehman Brothers had precipitated a financial panic which heralded the beginning of the most serious economic recession in the USA and Europe since the 1930s. When children were prevented from living better lives than their parents, laissez faire capitalism had failed the test of human progress. Not surprisingly, those dissidents who'd held firm to their Bolshevik beliefs felt vindicated. As exemplified by the name of *Chto Delat?*, there'd always been admirers of Lenin and Trotsky on the Left even when the global economic system was booming. Now, after nearly two decades of being on the wrong side of history, these Russian revolutionaries' intransigent opposition to bourgeois democracy and capitalist markets no longer appeared anachronistic. The romance of Bolshevism was back in fashion. In a 21st century re-match, the losing side in the Cold War game might win this time around.

When we'd played *Reds versus Reds* at the Winter Palace, Class Wargames was making Situationist political propaganda against the Bolshevik recuperators of Situationism. Across the world, there were parties and sects which were still upholding the Leninist line within the labour movement. However, for the sophisticated attendees of *Cyberfest 2008*, their political tactics of selling newspapers, organising demonstrations and contesting elections were strictly old school. In St Petersburg as in London, a heady infusion of New Left theory had been required to sell the Bolshevik revival to these denizens of bohemia. Within the academy, Toni Negri, Slavoj Žižek and Alain Badiou were the intellectual gurus of this new iteration of the totalitarian 'Communist hypothesis'. Imitating the pranksters of Pop Situationism, they'd outraged the scholarly guardians of liberal democracy by praising the murderous regimes of Lenin, Stalin and Mao.[71] Alongside this punk tactic of provocation, they'd also enthusiastically embraced the technique of détournement. Back in the 1980s, in Žižek's homeland of

---

70   See Kevin Kelly, *New Rules for the New Economy*; and Peter Leyden, Peter Schwartz and Joel Hyatt, *The Long Boom*. For a more sceptical view, see Richard Barbrook and Andy Cameron, 'The Californian Ideology'.

71   For one of the more thoughtful responses from the Right to their enthusiasm for Bolshevik cruelty, see John Gray, 'The Violent Visions of Slavoj Žižek'.

Slovenia, the members of Laibach, Irwin and Red Pilot had pioneered the satirical remixing of the heroic Modernist past to question the conformist Post-Modern present: the retro-garde.[72] With their musicians dressed as 1940s Yugoslav Partisans, these artists from NSK launched a ferocious multi-media assault against not only the kitsch culture promoted by the bloodthirsty nationalists of the Balkans, but also the corporate art favoured by gallery curators in the West.[73] Copying this successful appropriation of Situationist tactics, the 2000s promoters of the totalitarian Communist hypothesis resurrected the discarded language of the Bolsheviks to critique the ideological hegemony of neoliberalism. In their 21st century détournement of the Cold War stand-off, there now was a Left alternative to the tyranny of the global financial markets: Lenin's Russia, Tito's Yugoslavia and Mao's China.[74] But, by returning to the Stalinist origins of semiotic structuralism, Negri, Žižek and Badiou had also proclaimed the concentrated spectacle as the only antidote to the integrated spectacle. Communism was a contemplative hypothesis not a lived activity. Once again, the Bolshevik intellectuals were the privileged few who would lead the indoctrinated masses forward into the totalitarian past: '... the authority of the [vanguard] Party is ... a new type of knowledge linked to a [revolutionary] collective political subject'.[75]

In the summer of 2008, while Class Wargames was preparing for its Russian expedition, an impassioned pamphlet was published in France which would codify this revival of vanguard politics for the youthful activists of the anti-capitalist protest movements: the Invisible Committee's *The Coming Insurrection*. Three decades before he'd joined up with Žižek and Badiou to champion the totalitarian Communist hypothesis, Negri had first gained notoriety as the prophet of the

---

[72] '... the *retro-principle* ... appropriates all those *texts* (signs, images, symbols and forms of rhetoric) which retrospectively have become identification signs for artistic, political, religious or technological 'salvation utopias' of the 20th century.' Inke Arns, 'Irwin (NSK) 1983–2002'. Emphasis in the original.

[73] NSK was the acronym of this retro-garde art movement: Neue Slowenische Kunst. For their adventures, see Alexei Monroe, *Interrogation Machine*.

[74] This nostalgia for militarised socialism led to the insistence that the greatest achievement of May '68 was the New Left's fascination with the vanguard politics of October 1917, see Alain Badiou, *The Communist Hypothesis*, pages 41–100.

[75] Slavoj Žižek, *Revolution at the Gates*, page 188.

left of the New Left in 1970s Italy: the Autonomists. Relegated to a subordinate role by the Cold War partition of Europe, this country's Stalinist party was revolutionary only in rhetoric and imagery. Imitating the Social Democrats, its pragmatic leaders had limited their ambitions to improving the living standards and political influence of the industrial working class within the Fordist system.[76] Not surprisingly, the May '68 generation was unimpressed by this reformist strategy. Like the Situationists, the Italian Autonomists dreamt of a more participatory form of politics. Rejecting parliamentary and trade union representation, these courageous activists adopted the revolutionary tactics of wildcat strikes, university occupations, street fighting and community media.[77] Frightened by this outburst of proletarian insubordination, the Stalinists had supported the Italian establishment's savage clampdown on the Autonomists in the late-1970s. Framed as a terrorist, Negri was forced into exile while other prominent members of the movement were jailed or went into hiding. The Italian New Left uprising had been crushed.[78] However, although temporarily defeated as practice, Autonomism would eventually triumph as theory. By the time that the 21st century arrived, the writings of Negri and his comrades had become essential reading for the opponents of neoliberal globalisation across the world. Crucially, they'd predicted that rioters, hackers, queers, squatters and ravers would replace the co-opted industrial proletariat as the revolutionary subject of history.[79] Empowered by the Net, this new iteration of the New Left would instigate the spontaneous uprising of the multi-faceted multitude against the monolithic hegemony of the neoliberal Empire.[80] Autonomism was the hipster intellectuals' theory of DIY politics.

---

[76]   For the successful implementation of these ameliorative policies at a local level, see Max Jäggi, Roger Müller and Sil Schmid, *Red Bologna*.

[77]   See Red Notes, *Italy 1977–8: Living With an Earthquake*; and Steve Wright, *Storming Heaven*.

[78]   For eyewitness accounts of this brutal state repression against the Autonomists, see Red Notes, *Italy 1980–81 After Marx, Jail!*

[79]   See the prophetic analyses of the post-Fordist recomposition of the working class in Sergio Bologna, 'The Tribe of Moles'; and Toni Negri, 'Archaeology and Project'.

[80]   See Michael Hardt and Toni Negri, *Empire*, pages 393–413; and Maurizio Lazzarato, 'General Intellect'.

In *The Coming Insurrection*, the Invisible Committee argued that a dedicated officer corps was now required to lead the nomadic army of the 21st century anti-capitalist revolution. Echoing Lenin, these Autonomists believed that the masses were too stupefied by bourgeois ideology to determine their own destiny without the guidance of this illuminated elite.[81] Until the world-historical moment of collective emancipation arrived, self-management was inevitably a minority affair. Fortunately, by embracing a bohemian lifestyle, the alter-globalisation activists were already anticipating the communist future in the neoliberal present.[82] From amongst the best and brightest of them, the Invisible Committee would recruit the members of its new vanguard party. Like the Bolsheviks who'd recuperated the Soviets, these Autonomists desired the spectacular annexation of participatory politics. Telling, in its earlier incarnation as Tiqqun, the Invisible Committee had condemned Debord while enthusing about Negri, Foucault, Deleuze and Guattari.[83] Derived from Stalin's sociolinguistics, the theoretical musings of these New Left philosophers justified the authoritarian assumptions of *The Coming Insurrection*. The chosen few must liberate the befuddled many. Military discipline was the precursor of direct democracy.[84]

By hosting the participatory performance of *Reds versus Reds* at the Winter Palace, Class Wargames provided the Situationist retort to both the academic and the Autonomist revivals of vanguard politics. In this key manoeuvre for the second phase of our campaign of ludic subversion, the two armies of toy soldiers were sent into combat against the self-appointed generals of the popular uprising against neoliberal

---

81   'An assembly [of workers] is not a place for decision, but for ... free speech exercised without a goal.' The Invisible Committee, *The Coming Insurrection*, page 81. Also see pages 22–27 for their sociological apologia for this anti-proletarian prejudice.

82   See The Invisible Committee, *The Coming Insurrection*, pages 65–68, 80–82.

83   Reversing the historical flow of influences between Situationism and Autonomism, they even claimed that '... Debord was an execrable middleman for all that was explosive in the [1970s] Italian situation ...' Tiqqun, *This is Not a Program*, page 21. For a Situationist dismissal of this sect's militarist obsession with revolutionary violence, see Jules Bonnot de la Bande, 'Advisory Concerning Spectacular Terrorism'.

84   'There is no such thing as a peaceful insurrection. Weapons are necessary; it's a question of doing everything possible to make using them unnecessary.' The Invisible Committee, *The Coming Insurrection*, pages 84.

capitalism. In his concluding remarks, Fabian emphasised that – although they could no longer exercise power in such a brutal fashion as the 28mm figurines of Trotsky and the two Bolshevik commissars had done during our recreation of the Kazan operation – too many of today's Left intellectuals and activists still fantasised about acting as decisively as these metal miniatures. It was their firm leadership that would decide between victory and defeat on the social battlefield. For this retro-garde tendency, the supersession of the integrated spectacle was the resurrection of the concentrated spectacle. In both tactics and strategy, the proponents of the totalitarian Communist hypothesis and the militants of the Invisible Committee had learnt well from the Situationists. Provocation and détournement were guided missiles against bourgeois complacency. With the demise of Fordism, the best class warriors were to be found amongst the quasi-criminal and over-educated elements of the proletariat. However, as revealed by their penchant for semiotic structuralism, these latter-day admirers of Bolshevism continued to hold the masses in contempt. Brainwashed by the media and repressed by the patriarchal family, the majority of the inhabitants of the consumer society were inherently conservative. Illuminated by the totalitarian Communist hypothesis, the Bolshevik intellectuals must give the orders to those who were destined to take orders. Countering this patronising attitude, the aim of our *Reds versus Reds* détournement of figurine wargaming was to shrink these would-be despots of the insurrectionary multitude down to 28mm scale. Transformed into toy soldiers, the Autonomist commissars of the networked vanguard were sent back to the tragic times that had given birth to them. As Fabian now revealed, this re-enactment of Russian revolutionary history was our Situationist remedy for the Bolshevik recuperation of Situationism.[85] It was better to play at being Trotsky than to make politics like Trotsky.

By refighting the conflict between the rival Red factions inside the Winter Palace, Class Wargames had returned to the birthplace of the militarised version of socialism that was newly fashionable amongst the 21st century Left. In 1917, as the Tsarist system collapsed in ignominy, the Bolsheviks had taken command of the key institution which would

---

[85] See Class Wargames, 'Communiqué #5'; and Mark Copplestone, 'Not Just A Game of Toy Soldiers'.

enable them to rebuild a more powerful and ambitious Russian state: the professional army.[86] During that momentous year, the competing Red parties had ostensibly fallen out over whether their new republic should be ruled by the Congress of Soviets or the Constituent Assembly. Yet, neither of these forms of democratic legitimation was capable of creating long-term political stability within Russia. Out in the countryside, the peasant majority of the population were instinctive anarchists. For them, the demise of the autocratic state meant the dispossession of the landowning aristocracy. Each village commune could now run its own local affairs without any outside interference.[87] Crucially, it was this peasant ethic of self-reliance that had inspired the audacious experiments in direct democracy within the cities. By holding mass meetings, workers could manage their factories and soldiers run their regiments. Joining this self-management movement, artists and intellectuals declared that they too wanted to control their own cultural and educational institutions.[88] In the Bolshevik mythology of the 1917 Russian Revolution, this flowering of participatory politics had culminated in the storming of the Winter Palace. Thanks to Lenin and Trotsky's skilful generalship, everyone could now take part in deciding the destiny of the nation: 'The Soviet system represents the maximum of democracy for the workers and peasants.'[89]

When he went to Russia in 1920, H.G. Wells – the English socialist author and wargames pioneer – had no difficulty in recognising the fallacy of this claim. Despite the language barrier, his visit to the Petrograd Soviet quickly revealed its deficiencies compared to the Westminster parliament. Above all, this talking shop lacked the legislative powers which could determine who formed the government of the country. Ironically, in practice, Russian proletarian democracy was less accountable than British bourgeois democracy. The Bolshevik leadership may have participated in the debates of the Petrograd Soviet,

[86] See Harold Nelson, *Leon Trotsky and the Art of Insurrection*, pages 93–124; and Mark von Hagen, *Soldiers in the Proletarian Dictatorship*, pages 13–21.

[87] See Jacques Camatte, *Community and Communism in Russia*, pages 16–25, 33–48; and Charles Bettelheim, *Class Struggles in the USSR*, pages 210–249.

[88] See Oskar Anweiler, *The Soviets*, pages 97–207; and Maurice Brinton, *The Bolsheviks and Workers' Control*, pages i–xv.

[89] V.I. Lenin, 'Fourth Anniversary of the October Revolution', page 503.

but their executive authority was derived from elsewhere.[90] In October 1917, it'd been the military that had decided which Red faction would control Russia. The weaponry of the Petrograd garrison was much more important than the votes of the city's population. Fighting for survival against internal and external enemies, Lenin's regime over the next few years rebuilt the regular army which had almost disintegrated during the revolutionary turmoil. Amongst the European Left, it had long been argued that only volunteers could be trusted with the defence of the nation. From bitter experience, they knew that professional soldiers led by career officers would obey orders to crush internal dissent with extreme violence. By democratising the army, Social Democrats believed that the threat posed by this repressive institution could be neutralised. When every worker was a part-time soldier, the men in uniform would be loyal to the Left.[91]

In 1917, like other revolutionary groups, the Bolsheviks had recruited its own militia forces in Petrograd and Moscow: the Red Guards. During that tumultuous year, these armed workers played a key role in ensuring that Lenin's party came out on top in the factional competition for state power. For a brief moment, the Bolsheviks were able to congratulate themselves for putting the European Left's proletarian military policy into practice.[92] Unfortunately, this commitment to a volunteer army proved to be as short-lived as their enthusiasm for universal suffrage. After some disastrous encounters with its German and White opponents, Lenin's regime soon relegated the Red Guards to policing duties. Despite their ardour, workers' militias from the cities lacked not only the numbers, but also, more importantly, the mindset to win the Russian Civil War. Even on the battlefield, these amateur soldiers still wanted to discuss with each other whether or

---

[90]   See H.G. Wells, 'Russia in the Shadows', pages 391–395. In contrast, Marx emphasised that: 'The [1871 Paris] Commune was ... executive and legislative at the same time.' Karl Marx, *Civil War in France*, page 40.

[91]   'The first decree of the [1871 Paris] Commune ... was the suppression of the standing army and the substitution for it of the armed people.' Karl Marx, *Civil War in France*, page 40. For the practical implications of this Social Democratic policy, see Friedrich Engels, 'The Prussian Military Question and the German Workers' Party'; and Jean Jaurès, *L'Armée Nouvelle*.

[92]   See Harold Nelson, *Leon Trotsky and the Art of Insurrection*, pages 108–124; and Mark von Hagen, *Soldiers in the Proletarian Dictatorship*, pages 13–24.

not they agreed with their commander's decisions before going into action.[93] Requiring more reliable troops, Trotsky – as the Bolsheviks' defence minister – instead conscripted the sons of the peasantry in their millions to serve under officers who'd learnt their trade in the Tsar's regiments. The Red Guards had been replaced by the Red Army. Military discipline was restored by using tried-and-trusted methods: a rigid hierarchy of ranks, smart uniforms, saluting superiors, medals for bravery and harsh punishments for trouble-makers including the death penalty for deserters. Substituting Bolshevik ideology for radical democracy, political commissars now enforced allegiance to the new Russian government amongst the rank-and-file soldiery.[94] Under Trotsky's leadership, orders were to be obeyed without any debates in the Red Army. The victory of the revolution had been bought at a terrible price: the defeat of the revolution.[95]

When the Tsar's regime had collapsed in February 1917, tight press censorship suddenly gave way to almost unrestricted media freedom. From the outset, the competing parties' newspapers were at the forefront of their struggle for political power. Not surprisingly, as instability increased, toleration for opposing viewpoints quickly diminished. Printing presses were now the arsenals of civil strife.[96] In October 1917, the Bolsheviks had launched their coup d'état in response to a bungled attempt by their Red rivals to close down one of their newspapers. As well as taking over the utilities, railway stations, telephone exchange and telegraph offices, Trotsky's troops also seized control of the Right's printing works. Within a few days, the new Bolshevik government had reintroduced press censorship and banned various conservative newspapers.[97] Over the next few years, media freedom soon disappeared

---

[93]   See Evan Mawdsley, *The Russian Civil War*, pages 46–51; and Mark von Hagen, *Soldiers in the Proletarian Dictatorship*, pages 24–5.

[94]   See Leon Trotsky, *Military Writings*, page 148–158; Isaac Deutscher, *The Prophet Armed*, pages 405–485; and Mark von Hagen, *Soldiers in the Proletarian Dictatorship*, pages 25–66.

[95]   See Ante Ciliga, *The Russian Enigma*, pages 283–291, 489–491; and Evan Mawdsley, *The Russian Civil War*, pages 377–403.

[96]   See Peter Kenez, *The Birth of the Propaganda State*, pages 29–35.

[97]   See Leon Trotsky, *History of the Russian Revolution*, pages 194–195, 210–211; and John Reed, *Ten Days That Shook the World*, page 166.

amidst the chaos and bloodshed of the Russian Civil War. Under military discipline, there could be no open expression of dissent. Even the critical voices on the Left had to be silenced.[98] What the Bolsheviks required instead was rousing propaganda which mobilised the masses to fight for the Soviet republic: the concentrated spectacle. Like the artistic avant-garde, the political vanguard was convinced that changing popular consciousness would inevitably transform the whole of society. In an influential interpretation of this fundamental human right, the Bolsheviks now claimed that their monopoly over intellectual and cultural life was the most advanced form of media freedom.[99] Armed with the correct political ideology, the 'firmly knit and monolithic' vanguard party was leading the peoples of the world into the utopian future.[100]

During the Russian Civil War, the intervention of avant-garde artists helped to decide which side would emerge victorious on the battlefield. By backing Lenin's party against its Red rivals, they'd identified the Bolsheviks' political monopolisation of the 1917 Revolution with the cutting-edge of aesthetic creativity. Through their posters, plays, paintings, films and publications, these Modernist propagandists motivated the conscripted peasantry to fight with fervour for the Soviet cause. Thanks to their hard work and commitment, radical artworks were transformed into deadly weapons against not only the Whites, but also other Red factions.[101] In the ferocious struggles of the Russian Civil War, Trotsky's armoured train covered with Constructivist designs became the icon of the Bolshevik synthesis of ideological and military shock tactics. Rushing from front to front, this mobile factory of the concentrated spectacle combined the persuasive power of the printing press, radio broadcasting and theatrical performances with the coercive

---

[98] See Peter Kenez, *The Birth of the Propaganda State*, pages 35–44; and Arthur Ransome, *The Crisis in Russia*, pages 35–43.

[99] See Peter Kenez, *The Birth of the Propaganda State*, pages 44–118; and Richard Barbrook, *Media Freedom*, pages 38–54.

[100] Commission of the CC of the CPSU(B), *History of the Communist Party of the Soviet Union*, page 140. Also see Susan Buck-Morss, *Dreamworld and Catastrophe*, pages 40–96.

[101] See Peter Kenez, *The Birth of the Propaganda State*, pages 95–118; and Mark von Hagen, *Soldiers in the Proletarian Dictatorship*, pages 89–114.

might of motorised infantry, guard cavalry and heavy artillery. Like the small teams of specialists who'd carried out the Bolshevik coup d'état, this elite detachment of the Red Army was living proof of the collective power of industrial production with its complex hierarchy of intellectual and practical skills. No enemy unit had been able to withstand its devastating fusion of ideological passion and military firepower for long. Within the agrarian society of early-20th century Russia, Trotsky's armoured train was a wondrous Constructivist premonition of the possibilities of the hi-tech future in the present.[102]

---

[102] See Leon Trotsky, *My Life*, pages 427–439; Arthur Ransome, *The Crisis in Russia*, pages 67–72; and David Elliot, *New Worlds*, pages 72–73.

2.4: THE TEMPTATIONS OF BOLSHEVISM

In 1921, the Red Army finally achieved its hard-won victory in the Russian Civil War. By purging their erstwhile comrades on the Left, the Bolsheviks had first taken exclusive ownership of the popular revolution which then – after great sacrifices – led to the annihilation of the aristocratic counter-revolution. Violence not voting had decided who would rule over the new republic.[103] Not surprisingly, the Red Army was now the most admired institution of this reborn Russian state. Under the Tsars, the military profession had been widely despised, especially amongst the Left. However, in 1917, these prejudices quickly disappeared when mutinous soldiers and sailors became the strongest supporters of the revolution. It was their commitment that enabled the Reds to overthrow the absolute monarchy which had brutally oppressed the Russian people for centuries. It was their bravery that would thwart the Whites' efforts over the next four years to restore the old order by force. In their life-and-death fight for survival, the Bolsheviks soon became devotees of '… the military virtues of honour, self-sacrifice and obedience'.[104] Direct democracy was now condemned for threatening the fragile unity of the nation against its domestic and foreign enemies. As on the battlefields of the Russian Civil War, an undisputed chain of command was needed for the efficient running of all political, cultural and economic institutions.[105] Intoxicated by victory, Trotsky in 1921 advocated mobilising the entire civilian population in labour armies to carry out the rebuilding of the devastated country. In this militarised recuperation of socialism, obeying orders issued by state planners became the Leninist substitute for trading commodities within the

---

[103] As the leader of the Bolshevik regime emphasised: '… the solution of the problems [in Russia] is effected not by means of the ballot, but by the class struggle in all its forms, including civil war.' V.I. Lenin, 'The Elections to the Constituent Assembly', page 481. Also see Leon Trotsky, *Terrorism and Communism*, pages 51–68, 119–125.

[104] Mark von Hagen, *Soldiers in the Proletarian Dictatorship*, page 279.

[105] See the unabashed enthusiasm for authoritarian 'one-man management' in V.I. Lenin, *The Immediate Tasks of the Soviet Government*; and Nikolai Bukharin, *Economics of the Transition Period*.

marketplace.[106] Reflecting this new wisdom, Bolshevik propaganda was saturated with the terminology of armed conflict. Workers and peasants were soldiers in the economic struggle to increase industrial and agricultural production. Avant-garde artists became fighters on the cultural front against ideological reaction. In revolutionary Russia, every citizen was a conscript in the Red Army: 'War Communism'.[107]

For the Bolsheviks, the defeat of the Whites in 1921 was their greatest moment of existential doubt. During the Russian Civil War, the advocates of Soviet democracy within the party had accepted that drastic measures were temporarily required to defend the revolution against its domestic and foreign opponents. Only too aware of the tragic fate of the 1871 Paris Commune, they knew that it was shoot first or be shot.[108] However, once the emergency was over, many on the Left believed that state repression against dissenters had lost its rationale. In a wave of strikes, workers in Petrograd demanded that the Bolsheviks should loosen their monopoly over political and economic power in Russia. Inspired by their example, the Kronstadt sailors who'd provided the elite troops for the October 1917 coup d'état and the 1918 Kazan campaign also rose in revolt against Lenin's regime. Drafting a manifesto for this new split within the Red cause, these rebels had one key demand that would enthuse the Situationists many decades later: 'Soviets without Bolsheviks.' In revolutionary Russia, direct democracy must now replace military discipline. Outraged by this proletarian insurrection, Lenin's regime first ruthlessly crushed the strikes in Petrograd and then massacred the defenders of the Kronstadt Soviet. Like the Paris Commune, this local experiment in self-management had been no match for a disciplined national army of peasant conscripts led by professional officers.[109] Having blocked any

---

[106] See Leon Trotsky, *Terrorism and Communism*, pages 140–182; and Isaac Deutscher, *The Prophet Armed*, pages 486–503

[107] See Roger Pethybridge, *The Social Prelude to Stalinism*, pages 73–131; and E.H. Carr, *The Bolshevik Revolution Volume 2*, pages 151–268.

[108] Writing on his armoured train in 1920, Trotsky claimed that: 'We are taking vengeance for the [1871] Commune and shall avenge it.' Leon Trotsky, 'The Paris Commune and Soviet Russia', page 46.

[109] See Ida Mett, *The Kronstadt Uprising*; Oskar Anweiler, *The Soviets*, pages 244–253; and Victor Serge, *Memoirs of a Revolutionary*, pages 115–156.

opening towards political pluralism, the Bolsheviks instead relaxed their controls over the Russian economy, especially within the countryside. Letting peasants trade in the marketplace was much less threatening to the privileges of this new ruling elite than allowing workers to vote in the Soviets.[110]

During the 1920s, the veterans of the Russian Civil War deplored the moral laxity encouraged by the increasing toleration of private enterprise.[111] According to Trotsky, his opponents within the Bolshevik party were guilty of preparing the way for the restoration of liberal capitalism. What he advocated instead was a return to the military virtues of the wartime Red Army. When state planning displaced market competition, discipline and commitment would supplant consumerism and selfishness.[112] In the bitter contest for the Bolshevik leadership that followed Lenin's death in 1924, Stalin eventually emerged as the new boss of bosses. Yet, despite this political setback, it was Trotsky who would win the ideological argument over the most effective development strategy for the Soviet republic.[113] In 1928, Russia was the first country to succumb to the traumatic economic crisis which would engulf the whole world over the next decade. When the markets were no longer able to provide enough food from the countryside to feed the cities, the Bolshevik government quickly rediscovered the military solutions which had secured its grip on power during the Russian Civil War. Appropriating Trotsky's programme as his own, Stalin now ordered the mobilisation of the whole population in a nationwide campaign to modernise agriculture and industrialise the economy. Compulsory military service provided the prototype for

---

[110] See Roger Pethybridge, *The Social Prelude to Stalinism*, pages 196–251; and E.H. Carr, *The Bolshevik Revolution Volume 2*, pages 269–357.

[111] See Mark von Hagen, *Soldiers in the Proletarian Dictatorship*, pages 166–168, 185–195.

[112] For the political and economic programme of the Left Opposition within Russia's governing party, see Leon Trotsky, *The New Course*; and Eugeny Preobrazhenksy, *The New Economics*.

[113] In 1931, one of his imprisoned followers eventually realised that: 'Trotsky... is ... the theorist of the regime which Stalin is carrying out in practice.' Ante Ciliga, *The Russian Enigma*, page 283.

this ruthless drive to proletarianise the Russian peasantry.[114] Like Red Army soldiers, the exploited and fearful servants of the Stalinist state were all equal in their subordination to the maximum leader. In this stern empire of the concentrated spectacle, they worked under strict discipline, received the same rations and were subjected to incessant ideological indoctrination. As Marx and Engels had foreseen in the late-19th century, the fatal flaw of the Russian Left was its obsession with 'barrack-room communism.'[115]

On that November 2008 evening at the Winter Palace, Class Wargames' performance was our Situationist exorcism of the vanguard party's counter-revolution within the proletarian revolution. For this second phase of our campaign of ludic subversion, the International's avant-garde art tactic of participatory creativity would be implemented to propagandise for the communist political strategy of direct democracy. With Trotsky having once again triumphed in our *Reds versus Reds* re-enactment, I now took over the commentator's role to introduce Debord's ludic antidote to the Bolshevik militarised recuperation of socialism: *The Game of War*. For the next contest at the Hermitage, Fabian and Ilze would play the South against Mark and Stefan as the North.[116] While the two sides were making their opening moves, I began to elucidate the political reasoning which had inspired this game. Born in 1931, Debord's childhood and adolescence had coincided with the apogee of Stalinist hegemony over the French Left. Before the Second World War, the Social Democrats had been the dominant force within working class politics.[117] But, when France was defeated in 1940, this mass party focused on winning elections, cultural agitation and trade union activism had suddenly become an irrelevance. Under Nazi occupation, any overt opposition was ruthlessly repressed. In such dangerous circumstances, the armed struggle against the fascist enemy had to be led by a disciplined revolutionary organisation: the

---

[114] See Mark von Hagen, *Soldiers in the Proletarian Dictatorship*, pages 295–343; and David Stone, *Hammer and Rifle*, pages 85–183.

[115] Karl Marx and Friedrich Engels, 'The Alliance of Social Democracy and the International Working Men's Association', page 120.

[116] The photographs of this game are in the Events 2008 section of the Class Wargames website.

[117] See Jean Lacouture, *Léon Blum*; and Julian Jackson, *The Popular Front in France*.

French Communist Party. Thanks to the courage and dedication of its members, the Germans and their collaborators paid an increasingly high price to keep control over the country until the arrival of the Allied armies in 1944 put an end to the conflict. By providing these elite troops of the French Resistance, the Stalinists had eclipsed their Social Democratic, Trotskyist and Anarchist rivals on the Left. In the elections held immediately after the Second World War, they were able to win almost a third of the popular vote. If women hadn't just been enfranchised, the French totalitarian Communists would have come close to securing a working majority of deputies in the National Assembly.[118]

When these ballots were cast in 1945–7, the prestige of the Soviet Union had never been higher. For four years, people across the world had been thrilled by the Russians' stubborn refusal to succumb to Nazi aggression. Under Stalin's leadership, the Red Army had fought back and – at a massive cost in lives and material – won the Second World War. His regime's brutal policy of forced industrialisation had built the factories that produced the tanks, planes, rifles and artillery which destroyed Adolf Hitler's empire. The fate of humanity had been decided on the Eastern Front.[119] Most appropriately, Yevgeny Khaldei's 1945 photograph of the hoisting of the red hammer-and-sickle flag of the Soviet Union on the Reichstag building in Berlin came to symbolise the final victory over fascism in Europe.[120] As I now explained to the audience of *Cyberfest 2008*, Debord and his comrades had grown up under the shadow of this triumph of militarised socialism. When the continent was partitioned between Russia and America at the 1945 Yalta conference, Stalin had consigned the French totalitarian Communists to permanent opposition. Prevented from taking state power, this vanguard party had instead concentrated its efforts on imposing the rule of the concentrated spectacle over the political, economic and cultural institutions of the Left. By the time that Debord became an activist in the late-1950s, the Cold War division of Europe

---

[118] See Serge Halimi, *Sisyphe est Fatigué*, pages 241–350; and R.W. Johnson, *The Long March of the French Left*, pages 23–51.

[119] See Richard Overy, *Russia's War*; and Evan Mawdsley, *Thunder in the East*.

[120] Like Eisenstein's *October*, this famous image was also doctored to conform to the requirements of Stalinist ideology, see Dean Lucas, 'Flag on the Reichstag'.

had ensured that: '… French Marxism … [was] identified completely with the Soviet Union and the "thought" of Joseph Stalin.'[121]

The dissidents of Debord's generation who'd founded the New Left had never completely escaped from the military glamour of Bolshevism. Like their Stalinist elders, many of these young French anti-Stalinists also saw themselves as the skilful generals of the proletarian vanguard. Having repudiated the Soviet despot, they'd then transferred their loyalties to another charismatic warrior intellectual of the concentrated spectacle: Trotsky, Mao, Castro or Pol Pot. The French Communist Party might have become compromised by its reformist policies in the postwar decades, but its wartime resistance against fascism still provided the best model for revolutionary militancy. Amongst the ranks of the New Left, many dreamt of returning to the hardline intransigence of the Bolshevik Left in its prime.[122] As in our *Reds versus Reds* game, these militants of May '68 continually re-fought the sectarian quarrels of the 1917 Russian Revolution and its aftermath amongst themselves. Instead of uniting against the common enemy, the French New Left during the 1970s became obsessed with its own sectarian divisions.[123] Defeat and disillusionment were the inevitable consequences of this ideological confusion. By the time that the 20th anniversary of May '68 arrived, most of these once youthful radicals had long since made their peace with bourgeois society. With the revolutionary overthrow of capitalism no longer on the agenda, the Post-Modernist celebration of cultural diversity was now the limit of their ambitions: '… [the] loss of the ability immediately to perceive what is significant and what is … irrelevant; what is incompatible and what could well be complementary; all that a particular consequence implies and at the same time all that it excludes …'[124]

---

[121] Arthur Hirsh, *The French Left*, page 11.

[122] See Christophe Bourseiller, *Les Maoistes*, pages 105–297; and A. Belden Fields, *Trotskyism and Maoism*, pages 41–130.

[123] For an exhaustive list from 1978 of these competing groups, see Roland Biard, *Dictionnaire de l'Extrême-Gauche*.

[124] Guy Debord, *Comments of the Society of the Spectacle*, page 30. For the intellectual targets of his scorn, see Jean-François Lyotard, *The Post-Modern Condition*; Jean Baudrillard, *Simulations*; and Gilles Deleuze and Félix Guattari, *A Thousand Plateaus*.

By playing *The Game of War* along with *Reds versus Reds* in the Winter Palace as the opening manoeuvre of the second stage of our campaign of ludic subversion, we were honouring the Situationists' discovery of a more subversive escape route from the dead end of Bolshevism. During the first decade of its existence, the International had mimicked the New Left's reborn vanguard parties in its ideological intensity with fierce debates over the correct political and cultural strategy decided through bitter splits and expulsions. Like Lenin, Trotsky and Stalin, Debord had also insisted upon ideological purity as the test of communist virtue.[125] Then, in May 1968, a revolution had taken place for real in France. During this momentous month, Debord became convinced that the Winter Palace of consumer capitalism was on the brink of falling to the insurgent proletariat. In a resurgence of direct democracy, the masses were creating their own institutions of social power: the workers' councils. For a brief moment, the Kronstadt rebels' demand for Soviets without Bolsheviks had become a practical possibility. Debord now understood that the Situationist International must finally free itself from all ideological taints of vanguard politics. Victory could no longer be won with an elitist military strategy on the new spectacular battlefield. Everyone must be involved in the revolutionary transformation of modern society. On the streets of Paris in May '68, the Situationists had the exhilaration of briefly experiencing the libertarian communist future in the present: 'Capitalised time stopped ... People strolled, dreamed, learned how to live. Desires began to become ... reality.'[126]

During our performance at the Hermitage, as Fabian and Ilze launched a devastating cavalry attack against their opponents, I took this opportunity to discuss how Debord had laid down these lessons of May '68 within *The Game of War*. In the immediate aftermath of this almost revolution, he'd had the moral strength to resist the temptations of Bolshevism. One of Debord's greatest achievements was his announcement of the dissolution of the Situationist International in 1972. By this daring move, he succeeded in preventing its admirers

---

[125] See Len Bracken, *Guy Debord*, pages 72–157; and Andrew Hussey, *A Game of War*, pages 156–230.

[126] René Viénet, *Enragés and Situationist in the Occupation Movement*, page 77.

from turning themselves into yet another New Left vanguard party. The strategy and tactics of the International were practical responses to the specific historical circumstances in which Debord and his comrades had found themselves. Asserting that their revolutionary adventures provided an infallible solution for all subsequent generations would transform Situationism from a subversive practice into a dogmatic ideology.[127] Intellectuals must be trained to resist their instinctive desire for recuperation by the concentrated spectacle. Debord was well aware that the working class movement was strengthened when dissident thinkers put their learning in the service of the revolution. But, as the attendees at *Cyberfest 2008* knew only too well, the tragic history of 20th century Russia was a dreadful warning to the Left across the world. The Bolsheviks – the leaders of the exploited – had all too easily become a new class of exploiters. By inventing *The Game of War*, Debord had provided his answer to how radicals after May '68 could stop themselves from also turning into a little Lenin, Trotsky or Stalin. This ludic battlefield was the Situationist antidote to the snares of Bolshevism.

Pointing to the board, I directed the *Cyberfest 2008* audience's attention to the South's audacious outflanking attack against the North's army. Laid out according to the Rio de Janeiro scenario shown in **Diagram 2** on page 224, the two sides had begun with their forces divided into three almost equal brigades. In a series of clever manoeuvres, Fabian and Ilze had utilised their cavalry pieces on their left flank to break through the North's defences. At a key moment in the game, they'd happily sacrificed one of these elite units to open the way to taking their opponent's western arsenal. As I now explained, Fabian and Ilze were in the ascendency because they clearly understood the political meaning of this Situationist simulation. For Debord, the four cavalry pieces symbolised the artists and intellectuals who'd committed themselves to the cybernetic communist cause. In *The Game of War*, the task of both North and South was to learn how to make the best use of these guard troops of the social battlefield without becoming Bolsheviks themselves. During the May '68 Revolution, the Situationist

---

127   See the impassioned diatribe against these would-be synthesisers of Situationism and Bolshevism in Guy Debord and Gianfranco Sanguinetti, *The Veritable Split in the International.*

International had gladly sacrificed itself to prepare the ground for the final assault of the proletarian army: '... I believe I can say that our formation as a whole never swerved from its line until it plunged into the very core of destruction.'[128] Like cavalry units in *The Game of War*, the members of the revolutionary vanguard were expendable pieces in the struggle to build a truly human civilisation. Inside the Winter Palace, the players of North and South were learning that there could be no leadership which placed itself above the working class as a whole. In this tabletop combat, the whole army had to work as one to achieve victory against the common enemy. By inventing *The Game of War*, Debord had supplied his ludic response to the totalitarian temptations of Bolshevism. When every proletarian could play at being Lenin, Trotsky and Stalin on its game board, then no intellectual would be tempted to become a little Lenin, Trotsky or Stalin in real life.

---

[128]   Guy Debord, *In Girum Imus Nocte et Consumimur Igni*, page 179. In this film, the International's role in May '68 was visually identified with the Light Brigade's suicidal charge against the Russian artillery which led to the British-French victory at the 1854 battle of Balaclava. For an account of this infamous moment in military history, see Mark Adkin, *The Charge*.

2.5: THE CHOSEN FEW

After the contest in the Hermitage was over, the members of Class Wargames were invited to a local restaurant by Dmitry Golynko and his friends to celebrate our decisive intervention at *Cyberfest 2008*. Over vodka and blinis, the conversation soon turned to the political meaning of *The Game of War*. Despite their recent arrival in the country, Situationist ideas were already finding local devotees. Drawn from the same bohemian milieu as *Chto Delat?*, the activists of Voina had just begun a daring campaign of public provocations against the mendacity and hypocrisy of the Putin regime. In this early-21st century Russian version, Situationism meant avant-garde performance art in the service of libertarian Left politics.[129] Not surprisingly, our Russian comrades were puzzled by Debord's decision to devote so much of his time to inventing a simulation of Horse-and-Musket warfare. Surely the chief theorist of the International should have spent his energies on something much more obviously political? If he did want to make a ludic critique of Bolshevism, why didn't he instead create a Situationist variant of Chris Peers' *Reds versus Reds* game? There were plenty of precedents for this approach. In 1933, A.S. Yurgelevich had produced a Soviet *Battle-Chess* which updated the original version by not only extending the board to 128 squares, but also replacing its monarchical pieces with new ones representing machine guns, tanks and aircraft.[130] Since the publication of SPI's *Russian Civil War* in 1976, there'd been a succession of board games which had modelled this key turning point in world history.[131] However, Debord hadn't imitated these more-or-less successful attempts to re-enact the Bolsheviks' rise to power. For some bizarre reason, his simulation was focused upon the military campaigns of over a century earlier. If Debord's goal really was to prevent leftists from becoming a little Lenin, Trotsky or Stalin, then why did *The Game of War* encourage its players to transform themselves into a little Bonaparte?

---

[129] For an account of their early actions, see Danila Rozanov, 'Voina: artists at war'.

[130] See Hans Bodlaender, 'Battle-Chess'.

[131] See Jim Dunnigan, *Russian Civil War*; Andy Lewis, Ted Raicer and Volko Runkhe, *Reds!*; David Dockter, *The Triumph of Chaos*; Brian Train, *Konarmiya*; and William Sariego, *Red Russia*.

As the vodka flowed, the questioning intensified. In the early-1960s, the Situationists' ludic manifesto had envisaged a co-operative playtime where everyone was a winner.[132] Yet, when we'd staged *The Game of War* that evening in the Hermitage, there could be only one victor – and there had to be a loser. For some people around the table in the restaurant, this miniature head-to-head combat reeked of the masculine competitiveness of bourgeois society. Inside the Winter Palace, its players had embraced the same aggressive militarist emotions that fuelled the recent US-led invasions of Afghanistan and Iraq. Debord's abandonment of the Situationist vision of non-competitive gaming might have been more understandable if his aim had been to recreate the iconic revolutionary uprisings of his own times. But, as we'd already realised back in 2007, his ludic masterpiece wasn't an abstraction of workers and students fighting against the cops on the streets of Paris in May '68.[133] *The Game of War* also didn't reproduce the struggles of the Algerian guerrillas against French colonialism or the Vietnamese partisans against American imperialism.[134] On the contrary, its pieces were divided into the famous 18th and 19th century military trinity: infantry, cavalry and artillery. As Debord had emphasised, his game was founded upon very specific 'voluntary historical limits'.[135] Within the confines of this miniature battlefield, its participants had to play at being Bonaparte. For both North and South, the prize of conquest was an emperor's crown.

When this discussion took place in St. Petersburg, Class Wargames still hadn't fully worked out our analysis of *The Game of War*. We could parry the harder questions from our Russian comrades, but weren't able to provide them with definitive answers. Luckily, on that November night, the copious flow of vodka had hidden these serious gaps in our knowledge. However, on our return to England, we knew that this problem would have to be rectified as soon as possible. Class Wargames must be able to give a convincing explanation of why Debord had

---

[132] See the Situationist International, 'Contribution à une Definition Situationniste du Jeu'.

[133] For a game of this revolution, see François Nedelec and Duccio Vitale, *Mai '68*.

[134] For examples of games inspired by these conflicts, see Brian Train, *Algeria*; and Nick Karp, *Vietnam*.

[135] Alice Becker-Ho and Guy Debord, *A Game of War*, page 24.

devised a Horse-and-Musket simulation. By the time that the second phase of our campaign of ludic subversion had commenced at *Cyberfest 2008*, we'd already understood that this avant-garde artwork was promoting libertarian communist politics. While moving its pieces across the board, the players of *The Game of War* were learning how to avoid the temptations of the 21st century revival of the Bolshevik vanguard. The promoters of the totalitarian Communist hypothesis and the militants of the Invisible Committee were both mythologists and amnesiacs of the tragic history of the 1917 Russian Revolution. Fortunately, Class Wargames' participatory performances could enable the inhabitants of the present to experience this formative moment of the past in person. Proletarian memory was the death knell of the integrated spectacle.

Prodded by the questioning of our Leningrad comrades, Class Wargames realised that we would now have to delve deeper into the Situationist politics of revolutionary history. Having successfully made the link between 2008 and 1917 with our performances at the Winter Palace, our next task would be to go further back in time to the much earlier epoch of Horse-and-Musket warfare replicated by *The Game of War*. From our research, we knew that Debord hadn't been alone in his deep fascination with the military career of Bonaparte. The Napoleonic era had been the most popular historical period amongst the wargaming subculture in the 1960s and 1970s. The collectors of toy soldiers loved the bright and colourful uniforms which had aided recognition of who was who on these smoke-filled battlefields.[136] The fans of Avalon Hill games had ensured that *Waterloo* was one of its best-selling releases during this period.[137] For these hobbyists, this almost modern moment in military history had the attraction of being neither too distant nor too recent in time. Re-staging the battles of the Greeks and Romans required an understanding of a socio-economic system which was very different from that of late-20th century capitalism. Re-fighting the campaigns of the First or Second World Wars evoked painful family memories for many people. Fortunately, the era of Horse-and-Musket

---

[136] See Barrie Quarrie, *PSL Guide to Wargaming*, pages 86–87.

[137] See Lindsley Schutz and Thomas Shaw, *Waterloo*; and Jim Dunnigan, *The Complete Wargames Handbook*, page 147.

warfare was both close enough to be familiar and far enough away to be enchanting. Above all, these Napoleonic wargames offered the opportunity for hobbyists to play the most romantic warrior hero of them all: Napoléon Bonaparte. Whether with toy soldiers or cardboard counters, they too could be victorious at Marengo, Austerlitz and Wagram. This time around, they would annihilate the enemy's army at Borodino, Leipzig and Waterloo. For Debord's generation, pretending to be Bonaparte was their ultimate wargaming experience: 'There are amateur tacticians who want to prove that they could have bettered Napoleon in some battle or campaign (there may even be some who believe that they are Napoleon!) ...'[138]

In 1960s and 1970s France, this ludic obsession had been an identifier of reactionary politics. The connoisseurs of toy soldiers revered the upstart emperor as the forerunner of the two uniformed saviours who'd defined the bitter split within the authoritarian Right during the mid-20th century: Phillipe Pétain and Charles de Gaulle. Among the followers of both factions, manoeuvring beautifully painted figurines in historically correct uniforms across a miniature Napoleonic battlefield became their aesthetic rejection of the equalitarian ethos of the modern world.[139] By publishing *The Game of War*, Debord deployed the Situationist tactic of provocation against these guardians of the established order. The abstract design of its pieces made no attempt to reproduce the splendid finery of the imperial army. The board wasn't an accurate simulation of the terrain from one of the emperor's famous battles. Above all, in his recreation of Horse-and-Musket warfare, the military supremacy of Bonaparte was firmly reconnected to the political energy of the 1789 French Revolution. For the Right, the rule of the emperor was commemorated as a high point in the nation's history: civil order at home and absolute hegemony over the European continent.[140] But, on the Left, the legacy of Bonaparte's regime had always been much more contentious. On the one hand, this charismatic general had consolidated the social gains of the 1789

[138]   John Sanders, *An Introduction to Wargaming*, page 10.

[139]   See Harry Pearson, *Achtung Schweinehund!*, pages 161–3.

[140]   See Michel Franceschi and Ben Weider, *The Wars against Napoleon*; and Alistair Horne, *The Age of Napoleon*.

French Revolution: the abolition of feudal privileges, the redistribution of land to the peasantry and the codification of legal equality. Yet, on the other hand, his seizure of power had also marked the end of the republican experiment in political democracy: the restoration of the monarchy, the curtailment of civil liberties and the restriction of the electoral franchise. The people's emperor was the enforcer of the dictatorship of the bourgeoisie.[141]

Most worryingly of all, like Stalin, Bonaparte had first risen to prominence as a fervent supporter of the Left before reinventing himself as the supreme leader of the Right. By synthesising these two opposites in his regime, he'd succeeded in embodying both the realisation and the negation of the 1789 French Revolution.[142] Not surprisingly, this Napoleonic myth was the instigator of political confusion long after his death. Even the fiercest opponents of monarchy have been able to find something to admire in the career of this crowned autocrat.[143] By publishing *The Game of War*, Debord provided his ludic response to the Left's confusion over whether Bonaparte should be admired as an enlightened despot or castigated as a corrupt tyrant. Embedded within the ebb-and-flow of its play was a Situationist lesson in European history. Through Debord's ludic invention, every proletarian could learn that there was no doubt about the emperor's guilt. Tellingly, echoing Marx's famous quip, the pieces of *The Game of War* were reminders of Bonaparte's hijacking of the 1789 French Revolution: '… the republic's motto, … [Liberty, Equality, Fraternity, had been] replaced by the unambiguous words: Infantry, Cavalry, Artillery!'[144]

During the discussions with our Russian comrades after *Cyberfest 2008*, we still hadn't fully realised the theoretical implications of

---

[141] See Pieter Geyl, *Napoleon For and Against*, pages 25–33, 125–126, 232–277, 319–323, 376–400.

[142] Anticipating the Post-Modernist mixing of opposites, Bonaparte boasted that his regime combined the best elements of monarchy and republic, see Emmanuel de Las Cases, *Mémorial de Sainte-Hélène*, pages 367–368, 558–561. Also see Georges Lefebvre, *Napoleon*, pages 71–94; and Isser Woloch, *Napoleon and his Collaborators*, pages 36–65.

[143] For the early-19th century origins of the Bonapartist cult, see Sudir Hazareesingh, *The Legend of Napoleon*.

[144] Karl Marx, *The Eighteenth Brumaire of Louis Bonaparte*, page 67.

this design decision. *The Game of War* and *Reds versus Reds* might have been simulating different periods in military history, but they were teaching the same political lesson to their players: the leaders of the oppressed can all too easily become their new oppressors. From our performances of both games, we'd understood how Debord's masterpiece was a ludic meditation on the Bolsheviks' recuperation of the 1917 Russian Revolution. On that night in Leningrad, what we hadn't yet comprehended was why this game was also a fierce critique of Bonaparte's hijacking of the 1789 French Revolution. Nearly two decades after the end of the Cold War, it was easy for the people sitting around the table inside that St. Petersburg restaurant to forget the enthusiasm with which the Left in France had once identified these two world-historical turning points with each other. When Debord first became politically active in the 1950s, the competing Bolshevik sects had taken pride in tracing their lineage back to the radical republicans of 1792–4: the Jacobins. For them, far from being a foreign import, the vanguard party was the contemporary manifestation of a long and admirable French revolutionary tradition. After their fall from power, the Jacobins had been forced to organise themselves as secretive conspiracies to survive under the authoritarian regimes that controlled 19th century France. What had begun as a tactical necessity for the republican Left was soon transformed into a political virtue. The members of the revolutionary conspiracy were a select band of activists, artists and agitators who'd succeeded in freeing themselves from the shackles of bourgeois ideology.[145] Regrettably, the rest of the French population still remained befuddled by the false ideas promoted by the media, the church and the academy. The political implications of this elitist analysis were clear. Before they could rule themselves, the French people must first be re-educated in republican principles under the tutelage of the Left's concentrated spectacle.[146] During the 1789 Revolution, religious devotion had deluded the inhabitants of the Vendée region into fighting for their aristocratic exploiters. After the 1848 Revolution, the Napoleonic myth had convinced the majority of the peasantry to support his nephew's grab for the imperial

---

[145] See Phillipe Buonarroti, *Babeuf's Conspiracy for Equality*; and Alain Maillard, 'De Babeuf au Babouvisme'.

[146] See Louis-Auguste Blanqui, 'Defence Speech', pages 33–35; and Richard Barbrook, *Media Freedom*, pages 28–37.

crown. Conspiratorial politics was the French Left's response to these reverses. For the Jacobins, imposing a revolutionary dictatorship in the short-term was the necessary precondition for creating a democratic republic in the long-term. The vanguard party was the prophecy of the libertarian future in the monarchical present. Only the few could emancipate the many.[147]

At the 1920 Congress of Tours, the French Socialist Party had split over whether it should emulate the new Russian manifestation of Jacobinism: the Bolsheviks. Having been temporarily eclipsed by the parliamentary strategy of Social Democracy and the syndicalist struggles of Anarchism in the decades before the First World War, the conspiratorial politics of the inheritors of the 1789 Revolution were once again in the ascendency.[148] Over the next three decades, the rise of fascism, the Nazi occupation of France and the Cold War would confirm the historical necessity of this Jacobin revival. By the 1950s, being a revolutionary meant being a Bolshevik.[149] Despite their contempt for Stalinism, Debord and his comrades had found it very difficult to extricate themselves completely from this seductive political identity. This fascination with vanguard politics wasn't entirely irrational. As demonstrated by their contemporaries on the Left who in middle age would become revisionist historians, the outright repudiation of the Jacobin legacy could all too easily lead to political retrogression. Frightened by May '68, these repentant Stalinists would rehabilitate the conservative chroniclers of 1789 French Revolution to justify their accommodation with late-20th century neoliberalism. For the Right, the bloodletting of the Jacobin and Bolshevik regimes had always been their best argument against any attempts to abolish social inequality and implement direct democracy. By tracing the vanguard party back to its original version, these revisionist historians identified the 1789 French Revolution with the 1917 Russian Revolution to condemn the Left as the avowed enemy of liberty. Reversing the Bolsheviks'

---

[147]   See Louis-Auguste Blanqui, 'Organisation of the Society of Families'; and Samuel Bernstein, *Auguste Blanqui and the Art of Insurrection*, pages 56–84, 134–208.

[148]   See Jean Lacouture, *Léon Blum*, pages 146–168; and Serge Halimi, *Sisyphe est Fatigué*, pages 52–68.

[149]   See Serge Halimi, *Sisyphe est Fatigué*, pages 241–350; and R.W. Johnson, *The Long March of the French Left*, pages 23–51.

argument, all socialists were tainted by their Jacobin heritage. What had once been a positive had now become a negative.[150]

Ironically, these revisionist historians of the 1789 French Revolution were obsessed with a conspiratorial style of politics that was their own country's most influential ideological export. In 19th century Russia, the Left had modelled itself on the Jacobins who'd succeeded in overthrowing an absolute monarchy and founding a democratic republic. Small groups of intellectuals had tried to replicate this insurrectionary strategy by experimenting with every tactical option: military coups, avant-garde art, terrorist outrages, bohemian communes, peasant revolts and proletarian strikes. As Mikhail Bakunin – the founding father of Anarchism – had emphasised, their task was to create the 'invisible dictatorship' that would guide the spontaneous insurgency of the impoverished Russian masses to total victory over their aristocratic oppressors.[151] When the Tsarist autocracy finally collapsed during the First World War, the Bolsheviks were ready to fulfil this role of the Jacobins of the revolutionary crisis. Under Lenin's leadership, the illuminated few would open the way towards the hi-tech future for the ignorant masses. Not surprisingly, when the utopian promises of the October 1917 Revolution were disappointed, the Russian Left looked back to the history of the 1789 French Revolution to understand its predicament. In a re-enactment of the past, the radicalism of the Bolsheviks had been sabotaged by opportunists within their own ranks: a new iteration of the Thermidor faction who'd taken over the Jacobin republic in 1794. Once again, securing the abolition of aristocratic privilege had been achieved by sacrificing political democracy. Almost inevitably, this counter-revolution within the revolution culminated in the emergence of a new Bonaparte. The militarised version of socialism required an undisputed hierarchy of command under a maximum leader. After the death of Lenin in 1924, Trotsky and Stalin had vied

---

[150] In a revealing confession, the leading proponent of this Right rewriting of history admitted that: '... the inventory of the Jacobin legacy was overlaid with an implicit discourse for or against Bolshevism, a development that hardly made for intellectual flexibility.' François Furet, *Interpreting the French Revolution*, page 7. For a critique of this liberal historiography, see George Comninel, *Rethinking the French Revolution*.

[151] See Mikhail Bakunin, 'Letter to Albert Richard'; and Sergei Nechaev, *Catechism of the Revolutionist*. Also see Franco Venturi, *Roots of Revolution*, pages 36–62, 232–468.

with each other over who would become the next emperor of Soviet Russia. The defeated generalissimo would denounce his rival as the embodiment of his own thwarted ambition: the new Bonaparte of the Thermidor reaction. The rise and fall of the 1917 Russian Revolution was a recapitulation of the 1789 French Revolution.[152]

By making *October*, Eisenstein created the cinematic spectacle which drew upon this elision in time and space. In a series of evocative montages, he caricatured Alexander Kerensky – the leader of the Red faction whose government was overthrown by the Bolsheviks' coup d'état – as a vainglorious popinjay by cross-cutting the actor playing him with a white porcelain statue of Bonaparte. Above all, this film transformed the Petrograd garrison occupying the almost undefended Winter Palace into the Russian equivalent of the popular uprising which – on 14th July each year – is still commemorated as the defining moment of the 1789 French Revolution: the seizure of the Bastille prison in Paris which shattered the absolute rule of the Bourbon kings. For the domestic audience, *October* confirmed the Soviet regime's replacement of lived experience with its artistic re-enactment. The Bolshevik spectacle of the 1917 Russian Revolution had become the documentary coverage of authentic history. When *October* was shown in French cinemas, this Jacobin fantasy was then exported back to its country of origin. The ideological imperative had come full circle. On the screen, the French Left witnessed its own 1789 Revolution re-imagined as the 1917 Russian Revolution. The fall of the Bastille had been updated into the storming of the Winter Palace. The political message of Eisenstein's film was emphatic. Jacobinism was the 18th century anticipation of Bolshevism – and Bolshevism was the 20th century incarnation of Jacobinism. By watching *October*, two generations of the French Left were able to discover their own destiny within the forward movement of world history. The vanguard party was leading the workers and peasants into the communist future. Their task as officers of the revolution was to make the inevitable come true.

In the mid-1970s, New Left activists started sorrowfully recanting their Bolshevik sins. Most wickedly, they'd succumbed to the totalitarian

---

[152] See Leon Trotsky, *Revolution Betrayed*, pages 86–114. Also see Tamara Kondratieva, *Bolcheviks et Jacobins*; and Mark Hoskisson, 'The Red Jacobins'.

temptations of the vanguard party. Like Lenin, Trotsky and Stalin, they too had dreamt of imposing their will upon the grand narrative of history. In their confessions, these penitents blamed their political errors on the Left's profound misunderstanding of contemporary French society. Under Fordism, its old ideology which emphasised the class struggle between the impoverished masses and the greedy bourgeoisie was no longer relevant. With their basic material needs now being satisfied by consumer capitalism, people were instead devoting their energies to the multivalent politics of identity: age, gender, sexuality, culture, ethnicity and lifestyles.[153] In their meditations, the Post-Modernist recuperators of the New Left tried to make sense of their generation's experience of the traumatic transformation of France from a rural into an urban society. When they'd been born in the mid-20th century, the majority of the population were still living in the countryside. During their formative years, the double reflection between the 1789 French Revolution and the 1917 Russian Revolution had made sociological sense. The New Left's fascination with the vanguard party was inspired by the treasured historical memory of how the peasantry had been the decisive force in the overthrow of the absolute monarchy. By rebelling against their masters at the key moment, they'd deprived the aristocracy of the troops that had crushed previous urban insurrections. There was no repeat of the 1572 St. Bartholomew's Massacre in the rebellious Paris of 1789. Yet, despite this critical intervention, the French peasantry had never been able itself to take control of the revolutionary process. Divided into village communities, the rural population only aspired to liberty at a local level. Led by the inhabitants of Paris, the creation of the democratic republic had been a predominantly urban phenomenon.[154]

Paradoxically, in both the 1789 French Revolution and the 1917 Russian Revolution, the social pre-eminence of the peasantry had concentrated political power in the capital city. The fate of the nation was decided by whichever Left faction could seize control of Paris or Petrograd. Whether as Jacobins or Bolsheviks, a small group

---

[153]   See Jean-François Lyotard, *The Post-Modern Condition*; Jean Baudrillard, *The Mirror of Production*; and Gilles Deleuze and Félix Guattari, *A Thousand Plateaus*.

[154]   See Daniel Guérin, *Bourgeois et Bras Nus*; and Albert Soboul, *The Sans-Culottes*.

of activists, artists and agitators had been able to assert its right to rule in the interests of the disorganised and uneducated majority in the countryside. Under their enlightened guidance, the backward peasantry would be turned into civilised citizens. In this interpretation of the grand narrative of history, revolutionary dictatorship became the fast route to direct democracy.[155] When the New Left militants were children, this Bolshevik programme of rapid modernisation still hadn't lost its radical edge within a largely agrarian society. But, by the 1960s, it was de Gaulle's conservative government that was enthusiastically carrying out the urbanisation and industrialisation of France.[156] On reaching adulthood, the New Left was confronted by the political consequences of this social transformation: what had once been subversive was fast becoming reactionary. The early-19th century strategy of the vanguard party was an anachronism on the battlefields of late-20th century Fordism.

As Debord understood, there was much to regret in the disappearance of the old France, including its revolutionary traditions. However, his questioning of the Jacobin inheritance took a very different form from that of Lyotard, Foucault, Baudrillard, Deleuze and Guattari. Crucially, by promoting the Post-Modernist remix of Stalin's socio-linguistic theory, their recantation of Bolshevism had carefully preserved the leading role of the intellectuals in the struggle for human emancipation under the integrated spectacle. Like their Jacobin forebears, they still believed that only the chosen few could liberate themselves from the ideological domination of corporate capitalism. These activists, artists and agitators were the officer corps of the confused multitudes who provided the foot soldiers of the autonomous social movements. Once again, direct democracy had been recuperated as a dogmatic ideology. In 1977, by publishing *The Game of War*, Debord issued his ludic refutation of this New Left remix of vanguard politics. From then onwards, there was a Situationist alternative to the perpetual hegemony of the revolutionary conspiracy. The pernicious remnants of

---

[155] For the original version of this prophecy, see Louis-Auguste Blanqui, 'To the Mountain of 1793! To the Pure Socialists, its True Heirs!'; and Samuel Bernstein, *Auguste Blanqui and the Art of Insurrection*, pages 67–83.

[156] See André Gauron, *Histoire Économique et Sociale de la Cinquième République*; and Henri Mendras, *Social Change in Modern France*.

the concentrated spectacle within the integrated spectacle could now be outflanked and routed. When every proletarian knew how to play at being Bonaparte and Trotsky, the historical epoch of Jacobinism and Bolshevism would finally be over.

2.6: THE CROSSING OF THE ALPS

By the time that Class Wargames was invited to participate in the 2010 *Chto Delat?* season at the ICA, we were fully engaged in the second phase of our campaign of ludic subversion. Our participatory performances of *The Game of War* were Situationist political pedagogy carried out through avant-garde art. By re-enacting the past, the players of North and South were learning about the spectacular stratagems of the vanguard party. We'd embarked on this stage of our campaign at the Hermitage by emphasising the close historical connections between its contemporary Autonomist manifestation with the earlier Bolshevik version. As we played contest after contest, our expositions on *The Game of War* went further back in time to the original version of the 1917 Russian Revolution. The Napoleonic theme of this military simulation was no whim. Debord's choice of infantry, cavalry and artillery units for its pieces had a serious political purpose. Before the Autonomists were the Bolsheviks – and, before them, there were the Jacobins. Tracing the spectacular recuperation of the Left back two centuries was the Situationist retort to the perpetual present of neoliberal globalisation. Playing with the past was understanding the historical origins of our contemporary predicament with ludic means. Above all, by re-enacting the turbulent events which shaped the modern world, rebellious proletarians could gain confidence in their collective ability to guide the course of time towards a better future.

At the ICA in 2010, for the next push in the second phase of our campaign of ludic subversion, Class Wargames played the Marengo scenario as a punk provocation against the newly fashionable revival of Bolshevik ideology. Like our Russian comrades from *Chto Delat?*, the European Left was still mesmerised by Lenin's vision of vanguard leadership. Revolutionary elitism was its only alternative to the shabby compromises of electoral politics. By adopting this opening deployment for *The Game of War* shown in **Diagram 3** on page 226, we wanted to return to the historical moment when the reactionary implications of this Jacobin strategy were fully exposed for the first time. During the most radical phase of the 1789 French Revolution, Bonaparte had risen to prominence as a political soldier devoted to defending the new republic against both its internal and external enemies. In 1793, he'd not only devised the strategy that crushed the anti-Jacobin uprising in Toulon which had given control of this important Mediterranean seaport to the British navy, but also published a widely-read pamphlet that had passionately argued the cause of democratic patriotism. At this early point in his career, Bonaparte had unequivocally identified himself with the austere leader of the Jacobin dictatorship: Maximilien Robespierre. Like its Ancient Greek and Roman predecessors, the French republic was the political expression of an egalitarian community of citizen-soldiers.[157] Not surprisingly, when the Thermidor faction overthrew the Jacobin government in 1794, Bonaparte suffered for his Left opinions. After a brief imprisonment, this unreliable officer was then demoted to a minor position within the army. However, Bonaparte quickly adapted himself to the new dispensation. By 1795, he was in charge of the Paris garrison when it ruthlessly put down a monarchist revolt against the Thermidor regime. As his reward, Bonaparte was next given command of the French forces in Italy. During 1796–7, he became a national hero by inflicting defeat after defeat on the numerically superior and better equipped Austrian army. As de facto ruler of Northern Italy, Bonaparte demonstrated his growing political skills by adopting a liberal policy of conciliating the aristocracy and clergy which successfully neutralised local opposition to French rule.[158] Leading an expedition to Egypt in 1798, his victories in this exotic location further enhanced his celebrity status back home.[159] For the French public, this combination of political commitment and military genius became very seductive. Compared to the venal and squabbling leaders of the Thermidor faction, Bonaparte was the incarnation of republican virtue: 'Robespierre on horseback'.[160]

In 1799, France faced the imminent threat of foreign invasion. Due

---

[157] See Emmanuel de Las Cases, *Mémorial de Sainte-Hélène*, pages 55–57, 101–102, 194. Also see Steven Englund, *Napoleon*, pages 36–80; and David Chandler, *The Campaigns of Napoleon*, pages 3–29.

[158] See Emmanuel de Las Cases, *Mémorial de Sainte-Hélène*, pages 69, 295–297, 531.

[159] See Steven Englund, *Napoleon*, pages 83–160; and David Chandler, *The Campaigns of Napoleon*, pages 29–130, 205–249.

[160] Ironically, in his St Helena exile, Bonaparte vehemently repudiated Germaine de Staël's characterisation of this public image which had helped to elevate him to absolute power. See Emmanuel de Las Cases, *Mémorial de Sainte-Hélène*, pages 183–185, 575–576.

to the incompetence of the Thermidor government, the armies of the Second Coalition were rolling back the territorial gains that had created a protective cordon of 'sister-republics' around the mother country.[161] Returning from Egypt, Bonaparte offered himself as the saviour of the nation at this moment of deep crisis. Recruiting supporters from the rival Thermidor and Jacobin factions, this military hero promised to provide firm leadership both at home and on the battlefield.[162] By securing the loyalty of the Paris garrison, Bonaparte was soon able to seize control of the French republic in a coup d'état. Anointing himself as First Consul, he systematically concentrated all executive authority into his own hands.[163] But, like the Bolsheviks after their coup over a century later, Bonaparte's new regime had initially lacked democratic legitimacy. Thanks to his victories in Italy and Egypt, there was genuine admiration for the First Consul's great abilities. Having served loyally under both Jacobin and Thermidor governments, he could appeal to a large constituency amongst the French population who were tired of the bitter sectarian squabbles within the republican movement. Although its results were massaged, Bonaparte did obtain a large majority in the 1800 referendum that ratified the new constitution which gave dictatorial powers to the First Consul.[164] However, he was well aware that his hold on state power was still insecure. There were other enterprising generals and a Bourbon pretender to the throne waiting to take his place if he ever lost the confidence of the French people. Bonaparte knew that the most effective method of dealing with these rivals was to win a decisive victory against the armies of the Second Coalition. When he'd assembled his forces for the Marengo campaign in 1800, the First Consul was preparing to fight against a

---

[161] See Carl von Clausewitz, *Campagne de 1799 en Suisse et en Italie*, pages 13–359; and Owen Connelly, *The Wars of the French Revolution and Napoleon*, pages 107–110.

[162] After Thermidor, Bonaparte had quickly become '... a classic "political general" ... who unapologetically put his own interests ahead of ideology and campaigned for political influence in Paris as vigorously as he did for enemy territory.' David Bell, *The First Total War*, page 189. Also see Philip Dwyer, 'Napoleon Bonaparte as Hero and Saviour', pages 398–402.

[163] See Stendhal, *A Life of Napoleon*, pages 44–57; and Georges Lefebvre, *Napoleon*, pages 60–94.

[164] See Isser Woloch, *Napoleon and his Collaborators*, pages 3–89; and Georges Lefebvre, *Napoleon*, pages 71–77.

foreign enemy so he could thwart his opponents at home. The destiny of France would be decided on the fields of Italy.[165]

Two decades later, when the coffin of the exiled emperor was being lowered into his grave at St. Helena, the body of Bonaparte was wrapped in the grey cloak that he'd worn at the Battle of Marengo.[166] For devotees of the Napoleonic myth, this town in Piedmont has always been the sacred site of the key turning-point in their idol's life story. Before 14th June 1800, Bonaparte was an ambitious general who'd temporarily struck lucky when – by being in the right place at the right time – he'd become the military dictator of the French republic. It was winning a decisive victory at Marengo that had changed everything for this renegade Jacobin soldier. After that fateful day, Bonaparte's absolute control over the French state was unassailable. Within a year, he'd extended the term in office of the First Consul from 10 years to his own lifetime. By 1804, Bonaparte had succeeded in crowning himself as the emperor of the French. With his ascendency to the imperial throne confirmed in a popular referendum and blessed by the Pope, this bourgeois despot was convinced that he'd successfully fused the new democratic and old aristocratic forms of political legitimacy within his own person.[167] Having neutralised his opponents at home, Bonaparte then devoted the next decade to trying to achieve mastery over Europe. By uniting the continent under a single currency, one legal code and the metric system, his liberal autocracy would bestow the fruits of peace and prosperity on all of its different peoples.[168] When reviewing the troops of the imperial army on these campaigns of European conquest, Bonaparte was almost always mounted on

---

[165] The First Consul's personal secretary recollected that: 'It was Bonaparte's policy [in 1800] .. to buy security at home by battle and victory abroad. ... something must be done in Europe, worthy of [his 1796–7 Italian military successes before] ... he could hope to be seated firmly on his *throne*.' Louis de Bourrienne, *Memoirs of Napoleon*, . page 153. Emphasis in the original.

[166] See James Arnold, *Marengo & Hohenlinden*, page 268.

[167] See Emmanuel de Las Cases, *Mémorial de Sainte-Hélène*, pages 470–471.

[168] See Emmanuel de Las Cases, *Mémorial de Sainte-Hélène*, pages 433–434, 559–560. Also see Steven Englund, *Napoleon*, pages 209–355; and Geoffrey Ellis, 'The Nature of Napoleonic Imperialism'.

his favourite white stallion which he'd proudly named Marengo.[169] According to the Napoleonic legend, he had founded his dynasty on this Italian battlefield. Fulfilling the destiny revealed by this martial triumph, the task of the house of Bonaparte was to impose its political authority over the whole of Europe. Discarding its earlier incarnation as the Jacobin republic, the dictatorship of the bourgeoisie had now become the venal rule of one family.[170]

The acolytes of the Napoleonic cult were correct to celebrate the Marengo campaign. In 1800, Bonaparte had won a decisive victory through his almost uncanny ability to combine daring, intelligence and good fortune that would make him into the dominant personality of his generation. At the beginning of that year, the First Consul had been confronted by a very difficult political and military conundrum. During 1799, despite losing control of most of Italy, the French republic had managed to repulse the invasion of its Dutch and Swiss allies by the armies of the Second Coalition. After these embarrassing reverses, the Russian Tsar had decided to withdraw his troops from Western Europe.[171] However, as Bonaparte knew only too well, the outcome of this bloody conflict was still not yet decided. With the Royal Navy controlling the seas and the 1798 Irish Revolution having failed, the British isles were invulnerable to attack. If the French wanted to defeat the Second Coalition, the First Consul's only option was to knock the Austrians out of the war. As we replicated in our Marengo scenario for *The Game of War*, their forces had begun the 1800 campaigning season with a double-pronged offensive in Southern Germany and Northern Italy. While the French troops defending these two fronts slowly fell back, Bonaparte took command of the powerful reserve army which his administration had been secretly training and equipping over the winter. His first and most important decision was where to launch the counter-attack against the Austrian empire. In 1805 and 1809, Bonaparte was able to choose the most direct and easiest route towards the enemy's heartland: Southern Germany. But, in 1800, adopting

---

[169] For the biography of this famous horse and its owner, see Jill Hamilton, *Marengo*.

[170] See Stendhal, *A Life of Napoleon*, pages 135–147; and Steven Englund, *Napoleon*, pages 298–384.

[171] See Carl von Clausewitz, *Campagne de 1799 en Suisse et en Italie*, pages 363–618.

the best military strategy was politically difficult. The French army defending the Rhine border was led by a popular general who was Bonaparte's most serious rival for the job of First Consul: Jean Victor Moreau. Committing the reserve to this front might weaken rather than strengthen his regime. Being a skilled politician, Bonaparte without hesitation picked the riskier military strategy: an invasion of Northern Italy. If the French army could win a stunning victory over the Austrians on the plains of Piedmont, the glory would be his alone.[172]

During a meeting in Paris to plan the offensive, Bonaparte had predicted that the decisive battle of the war would take place at the key crossroads of Marengo.[173] Under Michael von Melas, the Austrian forces were already making rapid progress in spring 1800 as they'd advanced across Northern Italy. By April, only the stubborn resistance of Masséna's garrison in Genoa was preventing the enemy from crossing into France itself. Faced with this crisis, a cautious commander might have committed his reserves to relieving this last line of defence before the republic's southern bastion in Marseille. But, instead of coming to his colleague's rescue, Bonaparte devised a much more audacious strategy. Seizing the initiative, the French army would move into Switzerland, cross the Alps and, once in Northern Italy, cut the Austrians' lines of communications to their supply bases in Trieste and Vienna.[174] In the classrooms of 19th century military academies, the Marengo campaign was taught as the essence of Bonaparte's genius as a general: 'the manoeuvre onto the enemy's rear'. Yet, few of these pupils would ever have the courage to put this theory into practice when they became commanders in the field. Unlike their role model, these soldiers hadn't learnt their trade by fighting revolutionary warfare.[175]

In 1800, Bonaparte had repeatedly risked everything to achieve a

---

[172] See Georges Lefebvre, *Napoleon*, pages 96–99; and Reginald Burton, *Napoleon's Campaigns in Italy*, pages 104–106.

[173] See Louis de Bourrienne, *Memoirs of Napoleon*, page 154.

[174] The success of this daring strategy exemplified how '... rashness in war becomes a veritable proof of genius.' Louis de Bourrienne, *Memoirs of Napoleon*, page 163.

[175] See Antoine-Henri de Jomini, *The Art of War*, pages 62–125; and David Chandler, *The Campaigns of Napoleon*, pages 161–170.

decisive victory. Advancing into Switzerland meant exposing his lines of communications to an attack by the Austrian forces in Southern Germany. The crossing of the Alps was almost prevented by a hostile fort that had blocked the path over the St. Bernard pass. Masséna had to hold out long enough in Genoa to keep the Austrians distracted while the French army was able to complete its deployment in the Po valley. On 14th June, Bonaparte's repeated gambling for high stakes nearly did end in disaster. Having at last taken Genoa, von Melas had quickly turned his forces around to confront the threat to his lines of communications. Underestimating his opponent, Bonaparte had scattered his troops across the Piedmont countryside to close off the Austrians' remaining supply routes. When von Melas launched an assault on that morning against the French forces around Marengo, the First Consul had initially found himself at a serious tactical disadvantage. Taken by surprise, the French army was almost overwhelmed by its more numerous opponent. Despite fighting tenaciously, its soldiers couldn't prevent the Austrians breaking through their line. Then, at the very moment when the conflict seemed lost, Louis Desaix arrived with his division to reinforce Bonaparte's faltering regiments. Fortunately, the superior strategic position of the French army in Northern Italy had compensated for its tactical weakness in the environs of Marengo. Without waiting for orders, this general had rushed his troops towards the battlefield on hearing the sound of fighting in the distance. Organising a counter-attack with fresh troops, Desaix – at the cost of his own life – soon pushed back the Austrian army whose troops were too exhausted after hours of hard fighting to resist.[176] As the battle of Marengo came to its conclusion, François Kellerman led the cavalry charge which finally routed the enemy. In a letter to a friend, this brave warrior recollected with pride what Bonaparte's soldiers had accomplished on that summer day in 1800: '[the French army had] placed the crown on his head.'[177]

Six months later, the war of the Second Coalition was concluded when Moreau defeated the Austrian forces in Southern Germany at the battle

---

[176] See James Arnold, *Marengo & Hohenlinden*, pages 100–186; and David Chandler, *The Campaigns of Napoleon*, pages 286–298.

[177] François Kellerman in James Arnold, *Marengo & Hohenlinden*, page 284.

of Hohenlinden. By 1801, France was at peace for the first time in almost a decade with all of the great powers of Europe, including Britain. As one of its many displays of gratitude to Bonaparte's impressive achievement, the republic's parliament commissioned an official history of the Marengo campaign.[178] But, by the time that this book was ready for publication, an accurate account of what had happened in 1800 on the plains of Piedmont was no longer required. Having transformed the French republic into the empire of the French, Bonaparte was now determined to project an image of unimpeachable infallibility. As Debord pointed out, his project of 'monarchically directing the energies of memories' would anticipate the ubiquitous manipulation of the past under late-20th century spectacular capitalism.[179] Bonaparte was the original version of not only Stalin, but also de Gaulle. While commanding the army in Italy in 1796–7 and the expeditionary force to Egypt in 1798, this political soldier had learnt how to be a superb propagandist in his own cause.[180] He'd published newspapers both to motivate his own troops while they were on campaign and to publicise their accomplishments to the public back home. He'd seduced the leading intellectuals of republican France by joining their salons, appropriating artworks in Italy for the new Louvre museum and inviting a team of researchers to accompany his expedition to Egypt. During these early days of his career, Bonaparte had revelled in the cut-and-thrust of intellectual debate. As a former Jacobin serving the Thermidor regime, he was able successfully to promote himself as a warrior intellectual who could work with all factions of the republican movement.[181]

Not surprisingly, once he'd seized absolute power, Bonaparte quickly acquired a distaste for anyone who questioned the moral and political deficiencies of the established order: the 'ideologists'. Under his prototype of the concentrated spectacle, censorship was steadily tightened over all forms of art and media. Whether in print, on the

---

[178] See James Arnold, *Marengo & Hohenlinden*, pages 197–264.

[179] Guy Debord, *The Society of the Spectacle*, page 76.

[180] See Philip Dwyer, 'Napoleon Bonaparte as Hero and Saviour', pages 384–389.

[181] See David Bell, *The First Total War*, pages 198–201; and Timothy Wilson-Smith, *Napoleon and his Artists*, pages 64–84.

stage or in the gallery, the glorification of the emperor became the highest duty of the creators of culture.[182] Inadvertently, the writers of the official history of the 1800 Marengo campaign now found that they'd become dangerous opponents of the French state. Any truthful chronicler of the battle would recount that Bonaparte had made a near disastrous mistake when he'd divided his army into a widely dispersed line to cut off von Melas' supply lines. It is this tactical blunder which has made the battle of Marengo into a favourite subject for board game designers over the past few decades. In these simulations, the Austrians always have an excellent chance of prevailing over the First Consul.[183] However, Bonaparte had no desire to admit that another outcome to this confrontation on the Piedmont plains might have been possible. Determined to prevent any criticism of his military genius, the emperor not only banned the publication of the French parliament's study into the Marengo campaign, but also ordered the destruction of its proof copies. In the new official history, Bonaparte had led the Austrians into a clever trap by splitting his forces. Even when he was in error, the emperor was always correct.[184]

In 1801, Jacques-Louis David exhibited a painting that would become the icon of this rewriting of the Marengo campaign to serve the Napoleonic cult: *The First Consul Crossing the Alps by the St. Bernard Pass on 30th Floréal Year VIII*. Astride a rearing white horse, Bonaparte in a glamorous blue-and-gold uniform with a cloak flowing out behind him raised his arm to point the way forward into Italy to the French troops pushing an artillery piece up the mountain in the background. Inscribed in the rocks beneath him alongside his own name were those of two illustrious warriors from the past: Hannibal and Charlemagne. Reproduced as a print, David's painting quickly became the most famous visual image of Bonaparte across the whole of Europe. Two

---

[182] Bonaparte in 1799 confessed that: 'If I gave the press free rein, I would not stay in power for three months.' Michael Sibalis, 'The Napoleonic Police State', page 82. Also see Emmanuel de Las Cases, *Mémorial de Sainte-Hélène*, pages 124; and Isser Woloch, *Napoleon and his Collaborators*, pages 205–213.

[183] See David Naquin, *Battles of the First Empire: Marengo*; Dean Essig and David Powell, *Marengo*; Bowen Simmons, *Bonaparte at Marengo*; and Eric Harvey, *Marengo*.

[184] See James Arnold, *Marengo & Hohenlinden*, pages 264–265.

centuries later, *The First Consul Crossing the Alps* is still the authorised version of the Napoleonic myth in the mass media. Made just before photography was invented, this exhilarating painting has become our faithful record of the appearance of the greatest celebrity of those revolutionary times. Yet, like Eisenstein's *October*, David's *The First Consul Crossing the Alps* was an artistic fantasy that has succeeded in supplanting historical reality. Far from riding a white horse, Bonaparte had been seated on a mule when he'd led his troops across the St. Bernard Pass.[185] Tellingly, this painting wasn't a documentary record of what a war artist had observed at the time. Instead, working in his Paris studio, David had created the rearing horse from drawings of the equestrian statues of Marcus Aurelius in Rome and Peter the Great in St. Petersburg. When this artist had asked Bonaparte to sit' for the painting, the First Consul had dismissed his request with a revealing reply: 'Alexander [the Great] never posed for [the Ancient Greeks' leading artist] Apelles.' Although he'd provided his general's uniform to give authenticity to the project, he expected David to portray his flawed features in an idealised form. The painter's skill was to give a simulacrum of realism to the transformation of this political soldier into the saviour of the nation.[186] In *The First Consul Crossing the Alps*, Bonaparte became the spectacular embodiment of the bourgeois recuperation of the 1789 French Revolution. After a decade of turmoil and war, a charismatic hero had come to restore order at home and impose peace upon Europe. The absolute power of one man was now necessary to ensure that everyone else could enjoy liberal freedoms.[187] Five years after David's painting was first exhibited, Georg Hegel witnessed the emperor's triumphal entry into Jena after he'd destroyed the Prussian army outside this town. Convinced that this portrait had come to life before his eyes, the great philosopher proclaimed with enthusiasm that Bonaparte was now the guiding force of historical progress: 'I saw the emperor, this World Soul ... on horseback ... [who]

---

[185] This prosaic scene is portrayed in Hyppolite Delaroche's 1850 painting: *Bonaparte Crossing the Alps*. Also see James Arnold, *Marengo & Hohenlinden*, pages 90–91.

[186] See Warren Roberts, *Jacques-Louis David, Revolutionary Artist*, pages 143–146; and Timothy Wilson-Smith, *Napoleon and his Artists*, pages 87–90.

[187] See Thomas Carlyle, *Heroes and Hero Worship*, pages 258–262, 303–311; and Domenico Losurdo, *Liberalism*, pages 323–325.

reaches out over the entire world and masters it.'[188] The spectacle had been made flesh.

[188] Georg Hegel in Terry Pinkard, *Hegel*, page 228. Embracing this role, Bonaparte believed that the Alexander, Julius Caesar and other warrior heroes of the past had shaped human destiny through the strength of their own minds, see Emmanuel de Las Cases, *Mémorial de Sainte-Hélène*, pages 572–573.

2.7: THE GENERAL'S WILL

In its October 1955 issue, *Potlatch* reported back on a lively meeting of
the Lettrist International which had discussed ideas for improving the
urban environment in Paris. Everyone was in agreement that the metro
should be kept running all night to facilitate their nonconformist
lifestyles. Debord and Gil Wolman had argued over whether the group
should demand the demolition or secularisation of the city's churches.
Echoing the 1909 Futurist manifesto, the Lettrists proclaimed their
avant-garde contempt for the cultural establishment by advocating the
'abolition of museums and the distribution of their artistic masterpieces
to the bars' of Paris.[189] Enthused by cheap wine and good company, they
picked out one iconic painting which should be immediately moved
from its prominent position in the Louvre gallery to their bohemian
haunt at the Tonneau de la Montagne-Geneviéve: David's 1807 *The
Coronation of Napoléon and Joséphine*.[190] Five years before this meeting
took place, the Lettrists had outraged the French Right by preaching
atheism from the pulpit of Notre Dame cathedral. Now they dreamt of
detourning the visual commemoration of the crowning of Bonaparte's
bourgeois dictatorship inside this holy Catholic shrine. When placed
on the wall of their favourite Left Bank café, David's massive 621 x
979cm canvas would be transformed into a dreadful warning to the
political and artistic dissidents who looked up from their tables at it.
Surrounding the parvenu emperor in this famous painting were the
members of the new elite who'd done well out of the 1789 French
Revolution. Their splendid outfits at Bonaparte's coronation in 1804
were hiding the shameful abandonment of their republican beliefs.
Seduced by wealth and power, these once fervent revolutionaries had
become sleazy guardians of law and order. If the young radicals of the
1950s wanted to avoid the horrors of recuperation, they must learn
the lessons of the historical defeat on vivid display in David's *The
Coronation of Napoléon and Joséphine*. Unlike the Bonapartists or their

---

[189] See *Potlatch 1954/1957*, pages 110–111. Also see Filippo Marinetti, 'The Founding
and Manifesto of Futurism'.

[190] See *Potlatch 1954/1957*, page 111. For the making of this Bonapartist painting, see
Warren Roberts, *Jacques-Louis David, Revolutionary Artist*, pages 151–164.

latter-day Stalinist imitators, the Lettrists wouldn't trade their political integrity for the trinkets of worldly success.

In his painting of the investiture at Notre Dame, David had included himself among the 140 portraits of the key personalities of the new French empire. Throughout Bonaparte's reign, he would remain the pre-eminent artist of the imperial court. By the 1800s, David had become a superstar whose work was admired even by those who loathed his politics. He was the first artist in France who could make money by holding exhibitions of his latest paintings. David's studios at the Louvre were filled with the best-and-brightest students from across Europe.[191] Revealingly, it was a coterie of his pupils that would found the primordial avant-garde art movement in human history: the Barbus. Creating the template for generations to come, these students of David dedicated themselves to fermenting cultural rebellion against bourgeois conformity. In an abandoned monastery on the outskirts of Paris, the Barbus pioneered the leitmotifs of the bohemian artist: outrageous fashions, debauched parties, sexual promiscuity, chemical experimentation and communal living. Like the Surrealists, Constructivists and Situationists in the 20th century, one of their greatest creations was their own personalities.[192] Responding to this overt disdain for conventional morality, Bonaparte's police made clumsy attempts to clamp down on these aesthetic dissidents. In 1806, the male students of David unfortunate enough to be busted at an avant-garde gathering in the Bois de Boulogne had their long hair forcibly shaved off and their female companions were threatened with being prosecuted as prostitutes. For the enforcers of Bonaparte's regime, there was no doubt that these dissolute pupils of its most celebrated propagandist were guilty of undermining the social stability of the French empire.[193]

Not surprisingly, the Barbus took their teacher as the role model of artistic subversion. When David began his career before the 1789

---

[191] See Warren Roberts, *Jacques-Louis David, Revolutionary Artist*, pages 118–119, 123–125, 146–147; and Thomas Crow, 'Patriotism and Virtue', pages 38–48.

[192] See George Levitine, *The Dawn of Bohemianism*, pages 1–5, 55–72, 130–134; and Malcolm Easton, *Artists and Writers in Paris*, pages 8–18.

[193] See Malcolm Easton, *Artists and Writers in Paris*, pages 18–19.

French Revolution, the Classical motifs of the rococo style had been used to celebrate the decadent pleasures of aristocratic rule. Fortunately, given the chance to study in Rome, their hero had been able to break with this corrupt cultural orthodoxy. In his 1784 *The Oath of the Horatii* and 1789 *The Lictors Bringing the Bodies of his Sons to Brutus* paintings, David had won fame by presenting an austere vision of male citizen-soldiers stoically doing their duty while the women of the household mourned the tragic consequences of their actions. By returning to the original version of rococo in Ancient Rome, he'd been able to invent a politicised form of art: Neo-Classicism.[194] Crucially, for his contemporaries, these paintings of David were seen as prophecies of the 1789 French Revolution. Admiring *The Oath of the Horatii* at the 1791 Salon exhibition in Paris, a peasant infantryman had exclaimed with awe: "It made one think!" The republican virtues of the Classical past lived again in contemporary France.[195]

The popularity of his new style of painting led to David being commissioned to make a tableau of the rebirth of the nation: the representatives of the French people publicly dedicating themselves in 1789 to institute a liberal constitution at the Jeu de Paume in Versailles. Life had imitated his art – and his task was to commemorate this re-enactment of *The Oath of the Horatii* as an artwork. Unfortunately, David's determination to make an accurate depiction of this world-historic event couldn't keep pace with the tumult of the revolutionary process. By the time that he'd completed the initial drawings for his canvas in 1791, too many of the politicians who were to be depicted in *The Tennis Court Oath* had betrayed their ideals and were no longer worthy of official recognition.[196] Forced to abandon this project, David instead dedicated his brushwork over the next few years to honouring the martyrs of the new French republic. In 1793, he cleverly detourned the familiar images of the crucified Christ for a stunning

---

[194] See Warren Roberts, *Jacques-Louis David, Revolutionary Artist*, pages 11–38; and David Dowd, *Pageant-Master of the Republic*, pages 2–23.

[195] 'In these heroic Romans, he saw himself … taking the oath to be faithful to the nation. He felt, like them, a fanatical zeal to defend the Fatherland.' David Dowd, *Pageant-Master of the Republic*, page 1.

[196] See Warren Roberts, *Jacques-Louis David, Revolutionary Artist*, pages 51–59; and David Dowd, *Pageant-Master of the Republic*, pages 36–41.

portrayal of the brutal murder of one of his closest friends: *The Death of Marat.*[197] Distributed as a cheap print, David's painting quickly became the secular icon of revolutionaries across Europe. Instinctively, they understood that this masterpiece of Neo-Classical art heralded the inevitable victory of the democratic republic over its aristocratic enemies.[198]

In the immediate aftermath of the fall of the Bastille in 1789, David had thrown himself into the political struggle by organising an impassioned campaign against the monarchical monopoly over high culture. Under the old order, only the select few who'd been accepted as members of the Royal Academy of the Arts were allowed to exhibit and sell their works to the public. Excoriating this bastion of privilege, David and his allies argued that the liberal principles of free trade should be applied to the making of paintings and sculptures as elsewhere in the economy. To turn this demand into reality, these cultural revolutionaries championed the democratisation of the education system. Forming themselves into the Commune des Arts, they welcomed both fine artists and plebeian artisans into their ranks. Having finally persuaded the French government to abolish the Royal Academy in 1792, this group based in David's studio at the Louvre became the laboratory for a new republican approach to the teaching of painting and sculpture which laid down the template for progressive art education for generations to come.[199] Inspired by Jean-Jacques Rousseau's *Émile*, the Commune des Arts envisioned a mutual and egalitarian collaboration of masters and pupils that would overcome the old snobbish divisions between

---

[197] See T.J. Clark, *Farewell to an Idea*, pages 15–53. Jean-Paul Marat was the politician and journalist who'd led the radical Left of the Jacobin movement, see Clifford Conner, *Jean-Paul Marat*.

[198] See Warren Roberts, *Jacques-Louis David, Revolutionary Artist*, pages 78–84; and Thomas Crow, 'Patriotism and Virtue', page 36. For the popular reverence of the martyred Marat, see Albert Soboul, *Paysans, Sans-Culottes et Jacobins*, pages 189–196.

[199] 'The destruction of the [Royal] Academy was the great achievement of the world of art at the time of the French Revolution.' Carl Brun in Daniel Fox, 'Artists in the Modern State', page 376. Also see David Dowd, *Pageant-Master of the Republic*, pages 27–34, 38–39.

aesthetic appreciation and craft skills. Every French citizen must have the opportunity to become an artist if they so desired.[200]

Through this cultural agitation, David metamorphosed himself into a prominent politician. His contribution to the cause went far beyond creating memorial paintings of republican martyrs and designing the costumes of public officials. In 1791, David was elected as a Jacobin deputy of the French parliament for a Paris constituency. A year later, he was invited to become a member of the revolutionary government: the Committee of Public Safety. Outraged by their collaboration with the Austrian enemy, David enthusiastically voted for the execution of the traitorous king and queen. In defence of the French republic, he'd gladly signed the death warrants of its aristocratic and liberal opponents. As the most celebrated victims of the Terror were transported to the guillotine, David was there to make evocative drawings of their final public appearance. Shorn of her finery, Marie Antoinette Bourbon was caught with a few pencil lines on 16th October 1793 just before she met the violent end that she'd once wished upon the insurgent population of Paris. During these tumultuous years, David lived the fusion of radical art and revolutionary politics in its most intense form. For the Constructivists, Surrealists and Situationists over a century later, having the chance to share this wondrous experience would be their greatest ambition.[201]

As a member of the Committee of Public Safety, David was given responsibility for resolving the severe cultural crisis facing the new French republic. Three years earlier, in its conflict with the Royal Academy, the Commune des Arts had advocated the liberalisation of the creative economy. Free trade was the precondition of artistic autonomy. But, by the time that David took up his post, this faith in the magic of the markets had waned. Across France, the demise of aristocratic and clerical patronage had deprived artists and artisans of

---

[200] For the practical problems and theoretical arguments which shaped this revolutionary pedagogical programme of David and his colleagues, see George Levitine, *The Dawn of Bohemianism*, pages 10–20; and Jean-Jacques Rousseau, *Émile*, pages 165–208.

[201] See Warren Roberts, *Jacques-Louis David, Revolutionary Artist*, pages 66–91; and David Dowd, *Pageant-Master of the Republic*, pages 84–88.

their primary source of income. Traumatised by civil war and foreign invasions, the new bourgeois elite wasn't yet ready to take over this crucial role. As an emergency measure, the French government decided to provide assistance for its destitute supporters amongst the artistic community. Under David's direction, they were employed to make costumes, floats, banners and props in the Neo-Classical style for a series of revolutionary festivals. Over a century before the Bolsheviks' avant-garde re-enactments of the seizure of the Winter Palace took place, the Jacobin government was lavishly sponsoring public celebrations of important events in the brief history of the French republic: the storming of the Bastille, the abolition of the monarchy and its military victories over internal or external enemies. The artists and artisans who had once gratified the aristocracy with luxury goods were now devoting their imaginative skills to staging multi-media celebrations where the people could glorify the revolution.[202]

In his 1758 *Letter to Monsieur D'Alembert on the Theatre*, Rousseau had contrasted the passive contemplation of an audience of a play with the active involvement of the crowd at a carnival. Anticipating Debord's critique of the spectacle two centuries later, the sage of Geneva castigated the increasing division of labour in 18th century Europe between the producers and consumers of art. For this forefather of the Situationists, a flourishing republican democracy required the cultural underpinning of participatory creativity.[203] Enthused by Rousseau's text, David and his colleagues from the Commune des Arts dedicated themselves to turning theory into practice. Their revolutionary festivals were much more than a job creation scheme for unemployed artists and artisans. For the first time, the masses were also invited to join the party. On 20th September 1793, one third of the entire population of Paris was involved in making a collective artwork to celebrate the anniversary of the founding of the French republic. Specialist skills

---

[202] See David Dowd, *Pageant-Master of the Republic*, pages 45–97; and Mona Ozouf, *Festivals and the French Revolution*, pages 33–125.

[203] '... let the spectators become an entertainment to themselves; make them actors themselves; do it so each sees and loves himself in the others so that all will be better united.' Jean-Jacques Rousseau, *Letter to Monsieur D'Alembert on the Theatre*, page 126. He also stressed the political importance of these public celebrations in *The Government of Poland*, page 14.

had been required to manufacture the stunning Neo-Classical floats, statues and costumes for this carnival. But, what made this day so memorable was the active involvement of large numbers of ordinary people on the day of the festival itself. Under the old order, the public had been confined to admiring from a distance extravagant displays of monarchical and clerical power. Now, with the triumph of the republic, it was the inhabitants of Paris themselves who were taking centre stage in this popular carnival. With David as their mentor, they'd dressed up, marched in the parade, carried banners, played music, appeared on floats and carried out ceremonial rituals. If only for a brief moment, the spectacle was superseded on the streets of Paris. Fulfilling Rousseau's prophecy, the 1789 French Revolution had turned every citizen into an artist.[204] Most wonderfully, the Situationist memory of this collective achievement is still an affront to the ideological apologists of the integrated spectacle.

On 10th November 1793, one and a half centuries before the Lettrists' infamous provocation, an exuberant crowd of radical artisans led by Jacques-René Hébert invaded Notre Dame cathedral and – as a deliberate act of sacrilege – took over this sacred space for a wild party: the *Festival of Reason*. As they drank, sang and danced to celebrate the official abolition of slavery in the French colonies, these fervent atheists tore down the high altar and replaced it with a shrine dedicated to the secular ideal of Liberty. Emphasising their rejection of Christian mysticism, they concluded this blasphemous ceremony by crowning one of their more beautiful activists as the Goddess of Reason.[205] The supporters of Hébert who organised this unauthorised carnival inside Notre Dame were drawn from the Left faction of the Jacobin movement. In the early phases of the 1789 French Revolution, liberal grandees had tried to create a new political settlement founded upon an English-style constitutional monarchy. Discredited by the king's treachery, they'd lost power in 1792 to the more radical representatives of the bourgeoisie who understood that there could be no compromise

---

[204] See David Dowd, *Pageant-Master of the Republic*, pages 110–116; and Mona Ozouf, *Festivals and the French Revolution*, pages 83–84.

[205] See Daniel Guerin, *Bourgeois et Bras Nus*, pages 149–152; and Aimé Césaire, *Toussaint Louverture*, pages 201–203.

with the aristocracy. Instead, this new Jacobin government forged an alliance with the plebeian activists of the towns and countryside. Like the Bolsheviks during the Russian Civil War, their regime could only prevail against its internal and external enemies by mobilising the masses to fight on its behalf. Under the auspices of the Committee of Public Safety, the Jacobins adopted a series of measures designed to win popular support for the republican cause: punishing counter-revolutionaries, redistributing land, controlling prices and, last but not least, sponsoring public festivals. Best of all, this intransigent party of the French bourgeoisie had discovered a charismatic leader in Robespierre who was trusted by rebellious artisans and peasants across the nation.[206]

Facing a common danger, the social contradictions of the Jacobin movement weren't immediately apparent to its members. Like in Russia over a century later, the vicious political faction-fighting within the Left obscured the more fundamental divide between those who were profiting from the new regime and those who were still suffering from poverty and powerlessness. In 1792, the struggle between liberals and republicans for control of the French state had been finally decided by the direct intervention of the Paris mob. Emerging from their ghettos, the artisans, shopkeepers and labourers of the capital city had forcibly occupied the parliament building and expelled the advocates of compromise from the assembly. As a consequence, the new Jacobin regime derived its political legitimacy from two rival sources: representative democracy and direct democracy. On the one hand, the Committee of Public Safety was an executive chosen by the majority of deputies within the national legislature. On the other hand, Robespierre's administration was the collective expression of decisions made by citizens at local meetings in Paris and other republican strongholds.[207] In 1762, Rousseau had published a book that elucidated the stark difference between these two forms of democracy: *The Social Contract*. Contradicting the liberal admirers of the English parliamentary

---

[206] See Albert Soboul, *The Sans-Culottes*, pages 2–45, 251–264; and Norman Hampson, *The Life and Opinions of Maximilien Robespierre*, pages 120–191.

[207] See Daniel Guerin, *Bourgeois et Bras Nus*, pages 22–32, 80–95, 117–123; and Albert Soboul, *The Sans-Culottes*, pages 92–134.

system, he argued that elected representatives were only interested in representing their own selfish interests.[208] As the son of a watchmaker from Geneva, he believed that the artisan trade community provided a far superior model of political organisation. With their wives looking after the household, male citizens would assemble in public to decide together how the state should be run. Through intense discussions, they could eventually come to a consensus which was agreed by all: the General Will. Above all, it was through this participatory process of taking decisions together that the citizenry became united in the implementation of these public policies. For Rousseau, the democratic republic was an interactive creation: '... the ... collective being cannot be represented by anyone but itself ...'[209]

When the monarchy was abolished in 1792, the plebeian Jacobins were convinced that they were now masters of the French state. Like the workers and soldiers attending the Russian Soviets over a century later, artisans and shopkeepers in the capital held daily meetings through which they administered their own neighbourhoods: the Paris Sections. Across the country, revolutionaries used popular assemblies to deprive the liberal notables of their local power bases. Improving on Rousseau's patriarchal concept of direct democracy, these Left Jacobins warmly welcomed female activists into their ranks.[210] Anticipating the 20th century's workers' councils, these experiments in popular participation sought to coordinate both the political and economic life of the nation. It was this flourishing of self-management that ensured the French people were directly involved in supporting the war effort. Campaigns were launched to collect provisions for the republic's armies: horses, food, saltpetre, shoes and clothing. Punishing the clergy for its royalist sympathies, militants stripped the churches of their bells and other metal ornaments to provide the raw materials for making muskets and

---

[208] See Jean-Jacques Rousseau, *The Social Contract*, pages 140–143.

[209] Jean-Jacques Rousseau, *The Social Contract*, page 69. For how Rousseau's artisan background inspired his political theory, see James Miller, *Rousseau*, pages 14–48.

[210] See Albert Soboul, *Paysans, Sans-Culottes et Jacobins*, pages 203–222; Gwyn Williams, *Artisans and Sans-Culottes*, pages xxxi–xxxv, 40–57; and Catherine Marand-Fouquet, *La Femme au temps de la Révolution*, pages 49–138.

other weaponry. For the Jacobins, Rousseau's writings had become a self-help manual for securing the survival of the revolution.[211]

More than anything else, this mass mobilisation enabled the French republic to create a new type of army that was able to defeat the forces of reaction at home and abroad. During the wars conducted under the absolute monarchy, the aristocratic officer corps had imposed rigid discipline upon a rank-and-file recruited from the outcasts of society. In 1789 as in 1917, it was the insubordination of these despised soldiers that had tipped the balance in favour of the revolution. Over the next few years, this politicisation of the French army became ever more intense. When the liberals established a National Guard, they'd allowed its bourgeois members to elect their own officers and discipline themselves. Under the impact of civil war and foreign invasion, the social exclusivity of this militia soon had to be discarded.[212] As Rousseau had emphasised, those who enjoyed the benefits of citizenship also had to share the risks of military service.[213] Like Red Guards in 1917, these plebeian soldiers saw themselves as first and foremost fighters for a political cause. In 1792, the Jacobin government raised a revolutionary army composed of loyal artisans from Paris and the other major cities to enforce price controls, requisition food and intimidate malcontents at home.[214] With Austrian, British, Russian and Prussian troops massing on the French borders, Robespierre's regime called upon all patriotic young men to join the army defending the integrity of the nation: the levée en masse. As in the Russian Civil War over a century later, the survival of the revolution now depended upon the martial prowess of its civilian supporters. Much to the surprise of the military experts,

---

[211] See Alan Forrest, 'La Patrie en Danger', pages 19–24; and Richard Cobb, *The People's Armies*, pages 416–479.

[212] See Albert Soboul, *Les Soldats de l'An II*, pages 9–64; and John Lynn, *The Bayonets of the Republic*, pages 43–96.

[213] In his artisans' republic, securing internal peace meant meeting the threat of external conflict: '… all must now fight in case of need for their country, but at least no one has any longer to fight for himself.' Jean-Jacques Rousseau, *The Social Contract*, page 78.

[214] See Richard Cobb, *The People's Armies*, pages 249–415: and Paddy Griffith, *The Art of War of Revolutionary France*, pages 252–255.

this influx of volunteers not only saved the Jacobin republic, but also transformed the nature of European warfare.[215]

Ironically, the defection of its aristocratic officers benefited the French army. Instead of obeying orders without question, its citizen-soldiers were now fighting for a political cause under leaders who they'd chosen themselves. Unlike the brutalised conscripts of the absolute monarchy, they would break and run during an engagement rather than stand in formation accepting heavy casualties. However, once they'd reached a place of safety, these volunteers would – to the amazement of their enemies – quickly rally and return to the attack. Slowly but surely, the French republican army developed the tactics which delivered victory over its aristocratic enemies. On the battlefield, swarms of skirmishers would cover the advance of massed columns of infantry backed up by artillery barrages and cavalry charges. On campaign, this new republican army was led by a group of elite troops whose moniker would soon be adopted by both the artistic avant-garde and the political vanguard: the advanced guard. Tellingly, these politicised warriors didn't have to wait for detailed orders from a commander-in-chief before they seized any opportunity to exploit the weaknesses of their royalist opponents. Again and again, the conscious self-discipline of citizen-soldiers triumphed over the blind obedience of professional troops. In warfare as in art and politics, participatory creativity had empowered isolated individuals with the collective strength of the General Will.[216]

In 1806, while the French and Prussian armies were manoeuvring outside Jena in preparation for battle, Hegel had been hurriedly making corrections to the manuscript of the book that would make his name amongst the German intelligentsia: *The Phenomenology of the Spirit*. By the time that the final version was ready to be dispatched to the

---

[215] See Albert Soboul, *Les Soldats de l'An II*, pages 67–122; and Alan Forrest, 'La Patrie en Danger', pages 8–16, 19–26.

[216] See Albert Soboul, *Les Soldats de l'An II*, pages 203–210; John Lynn, *The Bayonets of the Republic*, pages 163–260; and Paddy Griffith, *The Art of War of Revolutionary France*, pages 175–234.

publishers, the fate of central Europe had been decided. As he joined the joyful crowds cheering Bonaparte leading the victorious French army into this university town, the serendipity of the moment was perfect.[217] In his just completed text, Hegel claimed that the origins of human civilisation could be traced back to a primeval moment when class divisions had emerged for the first time. In the distant past, the members of barbarian tribes had been united by the equality of poverty and ignorance. Then, in the founding moment of history, an outburst of extreme violence had split human society into two irreconcilable groups: the masters and the slaves. People had fought bitterly against each other to determine who would be in which class. Those who were brave enough to risk death became the masters. Those who were not became the slaves. One class would do the fighting while the other did the work. From then onwards, the evolution of human civilisation had been driven by the repeated reiteration of this all-encompassing conflict between the masters and the slaves.[218]

In *The Phenomenology of the Spirit*, Hegel traced how this social dialectic had manifested itself across the centuries. Like David, he admired the political and cultural achievements of Ancient Greece and Rome. As a scholar, he was fascinated by the wonders of the medieval kingdoms of Europe and Asia. Yet, each of these great civilisations had been unable to overcome the primordial class conflict that had given them life. Even the one true religion of Christianity had only been able to reconcile these social divisions in a spiritual form. However, immersed in the crowds lining the streets of Jena, Hegel knew that he was a member of the lucky generation that were alive at the transformative moment when the slaves had successfully risen in revolt against their masters: the fall of the Bastille. Like many Germans in 1806, he enthusiastically celebrated the arrival of the genius general who now personified the ideals of the 1789 French Revolution. They were convinced that Bonaparte's decisive victory at the battle of Jena-Auerstädt had swept away the old order in central Europe. When both masters and slaves become citizen-soldiers of the crowned republic, the class divisions

---

[217] See Terry Pinkard, *Hegel*, pages 227–230.

[218] See Georg Hegel, *Phenomenology of the Spirit*, pages 111–119. Also see Alexandre Kojève, *Introduction to the Reading of Hegel*, pages 31–70; and Jean Hyppolite, *Genesis and Structure of Hegel's Phenomenology of Spirit*, pages 172–177.

which had shaped human civilisation had been superseded: the end of history.[219]

Hegel would remain a fervent admirer of Bonaparte for the rest of his life. During the brief French ascendency over Germany, he and his family were active collaborators with the imperial regime. Between 1808 and 1810, Hegel was the editor of a Bonapartist newspaper in Bavaria. Both his brother and his brother-in-law would lose their lives in the emperor's disastrous invasion of Russia in 1812.[220] Even after the final defeat and exile of Bonaparte, Hegel had remained true to his hero's cause. Inside his writings' esoteric terminology was hidden an intellectual vindication of the achievements of the French empire.[221] Anticipating the Post-Modernist philosophers of the late-20th century, he compensated for the disappointment of his political hopes by transforming them into literary abstractions. What couldn't be put into practice could be enjoyed as theory. In *The Phenomenology of the Spirit*, Hegel had already constructed a lofty philosophical apology for Bonaparte's venal dictatorship. Like other liberals in the 1800s, he'd been convinced that the key mistake of the Jacobin regime was its decision to make an alliance with the plebeian masses. Inspired by Rousseau, these artisan and peasant radicals had dreamt of a democratic republic that would impose political and social equality: Absolute Liberty. According to Hegel, by rejecting all forms of authority, the Left Jacobins had instead plunged the nation into anarchic chaos. For liberals, the 1793 *Festival of Reason* in Notre Dame was the epitome of this mob irrationality. Deprived of the moral disciplines of religious belief, civilised society in France had collapsed into brutal barbarism as everyone pursued their own selfish interests.[222]

---

[219] '... the French Revolution ... completes the evolution of the Christian World in the real (and at the same time symbolic) person of the god-Man Napoleon who is ... Creator-Head of the perfect State.' Alexandre Kojève, *Introduction to the Reading of Hegel*, page 73.

[220] See Terry Pinkard, *Hegel*, pages 194–195, 199–202, 212–213, 240–3, 285–286, 302–3.

[221] As a Freemason, Hegel knew how to dissimulate his political views in a mystical disguise. See Susan Buck-Morss, *Hegel, Haiti and Universal History*, page 17.

[222] See Georg Hegel, *Phenomenology of the Spirit*, pages 211–228. Also see Jean Hyppolite, *Genesis and Structure of Hegel's Phenomenology of Spirit*, pages 453–460; *Marx and Hegel*, pages 54–62.

As Hegel explained, the Left Jacobins' desire for Absolute Liberty had inevitably culminated in its opposite when Robespierre's regime was forced to restore order through the Absolute Tyranny of the Terror. As Hébert's faction was dispatched to the guillotine, these bourgeois revolutionaries marked the conclusion of the destructive phase of the 1789 French Revolution by anathematising all forms of atheism. On 8ᵗʰ June 1794, in a final flourish, David had organised a cast of thousands for a massive festival in Paris which celebrated the inauguration of a new republican religion: the Cult of the Supreme Being.[223] The plebeian experiments in participatory democracy were over. The concentrated spectacle had now been sanctified as eternal and immutable. Unfortunately for Robespierre and his intimates, the Right Jacobins had condemned themselves by this irrevocable break with their artisan and petit-bourgeois allies. Deprived of the legitimacy of direct democracy, executive authority was now solely derived from the representative democracy of the legislature. Seizing this opportunity, liberal and republican members of parliament had banded together and overthrown the Committee of Public Safety. Over the next five years, the Thermidor regime tried and failed to create a stable constitutional settlement for post-revolutionary France. Besieged by Jacobins on their Left and monarchists on their Right, most of these bourgeois politicians had welcomed Bonaparte's seizure of state power in 1799. Under his charismatic leadership, liberalism could now rule unimpeded by forging a third way to modernity out of the most enlightened elements of its two deadly rivals: democracy and aristocracy.[224]

On 14ᵗʰ July 1824, while visiting Dresden with his students from Berlin university, Hegel ordered the most expensive champagne from their hotelier to toast the anniversary of the fall of the Bastille. Even though a Bourbon king was once again on the throne of France, the author of *The Phenomenology of the Spirit* was still confident that this marvellous day in 1789 had marked the beginning of the end of

---

[223] See David Dowd, *Pageant-Master of the Republic*, pages 120–124; and Mona Ozouf, *Festivals and the French Revolution*, pages 106–115.

[224] Bonaparte was convinced that: 'When I became emperor, I never ceased to be a citizen.' See Emmanuel de Las Cases, *Mémorial de Sainte-Hélène*, page 88. Also see Isser Woloch, *Napoleon and his Collaborators*, pages 3–65; and Howard Brown, 'The Search for Stability'.

history. During the intervening decades, the slaves – by learning how to face death without flinching – had prevailed over their masters on the battlefields of Europe.[225] Under Bonaparte, the liberal ideals of the 1789 French Revolution had been given their definitive institutional expression: the codification of laws, civil equality, religious toleration, expert administration and promotion by merit. As Hegel took pleasure in pointing out, even the bitterest opponents of the deposed emperor had now embraced his constitutional settlement. In early-19th century Europe, the Bourbon monarchy could be restored, but not the old-feudal order. As a liberal intellectual living in 1820s Berlin, Hegel moved within a circle of friends that included the patriotic reformers who'd catalysed the 1813 German uprising against the French empire. Most notably, he regularly played games of *Whist* with a military theorist who'd left the Prussian army to fight on the opposite side to his doomed brother and brother-in-law in the 1812 Russian campaign: Carl von Clausewitz.[226] Like these Berlin colleagues, Hegel now understood that Bonaparte had destroyed himself through reckless ambition. Intoxicated by power, the emperor had tried to micro-manage the whole of Europe. When commanding an army at the gates of Moscow, Bonaparte was also running another war in Spain and dealing with the day-to-day administration of France.[227] At this point in his reign, any independent initiatives by his subordinates had become suspect. Fatally, by monopolising all decision-making, Bonaparte had deprived the French army of its organisational edge over its aristocratic rivals. In 1800, Desaix had saved the day at the battle of Marengo by marching his troops towards the sound of the guns before he'd received the First Consul's urgent summons for help. In contrast, Emmanuel de Grouchy's division failed to arrive in time to turn the tide at the battle of Waterloo in 1815 because he knew that his primary duty was

---

[225]   See Terry Pinkard, *Hegel*, pages 450–453. Also see Keith Sanborn, 'Postcards from the Berezina', pages 84–85.

[226]   See Peter Paret, *Clausewitz and the State*, page 316; and Terry Pinkard, *Hegel*, pages 502–503. For Clausewitz's account of Bonaparte's humiliating defeat, see Carl von Clausewitz, *The Campaign of 1812 in Russia*.

[227]   For an insider's account of the over-centralisation of the imperial bureaucracy, see Stendhal, *A Life of Napoleon*, pages 118–147. This was the fatal weakness of Bonaparte's empire: 'Unable to learn, it will, eventually, fall.' Ricardo Blaug, *How Power Corrupts*, page 13.

to follow the emperor's orders to the letter without any questioning.[228] As in an Ancient Greek tragedy, Bonaparte had been undone by the deadly vice of hubris. Even the most brilliant man of his age was incapable of deciding everything for everyone at all times everywhere. Like a modern Prometheus who'd challenged the gods and lost, the emperor would end his days as a lonely figure imprisoned on the barren Atlantic island of St. Helena. Yet, by enduring this humiliation, Bonaparte would purge himself of his multiple mistakes and bloody crimes in many people's eyes. What would survive was a pernicious legacy which would enthral generations to come: the romantic allure of the Napoleonic myth.[229]

In 1820, Hegel published a book which codified his own idealised vision of Bonaparte's empire: *The Philosophy of Right*. Living in the capital city of Prussia, he carefully disguised his devotion to this nation's greatest enemy. As at the emperor's coronation in Notre Dame in 1804, he dressed up the novelty of bourgeois rule in feudal clothing. His reactionary readers could take comfort that – in this intellectual reverie – the king was still on his throne and the landowners had kept their domination over the upper house of parliament. However, in its introduction, Hegel emphasised that these ancient institutions were now serving a modern purpose: 'the rational is real'.[230] Alongside them were the self-appointed bodies that represented the bourgeois elites who now dominated Europe. At the helm of Hegel's state was the select group of cultivated and efficient bureaucrats whose task was to guide the destiny of the nation: the civil service.[231] The aristocratic society of masters and slaves had become a technocratic civilisation of order-givers and order-takers. For its author, this manifesto of authoritarian liberalism was a Bonapartist reflection on the tumultuous

---

[228] Ungraciously, Bonaparte blamed Grouchy rather than himself for his defeat at Waterloo, see Emmanuel de Las Cases, *Mémorial de Sainte-Hélène*, pages 110–111, 578–579. Also see David Chandler, *The Campaigns of Napoleon*, pages 1057–1093; and Owen Connelly, *The Wars of the French Revolution and Napoleon*, pages 207–213.

[229] See Sudhir Hazareesingh, *The Cult of Napoleon*; and Barbara Ann Day-Hickman, *Napoleonic Art*.

[230] See Georg Hegel, *Philosophy of Right*, pages 14–36.

[231] See Georg Hegel, *Philosophy of Right*, pages 155–223. Also see Bernard Cullen, *Hegel's Social and Political Thought*, pages 73–96.

events that had just shaken Europe. In the early-1790s, the democratic zeal of the Jacobins had inadvertently unleashed the anarchy lurking within the egoism of liberal economics. Fortunately, during his early years in power, Bonaparte had been able to restore social order by creating political structures that mediated between the interests of the individual and the collective: the Senate, the Tribunate and the Council of State. Under his new empire, its notables were recruited on merit not birth: 'Every soldier ... carried a marshal's baton in his knapsack.'[232] But, by the end of his reign, Bonaparte's ambition had eviscerated the autonomy of these crucial intermediary institutions which he himself had brought into being. Unwilling to listen to those who'd known better, this demiurge had invaded Russia and ruined everything that he'd worked so hard to achieve.[233] Yet, as the final act of his illustrious career, Bonaparte had rescued his reputation by his return from exile in 1815. Welcomed by cheering crowds and defecting soldiers, the emperor's political legitimacy was confirmed by an almost bloodless seizure of power. Issuing the Additional Act for the imperial constitution, he dedicated his new regime to nurturing the political and civil rights of French citizens. His dictatorship after the 1799 coup had been an unfortunate and temporary necessity to defend the country against its internal and external enemies. The long-term goal of the Bonapartist cause was always to build a free and meritocratic society where enterprising individuals would be able to achieve their full potential. Exiled after the disaster of Waterloo, the fallen emperor won his final victory by popularising this seductive Napoleonic myth.[234] Enrolling in this cause, Hegel's goal in *The Philosophy of Right* was to rescue what was best from the wreckage of Bonaparte's empire for the elucidation of the next generation of European liberals. He was convinced that the restoration of the Bourbons was only a temporary block on the inevitable realisation of the end of history. Befuddled by his obscure language, German conservatives might deceive themselves

---

[232] Jean-Baptiste Vachée, *Napoleon at Work*, page 132. Also see Emmanuel de Las Cases, *Mémorial de Sainte-Hélène*, pages 470–471, 496–497, 553–554; and Isser Woloch, *Napoleon and his Collaborators*, pages 158–185.

[233] '[Bonaparte] ... let himself be defeated not by men, but his own pride and the climate ...' Stendhal, *A Life of Napoleon*, page 158.

[234] See Napoléon Bonaparte, 'Act Additional 22nd April 1815'; and Emmanuel de Las Cases, *Mémorial de Sainte-Hélène*, pages 208, 253–257, 583–584.

that his tome was an apology for the aristocratic regime of the King of Prussia. Little did they realise that *The Philosophy of Right* was Hegel's exposition of what might have been if Europe in the 1820s was instead living under the enlightened rule of a liberal oligarchy headed by Bonaparte's son and heir: the King of Rome.[235]

Exiled in nearby Brussels, David also mourned the disappointment of his Napoleonic dreams. Like Hegel, he too had believed that Bonaparte embodied the third way between the two extremes of aristocratic privilege and democratic levelling.[236] Under the liberal empire, this repentant Jacobin had devoted his artistic skills to promoting the emperor's authoritarian constitutional settlement. As his contemporaries knew only too well, David in *The Oath of the Horatii* had anticipated the egalitarian impulses of the 1789 French Revolution. Placed on the same horizontal plane on the left of this Neo-Classical painting, three sons were depicted pledging their lives to fight in defence of the Roman republic against its monarchical enemies in front of their proud father. Echoing Rousseau's patriarchal attitudes, the female members of this family on the right of the tableau were shown mourning the bloody cost of this imminent confrontation. Not surprisingly, like his sponsors, David also conceived *The Tennis Court Oath* as a modern celebration of male political bonding. In the centre of this unfinished painting, the leaders of the three old feudal estates – the aristocracy, the clergy and the bourgeoisie – grasped hands to affirm their new common identity as French citizens. Around them, the deputies of the National Assembly were depicted swearing allegiance to this liberal version of Rousseau's social contract. Tellingly, the only women in David's drawings for this painting were to be found amongst the audience looking down from the balconies of the Jeu de Paume. As would become evident over the next few years, only the extreme Left of the revolutionary movement had understood that everyone – not only rich and poor, but also male and female – was entitled to the full rights of citizenship.

---

[235] For the political settlement promised by the 1810 birth of Bonaparte's child by his new Austrian wife, see Steven Englund, *Napoleon*, pages 359–364; and Adam Zamoyski, *1812*, pages 1–11.

[236] See Warren Roberts, *Jacques-Louis David, Revolutionary Artist*, pages 131–207.

Two decades after he was given the commission for the *The Tennis Court Oath*, David exhibited the Bonapartist recuperation of his own republican past: *The Distribution of the Eagle Standards*. In this 1810 masterpiece, the self-crowned emperor was portrayed in his coronation robes receiving the acclamation of his loyal troops. Unlike the protagonists in *The Oath of the Horatii*, Bonaparte and his notables were elevated on a dais above the faithful warriors in peacock uniforms brandishing their regimental flags who were promising to fight for imperial hegemony over the whole of Europe.[237] Back in the early-1790s, the politicised citizen-soldiers of the French republic had risked their lives to liberate the continent from aristocratic oppression. But, as would happen with the Red Army a century later, they and their successors had by 1810 been corrupted by the plunder and baubles which rewarded victory on the battlefield. The political mission of the early-1790s Jacobin fighters for freedom was now long forgotten. Under Bonaparte's charismatic leadership, the French military had become a privileged caste dedicated to advancing its own self-interest: the army of honour.[238] After the victory at Marengo, they had championed the First Consul's elevation to the imperial throne as a confirmation of their own bravery. In *The Distribution of the Eagle Standards*, David used his paint to flatter this patriotic enthusiasm and martial pride. Once again, he carefully placed women in the background whose symbolic role was to admire a florid display of male prowess. The artistic prophet of republican virtue had become the visual propagandist of bourgeois vanity.[239]

When they'd demanded that *The Coronation of Napoléon and Joséphine* should be immediately moved from the Louvre to the Tonneau de la Montagne-Geneviéve, the Lettrist International had chosen well.

---

[237] '[Bonaparte] … *perfected* the *Terror* by *substituting permanent war* for *permanent revolution.*' Karl Marx and Friedrich Engels, *The Holy Family*, page 166. Italics in original.

[238] 'Napoléon's military genius blossomed on the terrain fertilised by the French Revolution. It began to decline when his political goals became antagonistic to its revolutionary heritage.' Albert Soboul, *Les Soldats de l'An II*, page 278. For the ideological and combat degeneration of the French soldiery, see Stendhal, *A Life of Napoleon*, pages 148–152; and John Lynn, 'Toward an Army of Honour'.

[239] See Warren Roberts, *Jacques-Louis David, Revolutionary Artist*, pages 164–167.

In contrast with David's other famous political paintings, women were now at the centre of its action. As an artistic prototype of the concentrated spectacle, this canvas captured the iconic moment when Bonaparte had crowned his wife as empress. Surrounding her were the female members of the new imperial family. However, these pampered princesses bore no resemblance to the militant republicans who'd partied inside Notre Dame only a decade earlier. The empress Josephine was not the Goddess of Reason. Unlike the Paris festivals of the early-1790s, Bonaparte's coronation in 1804 had been an exclusive event staged for the select few with the city's inhabitants confined to being passive observers of the spectacular procession to and from Notre Dame.[240] Led by David himself, the austere look of Neo-Classicism was already well on the way to being recuperated as the luxurious aesthetics of Empire Style.[241] Crucially, with liberal order imposed upon France, the next generation of radical artists had been denied the chance to experience the intoxicating synthesis of political revolution and cultural rebellion. Instead, David's pupils would have to preserve the memory of participatory creativity within their own bohemian milieu: the avant-garde movement. From the Romantics to the Surrealists, generation after generation of leftfield artists kept faith with this subversive legacy. One day, the people's carnival would return to the streets of Paris. By dreaming of detourning *The Coronation of Napoléon and Joséphine*, the Lettrists in 1955 had affirmed their adherence to this hallowed avant-garde prophecy. Yet, like the Barbus, they'd also mistaken their own marginalisation for political rectitude. Their vision of mass creativity still had to be transformed from intellectual dogma into proletarian practice. When compared to the Hébertists' 1793 *Festival of Reason* with its thousands of participants, the 1950 provocation by a handful of Lettrists at Notre Dame was an insignificant gesture. It would take the morphing of this group into the Situationist International to begin their escape from the avant-garde ghetto. The insurgency against spectacular capitalism would require not just the détournement of David's paintings, but also the critique of Hegel's writings. Only by deposing the emperor who still haunted its imagination could the Left

---

[240] See Warren Roberts, *Jacques-Louis David, Revolutionary Artist*, pages 152–164; and Steven Englund, *Napoleon*, pages 238–251.

[241] See Odile Nouvel-Kammerer, *Symbols of Power*; and Thomas Crow, 'Patriotism and Virtue', pages 48–54.

rediscover its emancipatory world-historical mission: the ascendency of direct democracy over all social institutions.

2.8: THE PASSION FOR VICTORY

On 2nd December 2011, a select group of people gathered at Raylab for the English launch of the Russian language version of *Class Wargames Presents Guy Debord's The Game of War*. Thanks to the hard work of Elena and Ilze, our audiovisual meditation on this Situationist ludic masterpiece was now accessible to audiences in the wild East.[242] Over the summer, Stefan had already hosted special screenings of the Russian cut of the Class Wargames movie to bohemian audiences in St. Petersburg, Moscow and Irkutsk.[243] Most appropriately, this promotional tour was concluding in a renowned London meeting point for artists and hackers from the opposite ends of Europe.[244] As our film emphasised, the Situationists' searing critique of spectacular capitalism had emerged from their lucid analysis of the defeat of the 1917 Russian Revolution. Two decades after the implosion of the Soviet Union, the once distinct systems of East and West were now fused into a single integrated form of domination which combined the ideological rigidity of Stalinism with the commodity conformism of Fordism. During the second phase of our campaign of ludic subversion, Class Wargames had become focused upon making our own distinctive contribution to the political analysis of this historical trajectory of spectacular domination. Through our performances and publicity, we'd aimed to provide a compelling – and entertaining – alternative to the Left's stultified debates over the tragic fate of the 1917 Russian Revolution. For far too long, Eisenstein's *October* had been accepted as an eyewitness documentary. Countering this Bolshevik myth-making, we'd sampled war films, costume dramas, political documentaries and sci-fi thrillers to provide evocative imagery for the voice-over elucidating the Situationist reasoning about these momentous events. Like the cavalry pieces in *The Game of War*, the vanguard intellectuals were only one section of the Red forces on the social battlefield. If everyone could play at being a little Lenin, Trotsky or Stalin, then nobody on the Left would be able to recuperate the next upsurge of participatory democracy – and become a new Lenin, Trotsky

---

[242] See Ilze Black, *Class Wargames представляет: Игра в войну Ги Дебора*.

[243] See the photographs of these matches in the Events 2011 section of the Class Wargames website.

[244] See the Raylab website for more details of this art and technology project.

or Stalin who oppressed the people in the name of the revolution. The lessons of proletarian history were there to be learnt on the game board.

After the first screening of the Russian version of our film in London was over, Class Wargames invited the audience at Raylab to participate in a collective performance of *The Game of War*. Earlier in the year, Stefan had themed our promotional events in St. Petersburg and Irkutsk around a famous Red Army hero of the 1917–1921 Russian Civil War: Vasily Chapayev. Imitating this Bolshevik cavalryman's eponymous updating of *Draughts*, either potatoes or onions were transformed into the pieces and terrain features of Debord's game. As in Victor Pelevin's 1996 satirical novel, Stefan had channelled the spirit of Chapayev to commemorate the disappointed hopes of the 1917 Russian Revolution.[245] For the film launch at Raylab, Class Wargames opted for another remix of Debord's game which had been played on 2nd July 2011 at Moscow's State Polytechnical Museum. In an avant-garde homage to Takako Saito's *Liquid Chess*, its infantry, cavalry and artillery pieces were represented by glasses filled with red or white vodka. Honouring Debord's devotion to alcoholic intoxication, the unfolding of this game was guaranteed to result in the players of North and South becoming very drunk. Each time that they took an enemy piece, they'd have to down the large shot of vodka in its symbolic glass. Like Chapayev in the 1934 biographical film, the players of *The Game of War* must revel in the emotional intensity of combat.[246]

For this contest, Elena and Fabian decided to command the army of the North. On the other side of the board, Marc Garrett, Lara Blazic and Alexei Blinov became the commanders of the South. As in the ICA bar a year earlier, the opposing sides' pieces were laid out in the opening positions for the 1800 Marengo campaign shown in **Diagram 3** on page 226. Like the Austrians in the original campaign, Elena and Fabian's pieces were split into two strong forces advancing on each flank. Recreating the French army's deployment, the bulk of Marc, Lara and Alexei's troops were held in reserve behind a defensive screen. Once

---

[245] See Victor Pelevin, *Chapeyev and Void*.

[246] See Georgi and Sergei Vasiliev, *Chapayev*. Debord heavily sampled the Russian Civil War battle scenes in this 1934 film for his 1973 movie version of *The Society of the Spectacle*.

again, a difficult problem in military strategy had been posed. How could the rival generals transform their very different opening positions on the battlefield into a decisive victory over the enemy? Despite first appearances, as shown by the ICA game, the French definitely had the strategic advantage. In 1800, Bonaparte had triumphed by concentrating his military might against a divided opponent. When playing South in our Marengo deployment, the task was to replicate this winning manoeuvre. Taking the offensive, Marc, Lara and Alexei began by moving their reserve forward towards the Austrian formation on the east of the board. As the First Consul had proved, the South's best plan was to overwhelm one of the North's exposed flanks as quickly as possible and then demolish the other at its leisure. A year before at the ICA, Elena and Fabian had won the game by faithfully imitating the master. This time, playing the North at Raylab, their conundrum was working out how to thwart Bonaparte's winning strategy. If they fumbled like von Melas had done in 1800, it would be Marc, Lara and Alexei who'd be claiming victory in *The Game of War*.

On 24th August 2011, I'd played the Austrians against Ken Wark as the French in the basement of the Housmans bookshop just before a promotional event for the first volume of his marvellous history of Situationism: *The Beach Beneath the Street*. In this contest, as I withdrew my right flank through the pass into the centre of the board, he'd advanced his reserve to seize my western arsenal. But, by taking Vienna, Ken had fallen into a trap. Moving my now united forces through the gap between the two mountain ranges, I'd launched an attack which eventually cut his army's line of communications to its own western arsenal. I'd proved that the more experienced player could win as the Austrians in the 1800 Marengo campaign. Learning from this encounter at Housmans, Elena and Fabian in the Raylab game responded to the South's offensive by conducting a fighting retreat on their right flank. Showing their tactical superiority, they inflicted significant casualties as they were forced to concede ground. By the time that the French reserve broke through into the centre of the board, Elena and Fabian had succeeded in concentrating their forces together. In a dramatic series of moves, both sides now took piece after piece from each other. Fortunately, before the vodka prevented any more play, the game was decided. Commanded by the more skilful generals, the Austrians had demolished the French in this Marengo rematch at Raylab. As Debord had intended, beating Bonaparte meant knowing how to fight better than Bonaparte.[247]

By the time that this key event in the second stage of our campaign of ludic mischief was held, Class Wargames had become adept at promoting *The Game of War* as Situationist political propaganda. Taking our inspiration from Bernstein's toy soldier tableaus, we were re-enacting revolutionary history to denounce the ideological eternities of the integrated spectacle. At our 2011 Raylab event, its combination of film screening and game playing emphasised the close political parallels between the two world-historical revolutions which had shaped Debord's political imagination: the 1789 French original and its 1917 Russian remix. The Bolsheviks had copied their Jacobin predecessors – and the Bolshevik sects in France as elsewhere had inherited this hallowed tradition of conspiratorial politics. David and his pupils had pioneered the heady fusion of avant-garde art and vanguard politics which the Constructivists and the Surrealists had later implemented with such expertise. Above all, it was obvious that Stalin had been the Bonaparte of the 1917 Russian Revolution. Like the upstart emperor, he'd also forged a third way to modernity which dispensed with both the Left's direct democracy and the Right's hereditary aristocracy. As Alexandre Kojève had explained to his French audiences at the time, Stalin was the mid-20th century manifestation of Hegel's vision of Bonaparte as the pitiless champion of human progress: the World Spirit on a T34 tank.[248]

In our performances and propaganda for this stage of the campaign, Class Wargames always highlighted how the New Left critics of Bolshevism were also fascinated by the historical parallels between the two revolutions in France and Russia. During May '68, the Situationists were convinced that their generation was on the verge of realising the most utopian demands of the plebeian militants of the early-1790s. Within the workers' councils, the direct democracy of the Paris Sections had reemerged in a more modern iteration. Like David's popular

[247] For photographs of both games, see the Events 2011 section of the Class Wargames website.

[248] For his influential late-1930s lectures on Hegel, see Alexandre Kojève, *Introduction to the Reading of Hegel*. Also see Michael Kelly, *Hegel in France*, pages 37–39.

festivals, the mass demonstrations taking place across France were joyful carnivals of participatory creativity. When they'd launched their campaign of agitation which would culminate in that general strike that momentarily threatened the survival of the Gaullist regime in France, the Situationists at Nanterre university adopted a moniker evoking the radical Left of the Paris Sections: the Enragés.[249] In his influential 1946 history of the 1789 French Revolution, Daniel Guérin had identified this plebeian movement as the precursor of the libertarian communist groups of his own times. Like workers' councils, the Paris Sections had been the institutional expressions of direct democracy in practice. Crucially, by studying the Enragés' pioneering attempts to implement this radical programme, the French Left would be able to inoculate itself against the temptations of both Jacobinism and Bolshevism.[250] In their eulogy to the 1871 Paris Commune, the Situationists emphasised that these daring moments of political rebellion in French history were also mass celebrations of creativity and sociability.[251] Symbolising the late-19th century's avant-garde art commitment to the insurrectionary cause, Gustave Courbet – the charismatic Realist painter – had been given responsibility for co-ordinating the Paris Commune's cultural policies. Like David in the early-1790s, his task was mobilising the population to defend the republic against its reactionary enemies. On 8th May 1871, Courbet had watched with pride as a large crowd held a boisterous party which culminated in the demolition of the militarist monument commemorating Bonaparte's 1805 victory over the Austrians at Austerlitz: the Vendôme Column. As its pieces were taken away to be displayed as a detourned artwork in the Invalides museum, the avant-garde humiliation of the skilful general who'd hijacked the General Will was complete. The dictatorship of the proletariat had toppled the bourgeois dictator.[252]

---

[249] See Situationist International, 'The Beginning of a New Era'; and René Viénet, *Enragés and Situationists in the Occupation Movement.*

[250] See Daniel Guerin, *Bourgeois et Bras Nus*, pages 13–39. Raoul Vaneigem included the Enragés alongside the 1871 Paris Commune and the 1921 Kronstadt Soviet in his timeline of libertarian communist struggles, see Raoul Vaneigem, 'Basic Banalities', page 93.

[251] See Guy Debord, Attila Kotányi and Raoul Vaneigem, 'Theses on the Paris Commune'.

[252] See Prosper-Olivier Lissagaray, *History of the Paris Commune*, pages 231–232; and Alistair Horne, *The Fall of Paris*, pages 349–352.

During the second stage of our campaign of ludic subversion, Class Wargames played *The Game of War* and *Reds versus Reds* in homage to this celebrated avant-garde performance. Bonaparte was shrunk down to a mounted general in Debord's game. Trotsky was now one of Copplestone Casting's 28mm toy soldiers. The celebrity academics of the Autonomist vanguards were only cavalry pieces or commissar figurines which would happily be sacrificed for victory. In both the French and Russian revolutions, the increasing militarisation of politics had brought about the demise of participatory democracy. However, at our events, this temporal process was reversed in ludic form. Playing at being Bonaparte and Trotsky was understanding that the order-givers must be prevented from dominating the social battlefield. By this point in the second stage of our campaign, we'd worked out the answer to the intriguing question which we'd dodged during the discussions in the St. Petersburg restaurant after our 2008 intervention at the Hermitage: why had Debord devoted so much time and energy to inventing a simulation of Horse-and-Musket warfare? As our Leningrad comrades had pointed out at the time, unlike *Reds versus Reds*, the theme of his ludic creation appeared to have no connection with the dramatic events which had taken place in their country in the early-20th century. *The Game of War* might be nothing more than a hobbyist exercise in military nostalgia. Two years on, we now understood the fallacy of this widely-held interpretation of Debord's masterpiece. The political and social struggles of the 1789 French Revolution had laid out the battle lines which would later reappear in a more intense manifestation during the 1917 Russian Revolution. By going back to this formative moment in the rise of spectacular domination, Class Wargames was mapping the historical growth of the alienated terrain over which today's class forces must fight. The skilful general should know how to master time as well as space.

Having tracked the emergence of revolutionary resistance to spectacular domination back from Russia in 1917 to France in 1789, the Situationists were able to identify the modern expression of this collective desire for self-emancipation: the workers' councils. As the heirs of David, Courbet and the Constructivists, the practitioners of avant-garde art had been given the vital task of proselytising for this revolutionary ideal. At its 1962 Fifth Conference in Stockholm, this new imperative had split the International into two irreconcilable factions. On one side, there were the politicised artists – the Nashists – who'd kept faith with the avant-garde revolt into style. On the other side, there were the artistic politicos – the Debordists – who were now focused on instigating the proletarian revolution.[253] Taking exclusive control of the brand, the Paris headquarters defined the primary mission of the Situationist International as making smart propaganda for the late-20th century's most advanced expression of participatory democracy: the absolute rule of the workers' councils.[254] Through their links with *Socialisme ou Barbarie*, Debord and his allies had already joined the growing number of 1960s New Left militants who were rediscovering the almost forgotten theoretical and historical writings of the 1920s Council Communists. Despite strongly disagreeing over the necessity of the Bolshevik dictatorship, these heterodox writers had all been united in their admiration for Soviet democracy. Updating Rousseau for the industrial age, they'd argued that the ordinary people of Russia had – if only briefly – successfully instituted participatory democracy in the state, schools, factories, farms, media and army. The Paris Sections had been revived as the Workers' and Soldiers' Soviets. David's festivals were restaged as Constructivist artworks. The order-takers had become the order-givers.[255]

Having been anathematised for decades after the Council Communists' defeat by the Bolsheviks in the early-1920s, this inspiring vision of human emancipation was reborn on 23rd October 1956 when the Hungarians rose in revolt against their Stalinist oppressors. Although subsequently recuperated by both sides in the Cold War as a purely nationalist uprising, what would give global significance to this rebellion were the insurgent proletarians who'd risked their lives for a new social revolution. For the Situationists, like the 1921 Kronstadt Soviet, the 1956 Budapest Workers' Council proved that there was a

---

[253] See Situationist International, 'The Fifth S.I. Conference in Göteborg'; 'Ideologies, Classes and the Domination of Nature'; and Stewart Home, *The Assault on Culture*, pages 31–44. Jörgen Nash was the celebrated painter who'd founded the International's Scandinavian Section.

[254] See René Riesel, 'Preliminaries on the Councils and Councilist Organisations'; and Mustapha Khayati, 'On the Poverty of Student Life', pages 331–337.

[255] See Anton Pannekoek, *Workers' Councils*; Paul Mattick, *Anti-Bolshevik Communism*; and International Communist Current, *The Dutch and German Communist Left*.

libertarian communist – and eminently practical – alternative to both state autocracy and market alienation.[256] During the heated arguments at the International's Stockholm Conference, Debord's most vocal ally was a veteran of the barricades from the 1956 Hungarian Revolution: Attila Kotányi. Unlike the other attendees of the meeting in Stockholm, this militant had experienced direct democracy in action at first hand. Learning the lessons from the Budapest Workers' Council, the Situationists must now become the catalyst of the spontaneous proletarian insurrections that would soon overthrow not only the Fordist capitalists of the West, but also the Stalinist bureaucrats of the East. At long last, Bolshevism had lost its ideological grip over the European Left. As Kotányi later emphasised, the Budapest Workers' Council had swept away any remaining illusions in these malefactors of the concentrated spectacle: 'We fought the Communists because they weren't communist.'[257]

As the May '68 uprising reached its peak, the Paris Situationists had called for the rebellious masses to take immediate control of all public and private institutions: the Committee for the Maintenance of the Occupations. When people began collectively managing the factories, offices, media, universities and neighbourhoods, spectacular capitalism in all of its multiple manifestations was on the brink of dissolution.[258] The Gaullist government's promises of wage rises and welfare improvements would change nothing fundamental. In 1960s France, the living conditions of the masses might have improved markedly compared to those of their grandparents, but they were now more dependent than ever on the capitalist system. For the Situationists, the one-way flow of television broadcasting was the exemplar of this relentless expansion of bureaucratic authority from the workplace into

---

[256] See René Riesel, 'Preliminaries on the Councils and Councilist Organisation'. Tellingly, one of Bernstein's 1963 toy soldier tableaus was entitled *Victory of the Workers' Councils of Budapest*.

[257] Attila Kotányi made this quip at the after-party for nettime's 1996 conference in Budapest. Also see Balazs Nagy, *How the Budapest Workers' Council Was Set Up*; and Andy Anderson, *Hungary '56*.

[258] 'The critique of everyday life successfully began to modify the landscape of alienation ... Everyone, in his own way, made his own critique of [capitalist] urbanism.' René Viénet, *Enragés and Situationists in the Occupation Movement*, page 82. Also see the Situationist International, 'The Beginning of a New Era'.

everyday life under Fordism. As Rousseau had warned, the passive consumption of culture was the bulwark of authoritarian politics. Fortunately, by learning from the long history of popular resistance to the imposition of spectacular domination, it was possible to devise the winning strategy and tactics for this final decisive battle in the class war. Like their illustrious ancestors in the Paris Sections, the Situationists were convinced that the revolutionary synthesis of direct democracy and participatory creativity could create a truly human civilisation: 'The power of workers' councils can be effective only if it transforms the totality of existing conditions and ... to be recognised – and *to recognise itself* – in a world of its own design.'[259]

Through the performances and publicity for the second stage of our campaign of ludic subversion, Class Wargames explained how Debord's fervent commitment to libertarian communism was deeply embedded within the rules of *The Game of War*. Because the pieces could only move and fight as long as their supply lines to the arsenals were unimpeded, each side had been set the difficult task of maintaining the stability of its own communication network while striving to disrupt that of its opponent. By going back in time from May '68 through the tempestuous events of 1917 to the founding moment of modernity in 1789, Debord's game wasn't just critiquing the Bonapartist pretensions of today's Bolshevik and Autonomist commissars. Above all, his ludic invention celebrated the unbroken revolutionary lineage from the early-1790s Paris Sections through the 1921 Kronstadt Soviet to the workers' councils of his own times. With the 20th century left far behind, these historical teachings found within Debord's game have never been more topical. What was once only briefly implemented in one city with the printing press could now be permanently realised in a much more sophisticated form on a global scale with the Net. By participating in our performances, the players of *The Game of War* were not only re-enacting the heroic revolutionary past, but also practicing at fighting for the emancipated future.

Paradoxically, as this second phase of our campaign of ludic subversion went from success to success, Class Wargames became increasingly

---

259 Guy Debord, *The Society of the Spectacle*, page 127.

aware of the limitations of promoting *The Game of War* and other military simulations as Situationist political propaganda. Since our founding in 2007, we'd faithfully retraced the trajectory of Debord's seditious career from avant-garde artist to revolutionary theorist. In the first stage of our campaign, we'd perfected the playing of *The Game of War* as the ludic realisation of the most dangerous tactic of Pop Situationism: participatory creativity. Well aware of both the antecedents of the International and the impact of its English interpretors, Class Wargames had adopted the strategy of avant-garde art to mock the recuperation of Debord and his comrades by the prissy mandarins of the academy and the gallery system. Moving into the second phase of our campaign, we'd then switched targets to a more serious opponent: the Left nostalgists for vanguard politics. Countering the simultaneous forgetting and mythologising of the past under the integrated spectacle, Class Wargames had played *The Game of War* and *Reds versus Reds* to pay respect to the hard-won accomplishments of our mutinous ancestors. By going back two centuries, we'd not only traced the origins of our avant-garde art interventions through Deller, the Sex Pistols, Fluxus, the Surrealists and the Constructivists to Courbet's toppling of the Vendôme Column and David's popular festivals of republican virtue. More importantly, we were now also able to explain how the early-1790s Paris Sections were reiterated in the 1871 Paris Commune, the 1921 Kronstadt Soviet, the 1956 Budapest Workers' Council, the May '68 occupations and the anti-capitalist rebellions of our own times. The Situationist lessons of revolutionary history were there to be learnt on the game board.

In the immediate aftermath of May '68, Debord and his colleagues' could have easily turned themselves into leaders of a New Left version of the vanguard party. By then, the Situationists possessed enough notoriety to have found a receptive audience amongst the radicalised hippie generation in Western Europe. Not surprisingly, there were those who had less inhibitions about institutionalising May '68's fleeting moment of direct democracy. Like the Jacobins establishing the Cult of Supreme Being, these New Left vanguards offered a mystical solution to the forcible reassertion of social alienation. Prevented from running their own lives in practice, the masses would instead find solace in its spectacular facsimile: the Bolsheviks' cultural revolution.[260] By the early-1970s, Gauche Proletarienne – a 'Mao-spontex' group – was selling 150,00 copies of its weekly newspaper in France that promoted an almost coherent melding of these two incompatible positions.[261] Yet, despite having developed a far superior analysis of modern capitalism, the Situationists were never tempted to imitate this impressive feat of New Left proselytising. On the contrary, Debord retreated into the countryside and – after expelling its few remaining members – dissolved the International in 1972.[262] According to the Pop Situationist canon, this refusal to lead the New Left vanguard marked his rejection of proletarian politics. From then onwards, staying true to his libertarian communist ideals became a signifier of his avant-garde authenticity. Ironically, although they fiercely denounced this recuperative misrepresentation, the admirers of Debord's insurrectionary politics have over the last four decades also romanticised his unwavering commitment to the absolute rule of the workers' councils. While almost all of the other gurus of May '68 would sooner or later make their accomodation with spectacular capitalism, this Situationist stood firm in his unambiguous rejection of the rewards of money and fame until the end of his life. Even if they could not fully live up to this exacting example, Left intellectuals now had a stirring role model in Debord. Like their Situationist idol, they too would be the special individual who exclusively possessed the esoteric revolutionary knowledge that could irrevocably change the world. Whether lauded as an avant-garde artist or a libertarian communist theorist, Debord had become the intransigent prophet howling in the wilderness.

When Class Wargames had performed *The Game of War* and *Reds versus Reds* at the *1968 & All That* conference in London's Conway Hall, it was heartening that the biggest audiences at this 40th anniversary commemoration of May '68 were for the sessions praising the Situationists as the cutting-edge theoreticians of this New Left

---

[260] See Patrick Kessel, *Le Mouvement Maoïste en France*; and Christophe Bourseiller, *Les Maoïstes*.

[261] See Roland Biard, *Dictionnaire de l'Extrême-Gauche*, pages 162–168.

[262] See Len Bracken, *Guy Debord*, pages 86–97; and Anselm Jappe, *Guy Debord*, pages 101–117.

rebellion. Unlike its Trotskyist and Maoist rivals during that iconic year, the International had understood that the modern proletariat lived within a media-saturated consumer society. Most wonderfully, their advocacy of the ascendency of the workers' councils during the May '68 uprising had anticipated the network politics of the 21st century's anti-capitalist movements. In contrast with the Post-Modernists and the Autonomists, Debord had never taken the 'linguistic turn' which now provided the philosophical justification for intellectual snobbery within the Left. Tellingly, instead of studying Lenin and Lacan with Althusser and Foucault like so many of his New Left peers, he'd discussed Hegel with Jean Hyppolite and debated Marx with Henri Lefebvre.[263] Four decades after May '68, dissident activists, artists and academics still had much to learn from the exciting adventures of the Situationist International.

Unfortunately, Debord had also left a legacy of fierce sectarianism to his heirs. The impressive political and theoretical advances of the Situationists had been gained – in part – by sharply distinguishing themselves from all other currents within the New Left. Devising the winning strategy and tactics to overthrow the society of the spectacle required the unrelenting denunciation of those in the 1960s who were determined to repeat the recuperative errors of the Social Democrats, Anarchists and Bolsheviks.[264] By carefully studying the Left's history, revolutionary proletarians could gain important insights from their illustrious predecessors' successes and mistakes. However, there were no eternal wisdoms to be found in the past. Each generation must appropriate the achievements of its predecessors to devise its own historically specific programme. When he'd closed down the International in 1972, Debord was convinced that he'd successfully thwarted any attempt to transform Situationism into an eternal ideology like Social Democracy, Anarchism and Bolshevism. The next

---

[263] For Lefebvre's rueful reminiscences of their brief collaboration, see Kristen Ross, 'Lefebvre on the Situationists'. Also see Len Bracken, *Guy Debord*, pages 86–97; and Anselm Jappe, *Guy Debord*, pages 73–81.

[264] 'Caught in the vortex of desacralisation and resacrilisation, we stand essentially for the negation of ... the [Left] organisation ... as a *spectacle* in which everyone denies himself.' Raoul Vaneigem, 'Basic Banalities (II)', page 121. Emphasis in the original.

generation must formulate a new strategy and tactics for combating a more advanced manifestation of spectacular domination.[265]

Despite his best efforts, Debord failed completely in this vital mission. Prevented from becoming card-carrying members of the International, radical intellectuals instead took sustenance from his romantic image as the intransigent solitary prophet.[266] Over the decades that followed its dissolution as a formal organisation, Situationism would be reborn as a New Left historical re-enactment society. By engaging in this live action role-playing of May '68, the imitators of Debord were able to savagely denounce the electoral compromises of Social Democracy, the bureaucratic manipulations of Bolshevism, the moralistic lifestyles of Anarchism and the intellectual pretensions of Autonomism. Like the citizen-soldiers of the early-1790s French republic, these Situationist revivalists hailed revolutionary violence as the sole authentic expression of revolutionary politics. As had been proved by the 1965 Watts uprising, urban riots were the most effective method for breaking the hegemony of the state and the commodity over everyday life.[267] All other forms of political activity were inevitably doomed to co-option by the devious masters of the integrated spectacle. Not surprisingly, Class Wargames' campaign of ludic subversion was no exception to this inflexible rule. At the *1968 & All That* conference, the editors of *Dialectica Principia* distributed a leaflet publicising their fringe meeting which sternly denounced our shameful recuperative failings: '... Barbrook ... and Tompsett want to remain frozen in time, because

---

[265] 'It is necessary to go beyond this partial defeat [of May '68]. ... All conclusions remain to be drawn; everything has to be recalculated.' Guy Debord, *Critique of Separation*, pages 38–39.

[266] These disciples '... see in the ... [Situationist International] .... simply extremist ideas; and not so much extremist ideas as the idea of extremism; and in the last analysis ... the *image* of extremist heroes gathered together in a triumphant community.' Guy Debord and Gianfranco Sanguinetti, *The Veritable Split in the International*, page 42. Emphasis added.

[267] 'The spontaneous and uncontrolled character of the rebellion [in the streets of 2008 Athens] was proved precisely by the lack of any political or economic demands whatsoever, by a complete negation of politics and trade unionism.' TPTG, 'The Rebellious Passage', page 118. Nearly three decades earlier, Fabian had also contributed to this influential interpretation of Situationism: Riot Not to Work Collective, *We Want to Riot not to Work!*.

they hope to make a few bucks ...'[268] When we'd played *The Game of War* and *Reds versus Reds* inside the Conway Hall, Class Wargames had owed more to McLaren's marketing techniques than to Debord's insurrectionary politics.

Of course, it was *Dialectica Principia* that was truly frozen in time. As with other Situationist re-enactors, this magazine's greatest contribution to the 21st century Left was its ideological inflexibility. By staying stuck in the revolutionary moment of May '68, these disciples of Debord could immediately recognise the reformist errors of their own times. Anything less than the immediate abolition of wage labour and the bourgeois state was a disgusting sell-out.[269] Ironically, this voluntarist concept of New Left politics led inexorably to a fatalistic interpretation of socio-economic determinism. While waiting for the glorious workers' uprising which would overthrow spectacular domination, all the fans of Situationism could do in the meantime was propagandise for their libertarian communist beliefs. Any attempts to ameliorate the capitalist present were inevitably doomed to failure. Like medieval Christian millenarians, they must patiently suffer the hardships of this sinful world while living in hope of the imminent arrival of a better one.[270] As Debord had feared, these Situationist re-enactors preferred the certainties of the past to the possibilities of the future. Ideology was in command.

As the second stage of our campaign of ludic subversion progressed, Class Wargames became increasingly aware that our performances and publicity might also be succumbing to this nostalgic adoration of Situationism. By playing *The Game of War* and *Reds versus Reds*, we were concentrating the attention of the audiences at our events on the fascinating historical narrative which led from the 1789 French

---

[268] *Dialectica Principia*, 'The Battle for Ideas'. At the 2011 Anarchist Book Fair in London, Michel Prigent from *Dialectica Principia* confidently told me that: '*The Game of War* is an irrelevance amongst Debord's works.'

[269] 'For the Left, the solution is always ... to rally uncritically to slogans such as 'the right to work is a human right.' ... people are increasingly waking up to the fact that such perspectives are ... regressive.' Principia Dialectica, 'A World on Fire', page 5.

[270] For this quietist interpretation of the apocalyptic tradition, see Bernard McGinn, *Visions of the End*, pages 28–36.

Revolution through the 1917 Russian Revolution to the May '68 Revolution. In successive reiterations, each of these spontaneous outbursts of participatory democracy had been recuperated by the cynical managers of spectacular domination. Every time, the charismatic leader who'd personified this reassertion of hierarchical rule was a skilful general: Bonaparte, Trotsky and de Gaulle. As evidenced by the Bolsheviks' brutal massacre of the 1921 Kronstadt Soviet, these uniformed guardians of bourgeois order were quite capable of employing the most extreme violence to achieve their nefarious goals. In May '68, de Gaulle had also made sure that the French army was – if necessary – willing to crush the insurrectionary movement by force. However, it was his adoption of a more sophisticated strategy for the Fordist epoch of spectacular warfare that would deliver victory for Right. Instead of intimidating the French population into submission, de Gaulle decided to hold fresh parliamentary elections. Crucially, the ballot papers didn't include the absolute rule of the workers' councils. Given the stark choice between Gaullism and Stalinism, an overwhelming majority of those who'd voted opted for the devil that they knew. The Right had succeeded in maintaining its grip on state power. Representational democracy had trumped direct democracy. Distraught like the Austrians after the 1800 Marengo campaign, the New Left now realised that de Gaulle had cunningly outmanoeuvred them on the social battlefield. The May '68 French Revolution was over.[271]

Having personally witnessed this debacle, Debord's *The Game of War* was a ludic warning that a new skilful general would almost inevitably emerge to threaten the next outbreak of proletarian insurrection. As we stressed at our performances, the players of his military simulation were teaching themselves the Situationist history of 1789, 1917 and 1968 so that they could avoid making the same political mistakes as the courageous fighters for these failed revolutions had done. Next time, the Left must win. In the second stage of our campaign, Class Wargames enthusiastically propagandised for this political utilisation of *The Game of War*. Through our performances and publicity, Debord's seditious interpretation of the past was sent into ludic combat against

---

[271] See Allan Priaulx, and Sanford Ungar, *The Almost Revolution*, pages 154–159; and Patrick Seale, and Maureen McConville, *French Revolution 1968*, pages 214–229.

the amnesiacs and fabricators of the integrated spectacle. But, in our enthusiasm to engage the enemy, we were now also in danger of turning into Situationist re-enactors ourselves. Like *Dialectica Principia*, Class Wargames had become a bunch of May '68 geeks.

By the time that the 2011 Raylab launch took place, the political weaknesses of this second phase of our campaign of ludic subversion were no longer in doubt. Over the summer of that momentous year, a spontaneous wave of mass protests had ousted the despicable dictators of Tunisia, Egypt and Libya – and badly shaken all of the other corrupt regimes in the Middle East: the Arab Spring. Across Europe, huge numbers of people were now taking part in strikes, occupations and demonstrations against the disastrous austerity policies imposed in the wake of the global financial crisis. From Tunis and Cairo to Athens and Madrid, the youthful activists who'd spearheaded these new improvised movements of popular resistance were united in their scepticism about the traditional structures of the Left.[272] In the 2010s, the Situationist revivalists of May '68 weren't an anomaly. Like hobbyist wargamers deciding to concentrate on refighting one particular historical period of warfare, each of the rival factions of the Left was obsessed by its own chosen moment of revolutionary valour from the last century. Bolsheviks wanted to relive the storming of the Winter Palace in 1917 Petrograd. Anarchists dreamt of fighting fascism on the streets of 1936 Barcelona. Social Democrats took inspiration from the crowds celebrating the election victory which would create the British welfare state in 1945 London. Autonomists imagined themselves in the front row of a rowdy demonstration of students and workers in 1977 Milan. Trapped in the past, these political ideologues didn't get the present let alone the future. The Left was nothing more than a historical re-enactment society.

For many young revolutionaries in 2011, the interactive capabilities of the Net showed how politics should be conducted in the modern hi-tech world. Everyone with a computer, tablet or mobile was now able to make their own media. Empowered by these network technologies, people no longer needed professional politicians to represent their views for them.

---

[272] See TPTG, 'The Rebellious Passage'; and Blaumachen and Friends, 'The Rise of the (Non-)Subject'.

Instead, they could collectively solve their mutual problems through open meetings and on-line forums. The horizontal communities of Net politics were now replacing the hierarchical bureaucracies of the traditional Left. There were no leaders when the whole population had an email address, a Facebook account and a Twitter handle.[273] Ironically, in their enthusiasm for the democratic possibilities of these digital technologies, the youthful rebels of 2011 were inadvertently engaging in their own form of historical revivalism. Back in the 1960s and 1970s, the boosters of McLuhanism had predicted that the inexorable convergence of computing, telecommunications and media into the Net would culminate in the advent of a new human civilisation: the information society. The national hatreds, class divisions and social isolation of the industrial epoch would soon be no more. In the global village of their imaginary future, everyone was going to have creative, fulfilled and prosperous lives.[274]

By the time that the Net became a mass phenomenon in the late-1990s, this McLuhanist prophecy had been annexed by the apologists for neoliberal globalisation. According to their Californian ideology, the rapid spread of the Net was creating a worldwide unregulated virtual marketplace where every entrepreneur with a good idea had the chance to become fabulously wealthy by founding their own dotcom company. As relics of the industrial age, the Left's parties and trade unions with their statist welfare policies were now obsolete.[275] Challenging this neoliberal version of the McLuhanist revelation, the Autonomists claimed that the decline of the industrial proletariat had led to the emergence of the new digital rebels of the information society: the 'immaterial labourers' of the creative, technical and educational sectors. In their mailing lists, clubs, websites, squats and shows, these leftfield activists, hackers and artists were prefiguring the libertarian future in the corporate present. Equipped with increasingly powerful network

---

273 See Paul Mason, *Why It's Kicking Off Everywhere*; and Joss Hands, *@ is for Activism*.

274 See Richard Barbrook, *Imaginary Futures*; and Frank Webster, *Theories of the Information Society*.

275 See Richard Barbrook and Andy Cameron, 'The Californian Ideology'; and Paulina Borsook, *Cyberselfish*.

technologies, this revolutionary multitude would soon bring about the fall of the neoliberal Empire. Milan in 1977 was the anticipation of the whole world in the new millennium.[276]

When we'd assembled at Raylab in December 2011, Class Wargames was facing an interesting dilemma. Like the Autonomists in the late-1990s, it would have been easy to update our Situationist ludic propaganda for the 2010s generation of network revolutionaries. As in May '68, general strikes, mass demonstrations and occupations of key points in the city had proved during that dramatic year to be effective tactics for combating the autocrats of the integrated spectacle. Organising their protests through social media, many of these young activists had already embraced the Situationists' strategic wisdom that the greatest threat to any popular revolution was the recuperative tendencies of the Left's own leaders. With a little tweaking, we would have had no difficulty in arguing that everyone who played *The Game of War* was celebrating the profound influence of the Situationist International upon the audacious practitioners of today's digital politics. But, what had prevented us taking this attractive option was our growing awareness that the second stage of our campaign of ludic subversion had reached the limits of its advance. Proselytising with ludic methods for the ascendency of the workers' councils was no longer sufficient. As emphasised by the more perceptive analysts of the Arab Spring and the European occupation movements, these leaderless revolutions had produced their own crop of skilful generals: the self-selected 'choreographers' of social media protests.[277] The absence of the formal structures of parties and trade unions had disguised the directing role within spontaneous uprisings of the on-line stars who were liked on Facebook, followed on Twitter and admired in blogs. As with the New Left before them, the 2011 insurgents had also discovered that direct democracy could quickly morph into vanguard politics: 'the

---

[276] See Maurizio Lazzarato, 'General Intellect'; and Michael Hardt and Toni Negri, *Empire*, pages 385–389, 409–411.

[277] See Paulo Gerbaudo, *Tweets and the Streets*, pages 134–157; and 'The Roots of the Coup', pages 110–112.

tyranny of structurelessness'.[278] Confounding the Autonomist remix of the McLuhanist prophecy, the new information society was just the latest upgrade of the old capitalist system.

By hosting participatory performances of *The Game of War* and *Reds versus Reds*, Class Wargames could remind the 21st century Left of the triumphs and traumas of its own glorious revolutionary history. David's popular festivals and the Constructivists' avant-garde artworks were preferred to the Empire Style and Socialist Realism. The 1790s Paris Sections were counterposed to Bonaparte – and the 1921 Kronstadt Soviet was the antithesis of Lenin, Trotsky and Stalin. By reliving this past, today's dissidents were able to recognise what was new and what was familiar about their own political situation. Instead of being mesmerised by the imaginary future of the information society, they should build upon the practical accomplishments of their heroic ancestors to devise their own vision of the shape of things to come. At this juncture of our campaign of ludic subversion, Class Wargames was now ready to move from its second phase of Situationist propaganda into the next stage of disseminating the skills of generalship to these anti-capitalist militants. The order-takers must learn how to become order-givers. Instead of the leaderless revolution, everyone should be a leader in the next iteration of the proletarian revolution. Four years after our opening engagement, Class Wargames now fully understood why Debord had designed *The Game of War* as a Clausewitz simulator. If the Left wanted to prevail over spectacular capitalism on the social battlefield, its activists had to be capable of fighting and winning as the collective skilful general. Our world-historic mission would be to teach this specialist knowledge to these dear comrades with the interactive pedagogical tools of military simulations. When the next May '68 took place, a new de Gaulle mustn't be able to outsmart the proletarian insurrectionaries. The third phase of Class Wargames' campaign of ludic subversion was about to get

---

[278] See Jo Freeman, *The Tyranny of Structurelessness*. Freeman's prophetic expose of the authoritarian tendencies within anti-authoritarian organisations was a reflection on her painful time within the late-1960s American feminist movement, see Jennifer Scanlon, 'Jo Freeman'.

underway: 'Our aim is ... to teach ourselves the knowledge that will secure the victory of cybernetic communism.'[279]

---

[279] Richard Barbrook and Fabian Tompsett, *Class Wargames Presents Guy Debord's The Game of War*, page 39.

NORTH

SOUTH

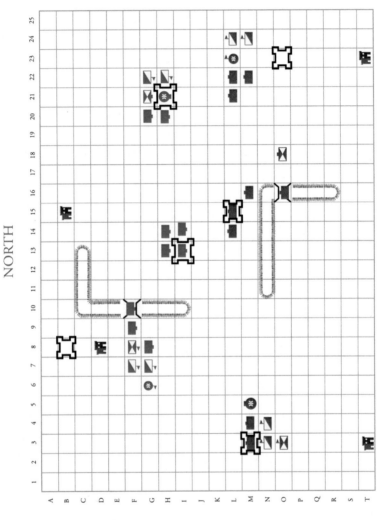

DIAGRAM 2

Rio de Janeiro opening positions for Guy Debord's *The Game of War*

AUSTRIANS

FRENCH

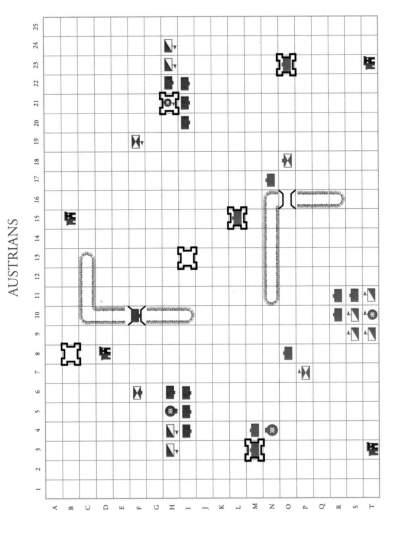

DIAGRAM 3

1800 Marengo campaign scenario for Guy Debord's *The Game of War*

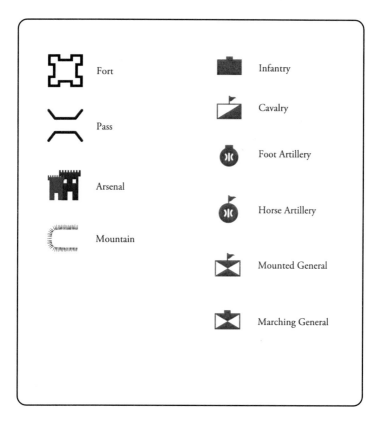

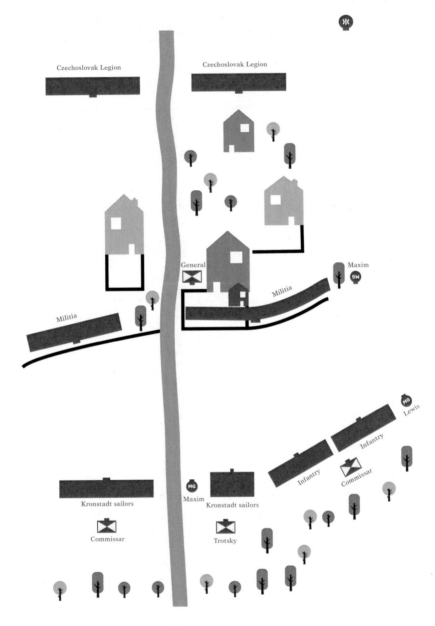

SOCIAL DEMOCRATS

Czechoslovak Legion

Czechoslovak Legion

General

Maxim

Militia

Militia

Maxim

Kronstadt sailors

Kronstadt sailors

Commissar

Trotsky

Infantry

Infantry

Lewis

Commissar

BOLSHEVIKS

DIAGRAM 4

1918 battle of Kazan scenario for Chris Peers' *Reds versus Reds*.

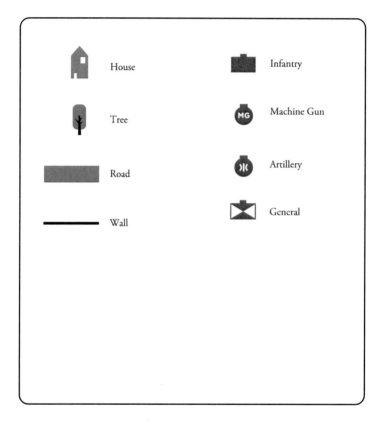

House

Tree

Road

Wall

Infantry

Machine Gun

Artillery

General

3.0: THE WORKERS' MILITIA

'Theory cannot equip the mind with formulas for solving problems, nor can it mark the narrow path on which the sole solution. is supposed to lie by planting a hedge of principles on either side. But it can give the mind insight into the great mass phenomena and their relationships, then leave it free to rise into the higher realms of action.'

Carl von Clausewitz, *On War*, page 698.

3.1: LA FORCE FAIT L'UNION

On 23rd and 30th June 2012, Class Wargames hosted two events for the *Invisible Forces* exhibition at Furtherfield's new space inside London's Finsbury Park. In this show dedicated to 'spontaneity, experimentation and [a] sense of adventure', Edward Picot, YoHa, Laura Oldfield Ford and other avant-garde artists tackled such pressing social issues as managerial mendacity, corporate surveillance and the gentrification of inner city neighbourhoods.[1] Alongside their installations, digital works and psychogeographic drawings, Furtherfield was – for the first time in its 15 year history – displaying a figurative oil painting in the gallery: Kimathi Donkor's *Toussaint L'Ouverture at Bedourete*.[2] Filling almost one entire wall of their space, this 136 x 183cm canvas depicted the charismatic general who'd led the revolutionary slaves of Haiti to victory over both the French and British imperialists. Created in the Neo-Classical style, Donkor's painting was conceived as a 21st century détournement of David's *The First Consul Crossing the Alps*. In the original version, the heroic figure of Bonaparte on a white stallion dominated the foreground while the rest of the French army was reduced to tiny figures in the background. However, in Donkor's remix, François-Dominique Toussaint L'Ouverture was depicted riding on horseback amongst his troops as they faced the dangers of the battlefield together. By rearranging the perspective of the tableau, this English artist had composed a visual meditation on the role of leadership in the revolutionary struggle. While David's painting of Bonaparte mythologised the 'genocidal maniac' who'd betrayed the republican cause by elevating himself into an emperor, Donkor's canvas celebrated Toussaint as the first among equals in a common fight for freedom.[3] When they'd defeated the European superpowers, the Haitian revolutionaries had demonstrated not only their military prowess, but also their political superiority over the enemies of human emancipation.

---

[1] Furtherfield, *Invisible Forces*, page 2.

[2] This painting is on the front cover of this book.

[3] Kimathi Donkor in Ilze Black, *Class Wargames Interviews Kimathi Donkor*, and Pablo Robertson de Unamuno, *Invisible Forces at Furtherfield Gallery*.

As our contribution to the *Invisible Forces* exhibition, Class Wargames decided to make two ludic artworks which would take their inspiration from Donkor's impressive painting. For the first of these events on 23rd June, we put on a participatory performance of Stefan's newly devised scenario for *The Game of War* shown in **Diagram 5** on page 336: the 1805 battle of Austerlitz. Having successfully adapted Debord's game to re-enact the 1800 Marengo campaign, its abstract engine was now manipulated to mimic Bonaparte's famous victory over the Austrian and Russian armies outside this Moravian village.[4] For many admirers of the French emperor, the battle of Austerlitz was his tactical masterpiece. Having lured the Austro-Russian forces into assaulting his right flank, Bonaparte waited until the crucial moment – and then launched his reserve in a devastating counter-attack against their weakened centre. Outmanoeuvred and outfought, the opposition was soon put to flight. Another astounding feat of military genius had been added to the Napoleonic legend.[5]

As the North and South teams were fighting our simulation of the battle of Austerlitz inside the Furtherfield gallery, Stefan elucidated the historical significance of this turning point in the 1803–1806 War of the Third Coalition. Like our commentaries for *The Game of War* and *Reds versus Reds* earlier in the second phase of our campaign of ludic subversion, his analysis of *Command & Colors: Napoleonics* was a Situationist lesson in political history. Pointing to Donkor's painting, Stefan explained that Bonaparte had been striving to build an empire in the East during this conflict because his empire in the West was no more. Three years before the French and Austro-Russian armies met in the Czech countryside, the First Consul had dispatched his brother-in-law Charles Leclerc with a large expeditionary force to retake the rebellious colony of Saint-Domingue in the Caribbean. Under the Bourbon monarchy, this island had been by far the most profitable

---

4   There have been numerous more-or-less successful attempts over the years to turn this decisive battle into a board game: John Young, *Austerlitz*; Dean Essig and David Powell, *Austerlitz*; Robert Markham, *Napoleonic Battles: Austerlitz 1805*; Kevin Zucker, *The Sun of Austerlitz*; and Bowen Simmons, *Napoleon's Triumph*.

5   See F.G. Hourtoulle, *Austerlitz*; and David Chandler, *The Campaigns of Napoleon*, pages 381–489.

outpost of the French empire.[6] Bonaparte was convinced that his well-equipped professional soldiers would easily be able to restore order and put its inhabitants back to work in the slave plantations. However, this nefarious scheme had been thwarted by the fierce resistance of the newly-born nation-people of Haiti. In 1804, the defeated and decimated French army of occupation was humiliatingly forced to evacuate the Caribbean island.[7] Tellingly, it was only a year later that the rest of Bonaparte's troops found themselves fighting against their Austro-Russian opponents at Austerlitz. The empire that had been lost in the West would now be conquered in the East. Yet, even the triumphant outcome of this famous battle proved to be ephemeral. As Stefan emphasised, Bonaparte would fight war after war over the next decade in the elusive search for final victory until he himself went down in defeat. The failed 1802 expedition to Haiti was a premonition of his disastrous 1812 invasion of Russia.[8] Crucially, by abandoning the democratic ideals of the Jacobins, Bonaparte had deprived his soldiers of their most potent weapon against the defenders of privilege: the support of the local population.[9]

For our next intervention at the *Invisible Forces* exhibition on 30th June, Class Wargames staged a ludic re-enactment of the confrontation depicted in Donkor's evocative painting: the 1802 battle of Fort Bedourete. Shockingly, despite its world-historical significance, we'd been unable to find any commercially available figurine rules or board games which simulated the 1791 Haitian Revolution. Rather than adapting Debord's ludic experiment again, we decided instead to make good this deficiency by hacking Richard Borg's *Commands & Colors: Napoleonics*. First published in 2010, this popular synthesis of figurine and board gaming already had a thriving on-line community

[6] '[In] ... 1783, Saint-Dominique ... comprised one-third of the foreign trade of France.' Thomas Ott, *The Haitian Revolution*, page 6. Also see Robin Blackburn, *The Overthrow of Colonial Slavery*, pages 163–166.

[7] For the history of this military catastrophe, see Thomas Ott, *The Haitian Revolution*, pages 139–187; and Martin Ros, *Night of Fire*, pages 151–201.

[8] See C.L.R. James, *The Black Jacobins*, pages 356–357.

[9] 'One of Napoleon's gravest miscalculations ... was to underestimate the extent to which liberty and equality had become the religion of the formerly enslaved [in Haiti] ...' Robin Blackburn, *The Overthrow of Colonial Slavery*, page 259.

of fans who were inventing their own battlefield scenarios.[10] In Alfred Auguste Nemours' *Histoire Militaire de la Guerre d'Independance de Saint-Domingue*, we'd found a detailed description of the day's fighting at Bedourete which allowed us to work out the terrain of this engagement, invent some special rules to add historical flavour and concoct the rival armies' opening positions shown in **Diagram 6** on page 338. On the southern side of the board, three columns of Haitian infantry were advancing in parallel while Toussaint and his Jacobin cavalry brought up the reserve. In the middle of the board, a lone French regiment was defending Fort Bedourete with the rest of the Bonapartist invasion force lined up across its northern side.[11] As in our Marengo and Austerlitz scenarios for *The Game of War*, the two sides had been set the challenge of optimising the military potential of both their very different starting dispositions and the geographical features of the battlefield. The winner would be the team that could master time and space under the emotional pressures of ludic combat.

For this game of *Commands & Colors: Napoleonics* at the Furtherfield gallery, the Haitians were commanded by Christian Nold and Tuesday Greenidge while Marc Garrett and David Bovill took charge of the French. In the first few moves, Toussaint's forces were in the ascendency as the Jacobins' centre column stormed into Fort Bedourete and their left flank moved forward to take the village on the western side of the board. However, learning from their experiences of playing *The Game of War*, Marc and David's team didn't lose their nerve. Ordering their troops to defend the woods on the north-west of the board, the French were able to halt the Haitian offensive with deadly firepower. Seizing the initiative, the Bonapartists next launched a vigorous counter-attack against their Jacobin opponent's right flank. Christian and Tuesday's team now committed the cavalry reserve to reinforce their exposed eastern position, but this gamble ended in disaster as they too were cut to pieces by the enemy's musket volleys. Eventually, as the casualties mounted on both sides, the Haitian losses became heavy enough to fulfil the French victory conditions. This time, the Bonapartists had

---

[10]   See GMT Games, *Commands & Colors: Napoleonics*.

[11]   See Alfred Auguste Nemours, *Histoire Militaire de la Guerre d'Independance de Saint-Domingue*, pages 348–358.

won the battle of Fort Bedourete against the Jacobins. As Richard Borg promised in the Scenarios booklet of *Command & Colors: Napoleonics*, history could be changed.[12]

A week earlier, immediately before our first performance for the *Invisible Forces* exhibition on 23rd June, Donkor had given a talk about the making of his illustrious painting. Back in 2004, he'd been outraged at the paucity of public celebrations of the 200th anniversary of the 1804 Haitian declaration of independence.[13] At the beginning of that year, an American-organised coup d'état had ousted Jean-Bertrand Aristide – the country's elected president – whose redistributive policies threatened the power and privileges of both the local oligarchs and overseas investors. Soon afterwards, using the United Nations as cover, the USA and its allies sent their troops to the island and recruited fascist paramilitaries to suppress any attempts by the locals to resist the destruction of democracy in Haiti.[14] Not surprisingly, in the Western media, the supporters of Aristide's Lavalas movement were castigated for their audacity in resisting neoliberal domination. Countering this racist condescension, Donkor set out to make a painting which would educate its viewers about Haiti's glorious revolutionary past. Two centuries earlier, this Caribbean island had been at the forefront of the global struggle for human liberation. Led by Toussaint, its rebellious slaves had not only freed themselves from servitude, but also advanced the cause of democracy in Europe. No wonder the 21st century adepts of the integrated spectacle wanted to erase the 1791 Haitian Revolution from popular memory. If the oppressed of South and North had successfully fought together against tyranny and exploitation long ago, their modern descendants might be tempted to imitate this courageous example today.[15] By painting *Toussaint L'Ouverture at Bedourete*, Donkor extolled this emancipatory

---

12   For photographs of this game, see the Events 2012 section of the Class Wargames website.

13   Kimathi Donkor in Ilze Black, *Class Wargames Interviews Kimathi Donkor*, and Pablo Robertson de Unamuno, *Invisible Forces at Furtherfield Gallery*.

14   See Peter Hallward, *Damming the Flood*; and Jeb Sprague, 'Paramilitaries in Haiti'.

15   According to the deposed Haitian president, 'Toussaint's fierce opposition to slavery, his leadership skills, his freedom-inspired writings ... bequeath to us [in 2008] a strategy for opposing injustice.' Jean-Bertrand Aristide, 'Introduction', page xxviii.

alternative to the established order. As the Haitian revolutionaries had proved, the insurgent masses were capable of overthrowing the most vicious of social systems. Countering the amnesia of the integrated spectacle, remembering the accomplishments of the past emboldens our ambitions in the present.[16]

When researching for his painting, Donkor had turned to his well-read copy of what is still the definitive historical account of the Haitian War of Independence: C.L.R. James' *The Black Jacobins: Toussaint L'Ouverture and the San Domingo Revolution*. It was within its covers that he'd found the stirring account of the battle of Fort Bedourete which would become the inspirational subject of his canvas.[17] Nearly a decade later, needing to work out the rival armies' positions at this engagement for our re-enactment at the Furtherfield gallery, Class Wargames tracked down Nemours' 1928 military history of the 1791 Haitian Revolution which James had used as his main source for this clash of arms.[18] Much to our surprise, we realised from its pages that the author of *The Black Jacobins* had subtly altered the original version to accentuate the heroic role of Toussaint at the battle of Fort Bedourete. In this influential book, history had been mythologised in the service of an admirable political cause. As Donkor's painting eulogised, Toussaint was '... the black Spartacus, the Negro ... who would avenge the outrages done to his race.'[19]

Growing up in the British colony of Trinidad in the early-20th century,

---

[16]   In 1962, the Martiniquean co-founder of the Negritude movement ended his biography of this Haitian revolutionary hero with these rousing words: '[Toussaint] ... well deserves the name given him by his compatriots of today: the Precursor.' Aimé Césaire, *Toussaint Louverture*, page 310.

[17]   See C.L.R. James, *The Black Jacobins*, pages 319–321. For the commander-in-chief's own account of this battle, see François-Dominique Toussaint L'Ouverture, *The Haitian Revolution*, pages 92–94.

[18]   For his intellectual debt to Nemours, see C.L.R. James, *The Black Jacobins*, pages v–vi, 382; and *Toussaint Louverture*, page 45.

[19]   C.L.R. James, *The Black Jacobins*, page 171. Spartacus was the leader of a 1st century BCE slave revolt against the Roman aristocracy which the early-20th century Left saw as the forerunner of their own socialist revolutions, see Frank Ridley, *Spartacus*; and Rosa Luxemburg, Karl Liebknecht, Clara Zetkin and Franz Mehring, 'Manifesto of the German Spartacists'.

James was fascinated as a child by the 1791 Haitian Revolution whose victory had helped to free his own ancestors from the horrors of slavery.[20] Moving to England in 1933, he'd become not only a prominent Trotskyist militant, but also the intellectual sage of the Pan-Africanist movement.[21] For James, it was the 1935 Italian invasion of Ethiopia that would give topical urgency to his historian's interest in the Haitian Revolution. Outraged by this Fascist atrocity, he hastily wrote an agitprop play about Toussaint's life which was given a short run at an avant-garde London theatre. With Paul Robeson taking the lead role, this drama of the Haitian independence struggle became his artistic cry of protest against the barbarism of Italian imperialism.[22] Turning his play into a book, James also endowed the historical narrative of *The Black Jacobins* with the emotional power of a Shakespeare play. According to Nemours' report of the battle of Fort Bedourete, the Haitian militiamen who were fighting for the French imperialists deserted in the aftermath of their side's defeat by the revolutionary army. However, in James' account, Toussaint rides up to these renegade soldiers at the key point in the engagement and – by the sheer force of his political arguments – persuades them to defect there and then to the cause of national liberation. By visualising this Pan-Africanist romanticisation of history, Donkor's painting was able to carry out a ruthless détournement of David's Bonapartist hagiography. Most wonderfully, *Toussaint L'Ouverture at Bedourete* became the Neo-Classical portrayal of a better past when the First Consul was an Afro-Caribbean Marat on horseback.[23] The artist imagined that – on receiving a commission at the presidential palace of the newly

---

[20] See Christian Høgsbjerg, 'Introduction', pages 6–7. For James' early years in Trinidad, see Kent Worcester, *C.L.R. James*, pages 3–26; and Richard Small, 'The Training of an Intellectual, the Making of a Marxist'.

[21] See Kent Worcester, *C.L.R. James*, pages 27–51; and Robert Hill, 'In England'. For an account of the pioneers of English Trotskyism, see Sam Bornstein and Al Richardson, *Against the Stream*.

[22] See C.L.R. James, *Toussaint Louverture*. For the story of this play, see Christian Høgsbjerg, 'Introduction', pages 10–28; and Nicole King, 'C.L.R. James, Genre and Cultural Politics'. Paul Robeson was a much loved left-wing African-American movie and music star of the 1930s, see Edwin Hoyt, *Paul Robeson*.

[23] In 1791, Marat was the first of the Jacobin leaders in Paris to call for the immediate abolition of slavery and the granting of independence to all French colonies, see Aimé Césaire, *Toussaint Louverture*, pages 175–176.

independent Haiti in 1804 – he'd been told how to paint the official portrait of the republic's martyred founding father: 'Do it in the French style!'[24]

During the 1950s, *The Black Jacobins* provided an instruction manual of anti-colonial rebellion for the charismatic leaders of the nationalist movements which would evict the bankrupt British empire from Africa: Kwame Nkrumah, Jomo Kenyatta and Julius Nyerere. In its portrayal of Toussaint, they'd found a stirring role model of an unimpeachable hero who'd sacrificed himself for the freedom of his people.[25] Returning the compliment, in the 1963 appendix to his book, James enthusiastically praised the emancipatory achievements of this new generation of revolutionary luminaries.[26] But, by the time that a new edition of *The Black Jacobins* appeared in 1980, this ardour for his Pan-Africanist admirers had long been disappointed.[27] Far from resembling Toussaint, they'd become modern equivalents of the military despots who'd ruled over the newly independent Haiti: Jean-Jacques Dessalines and Henry Christophe. During the next two centuries, the successors of these self-proclaimed monarchs failed not only to deliver prosperity for the majority of the population, but also to preserve the nation's sovereignty.[28] Most notoriously, during François 'Papa Doc' Duvalier's 1957–71 dictatorship, political stability in Haiti had been achieved through the enforced social and economic regression

---

[24] Kimathi Donkor in Ilze Black, *Class Wargames Interviews Kimathi Donkor*. Very appropriately for this task, his parents had named him in honour of Dedan Kimathi – the executed leader of the Mau-Mau guerrillas who'd fought against the British imperialists in 1950s Kenya, see Maina Wa Kinyatti, *Kenya's Freedom Struggle*.

[25] James had worked with both Kenyatta and Nkrumah before they returned home to lead their countries' independence struggles, see Robin Kelly, 'Introduction', pages 10–14; and Kent Worcester, *C.L.R. James*, pages 30–34.

[26] See C.L.R. James, *The Black Jacobins*, pages 396–399; and *Kwame Nkrumah and the Ghana Revolution*, pages 159–175.

[27] See C.L.R. James, *A History of Pan-African Revolt*, pages 109–136; *Kwame Nkrumah and the Ghana Revolution*, pages 10–17, 179–186. For a Trotskyist critique of James' infatuation with these anti-imperialist regimes, see Baruch Hirson, 'Communalism and Socialism in Africa'.

[28] See David Nicholls, *From Dessalines to Duvalier*, pages 33–164; and Peter Hallward, *Damming the Flood*, pages 9–16.

of the whole country.[29] In the late-20th century, the calamitous fate of this Caribbean island had provided a stark warning to the newly freed nations of the Third World. Expelling the colonial master was only the beginning of the liberation struggle. Without political democracy, economic modernisation and social justice, the people would never be able to control their own destiny. The revolution must be permanent.[30]

By recreating the battle of Fort Bedourete at the *Invisible Forces* exhibition, Class Wargames was not only challenging the deliberate forgetting of the heroic achievements of the Haitian Jacobins, but also interrogating this troubled heritage of insurgent leadership in the South. From the participatory performances of *The Game of War* and *Reds versus Reds* during the second stage of our campaign of ludic subversion, we'd understood that playing the past offered new insights into the difficult decisions forced upon the protagonists of key historical moments. Now, at our 30th June performance, the two sides were able to experience this 1802 clash of arms between the Haitian Jacobins and the French Bonapartists for themselves. Like Donkor's painting, our game was leftfield art in the service of political sedition. This hacked version of *Commands & Colors: Napoleonics* was an immersive tool for teaching the libertarian communist understanding of the 1791 Haitian Revolution. While the rival teams moved their pieces across the board, we'd kept up a continuous commentary which explained not only the tumultuous events which had led up to the battle of Fort Bedourete, but also the world-historical significance of the destruction of slavery in this Caribbean island. As James had stressed in *The Black Jacobins*, the democratic revolutions in France and Haiti were inextricably intertwined. In the 1790s, the radical movements on either side of the

---

[29]   See David Nicholls, *From Dessalines to Duvalier*, pages 191–238; and Edward Luttwak, *Coup d'État*, pages 180–1.

[30]   'One can only be for the time being for a socialist pattern [of society in Africa]. ... socialism ... demands a highly developed technological and industrial society. ... Now none of the underdeveloped countries have [yet] got that.' C.L.R. James, *Kwame Nkrumah and the Ghana Revolution*, page 169. Also see C.L.R. James, 'Black Power'.

Atlantic had risen and fallen together.[31] By the time that the Jacobins and Bonapartists met at Fort Bedourete in 1802, popular sovereignty had succumbed to military autocracy in both countries. Yet, there was still much at stake in this deadly combat. Bonaparte's troops were fighting for the restoration of human bondage within the French colonies. In contrast, Toussaint's soldiers were risking their lives for the equal rights of every citizen regardless of their skin colour.[32] As we explained to the audience at Furtherfield, the apostate emperor was the prototype of the nationalist revolutionaries who'd turned themselves into corrupt dictators in more recent times. But, as James' book and Donkor's painting celebrated, his Haitian adversary symbolised the better political option which was not taken. Even as Governor-General for Life, Toussaint had always been the servant of the people.[33]

---

[31] See C.L.R. James, *The Black Jacobins*, pages 85–144, 269–288. As a Trotskyist in the 1930s, he'd conceived of this 1790s alliance between the French and Haitian Jacobins as the anticipation of the Bolsheviks' 1920s call for proletarian insurrections in the North to be combined with anti-colonial rebellions in the South, see C.L.R. James, *World Revolution*, pages 62–68, 118–140.

[32] Title 2 of the 1801 Haitian Constitution guaranteed that: '... servitude is ... forever abolished. All men are born, live and die free ...' François-Dominique Toussaint L'Ouverture, *The Haitian Revolution*, page 46. Also see C.L.R. James, *The Black Jacobins*, pages 289–377; and Thomas Ott, *The Haitian Revolution*, pages 127–138.

[33] 'Since the revolution, I've done all that depended upon me to return happiness to my country and ensure liberty for my fellow citizens.' François-Dominique Toussaint L'Ouverture, *The Haitian Revolution*, page 65. Also see C.L.R. James, *The Black Jacobins*, pages 241–268.

3.2: GUIDING THE MASSES

As well as teaching the history of the 1791 Haitian Revolution, our participatory performance of the battle of Fort Bedourete scenario for *Commands & Colors: Napoleonics* was also a critique of Hegel's philosophy. During the second stage of our campaign of ludic subversion, we'd become proficient at combining factual exposition and theoretical analysis in the commentaries for our events. At the Furtherfield gallery, we were now ready to tackle the ambivalent legacy of this German speculative philosopher. When Hegel had cheered Bonaparte's entrance into Jena in 1806, he'd believed that this liberal dictator embodied the triumph of modern bourgeois society which had swept away the rigid class divisions between masters and slaves. However, only a few years earlier, the emperor of the French had sent an expeditionary force to subjugate Haiti's abolitionist republic.[34] For Bonaparte's regime, liberal rights were to be restricted to white people within the French colonies. As in the USA at that time, freedom for few was founded upon servitude for the many.[35] Far from representing the end of history, Hegel's Bonapartist politics contradicted his own philosophy of social evolution. As the Haitian Jacobins had proved in the 1800s, the practical realisation of the equality of all citizens would require more radical solutions.[36] Reflecting upon this conclusion, the next generation of dissident German intellectuals realised that bourgeois liberalism was only a temporary stage in the turbulent progress of humanity towards the truly emancipatory future:

---

[34] Hegel tried to justify the unjustifiable by claiming that the Africans' lack of bourgeois rationality condemned them to a life of chattel slavery, see Georg Hegel, *Lectures on the Philosophy of World History*, pages 173–190. For the elucidation of his confused politics, see Susan Buck-Morss, *Hegel, Haiti and Universal History*, pages 3–75; and Paul Gilroy, *The Black Atlantic*, pages 41–71.

[35] See Domenico Losurdo, *Liberalism*, pages 1–65; and Eugene Genovese, *The World the Slaveholders Made*, pages 118–244.

[36] 'Although the abolition of slavery [in Haiti] was the only logical outcome of ... [Hegel's] ideal of universal freedom, it did not come about through the revolutionary *ideas* ... of the French; it came about through the *actions* of the slaves themselves.' Susan Buck-Morss, *Hegel, Haiti and Universal History*, page 36. Emphasis added.

proletarian communism. Philosophical abstractions were no substitute for the material emancipation of the masses.[37]

Ironically, a century later, the left of the Left would find itself rediscovering what their illustrious predecessors had discarded. During his 1940s American sojourn, James had run a study circle for his comrades who were working in Detroit's car factories. Having split from the main Trotskyist party in the USA, they together embarked upon a careful reading of Hegel's writings to enable them to rethink their political strategy.[38] By the beginning of the 20th century, this philosopher's idealist abstractions had lost favour on the Left to more positivist interpretations of socialist theory.[39] But, when the old certainties in Europe collapsed under the impact of war and revolutions after 1914, there'd been a revival of interest in Hegel's theoretical concepts. As Marx had emphasised, dialectical reasoning was '... an abomination to the bourgeoisie and its doctrinaire spokesmen ... because it regards every historically developed [social] form as being in a fluid state ... and therefore grasps its transient aspect as well ...'[40] In his Geneva exile, Lenin had immersed himself in Hegel's *Logic* alongside Clausewitz's *On War* to understand the bewildering times of imperialist butchery within which he was then living.[41] Following the Bolsheviks' 1917 seizure of power, this esoteric philosophical position soon became the identifier of a distinct political identity. By downplaying the dialectic, the Social Democratic parties had abandoned their revolutionary heritage and prepared the way for their shameful collaboration with the slaughter of the trenches. Only by revitalising Marx with Hegel could the Left rediscover its emancipatory mission.[42]

---

[37]   See Karl Marx and Friedrich Engels, *The German Ideology*; and David McLellan, *The Young Hegelians*.

[38]   See Kent Worcester, *C.L.R. James*, pages 55–115; and Paul Buhle, 'Marxism in the USA'.

[39]   See Karl Kautsky, *The Class Struggle*; and Eduard Bernstein, *Evolutionary Socialism*.

[40]   Karl Marx, *Capital Volume 1*, page 103.

[41]   See V.I. Lenin, 'Conspectus of Hegel's book *The Science of Logic*'; 'The Collapse of the Second International'.

[42]   'The scientific theory of Marxism must become again what is was for the authors of the *Communist Manifesto* ... a theory of social revolution that comprises all areas of society as a totality.' Karl Korsch, *Marxism and Philosophy*, page 63.

During the 1920s, this theoretical synthesis became the leitmotif of the most iconoclastic intellectuals in Europe: György Lukács, Karl Korsch and Antonio Gramsci.[43] Even when Stalin temporarily recuperated dialectical materialism as the official ideology of Russian totalitarianism in 1938, Hegelian-Marxism had still retained its subversive potency.[44] Tellingly, for James and his Detroit comrades, it was their collective study of this philosophy of history during the 1940s that would enable them to escape from dogmatic Bolshevism.[45] As *The Black Jacobins* elucidated, the struggle for human emancipation hadn't begun with the 1917 storming of the Winter Palace in Petrograd. Although they continued to admire Lenin and Trotsky as revolutionary leaders, James' group now abandoned their former obsession with building the vanguard party. In its place, they focused their energies on preparing for the next explosive outbreak of popular sovereignty. From the Ancient Athenian agora through the Paris Sections to the Petrograd Soviet, the urban poor had repeatedly created socio-political institutions which allowed them collectively to run their own lives.[46] When the masses rose in revolt again, they would intuitively set up the modern expression of this instinctive desire for direct democracy: the workers' councils. In the past, the Left had formed vanguard parties because anti-capitalist activists were only a minority of the population. However, in the coming wave of social rebellion, it would be the overwhelming majority in their many millions who would carry out the radical transformation of society.[47] In 1940s Europe, the deadly

---

[43] See György Lukács, *History and Class Consciousness*; Karl Korsch, *Marxism and Philosophy*; and Antonio Gramsci, *Selections from the Prison Notebooks*.

[44] For this philosophical legerdemain, see Joseph Stalin, 'Dialectical and Historical Materialism'; and Loren Grahem, *Science, Philosophy and Human Behaviour in the Soviet Union*, pages 24–67.

[45] James and his comrades were searching for a smart theoretical analysis which could explain why the 'bureaucratic stranglers of the proletariat' now dominated the American Left's political parties and trade unions, see C.L.R. James, *Notes on Dialectics*, pages 181–184; and John McClendon, *C.L.R. James' Notes on Dialectics*, pages 181–238, 339–391.

[46] See C.L.R. James, 'Every Cook Can Govern'; *Notes on Dialectics*, pages 184–210.

[47] In 1950, he predicted that: '... from the beginning of the [imminent] social revolution, the proletariat *as a whole* will be organised to become the state and to manage production.' C.L.R. James, *State Capitalism and World Revolution*, page 56. Emphasis in original.

necessity to defeat Nazi Germany had almost banished such libertarian dreams from the political imagination. Fortunately, in their safe haven in faraway Detroit, James and his comrades were able to keep alive the theory of Hegelian-Marxism and the practice of Council Communism to pass on to the post-war generation of young subversives: the New Left. Most gratifyingly, within two decades, the hard work of this small study circle would be vindicated by the burgeoning tide of insurrectionary struggles that threatened the stability of the heartlands of the imperialist system. In May '68, the Bolshevik vanguard was finally made obsolete by the spontaneous eruption of popular sovereignty. The Hegelian dialectic of history had reasserted itself.[48]

At its 1962 Fifth Conference in Stockholm, the Situationist International decided to abandon avant-garde art for this modern expression of revolutionary politics. When they formulated their new position, Debord's faction was heavily influenced by their close association with the militants of *Socialisme ou Barbarie*. Like James and his Detroit comrades, these French socialists had also started out as Trotskyists who'd then begun to question the precepts of this Bolshevik heresy. Linking up with James and his comrades, they soon rediscovered the almost forgotten classics of 1920s libertarian communism.[49] Enthused by the 1956 Hungarian Revolution, this collaboration resulted in the publication of a prescient pamphlet: *Facing Reality*. Rejecting both Social Democracy and Bolshevism, its authors utilised Hegelian-Marxist theory to update the practice of Council Communism for the new Fordist dispensation. Political parties and trade unions had been recuperated into the bureaucratic hierarchies of consumer capitalism. The next upsurge of proletarian rebellion would reject these representative bodies in favour of the

---

[48] 'I know that [vanguard] parties are not necessary in [contemporary Europe] ... there are millions of people highly educated with fifty or a hundred years of practical experience behind them, so a party isn't necessary there [to lead them to communism].' C.L.R. James, 'Interviews', page 8.

[49] See Kent Worcester, *C.L.R. James*, pages 122–125, 139–140. For the story of *Socialisme ou Barbarie*, see Richard Gombin, *Les Origines du Gauchisme*, pages 127–151; and Arthur Hirsh, *The French Left*, pages 108–135.

self-management of all social institutions.[50] Taking their cue from James' Detroit experience, *Socialisme ou Barbarie* now primarily saw itself as a study circle and magazine publisher. The rule of the workers' councils could only be constituted once the revolutionary process was already underway. While waiting for this great day to arrive, the New Left had to resist the temptation to form vanguard parties which tried to impose their authority upon the class as a whole. As James had emphasised, the victory of the proletarian revolution required the participation of millions of people. Everyone must be involved in the building of the new society.[51]

Following the 1962 Stockholm scission, the Situationist International became enthusiastic propagandists for this heady combination of Hegelian-Marxist theory and Council Communist practice. In *The Society of the Spectacle*, Debord surpassed his mentors not only in his historical overview of the Left's squabbling political tendencies, but also in his denunciation of the solipsistic tedium of Fordist abundance. Best of all, after the May '68 French Revolution, his Situationist manifesto was widely praised for its intelligent anticipation of this unexpected outburst of participatory democracy. Yet, despite the blandishments of its newly acquired admirers, the Paris Section never expanded beyond a handful of members. Like James, Debord believed that the vanguard party was an anachronism in the late-20th century. Instead, the vital task of libertarian communists was to prepare the proletariat for its next spontaneous insurrection against spectacular capitalism.[52] By writing books, making films and designing games, Debord in his Auvergne exile demonstrated how James' politics could be put into practice even during the harder times of neoliberal ascendency in the 1970s and 1980s. Unlike many of his New Left peers, he never abandoned the subversive theory of Hegelian-Marxism for the elitist presumptions of semiotic

---

[50] See Grace Lee, Pierre Chalieu and J.R. Johnson, *Facing Reality*, pages 7–19. Also see Paul Cardan, *Modern Capitalism and Revolution*. Chalieu and Cardan were both pseudonyms of Cornelius Castoriadis who was the chief theoretician of *Socialisme ou Barbarie*. Johnson was James' political alias.

[51] See Paul Cardan, *Modern Capitalism and Revolution*, pages 91–95.

[52] See Guy Debord and Gianfranco Sanguinetti, *The Veritable Split in the International*, pages 67–71.

structuralism.[53] Above all, Debord argued that the recomposition of the working class under the integrated spectacle proved that there now was no credible alternative to the the the absolute rule of the workers' councils.[54] By unapologetically proclaiming this revolutionary analysis of modern society, the Situationists were providing their class with the theoretical and historical knowledge which would soon be used to carry out the radical transformation of everyday life: 'The *repressed* of the proletarian critique has come to light; it has acquired a memory and a language.'[55]

When we made our two ludic interventions at the *Invisible Forces* exhibition, Class Wargames was implementing Debord's politicisation of the historical imperative. Under the integrated spectacle, the enforced inability to imagine a better future was predicated upon the deliberate forgetting of the freedom struggles of the past. By playing the Austerlitz scenario of *The Game of War* and the battle of Fort Bedourete opening positions for *Commands & Colors: Napoleonics* at the Furtherfield gallery, Class Wargames was putting avant-garde art in the service of Situationist political propaganda. Fulfilling the aims of the second stage of our campaign of ludic subversion, the aesthetic pleasure of participating in these performances had become our interactive teaching tool. By re-enacting the revolutionary past on a game board, the competing teams were learning together about the hidden history which was depicted in Donkor's iconic painting. Emphasising Debord's intellectual debts to James and his Detroit comrades, our two ludic artworks challenged the neoliberal revisionists' erasure of the Haitian Jacobins from the academic chronicles.[56] As the 1793 *Festival of Reason* at Notre Dame celebrated, the oppressed of the South and the North had united, fought and won against their

---

[53] Back in the 1940s, James had also argued that Stalin's suspicion of Hegelian-Marxism exposed the Stalinist bureaucracy's fear of revolutionary social changes, see C.L.R. James, *Notes on Dialectics*, pages 98–106.

[54] See Guy Debord and Gianfranco Sanguinetti, *The Veritable Split in the International*, pages 13–34.

[55] Guy Debord and Gianfranco Sanguinetti, *The Veritable Split in the International*, page 14. Emphasis in original.

[56] Shamefully, there were no entries for Toussaint, Dessalines or Christophe in François Furet and Mona Ozouf, *A Critical Dictionary of the French Revolution*.

mutual enemy: the liberal bourgeoisie. Over two centuries later, the world outside the Furtherfield gallery in 2012 was being convulsed by a modern iteration of this global uprising against coercion and exploitation. By understanding what had happened in Toussaint's times through playing games, this new generation of dissidents could equip themselves with the accumulated combat experiences of their admirable forebears. Skilful generals must know how their opponents were once outsmarted.[57]

In *The Black Jacobins*, James had also drawn a parallel between the 1791 Haitian Revolution and the tumultuous events of his own lifetime. Like Bonaparte, Benito Mussolini – the Fascist dictator who instigated the Italian invasion of Ethiopia – was a renegade of the intransigent Left who'd traded his principles for power.[58] In his cruelty and crudeness, Dessalines was the prototype for Stalin's tyrannical rule over the Russian empire.[59] More than anything else, James identified the dramatic story of Toussaint with that of Trotsky. Most laudably, these two soldier politicians had successfully commanded the masses in their violent insurrection against the old social order. Unfortunately, they'd both also been Shakespearean tragic heroes who'd been brought down by their own personal flaws. Committing the same mistake as Trotsky, Toussaint had embraced the militarisation of politics. As the Governor-General for Life of Haiti, he'd centralised all decision-making into his own hands. Determined to rebuild the island's export economy, he'd ordered the former slaves back to work in the plantations as wage labourers. By the time that the French imperialists had invaded the island, Toussaint was facing widespread dissent amongst his own followers. Taking advantage of these internal divisions, the Bonapartists were able to depose, imprison and murder him. Like Trotsky in the 1920s, Toussaint had fallen from power because he didn't trust

---

57   See Class Wargames, 'Communiqué #9'; 'Communiqué #10'.

58   'We explain endlessly: fascism is Bonapartism. ...' C.L.R. James, *Notes on Dialectics*, page 177. For the Italian dictator's almost inevitable trajectory from one extreme of the political spectrum to the other, see Denis Mack Smith, *Mussolini*, pages 11–79; and Ernst Nolte, *Three Faces of Fascism*, pages 193–290.

59   See the close parallels in James' descriptions of these two dictators in *World Revolution*, pages 143–5; and *The Black Jacobins*, pages 289–377.

the masses. In Haiti as in Russia, the uniformed despots who then took control over the new state would build upon this authoritarian presumption to establish a vicious form of social domination.[60] By staging the 1802 battle of Fort Bedourete at the Furtherfield gallery, Class Wargames provided its ludic response to this sad tale of martyred heroes and lost opportunities. When everyone could play at being Toussaint, then no revolutionary leader would be irreplaceable.[61]

In his 1961 diatribe against French colonialism in Algeria, Frantz Fanon had championed an existentialist interpretation of Hegelian-Marxism for the anti-imperialist fighters of the South. The armed struggle was much more than a political strategy for overthrowing foreign rule. For Fanon, the oppressed must engage in revolutionary violence to rid themselves of their psychological submission to the oppressor. As Hegel had argued, the slaves could only live in a society without masters if they themselves were willing to risk death in combat.[62] Yet, two decades earlier, James in *The Black Jacobins* had already warned against the dangers of this fascination with militarised politics. Toussaint – like Trotsky – might have had the mental strength to hold fast to his revolutionary principles. However, Dessalines and Christophe – like Stalin – had succumbed to the bloodthirsty desire for absolute power. In Haiti as in Russia, the unquestioning loyalty required of soldiers on the battlefield was imposed upon every civilian of the new republic. The skilful generals had transformed themselves into revolutionary despots. Crucially, in *The Black Jacobins*, James argued that this military usurpation of the national liberation struggle wasn't inevitable. The impressive discipline of the Haitian citizen-soldiers had been learnt in the collective labour of the slave plantations. In contrast with their pre-industrial artisan, shopkeeper and peasant allies in France, they were modern proletarians who'd laboured in agricultural factories. Like the

---

[60] See C.L.R. James, *The Black Jacobins*, pages 224–288; and Kent Worcester, *C.L.R. James*, pages 36–42.

[61] See Class Wargames, 'Communiqué #9'; 'Communiqué #10'.

[62] See Frantz Fanon, *The Wretched of the Earth*, pages 27–84; *Towards the African Revolution*, pages 99–105, 144–149, 170–173.

workers of 1917 Petrograd, these Haitian rebels had also aspired to run their own lives collectively.[63] But, when they were prevented from democratically organising themselves by the post-independence ruling elite, their only alternative had been to become self-sufficient peasants. Although economically and ecologically disastrous in the long-run, the Haitian masses did temporarily succeed in winning a limited form of personal autonomy. The former slaves were now masters of their own small plots of land.[64]

By making parallels between the 1791 Haitian Revolution and the 1917 Russian Revolution, James was seeking a resolution of the conundrum of political leadership within participatory democracy. Back in 1872, Marx and his supporters had rejected Bakunin's vision of a conspiratorial elite directing the spontaneous rebellion of the masses against the established order. Instead, the Social Democrats dedicated themselves to building up the public institutions of the labour movement: the political party, trade unions and co-operatives. By pressing for social reforms in the short-term, these faithful Marxists believed that they were preparing for the communist revolution in the long-term. Workers were learning how to manage their own lives as party members, trade unionists and co-operative producers.[65] Yet, even before the disastrous collapse of this Social Democratic strategy in 1914, radical leftists had clearly identified its fatal flaws. Better organised than its constituents, the labour bureaucracy was much more interested in advancing its own interests within the existing system than risking everything to overthrow capitalism. For these salaried officials, reformism was an end in itself.[66] According to these questioners of orthodox Marxism, this

---

[63] See C.L.R. James, *The Black Jacobins*, pages 85–86, 392. Also see Aimé Césaire, *Toussaint Louverture*, page 34; and Robin Blackburn, *The Overthrow of Colonial Slavery*, pages 236–237.

[64] See David Nicholls, *From Dessalines to Duvalier*, pages 33–164; and Peter Hallward, *Damming the Flood*, pages 9–16.

[65] See Paul Thomas, *Karl Marx and the Anarchists*, pages 249–353; and Karl Kautsky, *The Class Struggle*.

[66] 'We now have a finely conservative [Social Democratic] party which ... continues to employ revolutionary terminology, but which in actual practice fulfils no other function than that of a constitutional opposition [to bourgeois rule].' Robert Michels, *Political Parties*, page 339. Also see Max Weber, *Essays in Sociology*, pages 196–244; and Eduard Bernstein, *Evolutionary Socialism*.

recuperation of socialist subversion was underpinned by the hegemony of bourgeois ideology over the proletariat. Trapped within capitalist social relations, ordinary people couldn't conceive of radically different ways of conducting politics or creating wealth. Their pragmatic vision of collective emancipation went no further than universal suffrage, higher wages and increased welfare spending. For them, the communist future was nothing more than a pious hope.[67]

In the immediate aftermath of the First World War, the charismatic leader and the vanguard party were both proclaimed as the modern antidotes to the passivity of the masses within industrial society. In 1920s Italy, defectors from Social Democracy and Anarchism hailed Mussolini as the longings of the people incarnated in a single person. Sweeping away the sordid comprises of parliamentary politics, this Fascist dictator was imposing his unflinching will upon the public and private bureaucracies which determined the nation's existence.[68] Similarly, in 1920s Russia, the Bolsheviks declared that the vanguard party was the anticipation of the imaginary future in the present. Enlightened by Lenin's doctrine, the totalitarian state would free the masses from the mystifications of bourgeois ideology and then lead them in the construction of the communist cornucopia.[69] But, by the time that James wrote *The Black Jacobins* in the late-1930s, both of these alternatives to Social Democracy had been discredited. Far from breaking with bureaucratic rule, the totalitarian regimes of Fascist Italy and Stalinist Russia were implementing the latest manifestation of bourgeois society: state capitalism. Following the implosion of the world market in 1914, all nations in the mid-20th century had been

---

[67] See V.I. Lenin, *What Is To Be Done?*; and Lars Lih, *Lenin*, pages 52–83.

[68] '... when Mussolini speaks, he translates into a naked and brilliant form the aims of the multitude. The multitude itself frantically acclaims [the charismatic leader], answering from the profundity of its own moral beliefs ...' Robert Michels, *First Lectures in Political Sociology*, page 126. Also see A. James Gregor, *Mussolini's Intellectuals*, pages 120–122, 148–155; and Max Weber, *Essays in Sociology*, pages 245–252.

[69] See Leon Trotsky, 'Theses on the Conditions of Admission to the Communist International'; and György Lukács, *History and Class Consciousness*, pages 295–342.

forced to adopt some variant of this autarchic system.[70] Ironically, as Debord later emphasised in *The Society of the Spectacle*, it was the Social Democrats who would prove to be the most sophisticated practitioners of this Fordist stage of capitalism. As advocates of one party dictatorship, both Fascists and Bolsheviks epitomised the less developed form of this new dispensation: the concentrated spectacle. In contrast, by combining political democracy with the mixed economy, their Social Democratic rivals were able to create a more progressive form of capitalist domination: the diffuse spectacle. In 1950s Europe, when forced to choose between West and East in the Cold War, the survivors of 1920s Council Communism had no hesitation in siding with the Social Democrats against the Stalinists. As Marx had prophecised, the proletarian revolution would take place first in the most advanced capitalist nations. In Cold War Europe, the West was undoubtedly the lesser evil.[71]

Like these 1920s veterans, by embracing the revolutionary zeal of Council Communism, the Situationist International at its 1962 Stockholm Conference had also tacitly accepted the reformist compromises of Social Democracy. Paradoxically, the deep political differences between these parliamentary and anti-parliamentary currents within the Left masked their common theoretical assumptions. For the acolytes of Lenin, Trotsky and Stalin, the overthrow of capitalism was a subjective act of political will that was carried out by the vanguard party. If the proletarian revolution hadn't yet taken place in a country, what was missing was the hardened nucleus of warrior intellectuals which could accomplish this world-historical task.[72] Rejecting this Bolshevik concept of voluntarist politics, Karl Kautsky – the intellectual champion of orthodox Marxism – had reaffirmed the programmatic outcome of the 1872 split between the Social

---

[70]　See C.L.R. James, *State Capitalism and World Revolution*, pages 1–54; 'Russia – a Fascist State'; and C.L.R. James, F.Forest and Ria Stone, *The Invading Socialist Society*, pages 23–32.

[71]　See Anton Pannekoek, *Workers' Councils*, pages 205–231; and International Communist Current, *The Dutch and German Communist Left*, pages 355–356.

[72]　See Grigory Zinoviev, 'The Role of the Communist Party in Proletarian Revolution'; and Leon Trotsky, *The Transitional Programme*, pages 11–14.

Democrats and the Anarchists within the European labour movement. While agitating for the liberation of humanity from oppression, the Left must always be acutely aware that its ambitions were limited by the objective circumstances within which it found itself.[73] As Marx had argued, capitalism could not be superseded until its progressive possibilities had been completely exhausted.[74] By campaigning for reforms in the present, Social Democrats were hastening the arrival of communist future. However, even with the most fervent ideological commitment, it was impossible to escape from capitalist exploitation until the time was right. If they understood Marx's grand narrative of history correctly, all Marxists must be socio-economic determinists. Their subjective desire for libertarian communism required the objective preconditions for proletarian emancipation. The Russian tragedy was a terrible warning to those who thought otherwise. By trying to leap over the objective historical circumstances by an act of subjective will in 1917, the Bolsheviks had created a monstrous state capitalist tyranny. The victory of the premature socialist revolution was a disastrous defeat.[75]

Opting to collaborate with the American empire at the outbreak of the Cold War, Social Democrats in 1950s Western Europe quickly shed their formal adherence to orthodox Marxism. In theory as well as practice, reforming capitalism had now become their only ambition.[76] Ironically, after the May '68 uprising, it was the left of the New Left that would revive the strategic wisdom of Marx's followers in the 1872 split. Through single issue campaigns, social movements and community media, the libertarian future could now be prefigured in

---

[73] See Karl Kautsky, *The Dictatorship of the Proletariat*, pages 1–58; *The Materialist Conception of History*, pages 450–464.

[74] 'No social order is ever destroyed before all the productive forces for which it is sufficient have been developed, and new superior relations of production never replace older ones before the material conditions for their existence have matured within the framework of the old society.' Karl Marx, *A Contribution to the Critique of Political Economy*, page 21.

[75] See Karl Kautsky, *The Dictatorship of the Proletariat*, pages 135–149; 'The Lessons of the October Experiment'.

[76] See Social Democratic Party, 'Basic Programme of the Social Democratic Party of Germany'; and Anthony Crosland, *The Future of Socialism*.

the capitalist present.[77] By the 1980s, these New Left activists were being recuperated within the institutions of the old parliamentary Left. As the years passed, they too would lose faith in the imminent arrival of the communist utopia. Slowly but surely, their adherence to Marxist fatalism transformed their interpretation of the Hegelian end of history into a more enlightened and pluralist version of neoliberal globalisation.[78] In contrast, exiled in the French countryside, Debord stubbornly refused to capitulate to the new orthodoxy. Like James in the 1940s, this Situationist veteran ruthlessly criticised the delusions of the competing factions of the European Left. Confirming his deterministic version of Hegelian-Marxism, their attempts to prefigure the self-managed future in the present had been inevitably recuperated. The proletarian institutions which would sweep away the integrated spectacle could only be built once the cataclysmic transformation of human society was already taking place for real. Until this world-historical moment arrived, the stoical duty of libertarian communists was to prepare for the spontaneous uprising which would bring the workers' councils to undisputed power: 'When the revolution is still far off, the difficult task of the revolutionary organisation is above all [the] *practice of theory*. [Only] when the revolution begins, its difficult task, more and more, is [the] *theory of practice*.'[79] Patience was a Situationist virtue.

Enthused by this insight, with our two interventions for the Invisible Forces exhibition at the Furtherfield gallery, Class Wargames embarked on a new phase of our campaign of ludic subversion against spectacular capitalism. Back in 2007, in the first stage of this assault, we'd started out performing *The Game of War* as the Situationist retort to the elitist pretensions of avant-garde art. By moving its pieces across the board, everyone was able to engage in participatory creativity. Inspired by our visit to *Cyberfest 2008* in St Petersburg, we soon became more interested

---

[77]   See George Katsiaficas, *The Imagination of the New Left*, pages 177–256; and Félix Guattari, *The Molecular Revolution*, pages 175–287.

[78]   See Michel Rocard, *À l'Épreuve des Faits*; and Stuart Hall and Martin Jacques, *New Times*.

[79]   Guy Debord and Gianfranco Sanguinetti, *The Veritable Split in the International*, page 68. Emphasis in the original. For the 21ˢᵗ century update of this Situationist analysis, see R.S., 'The Present Moment.'

in *The Game of War* as the Situationist antidote to the authoritarian assumptions of vanguard politics. In this second phase of our campaign of ludic subversion, we proclaimed that – when everyone was playing at being a little Lenin, Trotsky and Stalin – then nobody could become the Bolshevik dictator who oppressed the proletariat. By 2012, our understanding of *The Game of War* had deepened even further. After five years of hosting events on three continents, we were now ready to answer the key conundrum of why Debord firmly believed that this ludic invention was his greatest achievement. According to his hagiographers, the maximum leader of Situationism was just being facetious. For them, Debord's legacy must be his leftfield artworks, writings and films. At the very most, *The Game of War* was an eccentric homage to Duchamp's *Chess* obsession or a frivolous distraction made for his rural retirement. Playing military simulations might be an entertaining leisure activity, but it had no political importance for grown-up revolutionaries. Under spectacular capitalism, ludic subversion was a contradiction in terms.

At the Furtherfield gallery, Class Wargames took pleasure in refuting this snobbish assumption. After five years of active service in the field, Class Wargames could now explain why Debord's *The Game of War* was designed as a Clausewitz simulator. This mock battle was much more than an avant-garde artwork promoting Situationist ideas. For Debord, his ludic invention was a political solution for the dangerous problem of charismatic leadership within the proletarian revolution. During that summer of 2012, mass spontaneous uprisings against neoliberal austerity were taking place across the world. From Athens and Madrid to New York and Cairo, the boosters of these Occupy movements argued that a horizontal form of networked politics was now emerging to replace the corrupt hierarchical structures of the Social Democratic and Bolshevik parties. But, like the militants of May '68 before them, they too would soon discover that their leaderless revolution had produced its own unaccountable leaders. Within this new iteration of the New Left, Anarchists stubbornly denied the existence of the reborn invisible dictatorship while Autonomists loudly advocated their own hi-tech version of the Bolshevik vanguard. As the political and economic crisis worsened, growing popular support for a radical break with neoliberalism also encouraged other anti-capitalist activists to enter the electoral arena. With their elders' timid reformism discredited, this new generation of Social Democrats had rediscovered the more hardline parliamentary strategy of orthodox Marxism.[80] Ironically, the early-21st century's explosion of participatory politics had quickly turned into the Left's renewed commitment to representative politics in its multiple manifestations. Libertarian communism was still an imaginary future within the perpetual present.

For Debord, the rapid recuperation of the 2010s Occupy movements would have come as no surprise. Four decades earlier, he had observed the domestication of the New Left after the May '68 uprising with disdain. In non-revolutionary times, politics always remained the specialist activity of the privileged few. Spontaneous acts of rebellion were only brief premonitions of the coming hegemony of the workers' councils. Until this world-historical moment arrived, the hard duty of the Situationists was to provide the proletariat as a whole with both the practical skills and the theoretical understanding which would be required for successfully smashing the integrated spectacle.[81] In contrast, whether overtly or covertly, the Social Democratic, Anarchist, Bolshevik and Autonomist sects all assumed that only a self-selected minority was capable of fulfilling the vital task of guiding this fundamental transformation of modern society. As James had argued, the insurgent masses would inevitably elevate from their midst the revolutionary tribunes who could express their own emancipatory desires.[82] But, as Donkor's stunning painting reminded visitors to the Furtherfield gallery, the people's trust in these skilful generals had been disappointed again and again. Fortunately, Debord had an inspired solution to this intractable obstacle to human progress. By playing Situationist games, the millions of rank-and-file workers could now learn how to lead themselves in the collective struggle for libertarian communism. Ludic artworks were now dedicated to the service of the

---

[80] See Eric Olin Wright , 'Class Struggle and Class Compromise in an Era of Stagnation and Crisis'; and Christosforos Vernardakis, 'The Greek Left in the 2012 Elections'.

[81] 'The theory of revolution is judged by this sole criterion that its *knowledge* must become a *power*.' Guy Debord and Gianfranco Sanguinetti, *The Veritable Split in the International*, page 69. Emphasis in the original.

[82] '[The] ... people ... produced from themselves and their own resources the great body of leaders.' C.L.R. James, *Kwame Nkrumah and the Ghana Revolution*, page 61.

proletarian revolution. Like the 2008 performance of *Reds versus Reds* at the Winter Palace, we'd devised our 2012 détournement of *Commands & Colors: Napoleonics* as an interactive lesson in insurrectionary history. More importantly, having commenced the third phase of our campaign of ludic subversion, we also presented this simulation as an immersive exercise in military theory. By re-enacting the 1802 battle of Fort Bedourete, the Haitian and French teams were acquiring the virtuoso attributes of the skilful general in a simplified form. On that summer's day in the Furtherfield gallery, the Bonapartists had prevailed because they were better at maximising the destructive capabilities of their forces than their Jacobin opponents. Crucially, Class Wargames had discovered this practical application of ludic subversion through repeatedly playing *The Game of War*. By fighting the Marengo and Austerlitz scenarios, the participants at our performances were now able to learn the strategic and tactical insights derived from Clausewitz's writings built into Debord's simulation. After five years of frenetic activities, we'd finally understood why *The Game of War* was his greatest achievement: it was the Situationist cure for the oligarchical recuperation of participatory democracy. When every proletarian knew how to be a military captain, then revolutionary leadership could be exercised by the entire class.[83] In this third stage of our campaign of ludic subversion, Debord's Clausewitz simulator was teaching its leftist players to become like '... the ... adventurous ... general who understands and decides as much with instinct as with the available information ... [whose] genius and inspiration ... indicates a higher level of intellectual activity.'[84]

---

[83]   See Class Wargames, 'Communiqué #9'; 'Communiqué #10'.

[84]   Carl von Clausewitz, *Campagne de 1799 en Suisse et en Italie*, page 42.

3.3: THE CRAFT OF WARGAMING

During his Auvergne exile in the 1970s, Debord had pursued the two parallel and intertwined projects of book publishing and game development which were both inspired by the Napoleonic era. For the first part of this plan, he'd begun by persuading Lebovici to commission a new and improved French translation of Clausewitz's masterpiece: *On War*. He also arranged for their company to reprint this Prussian soldier's campaign chronologies as well as Bonaparte's maxims and Charles Napier's account of the 1809 Corunna operation. In contrast with the other left-wing publishers in 1970s France, Champ Libre stood out because its catalogue prominently featured classic texts of military theory and military history.[85] For the second half of this mission, Debord devoted his energies to completing *The Game of War*. In collaboration with Lebovici, he carefully planned the promotional campaign for his ludic masterpiece. Champ Libre published the players' manual which he'd written in collaboration with Becker-Ho. The gold-and-silver metal board and pieces provided iconic images for his *In Girum Imus Nocte* film. Just before Lebovici's murder ruined everything, Debord had been preparing the release of a cardboard version of his game for the mass market. Every Situationist admirer must be able to learn Clausewitz's military theory by playing *The Game of War* at their local bohemian cafés and workers' bars.

Revealingly, Debord described his new creation as a modern stripped-down version of *Kriegspiel*. By using this misspelt German term, he was endowing *The Game of War* with an illustrious historical pedigree.[86] According to the authoritative accounts, the ancestor of both professional and hobbyist wargaming was an early-19th century Prussian military simulation: *Kriegsspiel*.[87] First invented by Georg von Reisswitz in 1812 and then perfected by his son and namesake

---

85 For Champ Libre's publications, see Éditions Ivrea, 'Catalogue'. Also see Len Bracken, *Guy Debord*, pages 215–217; and Anselm Jappe, *Guy Debord*, page 114.

86 See Guy Debord, 'À Gérard Lebovici 24 Mai 1976'; and *Panegyric*, pages 63–7. Anticipating Debord, H.G. Wells had the same misspelling of *Kriegsspiel* in the subtitle of his *Little Wars* book.

87 See Peter Perla, *The Art of Wargaming*, pages 23–30; and Charles Grant, *The War Game*, page 15.

during the 1820s, this miniature version of Horse-and-Musket warfare was designed to teach and perfect the skills of ordering troops on the battlefield without the necessity of holding expensive field manoeuvres. When the younger von Reisswitz put on a demonstration of *Kriegsspiel* for the Prussian high command in 1824, the initially sceptical Chief of the General Staff exclaimed with enthusiasm at the end of the session: 'This is not a game, this is a war exercise! I must recommend it to the whole army!'[88]

What had made *Kriegsspiel* so distinctive on that Berlin evening was its abandonment of the mechanics of *Chess*. Long ago in 6th century South Asia, this board game had also started out as a military training exercise. The squared grid symbolised the open field where the two opposing feudal hosts had agreed to do battle with each other. The pieces represented the different types of troops who'd fought in the South Asian despots' armies: infantry, marines, cavalry and elephants.[89] However, gradually over time, the practical purposes of *Chess* were eclipsed by its intellectual pleasures. Inside the Arab and European courts of the medieval period, this military simulation was domesticated and feminised. For warrior aristocrats and their paramours, *Chess* now became '... the [poetic] metaphor of choice for the etiquette of lovers.'[90] With the queen as its most powerful piece, this ancient game had long ceased to be a teacher of the skills of generalship. In his 16th century Italian handbook for ambitious courtiers, Baldesar Castiglione warned against playing *Chess* too well in case it betrayed an unhealthy interest in frivolous matters. Serious people knew that board games were for relaxation not elucidation.[91]

Since medieval times, there'd been successive attempts to return *Chess* to its military origins. New pieces were added and different boards were devised, but these variants always retained the original's basic mechanics: perfect information about the opponent's deployment,

---

[88] Karl von Müffling in Bill Leeson, 'Origins of the Kriegsspiel'.

[89] See Richard Eales, *Chess*, pages 19–38.

[90] Marilyn Yalom, *Birth of the Chess Queen*, page 123. Also see Richard Eales, *Chess*, pages 38–70; and Class Wargames, 'Communiqué #6.

[91] See Baldesar Castiglione, *The Book of the Courtier*, pages 140–141.

moving only one piece at a time and combat as instant elimination.[92] The elder von Reisswitz's brilliant idea was to break completely with the *Chess* engine. Instead, he took his inspiration from the wartime experience of staff officers in their headquarters directing troops on the battlefield. Famously, Bonaparte had coordinated his army corps in devastating onslaughts against the enemy's forces by moving pins symbolising each unit across campaign maps.[93] But, by the time that the younger von Reisswitz demonstrated *Kriegspiel* to the Prussian General Staff, Europe was more or less at peace. It was now very difficult for its officers to receive the exhilarating on-the-job training that had transformed Bonaparte into the military master of the continent. Unable to fight real wars, von Reisswitz proposed that they instead should play his wargame. By training hard with *Kriegsspiel*, the Prussian General Staff would be at the peak of combat readiness when hostilities next recommenced in Europe.[94]

In its conception, von Reisswitz's game was an indoor version of tactical exercises without troops. Rather than officers riding across the countryside imagining where their regiments might attack or defend, *Kriegsspiel* simulated the look and feel of a staff headquarters at war. The two sides were placed in different rooms with maps which initially only showed the deployment of their own troops. Their pieces were divided into the infantry, cavalry and artillery units of a typical early-19th century army. Under the supervision of umpires, the rival teams ordered these forces forward until contact was made with the enemy. The complex rules of *Kriegsspiel* simulated the full-range of military activities: moving in column and line, crossing rivers, skirmishing, musket fire, artillery bombardments, hand-to-hand combat, fighting in towns, taking prisoners, retreating in panic and following up a victory. Special dice were thrown to calculate the casualties inflicted by different types of weaponry.[95] Within the safe environment of *Kriegsspiel*, the Prussian General Staff was now able by proxy to

---

[92] See Alfred Hausrath, *Venture Simulations in War, Business and Politics*, pages 3–5; Peter Perla, *The Art of Wargaming*, pages 16–19; and Andrew Wilson, *The Bomb and the Computer*, pages 2–3.

[93] See Jean-Baptiste Vachée, *Napoleon at Work*, pages 67–73.

[94] See Peter Perla, *The Art of Wargaming*, pages 25–30.

[95] See Georg von Reisswitz, *Kriegsspiel*.

experience the discord and unpredictability of war. As their miniature units moved across its maps, its officers were transforming themselves into the new Bonapartes of Europe.

In 1866, the potency of *Kriegsspiel* for the planning of military operations was dramatically confirmed by the crushing Prussian victory over the Austrians at the battle of Königgrätz. The skills acquired on map manoeuvres had given the edge to the players of von Reisswitz's game in this deadly confrontation. Not surprisingly, following the Prussian triumph at Königgrätz, armies across the world quickly introduced *Kriegsspiel* into their own military training programmes.[96] Crucially, for the new generation of professional officers, these simulations also became predictions of a future European conflagration as the long peace of the 19th century drew to a close. Echoing the popular invasion fantasy books of the period, their games speculated about the major powers engaging in a ferocious Napoleonic struggle for absolute hegemony over the continent.[97] It was by repeatedly playing simulations of a two-front war against both France and Russia that the German General Staff decided to concentrate their forces first in the West and – with this opponent defeated – then turn them on their adversary in the East: the Schlieffen Plan. After gaming its own version of this scenario, the British General Staff persuaded its political paymasters to make a formal alliance with France to prevent the military power of Berlin threatening London from the other side of the English Channel. *Kriegsspiel* was playing the future in the present.[98]

When the First World War broke out in 1914, what had first been simulated in military training exercises was now implemented for real with disastrous results. Far from delivering a quick victory in the West, the Schlieffen Plan resulted in the long stalemate of trench warfare which culminated in a humiliating defeat for Germany. Instead of

---

[96] See Peter Perla, *The Art of Wargaming*, pages 30–34; and Andrew Wilson, *The Bomb and the Computer*, pages 6–14.

[97] See I.F. Clarke, '*Dorking* Revisited'. In *The War of the Worlds*, H.G. Wells added a science fiction twist to this fashionable theme by replacing the Germans with Martians as the invaders of England.

[98] See Andrew Wilson, *The Bomb and the Computer*, pages 17–26; and Peter Perla, *The Art of Wargaming*, page 41 .

securing its global empire, Britain's military intervention into this continental conflict drained so much of the country's wealth and power that the USA emerged as the top nation on the planet by the end of the fighting. The seductive predictions of *Kriegsspiel* had proved to be false prophecies.[99] Despite these disappointments, admirals and generals still retained their enthusiasm for military planning with wargames. During the 1920s and 1930s, the US navy played detailed simulations to test out its plans for fighting against the British or Japanese fleets. Over in the East, the leaders of the Red Army devised the defence-in-depth strategy which would deliver victory in the next war by conducting exercises which experimented with different responses to an invasion of Bolshevik Russia from the West.[100] Above all, the German military kept faith with the predictive powers of *Kriegsspiel*. In 1940, its generals were able to discover the route through the Ardennes which led to victory over France through repeatedly playing wargames of this forthcoming confrontation.[101] Four years later, when the tables had been turned, the German General Staff was participating in a simulation of the expected Anglo-American crossing of the Rhine when suddenly news arrived that the Allies were making a probing attack nearby.[102] Switching from fantasy to reality, these officers now returned to playing the wargame which they couldn't possibly win. Before another year was out, Germany had gone down to an even more disastrous defeat as its battered forces were overwhelmed by double-pincer attacks from both the West and the East. Clever gaming tactics couldn't compensate for Hitler's self-destructive geopolitical strategy.

By the end of the Second World War, the peoples of Europe knew from bitter experience that German militarism was the most viciously reactionary political ideology on the continent. Yet, only a century and a half earlier, patriotic Prussian officers like Clausewitz were in the vanguard of their country's reform movement. The old fighting

---

99 For the horrific human and material costs of the First World War, see Eric Hobsbawm, *Age of Extremes*, pages 21–35.

100 See Peter Perla, *The Art of Wargaming*, pages 70–76; and Jacob Kipp, 'Soviet Military Doctrine and the Origins of Operational Art', pages 110–114.

101 See Heinz Guderian, *Panzer Leader*, pages 90–92.

102 See Peter Perla, *The Art of Wargaming*, page 44; and Thomas Allen, *War Games*, page 129.

methods of the absolute monarchy had been discredited by defeat after defeat on the battlefield. If French domination was to be thwarted, the Prussian army would have to be modernised along French lines. Motivated citizens made better soldiers than brutalised mercenaries. Talent not birth should decide who became an officer. Above all, the commander-in-chief of the army must be its most skilful general rather than a royal flunky. In 1806, the immigrant artillery corporal who'd been elevated into the emperor of the French starkly exposed the military deficiencies of a political system based upon inherited privilege and smug ignorance. At the battle of Jena-Auerstädt, squabbling generals, obsolete tactics and meddling courtiers had doomed the Prussian cause. Like other nationalistic officers, Clausewitz understood that political reform was now the precondition for reversing this military debacle. The Prussian state could only beat Bonaparte by becoming Bonapartist itself.[103]

In the aftermath of Jena-Auerstädt, Clausewitz and his allies argued for two key innovations: the detailed education of officers and the mass mobilisation of citizen-soldiers. Not surprisingly, reactionaries at court denounced these liberal supporters of army modernisation as closet Jacobins. The professionalisation of the officer corps would weaken the aristocracy's preeminence over state institutions. The universalisation of military service could presage the democratisation of political power. Throughout his career, Clausewitz stayed a dissident within the Prussian military establishment.[104] Most notably, in 1812, he'd opted to fight with the Russians against Bonaparte whose invading army included a large contingent of troops supplied by his own king. Being a liberal, Clausewitz's sense of patriotism was defined by loyalty to the nation before the monarchy.[105] Over the next three years, his scandalous defection was vindicated as the Prussian army first switched sides and then took a leading role in the military annihilation of Bonaparte's empire. However, Clausewitz would always remain politically suspect for being prematurely correct. Fortunately, when peace was restored,

---

[103] See Carl von Clausewitz, *Notes sur la Prusse dans sa Grande Catastrophe 1806*, pages 3–47. Also see Peter Paret, *Clausewitz and the State*, pages 98–136; and Beatrice Heuser, *Reading Clausewitz*, pages 26–27, 50–52.

[104] See Peter Paret, *Clausewitz and the State*, pages 123–146, 288–292.

[105] See Peter Paret, *Clausewitz and the State*, pages 166–168, 209–228.

he was able to focus his energies on improving the education of young officers. Like his *Whist* partner Hegel, Clausewitz also wanted the Prussia state to be administered by an enlightened oligarchy of public servants. Both the fervent admirer and the bitter enemy of Bonaparte were agreed that bourgeois meritocracy provided the third way between the two political extremes of the 1789 French Revolution: levelling democracy and aristocratic privilege.[106]

As a military instructor, Clausewitz emphasised that leadership within the army was a skill that had to be learnt not only in the field, but also in the classroom. The popularity of *Kriegsspiel* within the Prussian officer corps exemplified the success of Clausewitz's progressive pedagogy. In contrast with their peers elsewhere, these peacetime soldiers were playing wargames as a training exercise for fighting wars. Using the insights of *Kriegsspiel*, they were carrying out strategic analyses which would enable them to defeat their nation's rivals. Although none of them had the individual brilliance of Bonaparte, these educated and meritocratic officers had created their own collective version of this genius general: the Prussian General Staff. In 1820s Berlin, Clausewitz became the intellectual mentor of this modernising state institution.[107] He wrote a series of fascinating campaign histories which elucidated the political imperatives and military options of the Napoleonic wars. By placing themselves in the commander-in-chief's position, his readers could study the successes and reverses of past conflicts to understand how to put these lessons into practice themselves. As in *Kriegsspiel*, re-enacting these historical engagements was making preparations for future conflicts.[108]

During his time at the Berlin academy, Clausewitz worked hard on his famous philosophical and practical meditation upon the 1789 French Revolution's radical transformation of military violence: *On War*. Like many German liberal intellectuals, he looked to dialectical

---

[106] See Peter Paret, *Clausewitz and the State*, pages 286–306.

[107] See Peter Paret, *Clausewitz and the State*, pages 270–285; and Beatrice Heuser, *Reading Clausewitz*, pages 12–13.

[108] See Carl von Clausewitz, *On War*, pages 162–163, 181–204. Also see Peter Paret, *Clausewitz and the State*, pages 307–355.

theory to unlock the secrets of the turbulent events of his times. For Clausewitz, the abstract concept of Absolute War provided his way into understanding the confusing practicalities of Limited War. Back in the mid-18th century, the European powers had ruthlessly struggled against each other for territory and prestige. However, possessing only small professional armies, they'd always been forced to curb their imperial ambitions. In this exemplar, Limited War was an aristocratic game with fixed rules and rigid conventions.[109] As the ideologue of the Prussian General Staff, Clausewitz's task was to explain why the storming of the Bastille brought this brief civilised interlude to a sudden end. In 1792, by mobilising the masses to defend the nation, the French republic had unleashed the martial energy of Absolute War upon the continent.[110] Fulfilling Rousseau's predictions, its citizen-soldiers quickly learnt how to overcome the mercenary troops of the old order. Composed of politicised volunteers, the French republic's army dreamt of liberating the whole of Europe from monarchical tyranny. Intoxicated with ideological fervour, these Jacobin warriors were endowed with the essential weapon for winning the opening round of this Absolute War: high morale.[111]

In his canonical text, Clausewitz argued that the strength of the modern nation-state was now measured by a new secular trinity: the army, the government and the people. When combined together effectively, political leaders were able to utilise military violence to realise their territorial and ideological ambitions.[112] As the armed prophet of the 1789 French Revolution, Bonaparte had perfected the cutting-edge strategy for Absolute War: the concentration of forces to win the decisive battle which utterly destroyed his opponent's main army. Once he'd achieved military superiority, this skilful general then occupied the enemy's capital city and dictated the terms of a humiliating peace

---

[109] See Carl von Clausewitz, *On War*, pages 738–745. Also see Peter Paret, *Clausewitz and the State*, pages 24–29.

[110] See Carl von Clausewitz, *On War*, pages 700–725. Also see Beatrice Heuser, *Reading Clausewitz*, pages 24–29.

[111] See Carl von Clausewitz, *On War*, pages 216–227.

[112] See Carl von Clausewitz, *On War*, page 101. Also see Beatrice Heuser, *Reading Clausewitz*, pages 52–56.

treaty.[113] During the 1806 Jena-Auerstädt campaign, Clausewitz had witnessed the effectiveness of this revolutionary method of fighting wars at first hand. Being a leading military reformer, he argued that the Prussian state must imitate the meritocratic and equalitarian ethos of Bonaparte's army: promotion by talent and mass conscription. Above all, he stressed that this rejuvenation of military power must also be accompanied by the renewal of the nation's political culture. The destruction of French hegemony over Europe required what the Prussian state had so obviously lacked in 1806: determined leadership from above and popular support from below. The fate of soldiers on the battlefield was determined by the attitudes of civilians in their homeland.[114]

When he wrote *On War*, Clausewitz was reflecting on his own dramatic experiences during the Napoleonic wars. In 1812, he'd been there when the deadly of combination of the Tsar's obstinacy and the peasantry's hostility had doomed the French invasion of Russia.[115] During 1813–4, he'd fought alongside the volunteer militias who had sparked off the national uprising against the French occupation of Germany.[116] In his masterpiece, Clausewitz explained why destroying Bonaparte had meant becoming like Bonaparte. In both 1814 and 1815, the methods of Absolute War were turned against their greatest practitioner. Uniting against the common enemy, the European powers had relentlessly pursued the upstart emperor until his army was destroyed and his capital city was occupied. After two decades of bloody conflict, a political peace was finally imposed upon France through overwhelming military force.[117] For Clausewitz, the downfall of Bonaparte had been a historical moment that provided theoretical illumination. The cruelty and chaos of armed combat had resulted in

---

[113] See Carl von Clausewitz, *On War*, pages 265–321, 700–703. Also see Jean-Baptiste Vachée, *Napoleon at Work*, page 128, 160–178.

[114] See Charles Esdaile, *The Wars of Napoleon*, pages 182–216.

[115] See Carl von Clausewitz, *The Campaign of 1812 in Russia*. Also see Peter Paret, *Clausewitz and the State*, pages 222–254.

[116] These citizen-soldiers were more of a political than military threat to the Napoleonic imperial system, see Daniel Moran, 'Arms and the Concert'.

[117] For his account of the destruction of Bonaparte's empire, see Carl von Clausewitz, *Campagne de 1814*; and *Campagne de 1815 en France*.

the establishment of a stable constitutional settlement in Europe. In what would become his most famous phrase, Clausewitz revealed the rationality of power within the irrationality of violence: ' ... war ... is a continuation of political intercourse, carried on with other means.'[118]

On 26th November 1812, the two greatest military theorists of the Napoleonic era had faced each other in battle on opposite banks of the Berezina river in Belarus. Amongst the pursuing Russian army, Clausewitz was serving as a staff officer in the Tsar's crusade against the heathen invaders. On the far side of river with the bedraggled remnants of the retreating French army was a Swiss soldier who was an aide-de-camp to one of Bonaparte's marshals: Antoine-Henri Jomini.[119] Although they'd never meet in person, these two intellectuals in uniform would over the next few decades become the gurus of rival pedagogies within the army academies. In *On War*, Clausewitz emphasised that military theory was a conceptual toolbox to analyse the social and political implications of military history.[120] Absolute War was an abstract formula which could never be fully realisable in practice. Even the skilful general with enthusiastic troops could find his most brilliant plans going awry due to circumstances beyond his control. Political ambitions were always being frustrated by the 'friction' of war.[121] According to Clausewitz, the purpose of dialectical theory was pragmatic. In military history, all wars were more or less Limited Wars. Yet, only the abstract concept of Absolute War allowed the warrior intellectual to understand the rational strategy and tactics which had enabled one side to triumph in these eruptions of armed violence. From this theoretical insight, Clausewitz was able to draw practical conclusions for his pupils at the Berlin academy. Whether playing *Kriegsspiel* or fighting on campaign, these Prussian officers could use his dialectical philosophy to discover the best solutions for resolving

---

[118] Carl von Clausewitz, *On War*, page 99. Also see Beatrice Heuser, *Reading Clausewitz*, pages 33–41.

[119] See Christopher Bassford, 'Jomini and Clausewitz', page 5. Clausewitz gave his own account of this battle in *The Campaign of 1812 in Russia*, pages 206–212. Also see Adam Zamoyski, *1812*, pages 458–480.

[120] See Carl von Clausewitz, *On War*, pages 153–171, 181–198.

[121] 'War ... is movement through a thick medium.' Carl von Clausewitz, *The Campaign of 1812 in Russia*, page 185. Also see Carl von Clausewitz, *On War*, pages 138–140.

practical military problems: establishing lines of communications, positioning arsenals, defending mountain passes and, last but not least, crossing rivers. As Clausewitz's *On War* explained, these geographical obstacles weakened the defender more than the attacker because its forces were dispersed to cover multiple bridges and fords.[122] At that 1812 engagement on the Berezina, Clausewitz watched his theory become reality as Jomini and the rest of the French army had escaped from the encircling Russian forces. Much to the chagrin of this Prussian patriot, Bonaparte had survived to fight another day.[123]

When peace eventually came, Jomini was able to write his best-selling instruction manual which systematised the strategical and tactical innovations of the Napoleonic period: *The Art of War*. In contrast with Clausewitz, he wasn't much interested in the political and social reasons why the nations of Europe had been involved in such destructive armed conflicts with each other.[124] Instead, he saw warfare primarily as a set of technical skills that defined the professional officer corps. In the field and in the classroom, cadets learnt how to imitate Bonaparte's favourite manoeuvres of outflanking the enemy or breaking through the centre of his line.[125] Within the military academy, Jomini became the geometrician of Horse-and-Musket warfare. His textbook was intensely practical with no unnecessary political or philosophical reflections to disturb its more conservative readers. Wars between nations were decided by the size of their armies, the firepower of their weaponry, the morale of the soldiers and, above all else, the capabilities of their commanders. By studying Jomini, the diligent student

---

[122] For his analysis of the pitfalls of river defences, see Carl von Clausewitz, *On War*, pages 522–540. Also see Napoléon Bonaparte, *Military Maxims*, pages 41–46.

[123] Not surprisingly, his rival praised the 'truly wonderful' crossing of the Berezina river by the French army, see Antoine-Henri Jomini, *The Art of War*, page 228. We were delighted that the 2013 *Russian Army Expansion* set of *Commands & Colors: Napoleonics* contained a scenario for refighting this fascinating engagement.

[124] Jomini quickly rushed through the different causes and types of warfare in the opening section of *The Art of War*, pages 1–26.

[125] See Antoine-Henri Jomini, *The Art of War*, pages 56–254.

could become a little Bonaparte without any taint of Jacobinism.[126] Victory was secured through mathematical formulas which were only understood by professional officers. The players of *Kriegsspiel* were the experts of the military trade and politicians shouldn't interfere in their business. Within bourgeois society, war was an end in itself.

---

[126] 'Jomini ... saw the revolutionary warfare which he himself had participated as merely the technical perfection of a fundamentally unchanging phenomenon, to be modified only by superficial matters like the list of *dramatis personae*, technology and transient political motivations.' Christopher Bassford, 'Jomini and Clausewitz', page 4.

3.4: GAMING THE FUTURE

In 1876, Julius von Verdy du Vernois published a new type of *Kriegsspiel* which dispensed with the rules and dice of von Reisswitz's 1824 version. In their place, this German staff officer relied upon the game's umpires to decide the progress of the action. From their military experience in Prussia's recent wars against Denmark, Austria and France, his colleagues were able to determine the speed of movement of the rival armies and the likely outcome of any combat between them.[127] For von Verdy, this 'free' form of *Kriegsspiel* solved the problem of its players gaming the game. Instead of concentrating on simulating warfare, far too many of them were using quirks in von Reisswitz's rules to gain an advantage over their opponents. But, by transforming this 'rigid' military simulation into a role-playing exercise, von Verdy's umpires were able to prevent any unrealistic outcomes thrown up by these ludic anomalies.[128] Just as importantly, participating in *Kriegsspiel* was now much easier for busy officers who already had too many commitments on their time. With no rules to master, they instead played the game by simply telling the umpires where they wanted their forces to move and fight. If organised correctly, this version of *Kriegsspiel* was a facsimile of working at army headquarters under battlefield conditions.[129]

Impressed by Prussia's victories in Europe, the Japanese military also became ardent wargamers as this country's rulers embarked upon the conquest of East Asia. Both the winning strategy in the 1905 war against Russia and the 1941 airborne assault on the US fleet in Hawaii were devised with the help of detailed simulations. However, the Japanese General Staff's enthusiasm for the free version of *Kriegsspiel* would eventually lead to disaster at the 1942 battle of Midway. Seeking to please their superior officers, the umpires of the game held to plan this operation decided that its side's aircraft carriers were invulnerable

---

[127] '... what the [War] Game especially requires is a knowledge of the capabilities and fighting power of all arms, as well as their principal accepted formations.' Julius von Verdy du Vernois in John Curry, *Verdy's Free Kriegspiel*, page 14.

[128] See Peter Perla, *The Art of Wargaming*, pages 31–34; and Andrew Wilson, *The Bomb and the Computer*, pages 6–7.

[129] See von Verdy's blow-by-blow account of his Connewitz game in John Curry, *Verdy's Free Kriegspiel*, pages 23–100.

to torpedo attacks by American fighter planes. Unfortunately for the Japanese navy, when the battle was fought for real four weeks later, their opponents quickly exposed the fallacy of this subjective judgement. After a series of devastating raids by the US airforce, two-thirds of its carrier fleet had been sunk – and the war in the Pacific was lost. Contrary to von Verdy's expectations, abolishing the rules and dice of *Kriegsspiel* didn't stop its players gaming the game. The desire to win an imaginary victory had resulted in the worst defeat in Japanese military history.[130]

During the Second World War, the US navy benefited from its many peacetime simulations of potential conflicts in the Atlantic and Pacific. Like their German and Japanese rivals, its commanders also extensively used wargames to work out the best strategy and tactics for forthcoming operations against the enemy. However, the Americans much preferred the rigid versions of *Kriegsspiel* over its free variants.[131] This positivist bias was confirmed when the US navy's wargamers discovered their British ally's cutting-edge weapon in the battle of the Atlantic: operational research. In this pioneering form of systems analysis, scientists constructed mathematical models to discover the optimal routes for supply convoys and the most effective deployment of anti-submarine patrols. By incorporating this empirical data into their military simulations, American sailors were now able to formulate much more realistic rules for their manoeuvres with maps. Rather than rely on the subjective judgement of umpires, the US navy's wargames were based upon the cold logic of mathematical equations.[132]

In its bitter struggle against Germany and Japan, the American government mobilised patriotic scientists to develop the advanced weaponry that would win the anti-fascist struggle: tanks, airplanes, radar, code-breaking and the atomic bomb. By the time that the

---

[130] See Peter Perla, *The Art of Wargaming*, pages 45–48; Alfred Hausrath, *Venture Simulations in War, Business and Politics*, pages 30–32; and Andrew Wilson, *The Bomb and the Computer*, pages 32–35.

[131] See Alfred Hausrath, *Venture Simulations in War, Business and Politics*, pages 32–35, 61–71; and Peter Perla, *The Art of Wargaming*, pages 63–76.

[132] See Alfred Hausrath, *Venture Simulations in War, Business and Politics*, pages 39–44; and Andrew Wilson, *The Bomb and the Computer*, pages 36–43.

Cold War broke out in 1948, these once marginalised academics had become honoured members of the ruling elite. Crucially, it had been in their laboratories where the formulas of physics were transformed into a military technology which was capable of wiping out entire cities in one blow. Not surprisingly, the US state now looked to these warrior intellectuals to maintain its preeminence over the new Russian enemy.[133] Alongside the natural scientists who were involved in armaments research, social scientists were also recruited for the American team in this geopolitical confrontation. Generously funded by the US airforce, the RAND think-tank was set to work on solving what was the most important challenge facing the nation's leadership: devising a credible strategy for fighting the Cold War.[134] Both superpowers now possessed atomic bombs which could inflict massive damage on its rival. By the early-1950s, Clausewitz's Absolute War was no longer an abstract theoretical concept. Instead, it had become a terrifying premonition of the genocidal logic of nuclear conflict. If the two superpowers did start fighting each other, the US military's primary task was to carry out the total annihilation of Russia's cities and their unfortunate inhabitants. But, because their Eastern opponent could also retaliate in kind, any attempt to use these atomic bombs would be suicidal. The most powerful weapon in the world was also its most impractical.[135]

During the early-1950s, RAND's intellectuals tried to make sense of this military conundrum. From Clausewitz, they understood that fighting wars was carrying out politics with violent methods.[136] Their biggest problem was how to apply this brilliant theoretical insight to the genesis of US nuclear strategy when there were no historical precedents for two sides fighting each other with atomic weapons. While Clausewitz had theorised war by studying the past, his admirers at RAND had instead to analyse the superpowers' nuclear confrontation by simulating the

[133] See Stuart Leslie, *The Cold War and American Science*; and André Schiffrin, *The Cold War and the University*.

[134] See Fred Kaplan, *The Wizards of Armageddon*, pages 51–84; and Irving Louis Horowitz, *The War Game*, pages 13–16.

[135] In 1960, RAND predicted that up to 90 million Americans could be killed in a full-scale nuclear war with Russia, see Herman Kahn, *On Thermonuclear War*, page 113.

[136] See Fred Kaplan, *The Wizards of Armageddon*, pages 79; and Beatrice Heuser, *Reading Clausewitz*, pages 152–168.

future. As the mentor of this think-tank, Johnny von Neumann – the Hungarian émigré who'd helped to invent both the computer and the atomic bomb – championed the mathematical modelling of the USA's geopolitical strategic choices: game theory. Back in the 1920s, he'd argued that smart *Poker* players epitomised the rational egoism of bourgeois society. As in the neo-classical economists' musings about the free market, each of them competed for their own gain by observing a common set of rules.[137] The RAND academics already knew that Clausewitz had compared fighting battles with both playing at cards and making business deals.[138] Now, in its early-1950s updating, game theory became their favoured scientific method of analysing the Cold War. With its dispassionate calculations, the irrationality of risking the nuclear apocalypse could now be rationalised as a series of excellent *Poker* moves. Both superpowers would gain if they mutually disarmed, but neither could trust the other to keep any deal because the rewards of trickery were too great in the atomic age. When expressed as a mathematical formula, games theory revealed that the USA's most rational strategy was to keep on building more and more nuclear weapons: the Prisoners' Dilemma.[139] Simulating the future had told RAND's paymasters what they wanted to hear. It was now scientifically proven that the US airforce required a much bigger bomber fleet.[140]

Named in homage to Clausewitz's masterpiece, Herman Kahn's 1960 book – *On Thermonuclear War* – imagined a military technology that would come to define the kamikaze logic of the arms race between the two superpowers: the 'Doomsday Machine'. In this RAND-sponsored thought experiment, the Americans would construct a massive nuclear bomb which could wipe out all life on earth with radioactive fallout. If the Russians ever broke the rules of acceptable geopolitical behaviour, they'd run the risk of its computer program deciding to detonate the

---

[137] See John von Neumann and Oskar Morgenstern, *Theory of Games and Economic Behaviour*; and Steve Heims, *John von Neumann and Norbert Wiener*, pages 43–46, 79–95, 193–194, 292–293.

[138] See Carl von Clausewitz, *On War*, pages 97, 111.

[139] See Anatol Rapoport, *Fights, Games and Debates*, pages 15–46; and Irving Louis Horowitz, *The War Game*, pages 16–28.

[140] See Fred Kaplan, *The Wizards of Armageddon*, pages 85–110.

weapon which would bring about the extinction of humanity.[141] In this RAND remix, Clausewitz's theoretical concept of Absolute War had inspired the practical strategy of atomic armageddon: 'mutually assured destruction'. Acting as rational players, both America and Russia continually increased their nuclear stockpiles to ensure that neither side could deprive the other of its instruments of human genocide. Global stability was now founded upon a suicide pact between the two superpowers.[142]

In parallel to this research, Kahn and his RAND colleagues also investigated how Clausewitz's Limited War could be fought with atomic bombs. Adopting the terminology of game theory, they speculated that a single nuclear strike against Leningrad might be the most effective method of 'signalling' disapproval of any Russian attack on US-controlled West Berlin. In this 'tit-for-tat' strategy, the Americans would continue wreaking atomic destruction on their enemy until the geopolitical stalemate in Europe was restored.[143] For the RAND academics, nuclear weapons were welcome as the most powerful pieces on the board of the Cold War game. By the mid-1960s, Kahn was appearing at public meetings in towns and cities across America to explain the 44 rungs of his 'escalation ladder' which began with an 'Ostensible Crisis' and ended with a devastating 'Spasm or Insensate War'.[144] Thanks to game theory, the unthinkable had become thinkable. As a consequence, RAND's intellectuals became convinced that America could fight and win this nuclear version of Limited War. As long as enough fallout shelters were constructed, US civilian casualties might be limited to only two million dead. As Kahn kept emphasising, American know-how and entrepreneurship would ensure that the nation recovered quickly from the traumas of atomic warfare.[145] According to RAND's calculations, the USA's most

---

141   See Herman Kahn, *On Thermonuclear War*, pages 144–160. Stanley Kubrick satirised this RAND dystopian fantasy in his 1964 *Dr Strangelove* movie.

142   See Herman Kahn, *On Thermonuclear War*, page 28; and Jeremy Isaacs and Taylor Dowling, *Cold War*, pages 230–243.

143   See Herman Kahn, *On Thermonuclear War*, pages 126–144.

144   See Fred Kaplan, *The Wizards of Armageddon*, pages 222–224. For the book of this lecture tour, see Herman Kahn, *On Escalation*.

145   See Herman Kahn, *On Thermonuclear War*, pages 74–100.

powerful military technology was now a functioning weapons system. Nuclear war was the late-20th century's iteration of Limited War.[146]

From the early-1950s onwards, RAND was a pioneer of complex computer games which simulated the global political and military confrontation between America and Russia. With Kahn's help, its researchers incorporated different nuclear manifestations of Limited War into these role-playing exercises.[147] The leaders of the USA must learn how to risk the atomic apocalypse if they wanted to prevail over their Russian enemy.[148] Yet, when they hosted their ludic predictions of this future, RAND's researchers soon discovered that the players always tried as hard as possible to avoid being the first side to use nuclear weapons. In this think-tank's 1961 game of a Russian attempt to take over West Berlin, the American team was dominated by hawkish intellectuals like Henry Kissinger. But, however disadvantageous the umpires made the US position in this crisis simulation, they too had refused to escalate beyond conventional warfare. Even as a fantasy, crossing the nuclear threshold was obviously a disastrous move.[149] Contradicting Kahn's prophecies, RAND's wargames had exposed that neither of the superpowers was going to take the potentially disastrous gamble of fighting a Limited War with atomic weapons. As its acronym confirmed, risking mutually assured destruction was madness.

The threat of a global nuclear genocide guaranteed the partition of Europe into hostile blocs. Unable to seize any more territory in the rich North, America and Russia increasingly shifted their rivalry to the poor South. As the European colonies gained their independence, the two superpowers fiercely competed for hegemony over these newly independent countries. Each side energetically promoted its

---

[146] See Adrian Lewis, *The American Culture of War*, pages 201–204; and Fred Kaplan, *The Wizards of Armageddon*, pages 197–219.

[147] See Thomas Allen, *War Games*, pages 148–150, 161–166; and Alfred Hausrath, *Venture Simulations in War, Business and Politics*, pages 226–229.

[148] These elite politicians, bureaucrats and academics saw themselves as: '... the warrior caste ... endowed with the temperament of a *Chess* player ...' Irving Louis Horowitz, *The War Game*, page 24.

[149] See Fred Kaplan, *The Wizards of Armageddon*, pages 301–2. Also see Thomas Allen, *War Games*, pages 43–57.

own path to industrial modernity within the agrarian South: Fordism or Stalinism. Crucially, by claiming to embody the imaginary future of humanity in the present, America and Russia were asserting their territorial control over the developing nations.[150] In this struggle for world domination, the US government once again turned to its warrior intellectuals for strategic advice. In the same way that RAND took the leading role in analysing the nuclear standoff, the Political Science department at MIT became the centre of research into how American power could be most effectively exercised within the South. Generously funded by the US military, its academics carried out detailed empirical studies of the major flashpoints in the superpower confrontation within the developing world: Latin America, Africa and East Asia.[151] Providing a theoretical framework for their endeavours, Walt Rostow wrote the MIT Political Science department's 'non-communist manifesto' which argued that poor countries could only reach prosperity by strictly observing the rules of the capitalist game: *The Stages of Economic Growth*. Unfortunately, as he admitted, there was a disgruntled minority of marginalised intellectuals, exploited workers and impoverished peasants who had been seduced by the rival Stalinist vision of modernity. By resisting American hegemony over the South, these psychologically disturbed subversives were sabotaging their fellow citizens' efforts to join the global consumer society.[152] Rostow and his MIT colleagues' mission was to stymie this growing Red menace within the developing nations. At the Political Science department, they had to devise the techniques which could bring victory to the American side on this new front of the Cold War. The future of humanity now depended upon their knowledge and skills.[153]

Inspired by their peers at RAND, MIT intellectuals created political-military games to test out different strategies and tactics for imposing US dominance over the South. Combining role-playing exercises with

[150] For how owning prophetic time enabled the control of political space in the South, see Richard Barbrook, *Imaginary Futures*, pages 200–218.

[151] See Max Millikan and Donald Blackmer, *The Emerging Nations*; and Myron Weiner, *Modernisation*.

[152] See Walt Rostow, *View from the Seventh Floor*, pages 113–114; *Essays on a Half-Century*, pages 99–103.

[153] See Walt Rostow, *Concept and Controversy*, pages 245–253.

computer simulations, these ludic models were endowed with the positivist aura of the quantitative social sciences. As in von Reisswitz's *Kriegsspiel*, their players experienced a believable facsimile of taking vital decisions under the intense pressure of crisis conditions.[154] By participating in these MIT games, members of the US elite could now learn the skills required to direct American foreign policy in the South. Long before they were appointed as National Security Advisors to the US President, both Rostow and Kissinger had proved their mettle in the struggle against the Russians by becoming excellent players of these political-military simulations.[155] Being obsessive gamers, MIT-trained intellectuals envisaged the superpower confrontation in the developing world as a two-player 'zero-sum' matrix. America and Russia were competing to take over the South whose nations were the pieces on the global board. One empire's gain was the other's loss. There was no neutral option in this Cold War game. Above all, both sides were rational players who always acted in their own self-interest.[156] Echoing the RAND appropriation of Clausewitz, these MIT simulations encouraged the militarisation of politics. As a superpower, the USA always had the option of using extreme violence if insistent persuasion didn't achieve its objectives in the South. Unlike with the nuclear confrontation, Clausewitz's concept of Limited War could be credibly applied to localised conflicts within the developing world.[157] America and Russia were able to fight each other over an impoverished territory in the South without risking the destruction of the North's industrial heartlands in an atomic holocaust.[158] Whatever their unfortunate inhabitants might think, these peasant nations were just pieces on the board to be won and lost in the never-ending Cold War game.

During the 1950s, the leaders of the American empire discovered a

---

[154] See Thomas Allen, *War Games*, pages 150–160; and Alfred Hausrath, *Venture Simulations in War, Business and Politics*, pages 230–234.

[155] See Thomas Allen, *War Games*, pages 164–165.

[156] See Anatol Rapoport, *Fights, Games and Debates*, pages 105–242.

[157] See Alfred Hausrath, *Venture Simulations in War, Business and Politics*, pages 165–187, 244–274; and Andrew Wilson, *The Bomb and the Computer*, pages 66–76.

[158] 'In theory, ... limited war ... provide[d] a safety valve for preventing explosions of any "doomsday" proportions.' Irving Louis Horowitz, *The War Game*, page 143. Also see Adrian Lewis, *The American Culture of War*, pages 224–227.

strategically marginal and economically irrelevant country which provided an excellent location for waging Limited War between the two superpowers: Vietnam. Most gratifyingly, the Red team was a serious opponent whose defeat would greatly enhance the Blue team's reputation. Across most of the developing world, the USA had successfully replaced the departing European colonialists with its own neo-colonial rule. However, having finally thrown out the French at great cost in 1954, the Vietnamese partisans were determined to resist the American attempts to take over the southern half of their country. With the support of the liberated north, revolutionary nationalists launched a rural guerrilla war against the USA's local allies: the corrupt and brutal oligarchy that had collaborated with the hated French imperialists.[159] By the time that John Kennedy won the 1960 US presidential elections, American advisors were already fighting against Maoist insurgents in southern Vietnam. Joining the new administration, Rostow applied MIT theory to improve his side's militarised political intervention within this backward country. Under American supervision, all nations must progress through the pre-ordained stages of growth towards the apotheosis of US-style modernity: representative democracy and consumer plenty. By winning a decisive victory over the Vietnamese peasant revolution, the Kennedy government could ensure that the Maoists' alternative path to the future had been blocked off across the whole South.[160]

At MIT, the Political Science department organised role-playing computer simulations to devise the optimal strategy and tactics for this key battleground in the Cold War game. The French had lost in Vietnam because they'd fought like 19th century European colonialists. Fortunately, the Americans now possessed 20th century technology to even the odds.[161] As both Clausewitz and Jomini had emphasised, the

---

[159] See Robert Taber, *The War of the Flea*, pages 59–72; and Neil Sheehan, *A Bright Shining Lie*, pages 145–172.

[160] See Walt Rostow, *The Diffusion of Power*, pages 451–459; and David Halberstam, *The Best and the Brightest*, pages 121–129. For how the American ownership of time depended upon keeping control over this particular piece of territory in the South, see Richard Barbrook, *Imaginary Futures*, pages 220–251.

[161] See W.W. Rostow, *The Diffusion of Power*, page 450; and David Halberstam, *The Best and the Brightest*, pages 122–124, 542–543.

outcome of most campaigns was decided by an arithmetic calculation of troop numbers and intensity of firepower. When incorporated into computer simulations, this formula happily predicted that a US victory in Vietnam was inevitable. By repeatedly playing *TACSPIEL* and other counter-insurgency games, MIT-trained researchers devised the best strategy and tactics for securing American control over this South-East Asian nation.[162] In 'search-and-destroy' missions, the US army would first eliminate the Maoist guerrillas in the countryside and then switch to winning the 'hearts-and-minds' of the peasantry with civil assistance programmes. By steadily intensifying its bombing campaign against the liberated north, the American empire was signalling disapproval of continued Vietnamese resistance to its occupation of their country.[163] In a gruesome calculation, the US military compiled monthly 'body counts' to measure its inexorable eradication of the Maoist forces.[164] Given its superior resources and technology, the American empire could keep on ratcheting up the pain until – sooner or later – the Vietnamese enemy would be forced to admit defeat in this Limited War. According to the US military's calculations, the peasant insurgency was on the verge of being crushed.[165]

In early-1968, Rostow spent many hours in the White House basement huddled with US President Lyndon Johnson over a sand table which had been modelled into a facsimile of the American airbase at Khe Sanh in Vietnam. Like two hobbyist wargamers, they were re-fighting the 1954 siege of Điện Biên Phủ in a new scenario which added the greater destructive power of modern weaponry. In the original encounter, the French regular army had been humiliatingly defeated by the Vietnamese guerrillas. But, this time around, the US airforce would drop so many bombs on the Maoist opposition that the outcome would be very different. American technology would prevail

---

[162] See Thomas Allen, *War Games*, pages 181–208; and Alfred Hausrath, *Venture Simulations in War, Business and Politics*, pages 253–264.

[163] See Fred Kaplan, *The Wizards of Armageddon*, pages 328–342; and Andrew Wilson, *The Bomb and the Computer*, pages 118–130.

[164] See Robert McNamara, *In Retrospect*, pages 48, 237–238; and Michael Maclear, *Vietnam*, pages 224–227.

[165] 'The other side is near collapse. ... The charts are very good ... Victory is very near.' Walt Rostow speaking in 1967 in Daniel Ellsberg, *Secrets*, page 184.

over the peasant revolution.[166] Ironically, while the attention of the US President and his National Security Advisor was distracted by the siege of Khe Sanh, the Vietnamese resistance launched a devastating surprise attack on the cities of the American-occupied zone of the country: the Tet Offensive. As the fighting intensified, Rostow told his boss that the statistics from the battlefield proved that the final victory over the peasant insurgency was now in sight. By coming out of their jungle hideouts, the Vietnamese guerrillas had exposed themselves to the superior firepower of the US army. According to the body counts which scored each sides' gains and losses, the American team had won this key round of the Cold War game in the South.[167]

When playing von Reisswitz's *Kriegsspiel*, Prussian officers had soon learnt how to game the game in their favour. In his 1876 free version, von Verdy dispensed with the rules to make this military simulation more closely resemble the chaotic experience of directing troops on campaign. But, by the 1950s, the rigid form of *Kriegsspiel* had been reinvigorated by the advent of computing. At RAND and MIT, the complicated rules of the game were hidden inside the program code. Through running these computer simulations, American academics now believed that it was possible to obtain scientifically proven predictions of the geopolitical future.[168] Unfortunately for them, Rostow and his colleagues didn't realise that the Vietnamese guerrillas weren't playing by the same rules as them. These MIT academics had simulated fighting a Limited War against the peasant revolution in the South. However, for the inhabitants of Vietnam, their military and political struggle for national independence was an Absolute War. Whatever their losses, they would continue fighting until victory was achieved. For the Red player, there was only one choice in their game theory matrix.

Inside the basement of the White House in 1968, the ludic spectacle of

---

166 See Thomas Allen, *War Games*, pages 209–211.

167 See Walt Rostow, *The Diffusion of Power*, pages 459–470; and Neil Sheehan, Hedrick Smith, E.W. Kenworthy and Fox Butterfield, *The Pentagon Papers*, pages 615–621.

168 In 1969, the players of a US military computer game of the Vietnam war were told that: *'You won in 1964!'* Thomas Allen, *War Games*, page 140. Emphasis in the original.

Điện Biên Phủ had obscured the disastrous reality of the Tet Offensive. By the time that the Vietnamese attacks were finally repulsed, the Maoist guerrillas had discredited the American population's naive belief in a quick victory. As public support for the war collapsed at home, US troops became increasingly mutinous until they had to be withdrawn from South-East Asia.[169] Refusing to concede the game, the American military embarked upon the indiscriminate bombing of the Vietnamese countryside to drive its inhabitants into the cities. In this genocidal strategy, the peasant insurgency would be defeated by exterminating the rebellious peasantry.[170] As the casualties mounted, the US military kept on playing for a stalemate result. Then, after three decades of bloody conflict, the outcome never predicted in the MIT computer simulations finally took place. On 30th April 1975, Vietnamese troops liberated the capital city of the Americans' puppet state and the guns fell silent at last.[171] The champions of two rival interpretations of Clausewitz had met on this South-East Asian battlefield – and the revolutionary practitioners of Absolute War had triumphed over the counter-revolutionary theorists of Limited War.[172]

---

[169] See Gabriel Kolko, *Anatomy of a War*, pages 359–367; and Jonathan Neale, *The American War*, pages 117–146.

[170] See Samuel Huntington, 'The Bases of Accommodation'; and Gabriel Kolko, *Anatomy of a War*, pages 465–469, 489–491.

[171] See Gabriel Kolko, *Anatomy of a War*, pages 538–544; and Michael Maclear, *Vietnam*, pages 452–468.

[172] See Beatrice Heuser, *Reading Clausewitz*, pages 168–178.

3.5: COMRADE CLAUSEWITZ

During our first event for the *Invisible Forces* exhibition, the conversation amongst the players of *The Game of War* turned at one point to a question that had been also posed four years earlier in the St Petersburg restaurant. Looking at Donkor's painting of the 1791 Haitian Revolution on the wall of the Furtherfield gallery, they were curious why Debord's ludic experiment didn't model the anti-imperialist struggles of his own times. In both Europe and America, New Left activists had identified their own battles at home with those being waged in the developing world. Crucially, many of them were radicalised by what became the defining cause of the May '68 generation: opposition to the murderous American invasion of Vietnam. These young radicals had to show solidarity with the guerrilla fighters of this small peasant nation who were heroically resisting the richest and most technologically advanced military power on the planet. As the New Left's leaders kept emphasising, its Maoist partisans were just one contingent of a global insurrection against US imperialism. From Cuba and Bolivia to Palestine and South Africa, revolutionary movements were fighting to liberate their nations from brutal American-backed regimes.[173]

Most notoriously, New Left militants inspired by Mao and Che created armed detachments of the insurgent South inside the metropolitan North: the Black Panther Party, Weather Underground, Rote Armee Fraktion and Brigate Rosse.[174] Ironically, as was observed both in the St Petersburg restaurant and at the Furtherfield gallery, the early-1970s peak of this campaign of urban terrorism had coincided with the development phase of Debord's *The Game of War*. If this Situationist had wanted to expose the follies of these New Left Maoists, making a tabletop version of Horse-and-Musket combat was not an obvious choice. Debord should instead have carried out the détournement of the binary Cold War logic of American hobbyist military simulations. Like its MIT predecessors, Nick Karp's 1984 *Vietnam* game was

---

173   For an overview of this emancipatory interconnection between North and South, see George Katsiaficas, *The Imagination of the New Left*, pages 29–82.

174   See Philip Foner, *The Black Panthers Speak*; Dan Berger, *Outlaws of America*; Stefan Aust, *The Baader-Meinhof Complex*; and Red Brigades, 'Strategic Resolution'.

a two player contest between Blue and Red – and the Reds had to be Maoists.[175] As suggested by Bernstein's toy soldier dioramas, the appropriate ludic response might have been to imagine the victory of the libertarian communist alternative to vanguard politics in South-East Asia: the 1945 Saigon Commune.[176] In this Situationist version of the Vietnam wargame, the anti-Maoist Reds should be able to win this time around. History can be changed in our favour.

However, in *The Game of War*, Debord had eschewed the faux-realism of Karp's *Vietnam* with its detailed hex map, myriad cardboard pieces and bewilderingly complex rules. Instead of detourning this American obsession with historically accurate military simulations, he'd invented a ludic abstraction of Clausewitz's theoretical and historical writings on warfare. When we'd debated the meaning of Debord's masterpiece in the St Petersburg restaurant, Class Wargames still hadn't fully understood the political implications of this design decision. Fortunately, by the time that our 2012 event in the Furtherfield gallery took place, we could reveal that *The Game of War* was – despite its outward appearance – a Vietnam war game. In this bloody conflict, the military intellectuals who'd led both sides had studied Clausewitz's *On War*. However, the Blue and Red teams championed very different methods for putting his ideas into practice. Tellingly, in *TACSPIEL* and other MIT simulations, the US player's political goal could only be achieved by the military destruction of the enemy's forces. In contrast, the Vietnamese partisans conceived of Clausewitz's famous dictum in a much more dialectical sense. For them, politics always took primacy over violence. When the US military invaded Vietnam in 1965, the two nations were not just fighting over territory. Crucially, the warrior intellectuals of Blue and Red also knew that: '... the stage was set for the test of the differing American and Maoist interpretations of Clausewitzian doctrine'.[177]

---

[175] The American player could win this simulation's 'The Battle for South Vietnam' scenario by holding out for more turns than the historical ending of the war in spring 1975, see the rules book of Nick Karp, *Vietnam*, page 45.

[176] See Ngo Van Xuyet, '1945: the Saigon Commune'; and Lu Sanh Hanh, 'An Account of the 1945 August Revolution'.

[177] William Staudenmaier, 'Vietnam, Mao and Clausewitz', page 79.

By the time that *The Game of War* was published in 1977, the US side had been decisively defeated in this trial by combat. With the American team temporarily out of the game, the Maoists had ensured that the Left was now the proud owner of Clausewitz's theoretical legacy. Yet, before the First World War, Social Democrats had little time for the thoughts of the German General Staff's favourite philosopher. As advocates of the citizen-soldier army, labour activists were highly suspicious of these professional officers with their bellicose imperialist politics. In place of Clausewitz, they'd turned to Engels' historical materialist analysis of military affairs. Paralleling the productive economy, the techniques and technologies of destruction had kept on increasing in efficiency over time. As a result, each social system had fought wars in its own distinctive ways.[178] Informed by this Marxist historical overview, Engels argued that the Left must now update its own defence policy. Having personally experienced defeat on the battlefields of the 1848 German Revolution, he didn't share the republican enthusiasm for civilian volunteer armies. Echoing Jomini, Engels stressed the vital importance of the craft skills of the military profession. At the outbreak of the American Civil War, most of the US army's officer corps had defected to the slaveholders' rebellion. Despite their greater numbers, the North's citizen-soldiers were only able to prevail over the better led South when they too had learnt how to fight like professionals.[179] Engels' analysis was confirmed by the tragic fate of the 1871 Paris Commune whose civilian militia had been no match for the French regular army. Since it would inevitably lose when fighting the military on the barricades, the Left should instead win over the rank-and-file soldiers to its cause: the 'workers in uniform'. Universal conscription was now the best guarantor of universal suffrage. By the time that the Social Democrats had achieved enough popular support to take state power, the skilled professionals of the regular army would already be on the side of the proletarian revolution.[180]

Unfortunately, this prognosis was not ready to be realised when

---

[178] See Friedrich Engels, *Anti-Dühring*, pages 190–220.

[179] For their collaborative analysis of this 1861–65 military conflict, see Karl Marx and Friedrich Engels, *The Civil War in the United States*. Also see Martin Berger, *Engels, Armies and Revolution*, pages 74–86, 109–113.

[180] See Martin Berger, *Engels, Armies and Revolution*, pages 154–170.

the First World War broke out in 1914. Instead of the military professionals joining the Left's peace campaign, the workers' movement rallied to the Right's nationalist crusade. Disorientated by this humiliating capitulation of European Social Democracy, Lenin studied Clausewitz's *On War* to discover a dialectical analysis of the decisive role of military violence within political struggles.[181] State power meant forcing your enemy to submit to your will.[182] Armed with this knowledge, Lenin set to work on updating the Bolsheviks' credo. In his 1916 *Imperialism* pamphlet, he claimed that the German war economy was the premonition of the socialist future in the present: state capitalism.[183] On his return to Russia in 1917, he insisted that the fate of the revolution would be decided by bullets not ballots. By 1921, like Clausewitz and Hegel, Lenin had also become convinced that the enlightened rule of the authoritarian bureaucracy was the most efficient form of government.[184] Stripped of their liberal politics, the writings of these two Berlin *Whist* players now vindicated the Bolsheviks' militarised version of socialist politics: Marxism-Leninism.

In 1858, while reading *On War*, Engels was amused to discover Clausewitz's observation that 'war resembles commerce'. Writing to Marx, he commented that this book also had 'an odd way of philosophising, but [was] per se very good.'[185] After the 1917 Russian Revolution, these throwaway remarks became the textual authority for the Bolsheviks' cult of Clausewitz. Ironically, they now quoted from Engels' letter to justify their abandonment of his proletarian military policy. As leader of the Red Army, Trotsky had rebuilt the

[181]   See Jacob Kipp, 'Lenin and Clausewitz', pages 185–186. In 1915, Lenin updated Clausewitz's famous phrase: '... *every* war ... [is] a continuation of the politics of given interested nations – and *various classes* inside of them – at a given time.' V.I. Lenin, 'The Collapse of the Second International', page 284. Emphasis in the original.

[182]   See V.I. Lenin, 'Socialism and War', pages 223–225. Also see the opening of Carl von Clausewitz, *On War*, pages 83–86.

[183]   See V.I. Lenin, *Imperialism*, pages 102–105, 145–152. Also see Nikolai Bukharin, *Imperialism and World Economy*, pages 116–129, 144–167.

[184]   See V.I. Lenin, 'Preliminary Draft Resolution Of The Tenth Congress Of The R.C.P. On Party Unity'. Also see E.H. Carr, *The Bolshevik Revolution Volume 2*, pages 269–380.

[185]   Friedrich Engels, 'Engels to Marx in London: 7th January 1858'.

professional officer corps with the training and discipline needed to win the Russian Civil War. But, unlike Engels, he was fiercely opposed to any democratic selection of this military cadre.[186] Instead, quoting Clausewitz, Trotsky championed the Bolsheviks' elitist politics of armed violence. In Soviet Russia, the vanguard party had become the general staff of the workers and peasants' revolution.[187] In the aftermath of their decisive victory over the Whites, Mikhail Frunze argued that the Bolsheviks had now developed their own distinctive military policy. With its unique combination of hi-tech weaponry and ideological fervour, the Red Army would soon be capable of breaking the capitalist encirclement of Russia by force.[188] As well as being more sceptical about exporting revolution into Europe, Trotsky also criticised this aggressive foreign policy for serving the self-interest of the military profession. Modernising the Russian economy should take precedence over increasing the defence budget. In Trotsky's reading of Clausewitz, the politicians must always give the orders to the generals. While soldiering was a craft skill that could be learnt by both Reds and Whites, directing the Bolshevik regime required an ideological education which was only available on the Left. It was the political vanguard that must decide whether to stay on the defensive or go over to the offensive. There were no inherently revolutionary strategies or tactics in warfare. As pragmatists, the Bolsheviks should adopt any military methods that helped to defeat their enemies on the battlefield.[189]

During the First World War, Clausewitz's trinity of the army, government and people had disintegrated within Tsarist Russia. By 1917, mutinous soldiers and sailors were at the forefront of the revolutionary overthrow of the old order. After their successful coup d'état, the Bolsheviks had quickly set to work on constructing their own version of the Prussian staff officer's secular trinity: the vanguard party mobilising the masses to fight for the Red Army. By winning

---

[186] See Leon Trotsky, *Military Writings,* pages 144–145. Also see Jacob Kipp, 'Lenin and Clausewitz', pages 187–189.

[187] See Leon Trotsky, *Military Writings,* page 36.

[188] See Mikhail Frunze, 'Unified Military Doctrine and the Red Army'. Also see Makhmut Gareev, *M.V. Frunze,* pages 79–142; and Jacob Kipp, 'Lenin and Clausewitz', page 189.

[189] See Leon Trotsky, *Military Writings,* pages 19–69, 109–133.

its war against the Whites, Lenin's regime popularised this new interpretation of Clausewitz amongst the radical Left across the globe. During the 1930s, Antonio Gramsci – the imprisoned leader of the Italian Communist Party – made his own illuminating contribution to the theoretical precepts of Bolshevism. Synthesising Clausewitz and Lenin, he argued that political power was exercised through both force and persuasion: hegemony.[190] Learning the lessons of 1917, the vanguard party must become the premonition of the Bolshevik trinity of army, state and people inside modern bourgeois society. Adopting Clausewitz's terminology, Gramsci contrasted two different strategies for fighting the class enemy: the 'war of manoeuvre' in Russia and the 'war of position' in Europe. While Bolsheviks in the developing world prioritised the armed struggle, their comrades in the metropolitan heartlands had to concentrate on the ideological contest.[191] By choosing the optimal combination of force and persuasion for each social terrain, the skilful generals of the vanguard party would be able to impose their hegemony upon the inhabitants of the modern world.

As his armies terrorised the nations of Europe, Hitler boasted that the Nazis were successfully implementing Clausewitz's teachings on political warfare.[192] However, by failing to study this Prussian soldier's history of Bonaparte's 1812 campaign, the German dictator also made the fatal mistake of invading Russia. Once again, the emperor of the West was utterly destroyed by his rival in the East. During the Second World War, Stalin's promotion of Russian nationalism led to Clausewitz being temporarily condemned as the chief ideologist of German militarism.[193] But, following the death of the Bolshevik despot, this Prussian soldier's deep influence on vanguard politics quickly reemerged into the open. Lenin's appropriation of Clausewitz was once again taught as orthodoxy in the Red Army's academies. Above all, his insights into the political goals of military violence now

---

[190] See Antonio Gramsci, *Selections from the Prison Notebooks*, pages 5–14, 57–58, 257–265. Also see Perry Anderson, 'The Antinomies of Antonio Gramsci', pages 12–26.

[191] See Antonio Gramsci, *Selections from the Prison Notebooks*, pages 229–239. Also see Carl von Clausewitz, *On War*, pages 606–629; and Perry Anderson, 'The Antinomies of Antonio Gramsci', pages 7–12, 55–78.

[192] See Heinz Guderian, *Panzer Leader*, page 378.

[193] See Beatrice Heuser, *Reading Clausewitz*, pages 143–144.

justified the Russian empire wasting huge resources on the Cold War arms race. Coercion was the deadliest weapon in the struggle for global hegemony.[194]

The Clausewitz revival in Russia was boosted by Mao's admiration for his teachings. Back in the late-1930s, the maximum leader of Chinese Bolshevism had carefully studied *On War* while codifying the most effective strategy and tactics for his rural guerrilla forces.[195] Like Lenin, Trotsky and Gramsci, Mao was convinced that the vanguard party prefigured the new socialist trinity of army, government and people. As the general staff of the peasant revolution, these Chinese warrior intellectuals fought with both political and military weapons against the oppressors of the masses: brutal landowners, greedy merchants, corrupt officials and foreign imperialists.[196] Building upon Clausewitz's analysis of Spanish and Russian resistance to French occupation, Mao described a three stage strategy of rural guerrilla warfare. At first, the revolutionary forces defended in depth by embedding themselves amongst the peasantry. As their strength increased, these partisans continually harassed the enemy's army. Finally, when the opposition was significantly weakened, the Chinese Bolsheviks went over to the offensive to take the urban centres that brought total victory. At each stage of this strategy, political mobilisation and military violence were combined to achieve victory over the better equipped and resourced Japanese and Nationalist armies.[197] As both Clausewitz and Mao celebrated, patriotic citizen-soldiers could prevail against mercenary professionals. Revolutionary warfare required revolutionary politics.

When he updated Clausewitz's great book, Mao dispensed with one of its key strategic and tactical principles: the concentration of forces.

---

194 See Harriet Fast Scott, 'Soviet Doctrine in the Nuclear Age'; and B. Byely et al, *Marxism-Leninism on War and Army*. Also see Beatrice Heuser, *Reading Clausewitz*, pages 145–150.

195 See Mao Zedong, 'On Protracted War', pages 266–268; and Philip Short, *Mao*, pages 363–365.

196 See Mao Zedong, 'Analysis of the Classes in Chinese Society'. Also see Philip Short, *Mao*, pages 117–178; and Beatrice Heuser, *Reading Clausewitz*, pages 53–54.

197 See Mao Zedong, 'On Protracted War', pages 232–253, 275–311; and Philip Short, *Mao*, pages 221–223, 363–365. Also see Carl von Clausewitz, *On War*, pages 453–466, 566–584; and Beatrice Heuser, *Reading Clausewitz*, pages 138–140.

Instead, this Bolshevik commander insisted that his troops must remain dispersed in the countryside until they were ready to launch the third offensive stage of rural guerrilla insurgency.[198] As a keen *Go* player, Mao already knew how to surround his opponent's army by placing pieces around the edges of the board and then building into its centre. When this ludic metaphor was applied to mid-20th century China, the game's grid symbolised the class geography of the peasant insurrection.[199] In the late-1920s, the vanguard party had opened its campaign amongst isolated rural communities on the corners of the board. After two decades of fierce struggles to control its four sides, the Chinese Bolsheviks concluded the game by attacking the rich and powerful cities in the middle of the grid. Despite their nine stone opening advantage, the Nationalists had been so thoroughly defeated by 1949 that they were left with only one surviving eye in Taiwan.[200] By translating his ideas into Chinese, Mao had promoted Clausewitz into a 1st dan *Go* player.

In 1965, the American elite was convinced of its theoretical and ludic superiority over the Vietnamese Bolsheviks. RAND and MIT intellectuals had developed the most modern understanding of Clausewitz's ideas. *TACSPIEL* was much better at modelling rural guerrilla warfare than *Go*. Unfortunately for these champions of the American empire, their self-confidence was totally misplaced. Leading the Vietnamese resistance was a very skilled practitioner of Mao's three stage strategy of rural insurrection: Võ Nguyên Giáp. Fighting against the US invaders, his partisans combined political mobilisation and military violence to wear down the foreign army of occupation.[201] In 1968, Giáp fulfilled Clausewitz's dictum that the skilful general 'rises above all rules [of war]'.[202] While the American leadership's attention

---

[198] See Mao Zedong, 'On Protracted War', pages 298–305. Also see Beatrice Heuser, *Reading Clausewitz*, pages 140–142; and Scott Boorman, *The Protracted Game*, pages 170–172.

[199] See Mao Zedong, 'On Protracted War', pages 253–258; and Scott Boorman, *The Protracted Game*, pages 38–51.

[200] See Scott Boorman, *The Protracted Game*, pages 52–153.

[201] See Võ Nguyên Giáp, 'The South Vietnamese People Will Win'; 'Great Victory, Great Task'. Also see Peter MacDonald, *Giap*, pages 78–83.

[202] Carl von Clausewitz, *On War*, page 157.

was focused upon the siege of Khe Sanh, the Vietnamese resistance suddenly attacked the major urban centres of the US-controlled south of the country. According to Mao's three stage strategy, the Tet Offensive was a premature move that foolishly risked the exposing the guerrilla army to the overwhelming firepower of the enemy. All good *Go* players knew to avoid playing too many pieces in the centre of the board before they'd secured its corners and sides.[203] Yet, despite their heavy casulties, the Vietnamese partisans still emerged triumphant on the South-East Asian battlefield. Unlike the RAND and MIT intellectuals, Giáp and his comrades understood that vanguard politics was in command of the armed struggle. By disappointing the American people's hopes of imminent victory, they'd succeeded in shattering the morale of the US conscripts who were fighting the war in Vietnam. As Clausewitz had emphasised, citizen-soldiers had to be motivated by their commitment to the nation's cause. However, his American acolytes' enthusiasm for hi-tech weaponry blinded them to this political imperative. When the US military's rank-and-file troops refused to fight anymore, the Vietnamese had won the American war on the battlefield.[204] The Maoists had passed the test – and proved the superiority of their interpretation of Clausewitz's doctrine.

By inventing *The Game of War*, Debord proclaimed his heretical status amongst the New Left generation. Inspired by the heroic rural guerrillas of the South, youthful revolutionaries had become seduced by the Bolshevik appropriation of Clausewitz's ideas. They too would take up arms to achieve their political goals in the metropolitan centres of the North. Like his comrade Sanguinetti, Debord presciently warned that these Maoist insurrectionists were being manipulated by the state's intelligence services. In late-1970s Italy, indiscriminate bomb attacks frightened the population into supporting repressive measures against

---

[203] See Scott Boorman, *The Protracted Game*, pages 87–89.

[204] 'The United States has a strategy based on arithmetic. They question the computers ... and then go into action. ... They can't get it into their heads that the Vietnam war has to be understood in terms of the [Maoist] strategy of people's war ...' Võ Nguyên Giáp, 'Their Dien Bien Phu Will Come', pages 329–330. Also see Võ Nguyên Giáp and Van Tien Dung, *How We Won The War*; and Adrian Lewis, *The American Culture of War*, pages 274–294.

all forms of political dissent: the 'strategy of tension'.[205] Dismayed by this disastrous infatuation with urban terrorism, Debord argued that the New Left must renounce its obsession with the Maoist interpretation of Clausewitz's ideas. Far from pioneering the socialist future, the rural guerrillas of the South were fighting to establish the first stage of capitalist modernity: the concentrated spectacle. As the Vietnamese Maoists' destruction of the Saigon Commune in 1945 had proved, the vanguard party was a bureaucratic obstacle to the ascendency of the workers' councils. Fortunately, by playing *The Game of War*, libertarian communists could now break the Bolshevik monopoly over Clausewitz's *On War*. Within this military simulation were materialised the key strategic and tactical principles of this Prussian staff officer's writings. Above all, *The Game of War* provided a safe environment for Situationist rebels to learn how to turn Clausewitz's theoretical insights into practice. Moving its pieces across the board was excellent training for the social upheavals to come. Every proletarian must acquire the craft techniques of skilful generalship. On those 2012 summer afternoons at the Furtherfield gallery, Class Wargames took inspiration from Debord's masterpiece for its two ludic contributions to the *Invisible Forces* exhibition. In this third phase of our campaign of ludic subversion, our task was to teach military theory to those who participated in our performances. Unlike the Japanese admirals or MIT intellectuals who'd deluded themselves with the superficial realism of their own simulations, Class Wargames was engaged in realising a much more dialectical ambition. While engaged in mock combat under the auspices of Donkor's *Toussaint L'Ouverture*, the players of *The Game of War* and *Command & Colors: Napoleonics* were learning how to be not only Situationists, but also Clausewitzians.

---

[205] See Guy Debord, *Comments on the Society of the Spectacle*, pages 52–56 and Gianfranco Sanguinetti, *On Terrorism and the State*. Also see Stuart Christie, *Stefano Delle Chiaie*.

3.6: THE ROMANCE OF COMBAT

On Friday 17th August 2012, four members of Class Wargames set out from London on an expedition to Haldon Forest Park on the edge of Dartmoor in Devon. Within this unlikely setting, our copies of Debord's *The Game of War* and H.G. Wells' *Little Wars* were starring in the first part of the *Games People Play* exhibition which was running over that summer at CCANW: the Centre for Contemporary Art and the Natural World. As well our contributions, this show also featured a fascinating selection of other historical ludic curiosities, including the precursors of contemporary family favourites like *Snakes & Ladders* and *Monopoly*. In the CCANW's programme, Clive Adams – the director of this venue – revealed his inspiration for the exhibition: 'Games hold a mirror to civilisation; they build bonds, trust and strengthen social relationships.'[206] Fulfilling this mandate, Class Wargames arrived at this gallery in a wood ready to host two participatory performances of our leftist military simulations over the weekend of 18th–19th August. After nearly five years of touring, we'd become veterans in the remixing of hobbyist games into avant-garde art installations. As we'd discovered throughout the first stage of our campaign of ludic mischief, the everyday could become extraordinary when placed inside a gallery setting.[207] Having moved onto the second phase of this campaign, we'd also become adept at explicating the seditious reasoning which could be found within these martial make-believes. Class Wargames was by now very experienced at both the aestheticisation and politicisation of wargaming.

On that Saturday evening, we began our intervention by playing *The Game of War* with the audience gathered inside the CCANW space. Taking charge of the rival teams were a brother and sister who were eager to try out Debord's Clausewitz simulator: Ben and Lisa Vanovitch. Much to Clive Adams' bemusement, this performance of *The Game of War* would be dedicated to strengthening their social bond of sibling

---

206   Centre for Contemporary Art and the Natural World, *Games People Play*, page 1.

207   '... artists are often just fortunate people who get acknowledged or rewarded for what a lot of other people are doing outside the context of art.' Jeremy Deller in Matthew Higgs and Jeremy Deller, 'In Conversation', page 185.

rivalry. When the pieces were laid out for the Marengo scenario as in **Diagram 3** on page 226 and the basics of the rules had been explained, the miniature battle was ready to begin. On one side of the board, Ben – assisted by Tara Woodyer – took on the role of commander of the South. Across from them, Lisa became the general of the South with Fabian as her aide de camp. The other members of Class Wargames and the audience were ready to join in the lively discussions which would take place around the board. From the outset of the game, Ben's team ensured that the South kept the initiative by aggressively moving their main reserve army from the back of the board into the central plain. But, despite losing some important units in the retreat, Lisa's side eventually did manage to concentrate the North's pieces in front of its eastern arsenal. With the immediate crisis over, the result of the game was now open with either side capable of emerging the victor. As the event was by now drawing to close, the two siblings agreed upon a draw. After an evening of friendly rivalry, family honour on both sides had been satisfied. At the CCANW, everyone was a winner of *The Game of War*.

On Sunday afternoon, hostilities recommenced with a public performance of H.G. Wells' *Little Wars* on the covered stage outside the gallery. In both its appearance and mechanics, this celebrated novelist's ludic invention was very different from Debord's minimalist artwork. While on family holidays at the Kent seaside in South-East England, Wells – helped by Jerome K. Jerome and other literary types – had devised a set of rules to fight imaginary battles with toy soldiers borrowed from his children's collection. In 1913, Wells published the results of their efforts along with an amusing account of one of their contests in a best-selling book: *Little Wars*. Since the late-19th century, Britains and other manufacturers had been mass producing 54mm military figurines for small boys who wanted to play at war – and those who had to buy presents for them.[208] Now, thanks to the rules provided in Wells' book, grown-ups could also join in the fun. Infantry, cavalry and artillery were all given fixed moves in imperial measures. Hand-to-hand fighting was resolved by numerical superiority. Best of all, both sides were required to fire metal pellets from model cannon at

---

[208] See James Opie, *Collecting Toy Soldiers*, pages 20–21.

their opponent's soldiers which were removed from the game when hit.[209] In the photographs inside *Little Wars*, Wells and his famous friends were shown happily aiming miniature Britains' artillery pieces while kneeling in the garden of his Sandgate house. Enthused by their example, lots of other adults soon also started fighting mock battles with toy soldiers. Most wonderfully, the publication of *Little Wars* had launched the modern hobby of figurine wargaming.

In the eponymous book of his game, Wells emphasised that his ludic creation was more than just an amusing pastime. For over a decade before *Little Wars* appeared, he'd been a prominent – and maverick – member of the Fabian Society which lobbied for the gradual socialist reform of British society.[210] During his lifetime, Wells' sci-fi novels and futurological texts would popularise their vision of the enlightened elite who would replace the poverty and ignorance of liberal capitalism with a new collectivist commonwealth constructed along rational and scientific lines.[211] Most admirably, in contrast with many of his Fabian colleagues, he was also openly contemptuous of the racial hierarchies of the British empire and its American imitator.[212] Although no Marxist, Wells' socialism was always internationalist. Like all of his writings, *Little Wars* was designed to promote these Left political beliefs. By following its rules, the players of this figurine wargame would soon understand that any conflict between the major powers fought with modern weapons would result in massive casualties on the battlefield. Devastated by cannon fire and hand-to-hand combat, there were very few toy soldiers left in either side's miniature army at the end of this ludic contest.[213] In his explanatory remarks in *Little Wars*, Wells even dreamt of luring the generals, politicians and industrialists who were

---

[209]   See H.G. Wells, *Little Wars*, pages 39–66. In our performances of his game, we've replaced these metal pellets with matchsticks for health and safety reasons.

[210]   See Michael Sherborne, *H.G. Wells*, pages 152–175; and George Bernard Shaw, Sidney Webb, Graham Wallas, Oliver Clarke, Annie Besant and Hubert Bland, *Fabian Essays*.

[211]   See H.G. Wells, *A Modern Utopia*; and *The Shape of Things to Come*.

[212]   See Michael Sherborne, *H.G. Wells*, pages 155, 164–5, 175–179.

[213]   'You only have to play at *Little Wars* three or four times to realise what a blundering great thing Great War must be.' H.G. Wells, *Little Wars*, page 106. Also see Harry Pearson, *Achtung Schweinehund!*, page 173.

then driving Europe towards a disastrous imperialist bloodbath into his Sandgate garden. Once there, he would divert their competitive instincts with his socialist alternative to the impending Great War: playing with Britains' figurines. Knocking over toy soldiers with metal pellets was much preferable to killing human beings with artillery shells.[214]

During the second phase of our campaign of ludic subversion, Class Wargames began putting on participatory performances of *Little Wars*. By emphasising its pacifist message, we were able to remind apolitical figurine gamers of the political ambitions of their hobby's founding father. Tragically, Wells' toy soldier simulation had failed to prevent the outbreak of the horrendous military conflagration in 1914. Now, as the centenary of this catastrophe approached, playing *Little Wars* became our ludic protest against the forgetting and mythologising of this imperialist Great War. On that Sunday afternoon at CCANW's *Games People Play* exhibition, Class Wargames was making Left propaganda with toy soldiers. For our match of this original version of *Reds versus Reds*, Ben and Lisa decided to join together to command the French forces. Facing them under the red canvas in control of the British army was Tara with Stefan acting as her military advisor. As Wells had intended, casualties rose very quickly as matchsticks from the six Britains' model cannons rained down on the toy soldiers of both sides. At the climax of this ludic prophecy of the First World War, Ben and Lisa had the brilliant idea of sheltering their troops behind two artillery pieces while moving them into an enfilading position. Facing fire from their front and outflanked on their right, the British were soon reduced to only one 54mm figurine. Even the opposing armies in the trench warfare of 1914–8 hadn't suffered such heavy casualties. Incapable of further resistance, Tara and Stefan ruefully conceded the match. On this summer's day at CCANW, sibling cooperation had delivered a memorable victory.

In the appendix to *Little Wars*, Wells provided an advanced set of rules which could be used in army training. Despite his pacifist principles, he'd been unable to resist the invitation to adapt his civilian diversion

---

[214] See H.G. Wells, *Little Wars*, pages 103–105; and Class Wargames, 'Communiqué #8'.

for the deadlier purposes indicated by the misspelt name of the pioneering military simulation in the book's subtitle: *Kriegsspiel*.[215] Although professional wargaming would become increasingly sophisticated over the decades, this close link with the hobbyist subculture was never completely broken. As Peter Young and his colleague from Royal Military Academy Sandhurst explained in their classic 1967 *Charge!* book, players of toy soldier simulations were able to learn the '... basic principles of war – surprise, the concentration of effort at the right place and the right time, an understanding of the capabilities of the enemy's forces and his intentions ...'[216] With our two performances of *The Game of War* and *Little Wars* for the CCANW's summer exhibition, Class Wargames was now ready to build upon this all-important insight. Commencing the third phase of our campaign of ludic subversion, our primary goal became the dissemination of these basic principles of military theory amongst Left activists. In the preceding two stages of this offensive, we'd followed Debord's personal trajectory from avant-garde artist to libertarian communist proselytiser. Now, in the third stage of our campaign, Class Wargames would realise the full seditious potential of *The Game of War* in our performances and publicity. Unlike the US inventors of hobbyist and professional simulations, Debord hadn't been obsessed with modelling past or future conflicts as realistically as possible. Instead, *The Game of War* was a ludic abstraction of the strategic and tactical insights of *On War*. Crucially, through its Napoleonic theme, Debord had challenged the then dominant Cold War orthodoxies about Clausewitz's ideas. By refuting both the American and Maoist interpretations, his game championed its own Situationist détournement of this Prussian soldier's philosophy. Debord believed that Clausewitz's writings didn't just provide smart theoretical and historical insights into the violent transformation of Europe carried out by the modernising forces unleashed by the 1789 French Revolution. When studied carefully, these texts also illuminated the social turmoil shaking the world in the wake of the May '68 Revolution. Like conflicts between nations, class struggles were also conducted with a combination of force and persuasion. In his introduction to Champ Libre's 1976 reissue of

---

[215]   See H.G. Wells, *Little Wars*, pages 107–116.

[216]   Peter Young and J.P. Lawford, *Charge!*, page 9.

Clausewitz's analysis of the 1806 Jena-Auerstädt campaign, Debord declared that: '... we live in an epoch in which the study of all forms of war, all forms of historical action, are of the greatest political and theoretical interest.'[217] By playing wargames, Situationists were learning the military principles which would be required to conquer the emancipated future.

When *The Game of War* was published in the late-1970s, *Pong* and other first-generation video games were already familiar items not only in bars and arcades, but also in living rooms and bedrooms.[218] However, Debord's invention didn't have any need of this technological advance. Made from card or metal, its analogue board and pieces were still able to fulfil his main aim: creating a competitive social relationship between the players.[219] In *On War*, Clausewitz had compared a battle between rival armies to a duel between two aristocrats. In both cases, one side imposed its will upon the other with extreme violence.[220] Despite playing *Whist* with Hegel, this Prussian soldier was entranced by a very stark version of dialectical reasoning. According to his concept of Absolute War, victory was secured by totally destroying their enemy's military might. For both his American and Bolshevik admirers, Clausewitz's martial theory had justified their ambition to monopolise political power through armed force. There could only be one winner – and the defeated had to leave the stage of history. However, in Hegel's *Phenomenology of the Spirit*, this duel to the death between two wills resulted in the division of humanity into two opposing classes: the masters and the slaves. According to his grand narrative of history, this game of social power had been played again and again until it culminated in the 1789 French Revolution. For a brief moment, the Jacobins had tried and failed to resolve the dialectic of human evolution

---

[217] Guy Debord in Carl von Clausewitz, *Notes sur la Prusse dans sa Grande Catastrophe 1806*, page ix.

[218] *Pong* was released as an arcade game in the USA in 1972 and the console version had been available in Europe since 1974. See David Winter, 'Welcome to Pong-Story'.

[219] Echoing Clausewitz's comparison between *Whist* and war, Debord explained that: 'I wanted to imitate *Poker* [in the design of *The Game of War*] – not the chance factor in *Poker*, but the combat that is so characteristic of it.' Alice Becker-Ho and Guy Debord, *A Game of War*, page 156.

[220] See Carl von Clausewitz, *On War*, page 83.

by elevating one of the two rival classes to undisputed dominance. Fortunately, under Bonaparte's enlightened rule, the masters and the slaves were now being melded into one people: bourgeois citizens. The end of history was authoritarian liberalism.

Within the rules of *The Game of War*, Debord detourned both of these variants of dialectical reasoning. As the audiences at Class Wargames' events soon discovered, there might be only one victor, but everyone who participated in these collective performances was a winner. True to the Situationists' avant-garde origins, *The Game of War* was politicised art in the service of aestheticised politics. The two teams of players were re-enacting Hegel's concept of the world-historical struggle for recognition between masters and slaves.[221] Above all, by teaching the strategic and tactical principles of Clausewitz and other military theorists, *The Game of War* democratised the esoteric knowledge of the Bolshevik elite. When everyone could play at being Bonaparte, then no one could become a little Lenin, Trotsky or Mao. Back in 1861, Engels had joked that French soldiers came from '... the nation of ... generals'.[222] With *The Game of War*, Debord created the ludic manifestation of this democratic dream. By moving its pieces across the board, the slaves could now acquire the military and political skills of the masters. Thanks to this Situationist training exercise, they were able to possess the knowledge required to seize control of grand narrative of modernity. The Limited War strategy of the Social Democrats and Stalinists had been discredited by these parties' pusillanimous behaviour during the May '68 Revolution. If the workers' councils were to prevail over spectacular capitalism, Left activists must now become experts in the Absolute War strategy of proletarian revolution.[223]

In the performances and publicity for the third phase of our campaign of ludic subversion, Class Wargames stressed that Debord's *The Game of War* was his practical critique of the Bolshevik interpretation of

---

[221] 'I know that Clausewitz was not directly Hegelian, [and] no doubt had not read Hegel. ... [but] simply by dominating the very reality of the strategic sphere, [Clausewitz came] to be something truly close to a Hegelian dialectician.' Guy Debord, 'To Jean-Pierre Baudet'.

[222] Friedrich Engels, 'Waldersee on the French Army', page 510.

[223] See Guy Debord, *Comments on the Society of the Spectacle*, pages 85–88.

Clausewitz's writings. When everyone was a player, direct democracy was no longer mythologised into the exclusive ideology of the vanguard party. Participatory creativity was realisable in the here and now. While training with *The Game of War*, revolutionary militants were already experiencing this imaginary future in the tangible present. Like *Chess* in medieval times, the socialisation taking place around the board was as important as the two players moving their pieces in attack or defence. Horrifying military violence had become an entertaining metaphor for mental duelling. When, in the game of their eponymous book, Becker-Ho had finally defeated her husband, this victory was a cause for mutual celebration. In their Situationist wargame, competitive play had stimulated psychological intimacy between these close comrades. Similarly, at our two CCANW performances in 2012, winning or losing were also equally pleasurable experiences.[224] By inventing *The Game of War*, Debord had made his sociable contribution to the collective striving for emancipatory understanding. Libertarian communism was directly embedded within its board and pieces. When North and South fought each other, the rules of the game temporarily took precedence over the disciplines of capitalism. For these brief moments in time, its players were living the most utopian demand of modern humanity: 'The abolition of the proletarian condition is the *self-transformation* of proletarians into immediately social individuals ...'[225]

---

[224] See Class Wargames, 'Communiqué #6'.

[225] Théorie Communiste, 'Much Ado About Nothing', page 203. Emphasis in original.

3.7: THE LUDIC LESSONS OF MILITARY HISTORY

By inviting the audiences at our events to play *The Game of War*, *Reds versus Reds*, *Commands & Colors: Napoleonics* and *Little Wars*, Class Wargames was teaching the smart Situationist appropriation of Clausewitz's writings. In this third stage of our campaign of ludic subversion, our vital task was to disseminate the basic principles of military theory amongst our Left comrades. When we presented Debord's ludic creation, we stressed that – unlike *Kriegsspiel* and *TACSPIEL* – *The Game of War* hadn't been designed as a role-playing exercise which modelled the Prussian General Staff's headquarters or the US President's National Security Council meetings. Instead, the abstract style of its game engine was much closer to *Chess* or *Go*: two sides taking alternate turns, perfect information about each other's positions and only one attack allowed in each move. As Debord confessed, this minimalist imperative had forced his simulation to omit two important factors that often determined the outcome of military confrontations: the soldiers' morale and the weather conditions. In recompense, the ability to move five pieces on each turn ensured that *The Game of War* was much more fluid and unpredictable in its outcomes than *Chess*.[226] By imitating Bonaparte, its best players would learn how to manoeuvre their infantry, cavalry and artillery units to maximise their combined offensive and defensive power. With mobility restricted to one third of their army, they'd also have to become adept at prioritising their ambitions. There were never enough troops to be strong everywhere on the board. By seizing one opportunity, others must be missed. Debord wanted every libertarian communist to learn the essential skill of making difficult choices: 'This war game – like war itself and all forms of strategic thought and action – tends to demand the simultaneous consideration of contradictory requirements.'[227]

As one of his maxims, Bonaparte laid down that aspirant generals should carefully study the feats of the great commanders of the past.[228] Following his advice, whether played with toy soldiers or cardboard

---

[226] See Alice Becker-Ho and Guy Debord, *A Game of War*, pages 24–26, 155.

[227] Alice Becker-Ho and Guy Debord, *A Game of War*, page 21.

[228] See Napoléon Bonaparte, *Military Maxims*, page 79.

counters, the designers of hobbyist simulations have dedicated themselves to producing historically accurate recreations of specific battles or campaigns. As our Marengo and Fort Bedourete scenarios revealed, both *The Game of War* and *Command & Colors: Napoleonics* could be adapted to re-enact politically resonant military conflicts from the past. But, this antiquarian chrome disguised the primary purpose of our participatory performances during the third stage of our campaign of ludic subversion: training Left activists in the abstract principles of *On War*. Back in late-1930s Vietnam, Giap had taught a course on this classic book and Bonaparte's campaigns to the elite leadership of the underground Bolshevik party.[229] Four decades later, Debord had published *The Game of War* to disseminate Clausewitz's theoretical analysis of these tumultuous historical events amongst the entire revolutionary movement. By playing his ludic invention and other military simulations, the third phase of Class Wargames' campaign was now dedicated to fulfilling this Situationist's greatest ambition. Breaking the vanguard party's monopoly over political subversion, rank-and-file proletarians must now become the collective skilful general whose mental agility could overcome the friction of war. Like Bonaparte, they too should know how to recognise the enemy's weaknesses and to correct their own mistakes. Within the spatial and temporal confines of these military simulations, the passive contemplation of Clausewitzian theory was transformed into the ludic celebration of Situationist practice. Deciding where to move the pieces on the board – or toy soldiers across a miniature terrain – was learning by doing.[230] Through the brief experience of being a little Bonaparte, the players of wargames were acquiring the intellectual stamina and calculated courage required to fight the modern iteration of Absolute War: the class struggle.[231]

When discussing his academic rival's methodology, Clausewitz

---

[229] See Peter MacDonald, *Giap*, page 23.

[230] 'Wargames have ... educational advantages for the study of war because students must grapple with real strategic and tactical dilemmas as they struggle to beat their colleagues, and games show that the historical outcome of a conflict was not bound to occur.' Philip Sabin, *Simulating War*, page 37.

[231] 'Daring has the value of gold amongst the warrior virtues.' Carl von Clausewitz, *Campagne de 1799 en Suisse et en Italie*, page 475. Also see *On War*, pages 700–703.

criticised the 'false elegance' of Jomini's geometrical theories of military strategy and tactics. For this Prussian soldier, there was only one brutal necessity underpinning Absolute War: breaking the enemy's will to resist with murderous violence.[232] From this fundamental abstract principle, Clausewitz had developed his dialectical exposition of the chaotic practicalities of armies fighting against one another. By studying the unfolding of the analysis within his classic text, generations of bourgeois officers have learnt the skills of commanding troops in the field. Now, thanks to Debord's ludic invention, proletarian revolutionaries could also become experts in this esoteric doctrine. Within the workings of *The Game of War*, this Situationist veteran had carefully incorporated the most important insights of *On War*. By playing his ludic invention and other military simulations, Class Wargames was now dedicated to teaching Clausewitz's five key strategic and tactical principles to today's Left activists:

- Coup d'oeil;
- Psyching the opponent;
- Concentration of forces;
- Outflanking the enemy;
- Hot pursuit.

In warfare, skilful generals know instinctively how to deploy their forces to maximise their effectiveness in a particular terrain of combat: coup d'oeil. For those fortunate enough to possess this ability, the outcome of an engagement can be decided even before the fighting commences. Taking advantage of the local geography, the different types of troops are positioned to provide mutual support for each other in both attack and defence. The army's lines of communications to its supply bases are well protected against outflanking attacks by the opposing side. The reserve is placed in a secure location until the time is ready for its decisive intervention into the combat.[233] Like Bonaparte, these military

---

[232] See Carl von Clausewitz, *Campagne de 1799 en Suisse et en Italie*, pages 288–289; *On War*, pages 85–86, 102–105.

[233] '... the relationship between warfare and terrain determines the peculiar character of military action ... To master it a special gift is needed ... It is the faculty of *quickly and accurately grasping the topography of any area* which enables a man to find his way about at any time.' Carl von Clausewitz, *On War*, page 127. Emphasis in the original.

commanders can instantly recognise the strengths and weaknesses of the enemy's deployment on the battlefield – and will ruthlessly take advantage of any mistake to beat them. Equipped with coup d'oeil, skilful generals always begin the battle with a distinct edge over their less sophisticated opponents.[234]

While planning the 1800 Marengo campaign, Bonaparte spotted immediately that the Austrians had foolishly launched a double-pronged offensive in both North Italy and South Germany. By dividing its military might into two equal parts, the enemy was now vulnerable to a concentrated counter-attack by the French reserve army. Long before the two sides met at this Piedmont town, Bonaparte's coup d'oeil had decided the result of the battle of Marengo. Despite his initial tactical errors, the First Consul's superior strategic position ensured that Desaix's reinforcements were able to arrive in time to save the day for the French cause.[235] At the culmination of the 1805 Austerlitz campaign, Bonaparte demonstrated a similar expertise in exploiting the psychogeography of a particular location. By hiding his reserves in the morning mist of the rolling Czech countryside, the newly crowned emperor accentuated the numerical inferiority of his own army. Tempted by this display of weakness, the Russians and Austrians were lured into leaving the security of their hilltop position and launching an attack against the French right. Then, as the sun burnt off the mist, Bonaparte's reserves suddenly emerged to make a surprise counter-attack against the exposed flank of the enemy's offensive strike. Celebrated in the Napoleonic legend ever since, the 1805 battle of Austerlitz was a triumph of coup d'oeil. By positioning his troops to take maximum advantage of the quirks of the terrain, Bonaparte had enabled the smaller French army to win a decisive victory against the larger Russian and Austrian opposition.[236]

---

[234] For Bonaparte's mastery of coup d'oeil, see Jean-Baptiste Vachée, *Napoleon at Work*, pages 162–163. Also see Friedrich Hohenzollern, *The King of Prussia's Instructions to his Generals*, page 13; and Rory Muir, *Tactics and the Experience of Battle in the Age of Napoleon*, pages 141–143.

[235] See James Arnold, *Marengo & Hohenlinden*, pages 100–186; and David Chandler, *The Campaigns of Napoleon*, pages 274–275.

[236] See F.G. Hourtoulle, *Austerlitz*; and David Chandler, *The Campaigns of Napoleon*, pages 409–439.

The Game of War is a ludic tool for practising coup d'oeil. Unlike *Chess* or *Go*, its board doesn't consist of a uniform grid of squares or intersections. Instead, when they sit down to play, North and South are faced by different spatial arrangements of forts, mountains, passes and arsenals. In contrast with the realist aesthetic of hobbyist and professional wargames, these two territories aren't faithful representations of specific historical or contemporary locations. Instead, in *The Game of War*, the abstraction of its terrain features focuses the players' attention on the theoretical analysis of coup d'oeil: the positioning of troops of different capabilities to take maximum advantage of the local psychogeography. When they laid out the pieces for their book's exemplary game in similar opening positions to the Pump House scenario shown in **Diagram 1** on page 110, Becker-Ho and Debord chose an initial deployment which optimised the territorial peculiarities of their side of the board. North began the game with its units placed in a block on the western escarpment of the vertical mountain range. With its left flank protected by this impassable obstacle, the infantry and artillery pieces were ready to swing into the central plain while the cavalry units out on the right flank had the option of either taking South's western arsenal by themselves or launching a combined shock attack with their compatriots into the middle of the board. Tellingly, her opponent mirrored this deployment with his forces concentrated around his central fort. From this pivotal position, South could either push forwards to seize the enemy's eastern arsenal or occupy the middle plain. When they opted for these opening layouts, both Becker-Ho and Debord could take pleasure in their expertise in the practical skill of coup d'oeil.[237]

According to the rules of *The Game of War*, the two players are allowed to choose their own initial deployment.[238] However, as Class Wargames soon discovered, this direction impels both sides to mass their forces into one large group which tends to slow down the pace of play. In our Marengo scenario shown in **Diagram 3** on page 226, the opening layout is instead decided for the two sides. With their pieces already placed on the board, North and South are set the task of practising

---

[237] See Alice Becker-Ho and Guy Debord, *A Game of War*, pages 39–59.
[238] See Alice Becker-Ho and Guy Debord, *A Game of War*, page 13.

their coup d'oeil through this ludic abstraction of military history. When refighting the Marengo campaign at our ICA event in 2010, Fabian's team had realised from the outset that the French main army at the back of the board has to attack as quickly as possible before two Austrian flanks could unite their forces in the central plain. Playing South on that night, he and Elena succeeded in smashing North's right wing before Russell had realised that his side's army was going down in defeat. A year later at Raylab, they found themselves instead commanding the Austrian side. Learning from their ICA victory as the French, Fabian and Elena conducted a cunning fighting retreat on their western flank until their army was massed in sufficient strength in the centre to launch the deadly counter-attack which decided the match. The skilful general could play as North or as South in the Marengo scenario – and win as both of them. With sufficient practice, every player of *The Game of War* can acquire the special gift of coup d'oeil.

In the 2008 *Reds versus Reds* contest at the Winter Palace, the commanders of the two rival armies of Russian Civil War figurines were also faced with the problem of working out how to take the best advantage of the terrain of battle. As shown in **Diagram 4** on page 228, Mark's Social Democrats began in what appeared to be a very strong defensive position. However, when my team of Bolsheviks was discussing tactics before play commenced, we noticed that the main road leading into the middle of the village had created a vulnerable opening in the centre of the enemy's line. If we pinned down Mark's left and right flanks with diversionary attacks, then our elite Kronstadt sailors could be sent in to assault this weak spot and – once they'd broken through – outflank the rest of the Social Democratic army's defences. Fortunately for us, this understanding of the strengths and weaknesses of the terrain resulted in a stunning success on the Kazan battlefield on that night at the Hermitage. Like *The Game of War*, playing *Reds versus Reds* was a practical lesson in coup d'oeil.

On the battlefield, skilful generals are able to intimidate and cajole their way to victory: psyching the opponent. As Clausewitz emphasised, the fighting quality of an army is decided as much by the morale of its troops as the numbers in its ranks. Armed combat is a test of will and resolution for both sides: whose nerve will break first?[239] Placed under intense physical pressure, military commanders require a special combination of mental toughness and emotional lucidity to make intelligent decisions at speed.[240] If blessed with this ability, they can benefit from the exponential rewards of success in warfare. While their own side's morale soars with each triumph, the enemy's soldiers and civilians are thrown further and further into despondency with every reverse.[241] Victory is always due as much to mental stamina as material superiority. Persuading the opponent to concede is the most elegant way to win.

During his 1800s rampages across Europe, Bonaparte demonstrated a supreme mastery in the skill of psyching his military antagonists. One after another, the armies of the great powers went down to catastrophic defeats at the hands of the French emperor. Facing this genius general who'd won so many battles, his enemies were already half-convinced that they'd lost before the two sides had even started fighting. Looking back at this dangerous period, the Duke of Wellington ruefully observed that '... [Bonaparte's] presence on the field made a difference of 40,000 men.'[242] What eventually shattered this aura of invincibility was the disastrous French invasion of Russia in 1812. After the retreat from Moscow, Bonaparte had lost not only most of his best troops, but also much of his military reputation. Slowly but surely, France's imperialist rivals combined their forces in the final titanic struggle against the upstart emperor. Still intimidated by Bonaparte's charisma, the leaders of the European powers relied upon overwhelming numbers to accomplish the overthrow of the scourge of Europe. Even during the 1814 and 1815 campaigns, when the odds were massively in their favour, their generals had only advanced against the French army with extreme caution. Right up to the very end of his

---

[239] See Carl von Clausewitz, *On War*, pages 216–228.

[240] See Jean-Baptiste Vachée, *Napoleon at Work*, pages 174–176; and Rory Muir, *Tactics and the Experience of Battle in the Age of Napoleon*, pages 149–150.

[241] See Carl von Clausewitz, *On War*, pages 300–305.

[242] Arthur Wellesley in Charles Esdaile, *The Wars of Napoleon*, page 66.

career, Bonaparte was unsurpassed in the military skill of psyching the opponent.[243]

At the beginning of Becker-Ho and Debord's exemplary game, the South sent two of his cavalry pieces forward in an attempt to seize North's eastern arsenal. However, when the opposition in response moved her army across the pass to reinforce the centre, he'd quickly retreated these units believing that their lines of communications were now vulnerable. Unfortunately, by making this decision, South had also taken the option which would eventually lose the game.[244] By repeatedly refighting this match between Becker-Ho and Debord during our 2007 training sessions, Class Wargames soon discovered that the best move instead would have been to risk everything by persevering with the cavalry attack against North's eastern arsenal. Once deprived of this supply base, the enemy's main army lost its manoeuvrability in the central plain – and was susceptible to being destroyed in detail. From our re-enactments of this model game, Class Wargames realised that the North had succeeded in bluffing the South into making a premature withdrawal. As its creator intended, by playing *The Game of War*, we'd become diligent students of Clausewitz's military theory of psyching the opponent. Unlike *Reds versus Reds* or *Commands & Colors: Napoleonics*, Debord's ludic invention made no provision in its rules for checking the morale of the two sides' units. Rather this mental struggle was recreated within the stressful ebb-and-flow of its competitive play.[245] Learning from Becker-Ho and Debord's game, Fabian took great pleasure in psyching his opponents whenever possible during our public performances. Like Bonaparte, he was an expert at making the other side believe that they'd lost the battle despite the outcome still being in doubt. Even after his mounted general had been removed from the board in the 2008 Pump House game, Fabian kept on claiming that his victory was inevitable until the very moment that he was forced to concede the match. At our 2010 ICA and 2011

---

[243] See Carl von Clausewitz, *Campagne de 1814*, pages 53–62; *Campagne de 1815 en France*, pages 23–31.

[244] See Alice Becker-Ho and Guy Debord, *A Game of War*, pages 51–59.

[245] See Alice Becker-Ho and Guy Debord, *A Game of War*, page 25.

Raylab games, this self-confidence had much more substance. Whether North or South, the army with Fabian on the team possessed the strategic and tactical skills to outwit with verve the less experienced players of the other side. When facing this genius general on the ludic battlefield, the opposition had good reason to be psyched.

During the opening moves of the 2012 match of our hacked scenario for *Command & Colors: Napoleonics* shown in **Diagram 6** on page 338, Christian and Tuesday's Haitian army quickly seized the initiative as their guard infantry regiments routed the defenders of Fort Bedourete and took control over the centre of the board. As their left flank rapidly moved up in support, these re-enactors of Toussaint confidently predicted that victory would soon be theirs. By demoralising the enemy, this success would inevitably lead to greater successes. Unfortunately for them, Marc and David refused to be psyched by their opponent. Regrouping the shattered French forces, they formed a defensive line which – after a fierce firefight – repelled the Haitian assault. As the Bonapartists began advancing across the battlefield, it was now Marc and David's turn to engage in Clausewitz's stratagem of psychological intimidation. With their best units having suffered heavy losses, the Haitians must accept that they had little chance of winning the battle. When Toussaint's cavalry reserve was wiped out, Christian and Tuesday were forced to agree with this dismal prognosis and conceded the game. This time, the enemy had been psyched.

In combat, skilful generals are focused upon massing their troops into the strongest possible fighting system: the concentration of forces. As both strategy and tactics, numerical superiority can deliver victory on its own. For Clausewitz, this imperative to achieve a quantitative advantage represents the fundamental principle of warfare.[246] Since defence is more powerful than attack, a larger sized army is usually required to overcome this qualitative edge. Military commanders understand that they must concentrate their offensive strike at one key point while making the enemy divide their forces as widely as

---

[246] '... there is no higher and simpler law of strategy than that of *keeping one's forces concentrated*. No force should ever be detached from the main body unless the need is definite and *urgent*.' Carl von Clausewitz, *On War*, page 240. Emphasis in the original.

possible along the frontline. If manoeuvred with boldness and finesse, this kinetic mass can overwhelm almost all resistance to its forward advance. By destroying the other side's defences, the concentration of forces is the most basic – and effective – method of winning a war.[247]

Throughout his illustrious career, Bonaparte demonstrated his expertise in this martial technique. Even with inferior numbers, he was able to achieve quantitative superiority at the vital location. While besieging Mantua during the winter of 1796–7, Bonaparte's smaller French army attacked and defeated in turn the divided columns of the much bigger Austrian army which were trying to relieve this North Italian city. At the 1807 battle of Friedland, the emperor overcame his numerical inferiority in comparison with the Russians by launching a massed infantry, cavalry and artillery attack which routed the enemy's exposed left flank.[248] As both a strategist and tactician, Bonaparte's skill at concentrating his forces again and again delivered the decisive blow against the opposition. In his maxims, he stressed that the good commander always commits as many soldiers as possible to the fray: 'A single battalion sometimes decides the day.'[249] However, eventually, the enemies of Bonaparte learnt how to become like Bonaparte themselves. At the 1813 battle of Leipzig, the Russians, Prussians and Austrians managed to commit twice as many troops to the fight as the French imperial army which gave a quantitative edge to them that no amount of clever manoeuvring could offset. During the 1814 campaign, these allies' numerical superiority had become so great that even a bravura display of Bonaparte's strategic and tactical brilliance was unable to halt their advance into the heartland of his realm.[250] In 1815, the emperor made one last attempt to reap the benefits of his artful skill at organising the localised concentration of forces. Before the Russians and Austrians were able to mobilise their troops, he'd launched a surprise attack against the British and Prussian armies in Belgium. By attacking each opponent in turn, the French would enjoy

---

[247] See Carl von Clausewitz, *On War*, pages 427–470, 753–755; and *Notes sur la Prusse dans sa Grande Catastrophe*, pages 90–91.

[248] See David Chandler, *The Campaigns of Napoleon*, pages 53–125, 572–585.

[249] Napoléon Bonaparte, *Military Maxims*, page 34.

[250] See Carl von Clausewitz, *Campagne de 1814*, pages 53–62, *On War*, pages 335–337, 764–771; and David Chandler, *The Campaigns of Napoleon*, pages 865–1004.

the quantitative advantage in both engagements. Yet, when the battle of Waterloo was fought, Bonaparte went down to defeat for failing to observe his own maxim. Overconfident, he'd foolishly detached one third of his troops to chase the Prussians who still managed to arrive at the key moment to reinforce the British line.[251] This skilful general had been outfoxed in his favourite military manoeuvre of the concentration of forces. The imitators of Bonaparte had triumphed over the original version.

The Game of War is a training tool for learning the necessity of massing troops. According to its combat table, infantry and artillery pieces are both much stronger in defence than attack. Only the cavalry units are endowed with superior offensive power.[252] In this ludic model of Clausewitz's military theory, the two sides must manoeuvre their equally balanced armies of 15 fighting pieces to achieve local superiority in firepower at vital points of the board. When the moment is correct, the players should launch combined attacks of infantry, cavalry and artillery units that are strong enough to batter down the opposition's defences.[253] In the play of their exemplary game, Becker-Ho and Debord implemented the Clausewitzian logic of this Situationist simulation. Both sides chose opening positions which grouped their pieces into one big block. North had massed her forces around the western arsenal. South's main army was positioned next to his central fort. Over the next two dozen moves, Becker-Ho and Debord tried to outmanoeuvre each other with faints and probes. By the end of the game, North and South were racing to concentrate their forces in centre of board for the final decisive battle. In this ludic abstraction of Clausewitz's military theory, the eventual winner was the player who'd gained quantitative dominance over these key squares on the board.[254] After re-enacting Becker-Ho and Debord's game many times, Class Wargames devised the initial layout of our Marengo scenario to prevent North and South from the outset concentrating their troops at the

---

251 See Carl von Clausewitz, *Campagne de 1815 en* France, pages 40–45, 139–158; and David Chandler, *The Campaigns of Napoleon*, pages 1008–1095.

252 See Alice Becker-Ho and Guy Debord, *A Game of War*, pages 12, 14–16.

253 See Alice Becker-Ho and Guy Debord, *A Game of War*, page 21.

254 See Alice Becker-Ho and Guy Debord, *A Game of War*, pages 22–23, 39–149.

most advantageous position on their side of the board. The Austrians are split equally into two forces on both flanks. The French main army starts on the back row of squares. During our 2010 ICA and 2011 Raylab performances, Fabian and Elena had won the game both times by skilfully manoeuvring their side's units to focus a concentrated offensive power on the weakest points in their opponent's defences. Even when retreating, they'd been able to launch sneaky counter-attacks that took pieces off the enemy. Like Bonaparte, Fabian and Elena were excellent practitioners of Clausewitz's military theory of the concentration of forces. Defence may be stronger than attack, but battles are only won by going over to the offensive.

During our 2012 performance of *Little Wars* at CCANW, the audience had included a boisterous group of small children who were very amused by the sight of serious grown-ups playing with toy soldiers. Yet, despite its simplistic rules, even H.G. Wells' ludic invention can be used to teach Clausewitz's principles of military theory. By calculating casualties in hand-to-hand combat according to the relative numbers on each side, *Little Wars* encourages the formation of big battalions by both sides. Above all, the players who can mass their Britains' artillery pieces to bombard the enemy's troops are almost always rewarded with success. In the CCANW game shown in **Diagram 7** on page 340, Ben and Lisa had instinctively understood this Clausewitzian imperative embedded within the rules of *Little Wars*. The French infantry assault on the British right flank had initially prevailed due to their superior numbers over the defenders until they were beaten back by deadly cannon fire. Happily, by bringing all three of their model artillery pieces to bear on Stefan and Tara's troops, Ben and Lisa were soon able to reverse this potentially disastrous set-back – and eventually emerge the winners of the match. Through this CCANW performance, Class Wargames had shown why Wells' toy soldier playtime wasn't just an entertaining diversion. As in *The Game of War*, the players of *Little Wars* were learning Clausewitz's stratagem of the concentration of forces on this ludic battlefield.

In warfare, skilful generals seek to manoeuvre their troops around the enemy's frontline to attack them in the rear: outflanking the enemy. As Clausewitz emphasised, it is very difficult to make victorious frontal assaults against inherently stronger defensive positions.[255] Fortunately, successful flanking stratagems will not only minimise the offensive side's losses, but also wreck the resisting side's morale. Modern warriors are adept at moving with great speed across the terrain to take advantage of any gaps in the opponent's defences: 'the war of manoeuvre'.[256] On the battlefield, their main force should pin down the enemy's forward troops until the reserve is ready to launch the decisive attack on the rear that will decide the day. As both strategy and tactics, turning the flank is the most effective method for negating the superior strength of the defence. All military commanders must be masters of this basic principle of armed aggression.[257]

Lacking the blind obedience of professionals, the citizen-soldiers of the French republican forces had been very reluctant to risk their lives in frontal attacks against enemy positions. Instead, they much preferred going around the royalist frontline to make an assault on its unprotected rear.[258] As a political general of this revolutionary army, Bonaparte embraced this spontaneous stratagem as his favourite manoeuvre.[259] In his military maxims, he laid down a clear instruction to his admirers: '... never to attack a position from the front which you can gain by turning.'[260] At the 1793 siege of Toulon, the Jacobin army had been repeatedly repulsed in its attempts to storm this Provençal city's walls. Taking command, Bonaparte instead ordered these troops to seize the hill which overlooked its harbour. As soon as his artillery were successfully positioned on this dominant position, the British and their local allies had no choice but to abandon Toulon to the besieging French republicans.[261] Similarly, during the 1796 battle of Castiglione, Bonaparte had craftily manoeuvred his forces around the Austrian army's left flank to launch the attack on its rear which had decided the

[255]   See Carl von Clausewitz, *On War*, pages 485–490.

[256]   See Carl von Clausewitz, *On War*, pages 622–625, 653–665.

[257]   See Carl von Clausewitz, *On War*, pages 394–415, 746–7.

[258]   See Paddy Griffith, *The Art of War of Revolutionary France*, pages 195–199.

[259]   See Carl von Clausewitz, *On War*, pages 284–290; and David Chandler, *The Campaigns of Napoleon*, pages 161–170.

[260]   Napoléon Bonaparte, *Military Maxims*, page 23.

[261]   See David Chandler, *The Campaigns of Napoleon*, pages 17–29.

engagement.[262] When planning the 1800 Marengo campaign, the First Consul applied this tactical principle at the strategical level. By first moving into Switzerland and then crossing the Alps, the French reserve was able to cut the line of communications of the Austrian army in North Italy. In 1805, Bonaparte secured one of his most celebrated victories through his expertise in this military technique. When the Austrian army in South Germany had advanced towards the Rhine, the emperor's soldiers carried out a daring manoeuvre around its right flank which completely severed its supply line with Vienna. Almost without a shot being fired, the Austrians were forced into a humiliating surrender at Ulm.[263] For aspirant generals, studying Bonaparte's brilliant career is the best possible lesson in the military efficacy of outflanking the opposition.

In the opening moves of their exemplary game, both Becker-Ho and Debord attempted to manoeuvre their units onto the enemy's rear. The North detached one cavalry piece which successfully destroyed South's western arsenal. However, Debord decided to abandon his assault against Becker-Ho's eastern arsenal when his lines of communications were threatened. From then onwards, South's position had deteriorated until the match was finally lost.[264] When Class Wargames replayed this contest at our 2007 training sessions, we were also slowly able to acquire the skill of carrying out outflanking attacks. Above all, we came to understand that practised players could win the game with this military technique without needing to take many of the opponent's pieces. When their link to the arsenals was broken, these units were helpless.[265] In the Marengo layout, both sides are given different starting positions for the tricky task of manoeuvring their pieces to smash their opponent's lines of communications. During our ICA performance, Fabian and Elena led the French to victory by committing their reserve to turning the Austrians' right flank. When playing the same scenario as North in Raylab, they'd launched a counter-attack in the centre which threatened South's line of communications to its western arsenal. As

[262] See David Chandler, *The Campaigns of Napoleon*, pages 191–201.

[263] See David Chandler, *The Campaigns of Napoleon*, pages 390–402.

[264] See Alice Becker-Ho and Guy Debord, *A Game of War*, pages 22–109.

[265] See Alice Becker-Ho and Guy Debord, *A Game of War*, pages 17–19.

Debord intended, *The Game of War* was the ludic manifestation of Napoleonic military theory. In this Clausewitz simulator, both sides must fiercely compete to realise the same difficult ambition: 'the flanker will be flanked'.[266]

Through our participatory performances, Class Wargames sought to teach this indispensable stratagem with other military simulations. When my team was formulating our tactics for the 2008 *Reds versus Reds* game at the Hermitage, we'd initially thought that the Bolsheviks should try to outflank the left of the Social Democrats' front line which was defended by unreliable peasant conscripts. However, after examining the layout of this miniature Kazan countryside in more detail, we decided instead to carry out this manoeuvre with a direct assault on the centre of the village. Once this open terrain had been successfully seized, the Bolsheviks' crack regiment of Kronstadt sailors was then able to outflank both wings of the Social Democratic army. Given his side's untenable position, Mark had to concede the game. Similarly, in the concluding moves of the 2012 *Commands & Colors: Napoleonics* contest at Furtherfield Gallery, Marc and David's French forces had launched a vigorous counter-attack against the right flank of the battered Haitian army. As their troops advanced along the river, they succeeded in pushing their opponent's remaining units into the centre of the battlefield. Deprived of any room to manoeuvre, a Haitian infantry regiment was destroyed soon afterwards when it was forced to retreat off the board. The French had now achieved their victory conditions and the game was won. Although lacking the theoretical sophistication of *The Game of War*, both *Reds versus Reds* and *Commands & Colors: Napoleonics* were teachers of Clausewitz's outflanking principle of military theory. Ludic détournement is Situationist enlightenment.

In combat, skilful generals know how to follow up a victory over the enemy's forces with relentless energy: hot pursuit. According to Clausewitz, the primary task of the triumphant army is ensuring that its opponent's demoralised troops don't have the opportunity to recover from any reverse. By maintaining the utmost pressure upon its rival,

---

[266] Alice Becker-Ho and Guy Debord, *A Game of War*, page 23.

the attacking side can force the complete dissolution of the defender's military might.[267] Total victory is the theoretical imperative of Absolute War.[268] For this Prussian officer, the military principle of hot pursuit must be realised with extreme urgency. Under the friction of war, each move forward into the opposition's terrain weakens the invading army. By preventing defeated troops from rallying, the determined attacker can maintain its advantage despite these losses until the enemy is finally forced to surrender. For its adepts, the successful implementation of hot pursuit is achieved through not only intellectual ingenuity, but also emotional strength. There can be no slackening of the pace up to the great moment when complete victory is achieved.[269]

During his military career, Bonaparte was an expert practitioner of hot pursuit. Both at the strategic and tactical levels, this clever general always kept reserves which could be committed to follow up any breakthrough against the opposition.[270] At the battle of Marengo, the Austrians failed to make the most of their initial surprise attack against the French troops around this Italian town. However, when Desaix's reinforcements arrived to save the day, the First Consul didn't make the same mistake. In successive counter-attacks, he routed the Austrians and took possession of the field.[271] During the 1806 Jena-Auerstädt campaign, Bonaparte demonstrated his mastery of hot pursuit as a strategic principle. After winning this famous battle, he unceasingly harried the defeated Prussians until their whole army disintegrated and surrendered.[272] Eventually, the tables were turned on Bonaparte himself. During the 1812 retreat from Moscow, the French army fell to pieces under the Russians' persistent attacks.[273] Refusing any compromise, the Tsar over the next two years pursued the upstart emperor all the way

---

[267] See Carl von Clausewitz, *On War*, pages 268–278, 312–321; *Campagne de 1815 en France*, pages 165–167.

[268] See Carl von Clausewitz, *On War*, pages 700–703.

[269] See Carl von Clausewitz, *On War*, pages 633–640, 684–688, 755–758.

[270] See Carl von Clausewitz, *On War*, pages 240–249.

[271] See David Chandler, *The Campaigns of Napoleon*, pages 286–301.

[272] See Carl von Clausewitz, *Notes sur la Prusse dans sa Grande Catastrophe*, pages 145–162; and David Chandler, *The Campaigns of Napoleon*, pages 479–506.

[273] See Carl von Clausewitz, *The Campaign of 1812 in Russia*, pages 98–100; and David Chandler, *The Campaigns of Napoleon*, pages 767–861.

to his lair in Paris. Total victory had been denied to the most skilful general of Absolute War.

The Game of War is a simulation which teaches the military theory of hot pursuit. When they gain the initiative on the board, the best players intensify their offensive to deprive their opponent of any opportunity to launch a counter-attack.[274] In Becker-Ho and Debord's exemplary game, South failed to follow through with his initial assault into the centre. Instead, North took the lead with her army's bold manoeuvre across the pass to defend the eastern arsenal. Once massed in the centre, these pieces were then able to push the South's army to the back of the board until the match was conceded. Relentless pursuit had delivered complete victory.[275] At our 2008 Pump House game, Fabian had uncharacteristically fumbled his application of this military technique when – despite securing the initial advantage – he'd lost his mounted general to my cavalry charge. However, when the Marengo scenario was played at both the ICA and Raylab, he and Elena demonstrated their superiority in the ludic implementation of hot pursuit. As the French, they'd kept up their assaults on the Austrian army until it was no longer able to defend itself. Switching sides to North at Raylab, Fabian and Elena had been at first forced to carry out a fighting retreat while concentrating their pieces in the centre. But, once this task was completed, they switched over to a succession of counter-attacks which destroyed South's offensive capability. In *The Game of War* as on the battlefield, relentless determination is the leitmotif of total victory.

When playing other military simulations, Class Wargames discovered how their game engines also favoured the players who could apply Clausewitz's principle of hot pursuit. In the 2008 *Reds versus Reds* match at the Winter Palace, my side had prevailed because one of our Bolshevik commissars had prevented a wavering regiment from retreating at a vital moment. Having survived this momentary crisis, this regiment of regulars was immediately thrown back into action against the Social Democrat conscripts defending Mark's left flank. With our elite Kronstadt sailors now advancing fast towards the

---

274   See Alice Becker-Ho and Guy Debord, *A Game of War*, page 23.

275   See Alice Becker-Ho and Guy Debord, *A Game of War*, pages 131–149.

centre of the village, the Bolsheviks soon won the battle of Kazan by maintaining constant pressure upon the enemy without allowing them any time to recover. Similarly, in the 2012 *Commands & Colors: Napoleonics* game at Furtherfield, Marc and David's French army had recovered from their initial reverses to launch a relentless counter-attack which ended up sweeping Christian and Tuesday's Haitian troops off the board. During the 2012 CCANW performance of *Little Wars*, Ben and Lisa's British troops had continued their advance under heavy fire until they'd been able to reduce Stefan and Tara's forces to one lonely toy soldier. In each of these three games, the winning side had been the best players of the military principle of hot pursuit.

During the third stage of our campaign of ludic subversion, Class Wargames promoted *The Game of War*, *Reds versus Reds*, *Commands & Colors: Napoleonics* and *Little Wars* as Clausewitz simulators for libertarian communists. By taking part in these mock combats, their players were learning the five key principles of this Prussian officer's military philosophy: coup d'oeil; psyching the opponent; concentration of forces; outflanking the enemy; and hot pursuit. Crucially, these participants were understanding by doing. When making choices over where to move their pieces on the board or their toy soldiers across the terrain, the rules rewarded them for successfully putting Clausewitz's theoretical insights into ludic practice. By repeatedly playing these military simulations, Left activists could train themselves in the skills of generalship required to prevail on the social battlefield. In a détournement of Augusto Boal's famous observation about community theatre, Class Wargames paid homage to Debord as the heroic pioneer of ludic subversion by proudly affirming that: 'Perhaps [*The Game of War*] is not revolutionary in itself; but have no doubts, it is the rehearsal of revolution!'[276]

---

[276] Augusto Boal, *Theatre of the Oppressed*, page 155.

3.8: MAKING HISTORY

In the early evening of Wednesday 31ˢᵗ October 2012, a small crowd gathered inside Housmans Bookshop in London to celebrate the launch of the new pamphlet which compiled the extended script for our 2009 film along with the nine Communiqués that we'd released to accompany our performances over the previous five years: Richard Barbrook and Fabian Tompsett's *Class Wargames Presents Guy Debord's The Game of War*. But, what for us on that autumn night should have been a joyous occasion was overshadowed by a terrible personal tragedy. Only a month earlier, Elena Vorontsova Duffield had been struck down by cervical cancer and suddenly died at the shockingly young age of 37. In the two years since the 2010 *Chto Delat?* event at the ICA, she'd become an integral member of our Situationist project. Above all, it'd been thanks to her translating and organising skills that we'd been able to produce the Russian language version of the Class Wargames movie in 2011. Now, almost inexplicably, Elena was no longer with us. At the Housmans launch, before we began our talk about the pamphlet, Fabian and I said a few poignant sentences in honour of our fallen comrade. However, there was nothing that could be put into words which would express the searing pain of this traumatic loss.[277] We somehow expected Elena to walk through the door of Housmans and, smiling mischievously, join in the festivities. Class Wargames deeply missed her presence in our ranks on that evening – and we still do to this day.

Not surprisingly, the horrible reality of Elena's demise forced us to reflect upon the macabre metaphors which animated our ludic artworks. In all of the four games that we played at our performances, the taking of pieces on the board symbolised the taking of lives on the battlefield. When the cruelty of losing a dear friend was fresh in the memory, pretending to kill and maim other human beings could seem to be in very bad taste. What is more, Class Wargames was launching its pamphlet in Housmans Bookshop which had been founded in 1945 by the Peace Pledge Union. For over six decades, pacifist groups based in this building had been campaigning against the British establishment's

---

[277] Pictures were better at communicating our grief: Ilze Black, *Elena – in Memoriam*.

expensive infatuation with nuclear weapons, regimental pride and imperialist adventures.[278] The more literal minded adherents of the Left might be forgiven for thinking that the performances of *The Game of War* and *Commands & Colors: Napoleonics* which Housmans had scheduled to promote our new pamphlet were completely incompatible with the founding principles of this pacifist venue. Even when staged as simulations, military violence must be an anathema to all civilised people.

While talking with the audiences at our events over the years, Class Wargames has been amused to discover that lots of male lefties – and a select few of their female comrades – were enthusiastic wargamers in their teens. Although they'd have no problem in declaring their admiration for Trotsky, Che and other glamorous men in uniform, they were almost always embarrassed to admit that they might still enjoy refighting battles from the past. By inventing *The Game of War*, Debord had challenged the political prejudices of not only the hobbyist and professional practitioners of military simulations, but also, most wonderfully, these bashful activists, artists and academics of the Left. Through our performances, exhibitions, publications, videos and website, Class Wargames was encouraging socialist wargamers to come out of the closet. There was no shame in playing with toy soldiers as an ideologically aware adult. As Debord had proved, wargames could be both avant-garde artworks and political proselytisers. Best of all, his ludic creation facilitated the democratisation of Clausewitz's military teachings amongst the civilian population. As pacifists, the staff and patrons of Housmans may have detested the butchery of the battlefield. But, they would be foolish if they refused learn the lessons of armed combat which had been revealed at such a huge cost in human suffering. By playing at war, fighters for peace were gaining the specialised knowledge of how to defeat the masters of war at their own game. When every proletarian becomes a skilful general, the bourgeoisie will no longer be able to dominate the global system through its martial prowess.

On the Sunday afternoon preceding the launch of our pamphlet

---

278   See Housmans Bookshop, 'The Story of Housmans'.

at Housmans Bookshop, Class Wargames hosted a participatory performance of the Marengo scenario for *The Game of War* shown in **Diagram 3** on page 226. After dividing the first time players at this event into two teams, Stefan took on the role of military attaché for the Austrians while Fabian mentored their French opponents. Over the next few hours, Clausewitz's combat theories were put into ludic practice. Pointing out the strengths and weaknesses of their starting positions on the asymmetrical board, Stefan and Fabian gave the first lesson in generalship to the newbie commanders of North and South: the importance of coup d'oeil. The Austrians might look strong advancing aggressively on both flanks against a weak defensive line, but their forces were vulnerable to a concentrated counter-attack by the French reserve. As Stefan now recommended, their opening moves must be focused on closing this worrying gap in the middle of the board. Imitating their predecessors in the 2011 Raylab game, the North team ordered their pieces on the right flank across the pass to meet up with the rest of their troops in the central plain. While this complex manoeuvre was happening, the South's reserve force was being moved forward at great speed to meet them. Within a dozen turns, the rival armies had become engaged in a fierce struggle around the forts in the middle of the board. As Stefan and Fabian's second lesson in Clausewitzian theory, the Austrian and French teams were now encouraged to engage in psyching the enemy. Boasting about the inevitability of their total victory in the game would spread despondency and defeatism amongst the other side. But, as the third and fourth principles of the Prussian warrior intellectual emphasised, this mental intimidation had to be backed up with decisive actions on the battlefield. By this point in the match at Housmans Bookshop, neither the North or the South were able to outflank their opponent's army with any hope of success. Instead, they would have to prevail by implementing Bonaparte's second favourite stratagem: the concentration of forces. In this race to control the middle of the board, it was the French who were able to achieve local superiority over the Austrians. Helped by Fabian's tactical expertise, they would eventually come out on top in the costly fighting within the central plain. Implementing the fifth lesson of this Clausewitz simulator, the soldiers of the South were soon in hot pursuit of the shattered army of the North. After a few more moves, unable to resist any further, the Austrians reluctantly conceded the match to the

French.[279] In Housmans Bookshop as in history, Bonaparte had won the Marengo campaign. More importantly, as Debord had planned, both teams were victorious in their mutual quest for Situationist knowledge. By playing *The Game of War*, the pacifists in Housmans Bookshop had overcome their abhorrence of military bloodletting and learnt how to conquer on the social battlefield. The Left must understand how to be a skilful general.

Three days later, as the preliminary to the launch of our pamphlet, Class Wargames organised a collective re-staging of the 1802 battle of Fort Bedourete remix of *Commands & Colors: Napoleonics* shown in **Diagram 6** on page 338. For this engagement at Housmans Bookshop, the Haitian Jacobins were led by Kateryna Onyiliogwu with Fabian as her trusted advisor while the French Bonapartists were commanded by James Moulding aided by Robin Halpin from *Dialectica Principia*. Although Richard Borg's board game was missing the theoretical depth of Debord's ludic invention, our hack could still be used to teach some basic military nostrums. As in the summer match at Furtherfield gallery, the Haitians in a bravura display of coup d'oeil opened hostilities by sending their centre column to seize control of Fort Bedourete with their left flank simultaneously moving up in support. Refusing to be psyched by the opponent, the French responded by launching a counter-attack to retake the eponymous bastion while also massing the troops on their left for a rapid advance forward. Unfortunately for them, James and Robin's clever schemes would soon be foiled by the other side's helpful order cards and lucky dice throws. Both their concentration of Bonapartist forces in the centre and their outflanking manoeuvre on the left ended in grief as these French units were decimated by the Haitians' dexterity in musketry and hand-to-hand fighting. Having achieved this tactical advantage, Kateryna and Fabian now committed their remaining troops to the hot pursuit of the enemy. Within a few more moves, the French had lost their Charles Leclerc piece and the game was definitely over for the Bonapartists.[280] In this re-enactment as in reality, Toussaint and his Jacobins were triumphant

---

[279] For photographs of this first game at Housmans, see the Events 2012 section of the Class Wargames website.

[280] For photographs of this second game at Housmans, see the Events 2012 section of the Class Wargames website.

at the battle of Fort Bedourete. This time around, the course of history hadn't been changed.

With these two performances at Housmans Bookshop, Class Wargames had decisively entered the third phase of its hard fought campaign of ludic subversion. Debord's *The Game of War* had been described as his most autobiographical work and – over the previous five years – we'd had the great pleasure of retracing the career of this Situationist insurgent through our exertions across three continents. In the first stage, we'd played *The Game of War* as an avant-garde artwork. The second period was focused upon propagating its political message of collective revolutionary leadership. Now, in its third manifestation, Class Wargames' interventions were devoted to teaching the skills of military combat to Left activists. Over these five years, the successive phases of our campaign of ludic subversion had always stayed true to its underlying unity of purpose: the theoretical and practical critique of the integrated spectacle. During the opening manoeuvres of our campaign, Class Wargames had acted as a homage to the English Section's punk appropriation of Situationism. We'd carried out the provocation of playing wargames within the pacifist culture of the Left. We'd detourned hobbyist military simulations for our own political advantage. We'd revelled in the psychogeography of both the locations of our performances and the game board itself. We'd facilitated transient moments of participatory creativity when every player of *The Game of War* and *Reds versus Reds* became an artist. In the lineage of the Sex Pistols, the Haçienda and Banksy, the first iteration of our campaign was an exhilarating fiesta of Pop Situationism.

While pleased at the enthusiastic reception for our interventions, Class Wargames was also aware of the inherent limitations of adopting this strategy of aesthetic dissidence within contemporary Europe. Over in Putin's Russia, the Situationists' four tactics of avant-garde art did still retain their potency as insurrectionary weapons. Trumping the Lettrists' 1950 intervention at Notre Dame, Pussy Riot's 2012 scratch performance of their *Punk Prayer* in Moscow's Cathedral of Christ the Saviour so enraged this nation's reactionary political and religious authorities that two of its members were sent to prison after a farcical trial.[281] As *Chto Delat?* emphasised, their comrades' Situationist shock tactic had succeeded in achieving its primary goal: disturbing the univocal spectacle of political hypocrisy within Russia.[282] Compared to this audacious action, Class Wargames' avant-garde art performances, exhibitions, films and publications were quite safe. Far from being persecuted, we were lauded for our expertise in the four techniques of Pop Situationist cultural rebellion. Most gratifyingly, Class Wargames was sometimes paid for putting on events, contributing to shows and making videos. More than three decades after the Sex Pistols first played in London, provocation, remixing, psychogeography and user generated content had been thoroughly recuperated in England as smart business techniques for cutting-edge artists and media entrepreneurs. With Deller now representing his country at the 2013 Venice Biennale, even our joyful mocking of the po-faced aesthetes' disdain for the hobbyist subculture of wargaming was no longer outrageous.[283] In the Post-Modernist funfair of avant-garde entertainment, everyone was given the opportunity to be a Pop Situationist.

Retracing the trajectory of the 1962 split in the International, Class Wargames responded to this recuperatory danger by opening the second phase of our campaign of ludic subversion. Inspired by our 2008 expedition to St Petersburg, we became focused upon how Debord had constructed *The Game of War* as his masterpiece of Situationist political propaganda. Before its publication in 1977, he'd fearlessly promoted the proletarian revolutionary cause in print, at exhibitions and on film. Now, with this ludic experiment, Debord had provided a more interactive – and subtle – method for learning about the theoretical concepts and practical solutions of libertarian communism. In this second phase of our campaign of ludic subversion, Class Wargames

---

[281] See Pussy Riot, *Punk Prayer*. For the global campaign deploring the band's harsh punishment, see the Free Pussy Riot website.

[282] 'This is exactly the kind of iconic image [that] the [anti-Putin] protest movement has been trying to avoid, with its emphatically anti-revolutionary rhetoric, its consolidation around patriotic ... values, and its respectful avoidance of any critique aimed at the Russian Orthodox Church as one of the state-ideological apparatuses that has filled the void left behind by the ...[Stalinist] Party.' David Riff, 'A Representation which is Divorced from the Consciousness.'

[283] For the artist's own thoughts about this show, see Mark Rappolt, 'Jeremy Deller Interview'.

took its inspiration from his pioneering work. At our participatory performances of *The Game of War*, by moving their pieces across its board, the rival teams of North and South could personally experience the Situationist refutation of vanguard politics. When they ordered their 28mm Bolshevik or Social Democrat figurines into combat, the two sides in *Reds versus Reds* were reliving the militarised recuperation of socialism into the concentrated and diffuse versions of spectacular domination for themselves. Playing games was debating politics by other means.

In this second stage of our campaign of ludic subversion, Class Wargames was determined to keep faith with Debord's historical imperative. While we were touring from Belo Horizonte to Irkutsk, popular resistance to the depredations of neoliberal globalisation was growing in numbers and intensity across the world. As C.L.R. James had predicted, only the mobilised masses in their millions possessed the social power to challenge the technocratic monopolisers of power and wealth. But, like the New Left before them, this emerging generation of radicals also had a big problem with history. On the one hand, for the McLuhanist boosters of social media, the Net was reconstructing politics in its own hi-tech image. There was no longer any need for revolutionary leaders when everyone had access to email, blogs, Facebook and Twitter. On the other hand, for the admirers of Left sects, the path to the utopian future meant returning to a mythical past. Eisenstein's fictional portrayal of the 1917 storming of the Winter Palace in his 1927 *October* movie was still the essence of 21ˢᵗ century vanguard politics. With the second phase of our campaign, Class Wargames launched its offensive against both of these ideological errors. As a disorientating outflanking manoeuvre, our interventions now lauded Debord's *The Game of War* and Peers' *Reds versus Reds* as analogue simulations of vanguard politics. After working as an alienated individual on a screen all day, the tactile and social pleasures of moving pieces or figurines were a refutation of futurist fantasies in themselves. However wonderful, new media technologies couldn't save humanity by themselves.

At our performances, the explanatory commentary always congratulated Debord for avoiding inventing a faddish game of his own times which replicated either the street fighting in Paris between students and gendarmes during the May '68 Revolution or rural guerrillas combatting the military might of American imperialism somewhere in the South. Instead, he'd deliberately chosen to model the armed conflicts of two centuries earlier during the traumatic birth pangs of capitalist Europe. Contrary to the McLuhanist prophecies, the new information society was just the latest upgrade of the old capitalist system. All of the competing currents of today's Left had their origins in the primordial politics of this distant past. Each new generation of radicals must build upon what had already been achieved by their forebears. Through our participatory performances, the players of *The Game of War* and *Reds versus Reds* were now able to trace the tumultuous events of May '68 in Debord's own lifetime back through the Bolshevik mythology of October 1917 to what – along with Hegel – he'd believed was the formative moment of the modern world: the 1789 French Revolution.[284] The Jacobins were the pioneers of the Bolshevik style of vanguard politics. Bonaparte's liberal autocracy was the forerunner of Stalin's totalitarian tyranny. The failings of the Left in the present had their roots in its mistakes in the past.

Emphasising this long view of history, Class Wargames created the 1802 battle of Fort Bedourete scenario for *Commands & Colors: Napoleonics* to add to our ludic repertoire. As Donkor's painting commemorated, the first global rebellion against exploitation and injustice had taken place over two hundred years ago in the common struggle of the Jacobins on both sides of the Atlantic. Above all, through the influence of James' writings, the Haitian slaves' desire for liberation from bondage had reemerged in the Situationists' enthusiasm for the ascendency of the workers' councils over everyday life. By playing *The Game of War*, *Reds versus Reds* and *Commands & Colors: Napoleonics*, the participants at our performances were absorbing these ludic lessons in revolutionary history. Understanding the victories and defeats of the past was the precondition for devising the successful strategy and tactics for prevailing on the social battlefields of the future. Everyone must experience the excitements and temptations of being a little Bonaparte, Trotsky or Che for themselves. As Debord recommended, perceptive remembering can liberate the mind from both the forgetting and the mythologising of the integrated spectacle.

---

[284] Based in London, Class Wargames would – one day – like to trace in ludic form this historical caesura further back to our own country's original version of 1789 and 1917: the 1642 English Revolution.

In this second phase of our campaign, Class Wargames became fascinated with how Debord's ludic invention materialised the Situationist critique of revolutionary leadership. The fatal flaw of all of the Left sects in the 2010s was that they were still minority movements. Whether they denied the occult choreography of spontaneous mobilisations or championed the enlightened guidance of the diffuse vanguard, their activists were perpetuating the hallowed tradition of finding comfort in the ideological exclusivities of Social Democracy, Anarchism, Bolshevism and Autonomism. As Donkor's painting so brilliantly highlighted, these elitist dreams of collective emancipation have all too often become embodied in the charismatic personality of the great revolutionary leader: Toussaint, Lenin and Nkrumah. If some of these heroes have shamefully failed their followers, the primary causes lay in their moral flaws and political megalomania: Bonaparte, Mussolini and Mao. Hopefully, armed with the latest version of the correct ideology, the next Marat on horseback might be able to lead the masses to ultimate victory. With the publication of *The Game of War* in 1977, Debord had offered his own idiosyncratic alternative to this old solution of the New Left. Learning from this founding father of ludic subversion, instead of pining for a 21st century update of Robespierre, Trotsky or Cohn-Bendit, today's militants must understand that they themselves have to become the skilful general who will guide the proletarian struggle to ultimate victory. In the second stage of our campaign of ludic subversion, Class Wargames propagated this Situationist wisdom amongst the participants of our performances. Gathered around its board, the players of *The Game of War*, *Reds versus Reds*, *Commands & Colors: Napoleonics* and *Little Wars* were anticipating the direct democracy of the workers' councils in microcosm. By competing fiercely with each other, these admirers of Debord were co-operating to learn how revolutionary leadership should be exercised collectively in the libertarian communist future. Playing wargames was making Situationist political propaganda in ludic guise.

By 2012, our campaign of cultural rebellion had reached its third phase of offensive operations. Having successfully performed *The Game of War*, *Reds versus Reds*, *Commands & Colors: Napoleonics* and *Little Wars* first as avant-garde artworks and then as proselytisers for libertarian communism, Class Wargames now embraced Debord's call for wargames to be played as interactive training exercises in Clausewitzian military theory. Unfortunately, during the May '68 French Revolution, the skilful generalship of de Gaulle had triumphed over the raw recruits of the New Left on the social battlefield. Next time, the militants of the workers' councils must be much better prepared. Unlike their Social Democratic, Anarchist, Bolshevik and Autonomist comrades, the Situationists remained suspicious of any attempts to prefigure the communist future within the capitalist present. Avoiding this recuperative temptation, Debord proposed that proletarian revolutionaries should instead concentrate on teaching themselves the five theoretical principles of Clausewitz's *On War*: coup d'oeil; psyching the opponent; concentration of forces; outflanking the enemy; and hot pursuit. By fighting each other with model armies, the players of North and South could acquire the craft skills of revolutionary leadership for themselves. The specialist knowledge of the chosen few was now being transformed into the common understanding of the insurgent masses. As *Socialisme ou Barbarie* had advocated, the division of labour between order-givers and order-takers within the Left must be overcome. While patiently waiting for the coming libertarian communist insurrection, Situationists would be training hard with Clausewitz simulators to ensure that the decisive victory was theirs next time around. For Debord, *The Game of War* was *On War* remixed into a board game. Our task was to build upon this insight by playing military simulations to educate the Left in the skills of Situationist generalship.

In the participatory performances for the third stage of our campaign of ludic subversion, Class Wargames counterposed Debord's détournement of Clausewitz's writings with the Cold War interpretations of this Prussian soldier's ideas championed by both Bolshevik autocrats and RAND consultants. Like *Kriegsspiel*, *The Game of War* was an immersive teaching tool which enabled its players to turn military theory into ludic practice. But, unlike the professional simulations which were designed for training the officer corps, Debord's creation was made for everyone. At our events, Class Wargames was almost always teaching first timers how to play the game. For the acolytes of both Lenin and Kahn, Clausewitz's military theory had been esoteric knowledge which elevated the ruling elite above the rest of humanity. But, by studying hard with *The Game of War*, the rebellious masses could now also become proficient in his five key concepts of armed combat. If interpreted with awareness, the co-operative experience of playing *Reds versus Reds*, *Commands & Colors: Napoleonics* and *Little Wars* at our events could also impart important strategic and tactical insights as well. When giving orders to their toy soldiers or wooden blocks, the commanders of these simulations' miniature armies were learning how to take the best advantage of terrain features, intimidate their opponent with bravado, manoeuvre around defensive positions, maximise numerical superiority in fighting and ensure that the enemy's retreating troops never had the opportunity to rally. Embarrassed that they might be mistaken for fascists or imperialists, hobbyist wargamers were obsessed with the nerdy historical details of the uniforms and weaponry of the valiant warriors of their chosen period. Inspired by Debord, Class Wargames challenged these apolitical enthusiasts to embrace the hidden subversive possibilities of this amusing leisure activity. Playing with toy soldiers democratised the specialist skills of generalship. When everyone was trained in Clausewitz's five principles of armed struggle, the insurgent proletariat would be capable of exercising revolutionary leadership collectively.

Alongside this détournement of hobbyist wargames, the third phase of our campaign of ludic subversion also targeted the Left's own mythologising of its glorious past. After five years of hosting participatory performances, Class Wargames had finally understood why so many adult activists had amassed large armies of toy soldiers lovingly painted in the correct uniforms when they'd been teenagers. Even if they refused to admit it now, their political identity as adults was profoundly influenced by these military simulations of their youth. Like hobbyist wargamers deciding to concentrate on refighting one particular historical period of warfare, each of the rival factions of the Left was fascinated by its own chosen moment of political emancipation from the last century: 1917 Petrograd, 1936 Barcelona, 1945 London and 1977 Milan. Like members of historical re-enactment societies, the adherents of Bolshevism, Anarchism, Social Democracy and Autonomism were – almost unconsciously – engaged in live action role-playing. In contrast to the McLuhanists who proclaimed that nothing can be learnt about the post-industrial future from the industrial past, they could only experience the present as a mythologised facsimile of their favourite transformative times from long ago. In the third stage of our campaign, Class Wargames offered its ludic antidote to these geeky fantasies which were constricting the political imagination of the Left. By recovering their teenage horde of toy soldiers left in their parents' house, grown-up militants could indulge their obsession with the high points of labour history without confusing the past with the present. Freeing themselves from the delusion of resurrecting Lenin's vanguard party in the 21ˢᵗ century, contemporary admirers of Bolshevism should instead purchase Russian Civil War figurines from Copplestone Castings and enjoy playing at being a little Trotsky with Chris Peers' *Reds versus Reds* rules. Best of all, unlike in real life, the only casualties of their anachronistic political practice on this simulated social battlefield would be their model soldiers. As we'd proved with our 2008 intervention at the Hermitage, re-enacting the 1917 Russian Revolution with 28mm miniatures was a most delightful – and efficacious – method of exorcising the temptations of Bolshevism amongst the members of today's anti-capitalist movements.

In the first stage of our campaign of cultural dissidence, Class Wargames had briefly thought about creating a May '68 version of *The Game of War*. Fortunately, Rod had dissuaded us from acting upon this naive misconception. Five years later, in the third phase of the campaign, we now fully understood why making this commemorative set would have been such a grave political error. Crucially, in the early-1970s, Debord had first ruthlessly purged and then peremptorily dissolved the International to sabotage any attempt to recuperate Situationism as a 1968 Paris historical re-enactment society. Realising that they were now living in harder times, many of today's young militants have sought solace in the intoxicating memory of their elders' experiences during this almost revolution. In *The Society of the Spectacle*, they've found the theoretical manifesto of what might have been in the 'Red Decades' of the 1960s and 1970s.[285] Surpassing their Social Democrat, Anarchist, Bolshevik and Autonomist rivals, the Situationists have now become the epitome of the extreme left of the New Left. However, Debord would have been horrified by such fervent adulation of the International. Tragically, these admirers were determined to freeze the distinctive Situationist programme in time. As good Marxists, the International had developed its innovative

---

[285] See McKenzie Wark, *The Spectacle of Disintegration*, pages 47–48.

329

theoretical insights and radical practical solutions in response to the very specific historical circumstances within which they'd been living between the 1950s and the 1970s. What had distinguished them from the rest of the Left was precisely their keen appreciation of the novelty of the Fordist stage of capitalism. Anticipating the ascendency of neoliberal globalisation, Debord argued that the 1970s generation must continue this permanent revolution in libertarian communist thought and practice to meet the unexpected challenges of their own times. New problems would demand new answers. Unfortunately, most of the contemporary groupies of Situationism are instead much more interested in transforming the temporary expedients of May '68 into a rigid ahistorical ideology. By asserting their ownership of this mythical past, they aspire to control the confusing circumstances of the present. Above all, like their Social Democrat, Anarchist, Bolshevik and Autonomist peers, these faux Situationists are another iteration of the persistence of vanguard politics within the Left.

In the second phase of our campaign of ludic subversion, Class Wargames had promoted *The Game of War* as Debord's antidote to his own recuperation. By moving its pieces across the board, the players of North and South were becoming little Toussaints, Trotskys and Cohn-Bendits. As the commentary at our participatory performances stressed, the Situationist politics of this ludic propaganda were unambiguous. When everyone was a skilful general, then no vanguard could monopolise the leadership of the proletarian revolution. By the time that we were engaged in the third stage of our campaign, Class Wargames was concentrating on the practical applications of not only Debord's *The Game of War*, but also *Reds versus Reds, Commands & Colors: Napoleonics* and *Little Wars*. While fighting battles in miniature with each other, libertarian communists were teaching themselves Clausewitz's five principles of armed combat. If revolutionary leadership was to be exercised collectively, then everyone must be educated in the craft skills of generalship.

Equipped with this Situationist knowledge, the Left could now free itself from its thrall to ahistorical ideologies. The political strategy and artistic tactics of the International might have been innovative when they'd first been applied. But, in the same way that the military opponents of Bonaparte eventually learnt how to beat the emperor by imitating his innovative strategy and tactics, much of what had been threatening to bourgeois order in Situationism has long been domesticated. In the third phase of our campaign, Class Wargames facilitated the dissemination of Debord's pedagogical remedy for the corrupting inevitability of political recuperation. By playing *The Game of War, Reds versus Reds, Commands & Colors: Napoleonics* and *Little Wars*, today's rebels were acquiring the mental discipline required to devise the novel strategy and tactics for winning their generation's struggle against the obtuse tyranny of neoliberal globalisation. If they wanted to master the passage of time, the activists of the Left must no longer be slaves to a dead ideology.

In this third stage of our cultural offensive, Class Wargames eulogised the self-obsolescence of the Situationist International. *The Game of War* was Debord's ludic lesson in Do-It-Yourself politics. By acquiring the technical skills of Clausewitzian generalship on its board, libertarian communists would then be able to play the different sects of the Left as the infantry, cavalry and artillery pieces of the social battlefield. Each tendency had combat modifiers which reflected its own strengths and weaknesses. Social Democrats were great for fighting elections, but no good at scrapping with the cops. Anarchists had big bonuses in rioting, but were heavily penalised when trying to get out the vote. Bolsheviks were excellent for organising demonstrations, but awful at persuading uncommitted people to join the cause. Autonomists gained extras for social media activism, but had a reduced score for mobilising outside their bohemian bastions. Above all, there were no – and never could be any – Situationist pieces on the board of this game of proletarian insurrection. As Debord boasted: 'I'm not a philosopher, I'm a strategist.'[286]

In the revolutionary army, there were reserve units of intransigent intellectuals who could be deployed to make fierce denunciations of any signs of recuperation amongst the Left sects. However, having finally left the 20th century, what truly fulfilled James and Debord's prophecies of mass insurrection were the increasing number of newbies

---

[286] Guy Debord in Giorgio Agamben, 'Difference and Repetition', page 313. Ironically, the author of this article didn't seem to realise that this quip made to him by Debord was carefully aimed against his own semiotic structuralist errors.

reinforcing the Red side of the board. By participating in Class Wargames performances, these first time players could teach themselves how to become the collective skilful general. Like hobbyists allocating points to choose how many infantry, cavalry and artillery figurines should make up a toy soldier army, their world-historic mission was to assemble the optimal mix of Left tendencies for the cataclysmic struggle ahead.[287] As taught in both *The Game of War* and *Commands & Colors: Napoleonics*, a combined attack of different pieces was the deadliest form of assault. This co-operative leader's first task was imposing some self-discipline upon the squabbling soldiery of the fractured Left. Fighting each other was the worst way to fight the enemy. Every piece on the board must contribute to the collective struggle. Just as a Horse-and-Musket wargamer would be foolish to pick an army consisting only of infantry, cavalry or artillery miniatures, the premier proletarian team in the class struggle also couldn't be composed solely of Social Democrats, Anarchists, Bolsheviks or Autonomists. Depending upon the specific historical circumstances and territorial peculiarities, each combat unit had its own advantages and disadvantages. Once these different regiments had been rallied under a common banner, then the revolutionary army would be ready for the fray. The collective skilful general must decide when, where and with what troops that it would be most advantageous for the Left to engage its capitalist opponent with protests, elections, strikes, riots, lobbying, sabotage, occupations and propaganda.[288] As Clausewitz taught, there were no fixed strategies and tactics in the long history of warfare. Each victory on the social battlefield must be won in its own unique way.

By this third stage of our campaign, Class Wargames was hosting participatory performances of not only *The Game of War*, but also other interesting political-military simulations. Following Debord's own career as a Situationist subversive, we'd opened our offensive with an assault against the elitism of avant-garde art, then moved on

---

[287] Chris Peers' *Reds versus Reds* game was derived from the Russian Civil War army lists created for his *Contemptible Little Armies* set of rules.

[288] '[Political] ... theories are only made to die in the war of time. Like military units, they must be sent into battle at the right moment; and whatever their merits or insufficiencies, they can only be used if they're at hand when they're needed.' Guy Debord, *In Girum Imus Nocte et Consumimur Igni*, pages 150–151.

to questioning the authoritarianism of vanguard sects and now, after five years of frenetic activity, found ourselves training the troops in Clausewitz's military thinking. As Debord intended, *The Game of War* was an excellent pedagogical tool. If played with intelligence, *Reds versus Reds*, *Commands & Colors: Napoleonics* and *Little Wars* could also provide fascinating tactical insights for new recruits to the libertarian communist cause. As long the Left sects defined their identity by being the re-enactment society of their favourite period of radical history, then refighting old battles with model soldiers was more politically honest. Unlike many Social Democrats, Anarchists, Bolsheviks and Autonomists, at least the protagonists at Class Wargames' performances knew that they were engaged in make-believe.

At the sessions of the *Ludic Science Club* in the Fleapit and Firebox cafés in London, we also explored the political savvy to be gained from playing some fascinating non-military simulations: Jim Dunnigan's *Chicago-Chicago!*; Brian Train's *Red Guard*; Anders Fager's *Comrade Koba*; Francis Tresham and Mick Uhl's *Civilization* and Martin Wallace's *Liberté*. Whether commended for their factual accuracy or castigated for misreading their chosen epoch, the empathy of immersion within these ludic re-enactments was always rewarding in itself. Instead of passively observing famous struggles from the past between classes, nations and personalities, players could now actively make the decisions which had changed the course of human history. The most effective pedagogy was learning by doing. Building on this experience, Fabian and I in 2011 initiated a module for the BA in Politics at the University of Westminster which required its students not only to study these commercially available games, but also to invent their own prototype simulations of real or imagined social struggles.[289] Inspired by Debord's ludic détournement of Clausewitz's *On War*, James Moulding and Kateryna Onyiliogwu from its 2013 cohort transformed Lenin's flawed 1917 booklet on imperialism into a

---

[289] '... the greatest insight to be gained from conflict simulations comes from designing them rather than merely playing them.' Philip Sabin, *Simulating War*, page 40. For more details about this module, see the SPIR608 Political Simulation and Gaming module's Wikiversity pages.

card-and-plastic space colonisation contest.[290] The smartest critique of Bolshevik political theory was still Situationist ludic practice.

After five years on campaign, Class Wargames had acquired much expertise in training Left activists in military reasoning. By learning Clausewitz's five principles of combat, they could avoid fighting on the battlefields of the future with the maps of past struggles. Coming together to play political simulations, these militants were practising at becoming the collective skilful general. Under their unifying command, the rival tendencies of Social Democrats, Anarchists, Bolsheviks and Autonomists would become different pieces on the board – each with its own pluses and minuses. Rejecting ahistorical ideologies, proletarian warriors must be committed to developing the innovative strategy and tactics required for fighting in the special circumstances of our own times. On the other side of the board, state, corporate and military bureaucracies have long been reliant on role-playing exercises and other simulations to plan their responses to national emergencies and geopolitical crises. With the formulas of game theory, their neoliberal ideologues even found mathematic rationality within the social irrationality of the winner-take-all mentality of capitalist competition. By the third phase of our campaign of ludic subversion, Class Wargames had discovered the Situationist answer to the riddle of history. If the modern Left wanted to challenge the dominant order, its activists would have to know how to beat the bourgeoisie at their own game. In this 21st century iteration of Hegel's world-historic contest between the masters and the slaves, victory will go to the most skilful protagonists. In training sessions with *The Game of War* and other political simulations, the collective leadership of the libertarian communist future is now being forged. Enthused by the utopian possibilities of the better times to come, new types of pieces with their own advanced combat modifiers are already beginning to appear on the Red side of the board. With the smartest players on its team, the revolutionary proletariat is making ready to transform our troubled world into a truly human civilisation.

'The Empire's been ripe to fall for decades; it needed a big push, but it

---

[290] For their account of the development of this game, see James Moulding and Kateryna Onyiliogwu, 'Imperialism in Space'.

could always go. [Above all] ... the [ruling class] game itself ... had to be discredited. It is what held the Empire together for all these years – the linchpin; but that made it the most vulnerable point too. ... You've spent all your life learning games; there can't be a rule, move, concept or idea ... [that] you haven't encountered ten times before in other games ... These guys never stood a chance.'[291]

[291]   Iain Banks, *The Player of Games*, page 296.

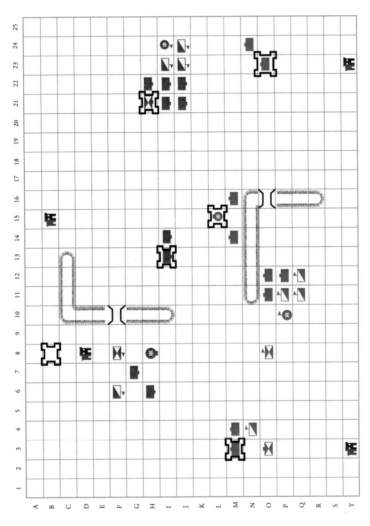

AUSTRIANS & RUSSIANS

FRENCH

336

DIAGRAM 5

1805 battle of Austerlitz scenario for Guy Debord's *The Game of War*

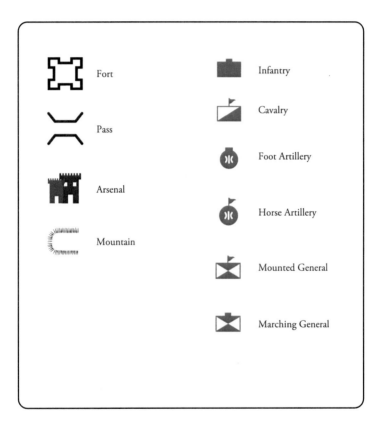

FRENCH

HAITIANS

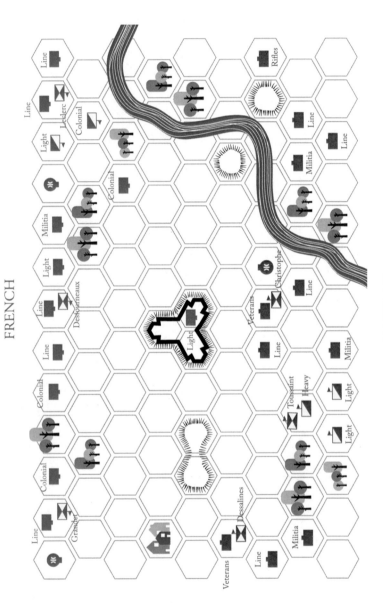

338

DIAGRAM 6

1802 battle of Fort Bedourete scenario for Richard Borg's *Commands & Colors: Napoleonics*

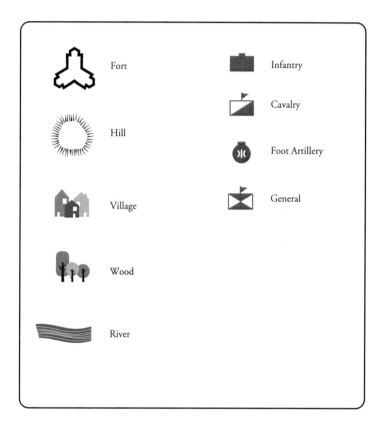

Fort

Hill

Village

Wood

River

Infantry

Cavalry

Foot Artillery

General

FRENCH

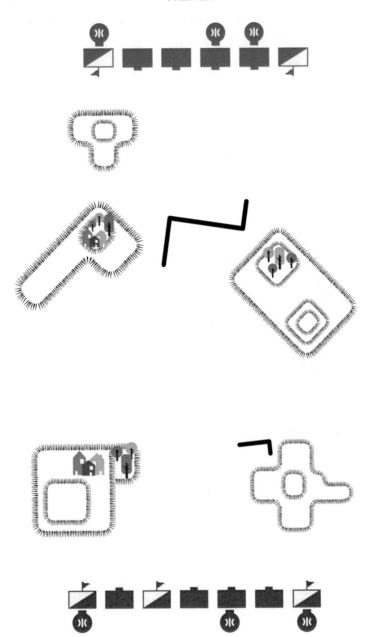

BRITISH

DIAGRAM 7

Haldon Forest opening positions for H.G. Wells' *Little Wars*.

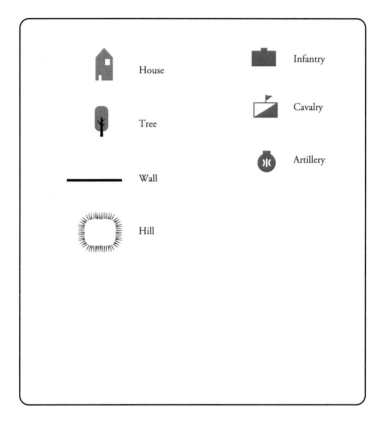

House

Tree

Wall

Hill

Infantry

Cavalry

Artillery

4.0: BIBLIOGRAPHY

'The most important principle for directing a war is that there is no shortcut to mastering its laws. ... if one uses the theory of dialectical materialism in observing and analysing the essence of war, one will discover that (whether on the offensive or defensive, with strong forces or weak) there are always two sides to a question, which are closely related and transform themselves into their opposites under certain conditions. Therefore, only when a commander engages in war can he [or she] gain insight into the objective factors that promote this transformation of opposites, and avoid disadvantages and make correct decisions leading to victory.'

Tao Hanzhang, *Commentary on Sun Tzu's The Art of War*, page 92.

Adams, Brook, Lisa Jardine, Martin Maloney, Norman Rosenthal and Richard Shone, *Sensation: Young British Artists from the Saatchi collection*, Royal Academy of Arts with Thames & Hudson, London 1997.

Adams, Tim, 'The Graffitist Goes Straight', *Observer*, 14th June 2009, page 33.

Adilkno (the foundation for the advancement of illegal knowledge), *Media Archive: world edition*, Autonomedia, New York 1998.

Agamben, Giorgio, 'Difference and Repetition: On Guy Debord's Films' in Tom McDonough (editor), *Guy Debord and the Situationist International: Texts and Documents*, MIT Press, Cambridge 2002, pages 313–319.

Allen, Thomas, *War Games: inside the secret world of the men who play at World War III*, Mandarin, London 1989.

Ali, Tariq, *The Coming British Revolution*, Jonathan Cape, London 1972.

Althusser, Louis, *Lenin and Philosophy and Other Essays*, New Left Books, London 1971.

Adkin, Mark, *The Charge: the real reason why the Light Brigade was lost*, Pimlico, London 1996.

Anderson, Andy, *Hungary '56*, Solidarity, London 1964.

Anderson, Perry, 'The Antinomies of Antonio Gramsci', *New Left Review*, Number 100, November 1976–January 1977, pages 5–78.

Angiolillo, Joseph (designer), *Napoleon's Italian Campaigns*, GTD, Manchester 1983.

Anweiler, Oskar, *The Soviets: the Russian workers, peasants and soldiers councils 1905–1921*, Pantheon, New York 1974.

Aristide, Jean-Bertrand, 'Introduction' in François-Dominique Toussaint L'Ouverture, *The Haitian Revolution*, Verso, London 2008, pages vii–xxxiii.

Armstrong, David, *A Trumpet to Arms: alternative media in America*, South End Press, Boston 1981.

Arnold, James, *Marengo & Hohenlinden: Napoleon's rise to power*, Pen & Sword, Barnsley 2005.

Arns, Inke, 'History Will Repeat Itself' in Inke Arns and Gabriele Horn (editors), *History Will Repeat Itself: strategies of re-enactment in contemporary (media) art and performance*, Hartware MedienKunstVerein and KW Institute for Contemporary Art, Dortmund/Berlin 2007, pages 37–63.

Arns, Inke, 'Irwin (NSK) 1983–2002: from "Was ist Kunst?" via Eastern Modernism to Total Recall', *ArtMargins*, <www.artmargins. com/index.php?option=com_content&view=article&id=316:irw in-nsk-1983-2002-from-qwas-ist-kunstq-via-eastern-modernism-to-total-recall&catid=111:articles&Itemid=68>, accessed 31st August 2013.

Arns, Inke, and Gabriele Horn (editors), *History Will Repeat Itself: strategies of re-enactment in contemporary (media) art and performance*, Hartware MedienKunstVerein and KW Institute for Contemporary Art, Dortmund/Berlin 2007.

Aust, Stefan, *The Baader-Meinhof Complex*, Bodley Head, London 2008.

Badiou, Alain, *The Communist Hypothesis: rethinking communism for the twenty-first century*, Verso, London 2011.

Bakunin, Mikhail, 'Letter to Albert Richard: 1st April 1870', *Selected Works*, Jonathan Cape, London 1973, pages 178–182.

Banks, Iain, *The Player of Games: a Culture novel*, Orbit, London 1989.

Banksy, *Wall and Piece*, Century, London 2005.

Barbrook, Richard, 'Cyber-communism: how the Americans are superseding capitalism in cyberspace', *Science as Culture*, Number 1, Volume 9, 2000, pages 5–40, <www.imaginaryfutures. net/2007/04/17/cyber-communism-how-the-americans-are-superseding-capitalism-in-cyberspace>, accessed 31st August 2013.

Barbrook, Richard, *Imaginary Futures: from thinking machines to the global village*, Pluto Press, London 2007.

Barbrook, Richard, *Media Freedom: the contradictions of communications in the age of modernity*, Pluto Press, London 1995.

Barbrook, Richard, *The Class of the New*, OpenMute, London 2006, <www.theclassofthenew.net>, accessed 31st August 2013.

Barbrook, Richard, 'The Hi-Tech Gift Economy' in nettime (editor), *Readme!: ASCII culture and the revenge of knowledge*, Autonomedia, New York 1998, pages 132–139; and *First Monday*, Volume 3, Number 12, 7th December 1998, <firstmonday.org/ojs/index.php/ fm/article/view/631>, accessed 31st August 2013.

Barbrook, Richard, 'The Holy Fools: revolutionary elitism in cyberspace', in Patricia Pisters (editor), *The Micropolitics of Media Culture: reading the rhizomes of Deleuze and Guattari*, Amsterdam University Press, Amsterdam 2001, pp. 159–175, <www. imaginaryfutures.net/2007/04/13/the-holy-fools-long-mix-by-richard-barbrook>, accessed 31st August 2013.

Barbrook, Richard, and Andy Cameron, 'The Californian Ideology' in Peter Ludlow (editor), *Crypto Anarchy, Cyberstates and Pirate Utopias*, MIT Press, Cambridge Mass 2001, pages 363–387, <www. imaginaryfutures.net/2007/04/17/the-californian-ideology-2>, accessed 31st August 2013.

Barbrook, Richard, and Fabian Tompsett, *Class Wargames Presents Guy Debord's The Game of War: the extended film script*, Unpopular Books, Poplar 2012.

Barker, John, 'Interview with the Author and Ilze Black', 15th June 2009.

Barker, John, 'Review Article: *Anarchy in the UK*', *Transgressions: a journal of urban exploration*, Issue 4, Spring 1998, pages 101–107, <www.katesharpleylibrary.net/4b8h98>, accessed 31st August 2013.

Barker, John (talk), 'The Weatherman Meets the Angry Brigade: Bill Ayers, John Barker and Hari Kunzru', Institute of Contemporary Arts, 26th February 2007.

Bassford, Christopher, 'Jomini and Clausewitz: their interaction', *The Clausewitz Homepage*, <www.clausewitz.com/readings/Bassford/Jomini/JOMINIX.htm>, accessed 31st August 2013.

Baudrillard, Jean, *Simulations*, Semiotext(e), New York 1983.

Becker-Ho, Alice, and Guy Debord, *Le Jeu de la Guerre: relevé des positions successives de toutes les forces au cours d'une partie*, Gallimard, Paris 2006.

Becker-Ho, Alice, and Guy Debord, *A Game of War*, Atlas Press, London 2007.

Bell, David, *The First Total War: Napoleon's Europe and the birth of modern warfare*, Bloomsbury, London 2007.

Berg, Aksel, 'Cybernetics and Education', *The Anglo-Soviet Journal*, March 1964, pages 13–20, <http://www.unz.org/Pub/AngloSovietJ-1964q1-00013>, accessed 31st August 2013.

Berger, Dan, *Outlaws of America: the Weather Underground and the politics of solidarity*, AK Press, Oakland 2006.

Berghaus, Günter, 'Happenings in Europe: trends, events and leading figures' in Mariellan Sandford (editor), *Happenings and Other Acts*, Routledge, London 1995, pages 310–388.

Bernstein, Michèle, 'Conversation with Author', 25th May 2013.

Bernstein, Eduard, *Evolutionary Socialism: a criticism and affirmation*, Schocken Books, New York 1961.

Bernstein, Samuel, *Auguste Blanqui and the Art of Insurrection*, Lawrence & Wishart, London 1971.

Bettelheim, Charles, *Class Struggles in the USSR: first period 1917–1923*, Harvester, Hassocks 1977.

Bey, Hakim, *T.A.Z.: the temporary autonomous zone, ontological anarchism, poetic terrorism*, Green Anarchist Books, Camberley 1996.

Biard, Roland, *Dictionnaire de l'Extrême-Gauche: de 1945 à nos jours*, Pierre Belfond, Paris 1978.

Black, Ilze (director), *Class Wargames Interviews Kimathi Donkor*, Class Wargames, London 2012, <vimeo.com/41627274>, accessed 31st August 2013.

Black, Ilze (director), *Class Wargames Presents Guy Debord's The Game of War*, Class Wargames, London 2009, <vimeo.com/17116481>, accessed 31st August 2013.

Black, Ilze (director), *Class Wargames представляет: Игра в войну Ги Дебора*, Class Wargames, London 2011, <vimeo.com/18822208>, accessed 31st August 2013.

Black, Ilze (director), *Elena – in Memoriam*, Class Wargames, London 2012, <vimeo.com/49071200>, accessed 31st August 2013.

Black Mask & Up Against The Wall Motherfucker, *The Incomplete Works of Ron Hahne, Ben Morea and the Black Mask Group*, Unpopular Books, London 1993.

Blackburn, Robin, *The Overthrow of Colonial Slavery 1776–1848*, Verso, London 1988.

Blanqui, Louis-Auguste, 'Defence Speech of Citizen Louis-Auguste

Blanqui before the Court of Assizes', *Selected Works*, EatDogEat, Lexington 2011, pages 29–43.

Blanqui, Louis-Auguste, 'Organisation of the Society of Families' in *Selected Works*, EatDogEat, Lexington 2011, pages 49–50.

Blanqui, Louis-Auguste, 'To the Mountain of 1793! To the Pure Socialists, its True Heirs!', *Selected Works*, EatDogEat, Lexington 2011, pages 91–100.

Blast Theory, *Blast Theory*, <www.blasttheory.co.uk>, accessed 31st August 2013.

Blaug, Ricardo, *How Power Corrupts: cognition and democracy in organisations*, Palgrave MacMillan, London 2010.

Blaumachen and Friends, 'The Rise of the (Non-)Subject', Blaumachen leaflet, 2012.

Boal, Augusto, *Theatre of the Oppressed*, Pluto, London 2000.

Bodlaender, Hans, 'Battle-Chess', <www.chessvariants.org/large.dir/chessbattle.html>, accessed 31st August 2013.

Bologna, Sergio, 'The Tribe of Moles: class composition and the party system in Italy' in Red Notes (editor), *Working Class Autonomy and the Crisis: Italian Marxist texts of the theory and practice of a class movement 1964–79*, Red Notes, London 1979, pages 67–91.

Bonaparte, Napoléon, 'Act Additional 22nd April 1815',<www.napoleon-series.org/research/government/legislation/c_additional.html>, accessed 31st August 2013.

Bonaparte, Napoléon, *Military Maxims*, Dover, Mineola 2004.

Bonnot de la Bande, Jules, 'Advisory Concerning Spectacular Terrorism', <libcom.org/library/advisory-concerning-spectacular-terrorism>, accessed 31st August 2013.

Boorman, Scott, *The Protracted Game: a Wei-Chi interpretation of Maoist revolutionary strategy*, Oxford University Press, New York 1969.

Bordwell, David, *The Cinema of Eisenstein*, Routledge, London 2005.

Borg, Richard (designer), *Commands & Colors: Napoleonics*, GMT Games, Hanford 2010.

Bornstein, Sam, and Al Richardson, *Against the Stream: a history of the Trotskyist movement in Britain 1924–38*, Socialist Platform, London 1986.

Borsook, Paulina, *Cyberselfish: a critical romp through the terribly libertarian world of high tech*, Little Brown, London 2000.

Bourdieu, Pierre, *Distinction: a social critique of the judgement of taste*, Routledge & Kegan Paul, London 1984.

Bourdieu, Pierre, and Alain Darbel, *The Love of Art*, Polity, Cambridge 1991.

Bourriaud, Nicholas, *Relational Aesthetics*, les presses du réel, Dijon 2002.

Bourrienne, Louis de, *Memoirs of Napoleon*, Hutchinson, London 1905.

Bourseiller, Christophe, *Les Maoïstes: la folle histoire des Gardes Rouges Français*, Plon, Paris 1996.

Bracken, Len, *Guy Debord – Revolutionary*, Feral House, Venice 1997.

Breton, André, 'Legitimate Defence', *What is Surrealism?: selected writings*, Pluto, London 1978, pages 31–42.

Breton, André, Diego Rivera and Leon Trotsky, 'Towards a Free Revolutionary Art' in Leon Trotsky, *Art & Revolution: writings on literature, politics and culture*, Pathfinder, New York 1970, pages 115–121.

Bridger, Sam (director), *Punk Britannia, 2: Punk 1976–1972*, BBC 2012.

Brinton, Maurice [Chris Pallis], *The Bolsheviks and Workers' Control: the state and counter-revolution*, Solidarity, London 1970.

Bristol Evening Post, 'Banksy Comes Home For Bristol Show', *Bristol Evening Post*, 12th June 2009, <www.thisisbristol.co.uk/news/Banksy-comes-home-Bristol/article-1071830-detail/article.html>, accessed 31st August 2013.

Brotchie, Alastair, and Mel Gooding, *Surrealist Games*, Redstone, London 1991.

Brown, Howard, 'The Search for Stability' in Howard Brown and Juliet Miller (editors), *Taking Liberties: problems of a new order from the French Revolution to Napoleon*, Manchester University Press, Manchester 2002, pages 20–50.

Buck-Morss, Susan, *Dreamworld and Catastrophe: the passing of mass utopia in East and West*, MIT Press, Cambridge 2000.

Buck-Morss, Susan, *Hegel, Haiti and Universal History*, University of Pittsburgh Press, Pittsburgh 2009.

Buhle, Paul, 'Marxism in the USA' in Paul Buhle (editor), *C.L.R. James: his life and work*, Alison & Busby, London 1986, pages 81–104.

Bukharin, Nikolai, *Economics of the Transition Period: with Lenin's critical remarks*, Bergman, New York 1971.

Bukharin, Nikolai, *Imperialism and World Economy*, Merlin Press, London 1972.

Buonarroti, Philippe, *Babeuf's Conspiracy for Equality*, August Kelly, New York 1965.

Bürger, Peter, *Theory of the Avant-Garde*, University of Minnesota Press, Minneapolis 1984.

Burton, Reginald, *Napoleon's Campaigns in Italy 1796–1797 & 1800*, Leonaur, Driffield 2010.

Byely, B., V. Dzyuba, G. Fyodorov, Y. Khomenko, T. Kondratkov, S. Kozlov, V. Kulakov, Y. Medvedev, V. Morozov, K. Spirov, Y. Sulimov, N. Sushko, S. Tyushkevich and D. Volkogonov, *Marxism-Leninism on War and Army*, Progress, Moscow 1972.

Camatte, Jacques, *Community and Communism in Russia*, David Brown, London 1978.

Cardan, Paul [Cornelius Castoriadis], *Modern Capitalism and Revolution*, Solidarity, London 1965.

Carlyle, Thomas, *Heroes and Hero-Worship*, Collins, London 1912.

Carolus Chess, 'Takako Saito', <sites.google.com/site/caroluschess/famous-people/artists/takako-saito>, accessed 31st August 2013.

Carr, E.H., *The Bolshevik Revolution 1917–1923 Volume 2: a history of Soviet Russia*, Penguin 1966, London .

Carr, Gordon, *The Angry Brigade: a history of Britain's first urban guerilla group*, Victor Gollancz, London 1975.

Castiglione, Baldesar, *The Book of the Courtier*, Penguin, London 1967.

Catlow, Ruth, Marc Garrett and Corrado Morgana (editors), *Artists Re:thinking Games*, FACT, Liverpool 2010.

Catlow, Ruth, *Rethinking Wargames: a chance to remaster conflict,*

<www.furtherfield.org/rcatlow/rethinking_wargames>, accessed 31st August 2013.

Catlow, Ruth, '*Let's Do Lunch* [2005]', <www.furtherfield.org/reviews/lets-do-lunch-2005>, accessed 31st August 2013.

Centre for Contemporary Art and the Natural World, *Games People Play: programme April–September 2012*, CCANW, Exeter 2012, <www.ccanw.co.uk/assets/files/CCANW_P18_WEB.pdf>, accessed 31st August 2013.

Centre for Contemporary Cultural Studies, *On Ideology: Working Papers in Cultural Studies 10*, University of Birmingham, Birmingham 1977.

Césaire, Aimé, *Toussaint Louverture: la révolution française et le problème colonial*, Présence Africaine, Paris 1962.

Chandler, David, *The Campaigns of Napoleon*, Weidenfeld and Nicolson, London 1967.

Chénieux-Gendron, Jacqueline, *Surrealism*, Columbia University Press, New York 1990.

Chernyshevsky, Nikolai, *What Is To Be Done?*, Cornell University Press, Ithaca 1989.

Chollet, Laurent, *L'Insurrection Situationniste*, Éditions Dagorno, Paris 2000.

Christie, Stuart, *Edward Heath Made Me Angry – the Christie File, part 3: 1967–75*, Christie Books, Hastings 2004.

Christie, Stuart, *Stefano Delle Chiaie: portrait of a black terrorist*, Refract Publications, London, 1984.

Chtcheglov, Ivan, 'Formulary for a New Urbanism' in Ken Knabb (editor), *Situationist International Anthology*, Bureau of Public Secrets, Berkeley 1981, pages 1–4.

Chto Delat?, 'A Declaration on Politics, Knowledge and Art', <www.chtodelat.org/index.php?option=com_content&view=article& id=766%3Aa-declaration-on-politics-knowledge-and-art&catid=212 %3Adeclaration&lang=en>, accessed 31ˢᵗ August 2013.

Ciliga, Ante, *The Russian Enigma*, Ink Links, London 1979.

Clark, T.J., *Farewell to an Idea: episodes from a history of Modernism*, Yale University Press, New Haven 1999.

Clark, T.J., 'Clement Greenberg's Theory of Art' in Francis Frascina (editor), *Pollock and After*, Routledge, London 2000, pages 71–86.

Clarke, I.F., '[*The Battle of*] *Dorking* Revisited', *Science Fiction Studies*, Number 38, Volume 1 – Part 1, March 1986, pages 84–86.

Clash, The, *Give 'Em Enough Rope*, CBS Records 1978.

Class Wargames, 'Communiqué #1: 23/10/07' in Richard Barbrook and Fabian Tompsett, *Class Wargames Presents Guy Debord's The Game of War: the extended film script*, Unpopular Books, Poplar 2012, pages 45–6; and <www.classwargames.net/?p=1509>, accessed 11ᵗʰ May 2014.

Class Wargames, 'Communiqué #5: 27/11/08' in Richard Barbrook and Fabian Tompsett, *Class Wargames Presents Guy Debord's The Game of War: the extended film script*, Unpopular Books, Poplar 2012, pages 57–61; and <www.classwargames.net/pages/?page_id=7>, accessed 31ˢᵗ August 2013.

Class Wargames, 'Communiqué #6: 25/07/09' in Richard Barbrook and Fabian Tompsett, *Class Wargames Presents Guy Debord's The Game of War: the extended film script*, Unpopular Books, Poplar 2012, pages 62–65; and <www.classwargames.net/pages/?page_id=7>, accessed 31ˢᵗ August 2013.

Class Wargames, 'Communiqué #7: 27/09/09' in Richard Barbrook and Fabian Tompsett, *Class Wargames Presents Guy Debord's The Game of War: the extended film script*, Unpopular Books, Poplar 2012, pages

66–69; and <www.classwargames.net/pages/?page_id=7>, accessed 31st August 2013.

Class Wargames, 'Communiqué #8: 18/09/10' in Richard Barbrook and Fabian Tompsett, *Class Wargames Presents Guy Debord's The Game of War: the extended film script*, Unpopular Books, Poplar 2012, pages 70–73; and <www.classwargames.net/pages/?page_id=7>, accessed 31st August 2013.

Class Wargames, 'Communiqué #9: 16/06/12' in Richard Barbrook and Fabian Tompsett, *Class Wargames Presents Guy Debord's The Game of War: the extended film script*, Unpopular Books, Poplar 2012, pages 74–77; and <www.classwargames.net/pages/?page_id=7>, accessed 31st August 2013.

Class Wargames, 'Communiqué #10: 13/04/13', <www.classwargames.net/pages/?page_id=7>, accessed 31st August 2013.

Clausewitz, Carl von, *Campagne de 1799 en Suisse et en Italie*, Éditions Champ Libre, Paris 1979.

Clausewitz, Carl von, *Campagne de 1814*, Éditions Champ Libre, Paris 1972.

Clausewitz, Carl von, *Campagne de 1815 en France*, Éditions Champ Libre, Paris 1973.

Clausewitz, Carl von, *Notes sur la Prusse dans sa Grande Catastrophe 1806*, Éditions Champ Libre, Paris 1976.

Clausewitz, Carl von, *On War*, Everyman's Library, London 1993.

Clausewitz, Carl von, *The Campaign of 1812 in Russia*, Da Capo Press, Cambridge 1995.

Cobb, Richard, *The People's Armies: the armées révolutionnaires – instrument of the Terror in the departments April 1793 to Floréal Year II*, Yale University Press, New Haven 1987.

Cockburn, Alexander, and Robin Blackburn (editors), *Student Power: problems, diagnosis, action*, Penguin, London 1969.

Cohn-Bendit, Daniel, and Gabriel Cohn-Bendit, *Obsolete Communism: the left-wing alternative*, Penguin, London 1969.

Collin, Mathew, with John Godfrey, *Altered State: the story of Ecstasy culture and acid house*, Serpent's Tail, London 1997.

Commission of the CC of the CPSU(B), *History of the Communist Party of the Soviet Union (Bolsheviks): short course*, Foreign Languages Publishing House, Moscow 1939.

Comninel, George, *Rethinking the French Revolution: Marxism and the revisionist challenge*, Verso, London 1987.

Connelly, Owen, *The Wars of the French Revolution and Napoleon 1792–1815*, Routledge, London 2006.

Conner, Clifford, *Jean-Paul Marat: tribune of the French Revolution*, Pluto, London 2012.

Copplestone Castings, <www.copplestonecastings.co.uk>, accessed 31st August 2013.

Copplestone, Mark, 'Not Just a Game of Toy Soldiers, <www.classwargames.net/?page_id=1503>, accessed 11st May 2014.

Coulter, Jim, Susan Miller and Martin Walker, *State of Siege: politics and policing in the coal fields – miners' strike 1984*, Canary Press, London 1984.

Coverley, Merlin, *Psychogeography*, Pocket Essentials, Harpenden 2006.

Crick, Michael, *Militant*, Faber & Faber, London 1984.

Critical Art Ensemble, *The Electronic Disturbance*, Autonomedia, New York 1994.

Crow, Thomas, 'Patriotism and Virtue: David to the young Ingres' in Thomas Crow, Brian Lukacher, Linda Nochlin, David Phillips and Frances Pohl (editors), *Nineteenth Century Art: a critical history*, Thames & Hudson, London 2007, pages 18–54.

Crosland, Anthony, *The Future of Socialism*, Jonathan Cape, London 1956.

Cullen, Bernard, *Hegel's Social and Political Thought: an introduction*, Gill and Macmillan, London 1979.

Curry, John, *Verdy's Free Kriegspiel including the Victorian army's 1896 war game*, History of Wargaming Project, Bristol 2008.

Cyland MediaLab, 'Cyberfest 2008 in Saint Petersburg', <cyland.ru/index.php?Itemid=48&id=67&option=com_content&task=view>, accessed 31st August 2013.

Davidson, Carl, *The New Radicals in the Multiversity and other SDS writings on student syndicalism*, Charles H. Kerr, Chicago 1990.

Davidson, Steef, *The Penguin Book of Political Comics*, Penguin, London 1982.

Day-Hickman, Barbara Ann, *Napoleonic Art: nationalism and the spirit of rebellion in France 1815–1848*, University of Delaware Press, Newark 1999.

Debord, Guy, 'À Gérard Lebovici 24 Mai 1976', *Correspondance Volume 5*, Arthème Fayard, Paris 2005, pages 350–358.

Debord, Guy, *Comments on the Society of the Spectacle*, Verso, London 1990.

Debord, Guy, *Considerations on the Assassination of Gérard Lebovici*, Tam Tam Books, Los Angeles 2001.

Debord, Guy, 'Letter to Floriana Lebovici, 25 Mars 1986',

Correspondance Volume 6, Arthème Fayard, Paris 2006, pages 387–389.

Debord, Guy, 'On *The Society of the Spectacle* (announcement of the film)', *Complete Cinematic Works: scripts, stills, documents*, AK Press, Edinburgh 2003, pages 220–222.

Debord, Guy, *Panegyric: volume 1*, Verso, London 1991.

Debord, Guy, 'Perspectives for the Conscious Alteration of Everyday Life' in Ken Knabb (editor), *Situationist International Anthology*, Bureau of Public Secrets, Berkeley 1981, pages 68–75.

Debord, Guy, 'Report on the Construction of Situations and of the International Situationist Tendency's Conditions of Organisation and Action' in Ken Knabb (editor), *Situationist International Anthology*, Bureau of Public Secrets, Berkeley 1981, pages 17–25.

Debord, Guy, *The Society of the Spectacle*, MIT Press, Cambridge 1994.

Debord, Guy, 'The Use of Stolen Films', *Complete Cinematic Works: scripts, stills, documents*, AK Press, Edinburgh 2003, pages 222–223.

Debord, Guy, 'Theory of the Dérive' in Ken Knabb (editor), *Situationist International Anthology*, Bureau of Public Secrets, Berkeley 1981, pages 50–54.

Debord, Guy, 'To Jean-Pierre Baudet: 26th October 1986', <www.notbored.org/debord-26October1986.html>, accessed 31st August 2013.

Debord, Guy (director), *Critique of Separation*, <www.ubu.com/film/debord_critique.html>, accessed 31st August 2013; and *Complete Cinematic Works: scripts, stills, documents*, AK Press, Edinburgh 2003, pages 29–42.

Debord, Guy (director), *Hurlements en Faveur de Sade*, Lettrism, France 1952, <www.ubu.com/film/debord_hurlements.html>, accessed 31ˢᵗ August 2013; and *Complete Cinematic Works: scripts, stills, documents*, AK Press, Edinburgh 2003, pages 1–11.

Debord, Guy (director), *In Girum Imus Nocte et Consumimur Igni*, Simar Films, France 1978, <www.ubu.com/film/debord_ingirum. html>, accessed 31ˢᵗ August 2013; and *Complete Cinematic Works: scripts, stills, documents*, AK Press, Edinburgh 2003, pages 133–205.

Debord, Guy (director), *On the Passage of a Few Persons Through a Rather Brief Unity of Time*, France 1979; and *Complete Cinematic Works: scripts, stills, documents*, AK Press, Edinburgh 2003, pages 13–27.

Debord, Guy (director), *The Society of the Spectacle*, France 1973, <www.ubu.com/film/debord_spectacle.html>, accessed 31ˢᵗ August 2013; and *Complete Cinematic Works: scripts, stills, documents*, AK Press, Edinburgh 2003, pages 43–109.

Debord, Guy, and Constant [Nieuwenhuys], 'La Déclaration d'Amsterdam', *Internationale Situationniste*, Number 2, December 1958, pages 31–32.

Debord, Guy, and Gianfranco Sanguinetti, *The Veritable Split in the International: public circular of the Situationist International*, B.M. Chronos, London 1985.

Debord, Guy, and Gil Wolman, 'Methods of Détournement' in Ken Knabb (editor), *Situationist International Anthology*, Bureau of Public Secrets, Berkeley 1981, pages 8–14.

Debord, Guy, Attila Kotányi and Raoul Vaneigem, 'Theses on the Paris Commune' in Ken Knabb (editor), *Situationist International Anthology*, Bureau of Public Secrets, Berkeley 1981, pages 314–317.

Deleuze, Gilles, and Félix Guattari, *A Thousand Plateaus*, Athlone, London 1988.

Deller, Jeremy (artist), and Mike Figgis (director), *The Battle for Orgreave*, Channel 4 Films 2002.

Deller, Jeremy, *The English Civil War Part II: personal accounts of the 1984–85 miners' strike*, Artangel, London 2002.

Derrida, Jacques, *Writing and Difference*, Routledge, London 1993.

Dery, Mark, 'Culture Jamming: hashing, slashing and sniping in the empire of signs', <markdery.com/?page_id=154>, accessed 31st August 2013.

Deutscher, Isaac, *The Prophet Armed: Trotsky 1879-1921*, Oxford University Press, Oxford 1954.

Dialectica Principia, 'The Battle for Ideas', *Dialectica Principia* leaflet for the *1968 & All That* conference, London 2008.

Dickinson, Rod, 'Rod Dickinson - Artist', <www.roddickinson.net/pages/index.php>, accessed 31st August 2013.

Dockter, David (designer), *Triumph of Chaos*, Clash of Arms, Sassamansville, PA 2005.

Dowd, David, *Pageant-Master of the Republic: Jacques-Louis David and the French Revolution*, Books for Libraries Press, Freeport NY 1969.

Dunnigan, Jim (designer), *Agincourt*, SPI, New York 1978.

Dunnigan, Jim (designer), *Chicago-Chicago: or "Mrs. O'Leary's cow, where were you when we really needed you?"* in *Strategy & Tactics*, Number 21, 1970.

Dunnigan, Jim (designer), *Russian Civil War: 1918-1922*, SPI, New York 1976.

Dunnigan, Jim, *The Complete Wargames Handbook: how to play, design and find them*, Quill, New York 1992.

Dwyer, Philip, 'Napoleon Bonaparte as Hero and Saviour: image, rhetoric and behaviour in the construction of a legend', *French History*, Volume 18, Number 4, pages 379-403.

Eales, Richard, *Chess: the history of a game*, Hardinge Simpole, Glasgow 2002.

Easton, Malcolm, *Artists and Writers in Paris: the bohemian idea, 1803–1867*, Edward Arnold, London 1964.

Éditions Ivrea, '[Champ Libre] Catalogue', <editions-ivrea.fr/catalogue-liste.php>, accessed 31st August 2013.

Elliot, David, *New Worlds: Russian art and society 1900–1937*, Thames & Hudson, London 1986.

Ellis, Geoffrey, 'The Nature of Napoleonic Imperialism' in Philip Dwyer (editor), *Napoleon and Europe*, Pearson, London 2001, pages 97–117.

Ellsberg, Daniel, *Secrets: a memoir of Vietnam and the Pentagon Papers*, Penguin, London 2003.

Eisenstein, Sergei, (director), *October 1917*, Mosfilm 1928.

Emberton, Wilfrid, *Skippon's Brave Boys: the origins, development and Civil War service of London's Trained Bands*, Barracuda Books, Buckingham 1984.

Engels, Friedrich, *Anti-Dühring: Herr Eugen Dühring's revolution in science*, Progress, Moscow 1947.

Engels, Friedrich, 'Engels to Marx in London: 7th January 1858', <www.marxists.org/archive/marx/works/1858/letters/58_01_07.htm>, accessed 31st August 2013.

Engels, Friedrich, 'The Prussian Military Question and the German Workers' Party' in Karl Marx, *The First International and After: political writings volume 3*, Penguin, London 1974, pages 121–146.

Engels, Friedrich, 'Waldersee on the French Army' in Karl Marx and Friedrich Engels, *Collected Works Volume 18: Marx and Engels 1857–1862*, International Publishers, New York 1982, pages 508–510.

English Section of the Situationist International, *The Revolution of Modern Art and the Modern Art of Revolution*, Chronos, London 1994.

English Section of the Situationist International [Tom Vague], *King Mob Echo*, Dark Star, London 2000.

Englund, Steven, *Napoleon: a political life*, Harvard University Press, Cambridge Mass 2004.

Esdaile, Charles, *The Wars of Napoleon*, Longman, London 1995.

Esposito, Vincent, and John Elting, *A Military History and Atlas of the Napoleonic Wars*, Greenhill, London 1999.

Essig, Dean, and David Powell (designers), *Austerlitz*, The Gamers, Homer 1993.

Essig, Dean, and David Powell (designers), *Marengo*, The Gamers, Homer 1995.

Etoy, 'The ToyWar-Story', <toywar.etoy.com>, accessed 31st August 2013.

Evans, Mike, *N.Y.C. Rock: rock 'n' roll in the Big Apple*, Sanctuary, London 2003.

Fager, Anders (designer), *Comrade Koba*, Gottick Games, Stockholm 2005.

Fairbairn, Geoffrey, *Revolutionary Guerrilla Warfare: the countryside version*, Penguin, London 1974.

Fanelli, Sara, *Tate Artist Timeline*, Tate Modern, London 2000.

Fanon, Frantz, *The Wretched of the Earth*, Penguin, London 1967.

Fanon, Frantz, *Towards the African Revolution (Political Essays)*, Grove Press, New York 1969.

Farren, Mick, *Give the Anarchist a Cigarette*, Pimlico, London 2002.

Fazakerley, Gordon, and Jacqueline de Jong with Jakob Jabobsen, 'Drakabygget: a Situationist utopia or meeting place for displaced persons' in Mikkel Bolt Rasmussen and Jakob Jakobsen (editors), *Expect Anything Fear Nothing: the Situationist movement in Scandinavia and elsewhere*, Nebula and Autonomedia, Copenhagen and New York 2011, pages 114–128.

Featherstone, Donald, *War Games: battles and manoeuvres with model soldiers*, Stanley Paul, London 1962.

Fields, A. Belden, *Trotskyism and Maoism: theory and practice in France and the United States*, Autonomedia, New York 1988.

Fisera, Vladimir, *Writing on the Wall – France May '68: a documentary anthology*, Allison & Busby, London 1978.

Flanagan, Mary, *Critical Play: radical game design*, MIT Press, Cambridge 2009.

Foner, Philip (editor), *The Black Panthers Speak*, Da Capo Press, Cambridge 1995.

Florida, Richard, *The Rise of the Creative Class: and how it's transforming work, leisure, community and everyday life*, Basic, New York 2002.

Forgács, Éva, *The Bauhaus Idea and Bauhaus Politics*, Central European University Press, Budapest 1991.

Forrest, Alan, 'La Patrie en Danger' in Daniel Moran and Arthur Waldron, *The People in Arms: military myth and national mobilisation since the French Revolution*, Cambridge University Press, Cambridge 2003, pages 8–32.

Foucault, Michel, *The Order of Things: an archaeology of human sciences*, Routledge, London 2001.

Fountain, Nigel, *Underground: the London alternative press 1966–74*, Routledge, London 1988.

Fox, Daniel, 'Artists in the Modern State: the nineteenth century background' in Milton Albrecht, James Barnett and Mason Griff (editors), *The Sociology of Art and Literature: a reader*, Gerald Duckworth, London 1970, pages 370–387.

Franceschi, Michel, and Ben Weider, *The Wars against Napoleon: debunking the myth of the Napoleonic wars*, Casemate, Newbury 2008.

Freeland, Chrystia, *Sale of the Century: the inside story of the second Russian Revolution*, Abacus, London 2006.

Freeman, Jo, *The Tyranny of Structurelessness*, Dark Star Press, London 1979.

Free Pussy Riot, <freepussyriot.org>, accessed 31st August 2013.

Frith, Simon, and Howard Horne, *Art into Pop*, Metheun, London 1987.

Fukuyama, Francis, *The End of History and the Last Man*, Penguin, London 1992.

Frunze, Mikhail, 'Unified Military Doctrine and the Red Army', <www-personal.ksu.edu/~stone/FrunzeDoctrine>, accessed 31st August 2013.

Furet, François, *Interpreting the French Revolution*, Cambridge University Press, Cambridge 1981.

Furet, François, and Mona Ozouf, *A Critical Dictionary of the French Revolution*, Harvard University Press, Cambridge 1989.

Furtherfield, 'Class Wargames – Game of War', *HTTP: house of technological termed practice*, <www.http.uk.net/events/gameofwar>, accessed 31st August 2013.

Furtherfield, *Invisible Forces: an exhibition about why contemporary life is so difficult for so many*, Furtherfield Press Release, May 2012.

Furtherfield, *Zero Gamer*, 01zero-one 22nd–27th November 2007 and the HTTP Gallery 2nd–18th November 2007, <www.http.uk.net/zerogamer>, accessed 31st August 2013.

Galloway, Alex, 'Debord's Nostalgic Algorithm', *Culture Machine*, Number 10, 2009, pages 131–156, <www.culturemachine.net/index.php/cm/article/view/350/352>, accessed 31st August 2013.

Garcia, David, and Geert Lovink, 'The ABC of Tactical Media', *ZKP 4*, nettime, Ljubljana 1997, pages 53–54, <www.ljudmila.org/nettime/zkp4/72.htm>, accessed 31st August 2013.

Gareev, Makhmut, *M.V. Frunze: military theorist*, Pergamon-Brassey's, McLean 1988.

Garratt, Sheryl, *Adventures in Wonderland: a decade of club culture*, Headline, London 1998.

Gauron, André, *Histoire Économique et Sociale de la Cinquième République: tome 1 – le temps des modernistes*, La Découverte/Maspero, Paris 1983.

Geldern, James von, *Bolshevik Festivals: 1917–1920*, University of California Press, Berkeley 1993, <publishing.cdlib.org/ucpressebooks/view?docId=ft467nb2w4;brand=ucpress>, accessed 31st August 2013.

Genosko, Gary, '[Review of] Vincent Kaufman, *Guy Debord: revolution in the service of poetry*', *Canadian Journal of Sociology Online*, November–December 2006, <www.cjsonline.ca/reviews/debord.html>, accessed 31st August 2013.

Gerbaudo, Paolo, *Tweets and the Streets: social media and contemporary activism*, Pluto, London 2012.

Gerbaudo, Paolo, 'The Roots of the Coup: it is political despair and lack of credible leadership that have led Egyptian revolutionaries to support the army's removal of Morsi', *Soundings*, Number 54, Summer 2013, pages 104–113.

Genovese, Eugene, *The World the Slaveholders Made*, Vintage, New York 1971.

Geyl, Pieter, *Napoleon For and Against*, Peregrine, London 1965.

Gillepsie, Gil, *The Naked Guide to Bristol*, Naked Guides, Bath 2004.

Gilroy, Paul, *The Black Atlantic: modernity and double consciousness*, Verso, London 1993.

GLA Economics, *Creativity: London's core business*, Greater London Authority, London 2002.

Golomstock, Igor, *Totalitarian Art in the Soviet Union, the Third Reich, Fascist Italy and the People's Republic of China*, Harper Collins, London 1990.

Goodman, Mitchell (editor), *The Movement Towards a New America: the beginnings of a long revolution*, Pilgrim Press/Alfred A Knope, Philadelphia/New York 1970.

Giáp, Võ Nguyên, 'Great Victory, Great Task', *The Military Art of People's War: selected writings of General Võ Nguyên Giáp*, Monthly Review Press, New York 1970, pages 285–307.

Giáp, Võ Nguyên, 'The South Vietnamese People Will Win', *The Military Art of People's War: selected writings of General Võ Nguyên Giáp*, Monthly Review Press, New York 1970, pages 185–225.

Giáp, Võ Nguyên, 'Their Dien Bien Phu Will Come', *The Military Art of People's War: selected writings of General Võ Nguyên Giáp*, Monthly Review Press, New York 1970, pages 328–332.

Giáp, Võ Nguyên, and Van Tien Dung, *How We Won The War*, Recon, Philidelphia 1976.

GMT Games, *Commands & Colors Napoleonics*, <www.ccnapoleonics. net>, accessed 31st August 2013.

Gombin, Richard, *Les Origines du Gauchisme*, Éditions du Seuil, Paris 1971.

Graham, Loren, *Science, Philosophy and Human Behaviour in the Soviet Union*, Columbia University Press, New York 1987.

Grant, Charles, *The War Game*, Ken Trotman, Huntingdon 2007.

Gramsci, Antonio, *Selections from the Prison Notebooks*, Lawrence & Wishart, London 1971.

Gray, Christopher (editor), *Leaving the 20th Century: the incomplete works of the Situationist International*, Rebel Press, London 1998.

Gray, John, 'The Violent Visions of Slavoj Žižek', *The New York Review of Books*, 12th July 2012, <www.nybooks.com/articles/archives/ 2012/jul/12/violent-visions-slavoj-zizek>, accessed 31st August 2013.

Green, Jonathon, *Days in the Life: voices from the English underground 1961–1971*, Minerva, London 1988.

Greenberg, Clement, 'Avant-garde and Kitsch' in Francis Frascina (editor), *Pollock and After*, Routledge, London 2000, pages 48–59.

Gregor, A. James, *Mussolini's Intellectuals: Fascist social and political thought*, Princeton University Press, Princeton 2005.

Griffith, Paddy, *The Art of War of Revolutionary France 1789–1802*, Greenhill, London 1998.

Guattari, Félix, *The Molecular Revolution: psychiatry and politics*, Penguin, London 1984.

Guderain, Heinz, *Panzer Leader*, Futura, London 1974.

Guérin, Daniel, *Bourgeois et Bras Nus 1793–1795*, Gallimard, Paris 1973.

Guilbaut, Serge, *How New York Stole the Idea of Modern Art: Abstract Expressionism, freedom and the Cold War*, University of Chicago Press, Chicago 1983.

Guy, Emmanuel, 'Où l'on Fait le Portrait de Guy Debord à Travers les Livres et son *Jeu de la Guerre*' in Emmanuel Guy and Laurence de Bras (editors), *Guy Debord: un art de la guerre*, Bibliotèque Nationale de France/Gallimard, Paris 2013, pages 172–184.

Hagan, Mark von, *Soldiers in the Proletarian Dictatorship: the Red Army and the Soviet socialist state 1917–1930*, Cornell University Press, Ithaca 1990.

Halberstam, David, *The Best and the Brightest*, Random House, New York 1969.

Halimi, Serge, *Sisyphe est Fatigué*, Robert Laffont, Paris 1993.

Hall, Stuart, and Martin Jacques (editors), *New Times: the changing face of politics in the 1990s*, Lawrence & Wishart, London 1989.

Hall, Stuart, and Tony Jefferson (editors), *Resistance through Rituals: youth subcultures in post-war Britain*, Hutchinson with Centre for Contemporary Cultural Studies University of Birmingham, London 1975.

Hamilton, Jill, *Marengo: the myth of Napoleon's horse*, Fourth Estate, London 2000.

Hampson, Norman, *The Life and Opinions of Maximilien Robespierre*, Basil Blackwell, London 1988.

Hands, Joss, *@ is for Activism*, Pluto, London 2011.

Hanh, Lu Sanh, 'An Account of the 1945 August Revolution' in

Simon Pirani, *Vietnam & Trotskyism*, Communist League (Australia), Petersham 1987, pages 61–72.

Hardt, Michael, and Antonio Negri, *Empire*, Harvard University Press, Cambridge 2000.

Hardwell, Peter, *Damming the Flood: Haiti and the politics of containment*, Verso, London 2007.

Harris, David, *From Class Struggle to the Politics of Pleasure: the effects of Gramscianism on Cultural Studies*, Routledge, London 1992.

Harris, John, *The Last Party: Britpop, Blair and the demise of English rock*, Fourth Estate, London 2003.

Hart Mathews, Jane de, 'Art and Politics in Cold War America' in Francis Frascina (editor), *Pollock and After: the critical debate*, Harper & Row, London 2000, pages 155–180.

Harvey, Eric (designer), *Marengo: morning defeat, afternoon victory*, Decision Games, Bakersfield 2010.

Hausrath, Alfred, *Venture Simulations in War, Business and Politics*, McGraw-Hill, New York 1971.

Hazareesingh, Sudhir, *The Cult of Napoleon*, Granta, London 2004.

Hegel, Georg, *Lectures on the Philosophy of World History: introduction*, Cambridge University Press, Cambridge 1975.

Hegel, Georg, *Phenomenology of the Spirit*, Oxford University Press, Oxford 1977.

Hegel, Georg, *Philosophy of Right*, Oxford University Press, Oxford 1967.

Heims, Steve, *John von Neumann and Norbert Wiener: from mathematics to the technologies of life and death*, MIT Press, Cambridge 1980.

Heuser, Beatrice, *Reading Clausewitz*, Pimlico, London 2000.

Hibbert, Christopher, *The French Revolution*, Penguin, London 1982.

Higgs, Matthew, and Jeremy Deller, 'In Conversation' in Jeremy Deller, *Joy in People*, Hayward Gallery, London 2012, pages 185–191.

Hill, Robert, 'In England 1932–1938' in Paul Buhle (editor), *C.L.R. James: his life and work*, Alison & Busby, London 1986, pages 61–80.

Hirsh, Arthur, *The French Left: a history and overview*, Black Rose, Montréal 1982.

Hirson, Baruch, 'Communalism and Socialism in Africa: the misdirection of C.L.R. James', <www.marxists.org/archive/hirson/1989/clr-james.htm>, accessed 31ˢᵗ August 2013.

Hobsbawm, Eric, *Age of Extremes: the short twentieth century 1914–1991*, Abacus, London 1994.

Hoggart, Richard, *The Uses of Literacy*, Penguin, London 1958.

Høgsbjerg, Christian, 'Introduction' in C.L.R. James, *Toussaint Louverture: the story of the only successful slave revolt in history*, Duke University Press, Durham 2013, pages 1–39.

Hohenzollern, Friedrich, *The King of Prussia's Instructions to his Generals*, Partizan Press, Leigh-on-Sea 1990.

Home, Stewart, *The Assault on Culture: utopian currents from Lettrism to Class War*, Aporia Press & Unpopular Books, London 1988.

Home, Stewart, *Cranked Up Really High: an inside account of punk rock*, CodeX, Hove 1995.

Home, Stewart, 'The Self-Mythologisation of the Situationist International' in Mikkel Bolt Rasmussen and Jakob Jakobsen (editors), *Expect Anything Fear Nothing: the Situationist movement in*

Scandinavia and elsewhere, Nebula and Autonomedia, Copenhagen and New York 2011, pages 205–214.

Horne, Alistair, *The Age of Napoleon*, Weidenfeld and Nicolson, London 2008.

Horne, Alistair, *The Fall of Paris: the siege and the Commune 1870–1*, Macmillan, London 1965.

Horowitz, Irving Louis, *The War Game: studies of the new civilian militarists*, Ballatine, New York 1963.

Hoskisson, Mark, 'The Red Jacobins: Thermidor and the Russian Revolution in 1921', *Permanent Revolution*, Issue 17, Summer 2010, pages 30–43.

Hourtoulle, F.G., *Austerlitz: the empire at its zenith*, Histoire & Collections, Paris 2003.

Housden, Martin, 'Interview with the Author and Ilze Black', 26th July 2009.

Housmans Bookshop, 'The Story of Housmans', <www.housmans. com/housmans_history.php>, accessed 31st August 2013.

Hoyt, Edwin, *Paul Robeson: the American Othello*, World Publishing, Cleveland 1968.

Huizinga, Johan, *Homo Ludens: a study of the play element in culture*, Beacon Press, Boston 1950.

Huntington, Samuel, 'The Bases of Accommodation', *Foreign Affairs*, July 1968, Number 4, Volume 46, pages 642–656.

Hussey, Andrew, *A Game of War: the life and death of Guy Debord*, Jonathan Cape, London 2001.

Hyppolite, Jean, *Genesis and Structure of Hegel's Phenomenology of Spirit*, Northwestern University Press, Evanston 1974.

Hyppolite, Jean, *Studies on Marx and Hegel*, Heinemann, London 1969.

ICA, 'Chto delat? (What is to be done?) – The Urgent Need to Struggle', <www.ica.org.uk/25668/Visual-Art/Chto-delat-What-is-to-be-done-The-Urgent-Need-to-Struggle.html>, accessed 31st August 2013.

International Communist Current [Phillipe Bourrrinet], *The Dutch and German Communist Left*, International Communist Current, London 2001.

International Communist Current, *The Italian Communist Left: 1927–45*, International Communist Current, London, 1992.

Invisible Committee, *The Coming Insurrection*, Natterjack Press, London 2009.

Isaacs, Jeremy, and Taylor Dowling, *Cold War: for 45 years the world held its breath*, Bantam, London 1998.

Jack, Andrew, *Inside Putin's Russia*, Granta, London 2005.

Jackson, Julian, *The Popular Front in France: defending democracy 1934–38*, Cambridge University Press, Cambridge 1988.

Jäggi, Max, Roger Müller and Sil Schmid, *Red Bologna*, Writers and Readers Publishing Cooperative, London 1977.

James, C.L.R., *A History of Pan-African Revolt*, PM Press, Oakland 2012.

James, C.L.R., 'Black Power', <www.marxists.org/archive/james-clr/works/1967/black-power.htm>, accessed 31st August 2013.

James, C.L.R., 'Every Cook Can Govern: a study of democracy in Ancient Greece – its meaning for today', <www.marxists.org/archive/james-clr/works/1956/06/every-cook.htm>, accessed 31st August 2013.

James, C.L.R., 'Extract From Transcript of Interviews with C.L.R. James: 5th September 1980', <pancaribbean.com/banyan/clr.htm>, accessed 31st August 2013.

James, C.L.R., *Kwame Nkrumah and the Ghana Revolution*, Alison & Busby, London 1977.

James, C.L.R., *Notes on Dialectics: Hegel-Marx-Lenin*, Alison & Busby, London 1980.

James, C.L.R., 'Russia – a Fascist State', <www.marxists.org/archive/james-clr/works/1941/04/russia-fascist.htm>, accessed 31st August 2013.

James, C.L.R., *The Black Jacobins: Toussaint L'Ouverture and the San Domingo Revolution*, Alison & Busby, London 1980.

James, C.L.R., *Toussaint Louverture: the story of the only successful slave revolt in history*, Duke University Press, Durham 2013.

James, C.L.R., *World Revolution 1917–1936: the rise and fall of the Communist International*, Humanities Press, New Jersey 1993.

James, C.L.R., with Raya Dunayevskaya and Grace Lee [Boggs], *State Capitalism and World Revolution*, Charles Kerr, Chicago 1986.

James, C.L.R., F. Forest [Raya Dunayevskaya] and Ria Stone [Grace Lee Boggs], *The Invading Socialist Society*, Bewick, Detroit 1972.

Jameson, Frederic, *Postmodernism: or the cultural logic of late capitalism*, Verso, London 1991.

Jappe, Anselm, *Guy Debord*, University of California Press, Berkeley and Los Angeles 1999.

Jaurès, Jean, *L'Armée Nouvelle*, L'Humanité, Paris 1915.

Johnson, R.W., *The Long March of the French Left*, MacMillan, London 1981.

Jomini, Antoine-Henri de, *The Art of War*, Dodo Press, London 2010.

Jorn, Asger, 'Critique of Economic Policy', *Transgressions: a journal of urban exploration*, Issue 4, Spring 1998, pages 13–35.

Jorn, Asger, 'Detourned Painting' in Elisabeth Sussman (editor), *On the Passage of a Few People Through a Rather Brief Moment in Time: the Situationist International 1957–1972*, MIT Press, Cambridge 1989, pages 140–147.

Josselson, Michael, and Diana Josselson, *The Commander: a life of Barclay de Tolly*, Oxford University Press, Oxford 1980.

Kahn, Herman, *On Escalation: metaphors and scenarios*, Frederick A. Praeger, New York 1965.

Kahn, Herman, *On Thermonuclear War*, Princeton University Press, Princeton 1960.

Kaplan, Fred, *The Wizards of Armageddon*, Touchstone, New York 1983.

Karp, Nick (designer), *Vietnam: 1965–1975*, Victory Games, New York 1984.

Katsiaficas, George, *The Imagination of the New Left: a global analysis of 1968*, South End Press, Boston 1987.

Kaufman, Vincent, *Guy Debord: revolution in the service of poetry*, University of Minnesota Press, Minneapolis 2006.

Kautsky, Karl, *The Class Struggle (Erfurt Programme)*, W.W. Norton, New York 1971.

Kautsky, Karl, *The Dictatorship of the Proletariat*, University of Michigan Press, Ann Arbor 1964.

Kautsky, Karl, 'The Lessons of the October Experiment', <www.

marxists.org/archive/kautsky/1925/x01/x01.htm>, accessed 31ˢᵗ August 2013.

Kautsky, Karl, *The Materialist Conception of History*, Yale University Press, New Haven 1988.

Kellein, Thomas, *Fluxus*, Thames & Hudson, London 1995.

Kelly, Kevin, *New Rules for the New Economy: 10 ways that the network economy is changing everything*, Fourth Estate, London 1998.

Kelly, Michael, *Hegel in France*, Birmingham Modern Languages Publications, Birmingham 1992.

Kelly, Robin, 'Introduction' in C.L.R. James, *A History of Pan-African Revolt*, PM Press, Oakland 2012, pages 1–33.

Kempton, Richard, *Provo: Amsterdam's anarchist revolt*, Autonomedia, New York 2007.

Kenez, Peter, *The Birth of the Propaganda State: Soviet methods of mass mobilisation 1917–1929*, Cambridge University Press, Cambridge 1985.

Kessel, Patrick, *Le Mouvement Maoïste en France: textes et documents 1968–1969*, 10/18, Paris 1978.

Khatib, Abdelhafid, 'Essai de Description Psychogéographique des Halles', *Internationale Situationniste*, Number 2, December 1958, pages 13–18.

Khayati, Mustapha, 'On the Poverty of Student Life' in Ken Knabb (editor), *Situationist International Anthology*, Bureau of Public Secrets, Berkeley 1981, pages 319–337.

King, Nicole, 'C.L.R. James, Genre and Cultural Politics' in Christopher Gair (editor), *Beyond Boundaries: C.L.R. James and postnational studies*, Pluto, London 2006, pages 13–38.

Kinyatti, Maina Wa, *Kenya's Freedom Struggle: the Dedan Kimathi papers*, St. Martin's Press, London, 1988.

Kipp, Jacob, 'Lenin and Clausewitz: the militarisation of Marxism, 1914–1921', *Military Affairs*, October 1985, pages 184–191.

Kipp, Jacob, 'Soviet Military Doctrine and the Origins of Operational Art, 1917–1936' in Willard Frank and Phillip Gillette (editors), *Soviet Military Doctrine from Lenin to Gorbachev, 1915–1991*, Greenwood Press, Westport 1992, pages 85–131.

Kirby, Michael, 'The First and Second Wilderness' in Mariellan Sandford (editor), *Happenings and Other Acts*, Routledge, London 1995, pages 89–93.

Kirby, Michael, 'The New Theatre' in Mariellan Sandford (editor), *Happenings and Other Acts*, Routledge, London 1995, pages 29–47.

Kollectiv, Pil, and Galia Kollectiv, *The Institute of Psychoplasmics*, Pump House Gallery, London 2008.

Kolko, Gabriel, *Anatomy of a War: Vietnam, the United States and the modern historical experience*, Phoenix Press, London 2001.

Kojève, Alexandre, *Introduction to the Reading of Hegel: lectures on the Phenomenology of the Spirit*, Cornell University Press, Ithaca 1969.

Kondratieva, Tamara, *Bolcheviks et Jacobins*, Payot, Paris 1989.

Korsch, Karl, *Marxism and Philosophy*, New Left Books, London 1970.

Kubrick, Stanley (director), *Dr Strangelove: or how I learned to stop worrying and love the bomb*, Columbia, Los Angeles 1964.

Lacouture, Jean, *Léon Blum*, Éditions du Seuil, Paris 1977.

Laflin-Barker, Sue, 'The History of Wargames Research Group: rules ancient and modern and other periods in between', <www.wrg.me. ukWRG.net/History/wrg.html>, accessed 31ˢᵗ August 2013.

Las Cases, Emmanuel de, *Mémorial de Sainte-Hélène*, Éditions du Seuil, Paris 1968.

Lazzarato, Maurizio, 'General Intellect: towards an inquiry into immaterial labour', <libcom.org/library/general-intellect-common-sense>, accessed 31ˢᵗ August 2013.

Lee [Boggs], Grace, Pierre Chalieu [Cornelius Castoriadis] and J.R. Johnson [C.L.R. James], *Facing Reality*, Correspondence, Detroit 1958.

Leeson, Bill, 'Origins of the Kriegsspiel', *Kriegsspiel News*, <79.170.44.85/kriegsspiel.inuk.co/index.php?option=com_content& task=view&id=15&Itemid=58>, accessed 31ˢᵗ August 2013.

Lefebvre, Georges, *Napoleon: from 18ᵗʰ Brumaire to Tilsit 1799–1807*, Routledge & Kegan Paul, London 1969.

Lefebvre, Henri, *Critique of Everyday Life Volume 1*, Verso, London 1991.

Lefebvre, Henri, *Everyday Life in the Modern World*, Transaction, New Brunswick 1984.

Lefebvre, Henri, *The Production of Space*, Blackwell, Oxford 1991.

Lefebvre, Henri, *Writings on Cities*, Blackwell, London 1996.

Lenin, V.I., 'Conspectus of Hegel's book *The Science of Logic – Book III (Subjective Logic or the Doctrine of the Notion)*', <www.marxists. org/archive/lenin/works/1914/cons-logic/ch03.htm>, accessed 31ˢᵗ August 2013.

Lenin, V.I., 'Fourth Anniversary of the October Revolution', *Selected Works Volume 6*, Lawrence & Wishart, London 1936, pages 500–508.

Lenin, V.I., *Imperialism: the highest stage of capitalism*, Communist Party of Great Britain, London 1929.

Lenin, V.I., 'On the Significance of Militant Materialism', <www.marxists.org/archive/lenin/works/1922/mar/12.htm>, accessed 31st August 2013.

Lenin, V.I., 'Preliminary Draft Resolution Of The Tenth Congress Of The R.C.P. On Party Unity', <www.marxists.org/archive/lenin/works/1921/10thcong/ch04.htm>, accessed 31st August 2013.

Lenin, V.I., 'Socialism and War: attitude of the Russian Social Democratic and Labour Party towards the War', *The Imperialist War: the struggle against social-chauvinism and social-pacifism 1914–1915*, International Publishers, New York 1930, pages 214–258.

Lenin, V.I., *State and Revolution*, Lawrence & Wishart, London 1933.

Lenin, V.I., 'The Collapse of the Second International', *The Imperialist War: the struggle against social-chauvinism and social-pacifism 1914–1915*, International Publishers, New York 1930, pages 273–322.

Lenin, V.I., 'The Elections to the Constituent Assembly and the Dictatorship of the Proletariat', *Selected Works Volume 6*, Lawrence & Wishart, London 1936, pages 463–485.

Lenin, V.I., *The Immediate Tasks of the Soviet Government*, Progress, Moscow 1970.

Lenin, V.I., 'To the Population', *Selected Works Volume 6*, Lawrence & Wishart, London 1936, pages 418–420.

Lenin, V.I., *What Is To Be Done?: burning questions of our movement*, Foreign Languages Press, Beijing 1975.

Lenin, V.I., and Yukko Rakhia, 'Theses and Report on Bourgeois Democracy and the Dictatorship of the Proletariat' in Bertil Hessel (editor), *Theses, Resolutions and Manifestos of the First Four Congresses of the Third International*, Pluto Press, London 1983, pages 7–20.

Leslie, Stuart, *The Cold War and American Science: the military-industrial complex at MIT and Stanford*, Columbia University Press, New York 1993.

Levin, Thomas, 'Dismantling the Spectacle: the cinema of Guy Debord' in Elisabeth Sussman (editor), *On the Passage of a Few People Through a Rather Brief Moment in Time: the Situationist International 1957–1972*, MIT Press, Cambridge 1989, pages 72–123.

Levitine, George, *The Dawn of Bohemianism: the Barbu rebellion and Primitivism in Neo-Classical France*, Pennsylvania State University Press, University Park 1978.

Lewis, Adrian, *The American Culture of War: the history of U.S. military force from World War II to Operation Enduring Freedom*, Routledge, New York 2012.

Lewis, Andy, Ted Raicer and Volko Runkhe (designers), *Reds!: the Russian Civil War 1918–1921*, GMT Games, Hanford 2001.

Lewis, Helena, *Dada Turns Red: the politics of Surrealism*, Edinburgh University Press, Edinburgh 1990.

Leyden, Peter, Peter Schwartz and Joel Hyatt, *The Long Boom: a future history of the world 1980–2020*, Texere, New York 2000.

Lih, Lars, *Lenin*, Reaktion, London 2011.

Lissagaray, Prosper-Olivier, *History of the Paris Commune*, New Park Publications, London 1976.

Livingstone, Marco, *Pop Art: a continuing history*, Harry N Abrams, New York 1990.

Lodder, Christina, *Russian Constructivism*, Yale University Press, New Haven 1983.

Losurdo, Domenico, *Liberalism: a counter-history*, Verso, London 2011.

Lucas, Dean, 'Flag on the Reichstag', *Famous Pictures: the magazine*, <www.famouspictures.org/mag/index.php?title=Flag_on_the_Reichstag>, accessed 31st August 2013.

Lukács, György, *History and Class Consciousness: studies in Marxist dialectics*, Merlin, London 1971.

Lutschinger, Stefan, *Malevich; A Suprematist board game*, Proll Positions, Vienna 2014.

Lütticken, Sven, *Life, Once More: forms of re-enactment in contemporary art*, Witte de With Center for Contemporary Art, Rotterdam 2005.

Lütticken, Sven, 'An Arena in Which to Re-enact' in Sven Lütticken (editor), *Life, Once More: forms of re-enactment in contemporary art*, Witte de With Center for Contemporary Art, Rotterdam 2005, pages 17–60.

Luttwak, Edward, *Coup d'État: a practical handbook*, Penguin, London 1969.

Luxemburg, Rosa, Karl Liebknecht, Clara Zetkin and Franz Mehring, 'Manifesto of the German Spartacists', <www.marxists.org/history/international/social-democracy/call/1919/30.htm>, accessed 31st August 2013.

Lydon, John, *Rotten: No Irish, No Blacks, No Dogs*, Coronet, London 1993.

Lynn, John, *The Bayonets of the Republic: motivation and tactics in the army of revolutionary France 1791–94*, Westview, Boulder 1996.

Lynn, John, 'Toward an Army of Honour: the moral evolution of the French army 1789–1815', *French Historical Studies*, Volume 16, Number 1, Spring 1989, pages 152–173.

Lyotard, Jean-François, *The Post-Modern Condition: a report on knowledge*, Manchester University Press, Manchester 1986.

MacDonald, Peter, *Giap: the victor in Vietnam*, Warner, London 1993.

Maclear, Michael, *Vietnam: the ten thousand day war*, Thames Methuen, London 1981.

Magun, Artemy, 'The Post-Communist Revolution in Russia and the Genesis of Representative Democracy', *Redescriptions: yearbook of political thought, conceptual history and feminist theory*, Volume 11, LIT Verlag, Jyväskylä 2007, pages 61–77.

Maillard, Alain, 'De Babeuf au Babouvisme' in Alain Maillard, Claude Mauzauric and Eric Walter (editors), *Présence de Babeuf: lumières, révolution, communisme*, Publications de la Sorbonne, Paris 1994, pages 261–279.

Malaparte, Curzio, *Technique du Coup d'État*, Bernard Grasset, Paris 1966.

Mao Zedong, 'Analysis of the Classes in Chinese Society', *Selected Works of Mao Zedong Volume 1*, Foreign Languages Press, Beijing 1967, pages 13–21.

Mao Zedong, 'On Protracted War', *Six Essays on Military Affairs*, Foreign Languages Press, Beijing 1971, pages 195–339.

Mao Zedong, 'Problems of War and Strategy', *Selected Works of Mao Zedong: Volume II*, Foreign Languages Press, Beijing 1965, pages 219–235.

Marand-Fouquet, Catherine, *La Femme au Temps de la Révolution*, Stock/Laurence Pernoud, Paris 1989.

Marcus, Greil, *Lipstick Traces: a secret history of the twentieth century*, Secker & Warburg, London 1989.

Marinetti, Fillipo, 'The Founding and Manifesto of Futurism' in Umbro Apollonio (editor), *Futurist Manifestos*, Tate, London 2009, pages 19–24.

Markham, Robert (designer), *Napoleonic Battles: Austerlitz 1805*, Avalanche Press, Irondale 2007.

Marx, Karl, *A Contribution to the Critique of Political Economy*, Progress, Moscow 1970.

Marx, Karl, *Capital Volume 1*, Penguin, London 1976.

Marx, Karl, *The Civil War in France*, Martin Lawrence, London 1933.

Marx, Karl, *The Eighteenth Brumaire of Louis Bonaparte*, George Allen & Unwin, London 1926.

Marx, Karl, and Friedrich Engels, *The Civil War in the United States*, International Publishers, New York 1937.

Marx, Karl, and Friedrich Engels, *The German Ideology*, Progress, Moscow 1964.

Marx, Karl, and Friedrich Engels, *The Holy Family or the critique of critical critique*, Foreign Languages Publishing House, Moscow 1956.

Marx, Karl, and Friedrich Engels with Paul Lafargue, 'The Alliance of Social Democracy and the International Working Men's Association' in Karl Marx, Friedrich Engels and Vladimir Lenin, *Anarchism and Anarcho-Synidicalism*, Progress, Moscow 1972, pages 106–123.

Mason, Paul, *Why It's Kicking Off Everywhere: the new global revolutionaries*, Verso, London 2012.

Mattick, Paul, *Anti-Bolshevik Communism*, Merlin, London 1978.

Mauss, Marcel, *The Gift: the form and reason for exchange in archaic societies*, Routledge, London 1990.

Mawdsley, Evan, *The Russian Civil War*, Birlinn, Edinburgh 2008.

Mawdsley, Evan, *Thunder in the East: the Nazi-Soviet war 1941–1945*, Bloomsbury, London 2007.

Mayor of London, *Cultural Metropolis: the Mayor's cultural strategy – 2012 and beyond*, GLA, London 2012.

McClendon, John, *C.L.R. James' Notes on Dialectics*, Lexington Books, Lanham 2005.

McGinn, Bernard, *Visions of the End: apocalyptic traditions in the Middle Ages*, Columbia University Press, New York 198.

McIver, Joel, *The Making of the Great Rock 'n' Roll Swindle*, Unanimous, London 2005.

McKay, George, 'DiY Culture: notes towards an intro' in George McKay (editor), *DiY Culture: party and protest in Nineties Britain*, Verso, London 1998, pages 1–53.

McLaughlin, Mark (designer), *War and Peace*, Avalon Hill, Baltimore 1980.

McLellan, David, *The Young Hegelians and Karl Marx*, MacMillan, London 1969.

McLuhan, Marshall, *Understanding Media: the extensions of man*, Routledge & Kegan Paul, London 1964.

McNamara, Robert, with Brian VanDeMark, *In Retrospect: the tragedy and lessons of Vietnam*, Times Books, New York 1995.

McPherson, James, *Battle Cry of Freedom: the Civil War era*, Oxford University Press, Oxford 1988.

Melly, George, *Revolt into Style: the pop arts in Britain*, Penguin, London 1970.

Mendras, Henri, with Alistair Cole, *Social Change in Modern France: towards a cultural anthropology of the Fifth Republic*, Cambridge University Press, Cambridge 1991.

Mension, Jean-Michael, *The Tribe*, Verso, London 2002.

Merrifield, Andy, *Guy Debord*, Reaktion Books, London 2005.

Mésa, *Mai 68 – Les Affiches de l'Atelier Populaire de l'ex-École des Beaux-Arts*, SPM, Paris 1984.

Mett, Ida, *The Kronstadt Uprising 1921*, Solidarity, London 1967.

Metzger, Gustav, *Damaged Nature, Auto-Destructive Art*, coracle @ workfortheeyetodo, London 1996.

Michels, Robert, *First Lectures in Political Sociology*, Harper Torchbooks, New York 1965.

Michels, Robert, *Political Parties: a sociological study of the oligarchical tendencies of modern democracy*, Free Press, New York 1962.

Miller, James, *Rousseau: dreamer of democracy*, Yale University Press, New Haven 1984.

Millikan, Max, and Donald Blackmer (editors), *The Emerging Nations: their growth and United States policy*, Little Brown, Boston 1961.

Monroe, Alexei, *Interrogation Machine: Laibach and NSK*, MIT Press, Cambridge 2005.

Moran, Daniel, 'Arms and the Concert: the nation in arms and the dilemmas of German liberalism' in Daniel Moran and Arthur Waldron (editors), *The People in Arms: military myth and national mobilisation since the French Revolution*, Cambridge University Press, Cambridge 2003, pages 49–74.

Morgana, Corrado, 'Introduction *Artists Re:thinking Games*' in Ruth Catlow, Marc Garrett and Corrado Morgana (editors), *Artists Re:thinking Games*, FACT, Liverpool 2010, pages 7–14.

Moulding, James, and Kateryna Onyiliogwu, 'Imperialism in Space: learn the concepts, not the rules – an educational game of Lenin's *Imperialism*', <imperialisminspace.uk>, accessed 31st August 2013.

Muir, Rory, *Tactics and the Experience of Battle in the Age of Napoleon*, Yale University Press, New Haven 1998.

Mulgan, Geoff, *Connexity: how to live in a connected world*, Chatto & Windus, London, 1997.

Nagy, Balazs, *How the Budapest Workers' Council Was Set Up: Hungary 1956*, Living History Library, Liverpool 2006.

Naquin, David (designer), *Battles of the First Empire: Marengo – 1800*, Historical Concepts, Boulder 1984.

Naumann, Francis and Bradley Bailey, *Marcel Duchamp: the art of Chess*, Readymade Press, New York 2009.

Neale, Jonathan, *The American War: Vietnam 1960–1975*, Bookmarks, London 2001.

Nechaev, Sergei [and Mikhail Bakunin], *Catechism of the Revolutionist*, AK Press, London 1989.

Nedelec, François, and Duccio Vitale (designers), *Mai '68: le jeu*, La Folie Douce, Paris 1980.

Negri, Toni, 'Archaeology and Project: the mass worker and the social worker', *Revolution Retrieved: selected writings on Marx, Keynes, capitalist crisis & new social subjects 1967–83*, Red Notes, London 1988, pages 203–228.

Nelson, Harold, *Leon Trotsky and the Art of Insurrection 1905–1917*, Cass, London 1988.

Nemours, Alfred Auguste, *Histoire Militaire de la Guerre d'Independance de Saint-Domingue: tome II les glorieux combats des divisions du Nord*, Berger-Levrault, Paris 1928.

Neumann, Franz, *Behemoth: the structure and practice of National Socialism 1933–1944*, Harper, New York 1966.

Neumann, John von, and Oskar Morgenstern, *Theory of Games and Economic Behaviour*, Princeton University Press, Princeton 1944.

Neville, Richard, *Playpower*, Paladin, London 1971.

Nicholls, David, *From Dessalines to Duvalier: race, colour and national independence in Haiti*, Rutgers University Press, New Brunswick 1996.

NME, *Punk 1975–1979*, NME Originals, London 2002.

Nolte, Ernst, *Three Faces of Fascism: Action Française, Italian Fascism, National Socialism*, Mentor, New York 1969.

Nouvel-Kammerer, Odile (editor), *Symbols of Power: Napoleon and the art of Empire Style*, Abrams, New York 2007.

Nuttall, Jeff, *Bomb Culture*, Paladin, London 1970.

Oberdorfer, Don, *Tet!: the turning point in the Vietnam War*, John Hopkins University Press, Baltimore 2001.

October – Association of Artistic Labour, 'Declaration 1928' in John Bowlt (editor), *Russian Art of the Avant-Garde: theory and criticism*, Thames & Hudson, London 1976, pages 273–279.

Ollman, Bertell (designer), *Class Struggle*, Avalon Hill, Baltimore 1980.

O'Malley, Jan, *The Politics of Community Action*, Spokesman, London 1977.

Opie, James, *Collecting Toy Soldiers in the 21ˢᵗ century*, Pen & Sword, Barnsley 2011.

Orchestra of the USSR Defence Ministry with the Bolshoi Theatre Choir, *Internationale*, Melodica 1980.

Ostrowska, Dorota, *Reading the French New Wave: critics, writers and art cinema in France*, Wallflower Press, London 2008.

Ott, Thomas, *The Haitian Revolution 1789–1804*, University of Tennessee Press, Knoxville 1973.

Overy, Richard, *Russia's War: A History of the Soviet Effort: 1941–1945*, Penguin, London 1998.

Ozouf, Mona, *Festivals and the French Revolution*, Harvard University Press, Cambridge 1988.

Pannekoek, Anton, *Workers' Councils*, Echanges et Mouvement, London undated.

Paret, Peter, *Clausewitz and the State: the man, his theories and his times*, Princeton University Press, Princeton 2007.

Parry, Richard, 'Preface' in Christopher Gray (editor), *Leaving the 20th Century: the incomplete works of the Situationist International*, Rebel Press, London 1998, pages v–vii.

Pearce, Celia, 'The Aesthetics of Play', *Visible Language*, Number 1, Volume 40, January 2006, pages 68–89.

Pearson, Harry, *Achtung Schweinehund!: a boy's own story of imaginary combat*, Little Brown, London 2007.

Peers, Chris (designer), *Contemptible Little Armies*, HLBS, Birmingham 2002.

Peers, Chris (designer), *Reds versus Reds: Russian Civil War rules – all the bits we need*, Copplestone Castings, Birmingham 2008, <www.classwargames.net/wp-content/uploads/2011/08/RCW_wargame_rules.rtf>, accessed 31st August 2013.

Pelevin, Victor, *Chapayev and Void* [*Buddha's Little Finger*], Penguin, New York 2001.

Perla, Peter, *The Art of Wargaming: a guide for professionals and hobbyists*, Naval Institute Press, Annapolis 1990.

Pethybridge, Roger, *The Social Prelude to Stalinism*, MacMillan, London 1974.

Pinkard, Terry, *Hegel: a biography*, Cambridge University Press, Cambridge 2000.

Plan 9, *Summer of Dissent: 7th July–2nd August 2009*, <www.plan9.org.uk/index.php?option=com_content&view=article&id=131:dissent&catid=2:past-&Itemid=12>, accessed 31st August 2013.

Plant, Sadie, *The Most Radical Gesture: the Situationist International in a postmodern age*, Routledge, London 1992.

Pollock, Ethan, *Stalin and the Soviet Science Wars*, Princeton University Press, Princeton 2006.

Porta2030, *You Are The Net, You Are Porta-Porter*, <richair.waag.org/porta2030>, accessed 31st August 2013.

Potlatch 1954/1957, Éditions Allia, Paris 1996.

Pountain, Dick, and David Robins, *Cool Rules: anatomy of an attitude*, Reaktion, London 2000.

Preobrazhensky, Eugeny, *The New Economics*, Oxford University Press, Oxford 1965.

Priaulx, Allan, and Sanford Ungar, *The Almost Revolution: France – 1968*, Dell, New York 1969.

Principia Dialectica, 'A World on Fire: editorial', *Principia Dialectica: enemies of utopia for the sake of its realisation*, Number 2, Autumn/Winter 2006, pages 4–5.

Priore, Michael and Charles Sabel, *The Second Industrial Divide: possibilities and prosperity*, Basic Books, New York 1984.

Pump House Gallery, 'About Us', <pumphousegallery.org.uk/about-us>, accessed 31st August 2013.

Pussy Riot, *Punk Prayer*, Moscow 2012, <www.youtube.com/watch?v=ALS92big4TY>, accessed 31st August 2013.

Pynchon, Thomas, *Against the Day*, Penguin, London 2006.

Quarrie, Barrie, *PSL Guide to Wargaming*, Patrick Stephens, Cambridge 1080.

Quattrocchi, Angelo, 'The Situationists are Coming', *OZ*, Number 20, 1969, pages 6–9.

Radcliffe, Charles, 'The Seeds of Social Destruction' in Franklin Rosemont and Charles Radcliffe (editors), *Dancin' In the Streets: Anarchists, IWWs, Surrealists, Situationists & Provos in the 1960s as recorded in the pages of Rebel Worker and Heatwave*, Charles H Kerr, Chicago 2005, pages 392–401.

Radcliffe, Charles, 'Two Fiery Flying Rolls' in Franklin Rosemont and Charles Radcliffe (editors), *Dancin' In the Streets: Anarchists, IWWs, Surrealists, Situationists & Provos in the 1960s as recorded in the pages of Rebel Worker and Heatwave*, Charles H Kerr, Chicago 2005, pages 326–380.

Rasmussen, Mikkel Bolt, 'To Act In Culture While Being Against All Culture' in Mikkel Bolt Rasmussen and Jakob Jakobsen (editors), *Expect Anything Fear Nothing: the Situationist movement in Scandinavia and elsewhere*, Nebula and Autonomedia, Copenhagen and New York 2011, pages 75–113.

Ransome, Arthur, *The Crisis in Russia 1920*, Faber and Faber, London 2010.

Rappolt, Mark, 'Jeremy Deller Interview', *Art Review*, <artreview.com/home/feature_jeremy_deller_venice_interview>, accessed 31st August 2013.

Raspaud, Jean-Jacques, and Jean-Pierre Voyer, 'Situationist Data (Data)' in Elisabeth Sussman (editor), *On the Passage of a Few People Through a Rather Brief Moment in Time: the Situationist International 1957–1972*, MIT Press, Cambridge 1989, pages 176–188.

Raylab, <www.raylab.com>, accessed 31st August 2013.

Red Brigades, 'Strategic Resolution', *The Ripening of Time*, Number 12, April 1979–December 1979, pages 31–46.

Red Notes (editor), *Italy 1977–8: Living With an Earthquake*, Red Notes, London 1978.

Red Notes (editor), *Italy 1980–81 After Marx, Jail!: the attempted destruction of a communist movement*, Red Notes, London 1981.

Reed, John, *Ten Days That Shook The World*, Penguin, London 1966.

Reid, Jamie, and Jon Savage, *Up They Rise: the incomplete works of Jamie Reid*, Faber & Faber, London 1987.

Reisswitz, Georg von (designer), *Kriegsspiel: the Prussian army wargame*, Too Fat Lardies, St Albans 2007.

Reynolds, Simon, *Rip It Up and Start Again: post-punk 1978–1984*, Faber and Faber, London 2005.

Richta, Radovan (editor), *Civilisation at the Crossroads: social and human implications of the scientific and technological revolution*, Australian New Left Review, Sydney 1969.

Ridley, Frank, *Spartacus: the leader of the Roman slaves*, Frank Maitland, Kenardington 1961.

Riesel, René, 'Preliminaries on the Councils and Councilist Organisation' in Ken Knabb (editor), *Situationist International Anthology*, Bureau of Public Secrets, Berkeley 1981, pages 270–282.

Riff, David, 'A Representation which is Divorced from the Consciousness of Those Whom It Represents is No Representation. What I do not know, I do not worry about', *Chto Delat?*, <www.chtodelat.org/index.php?option=com_content&view=article&id=1023%3Adavid-riff--a-representation-which-is-divorced-from-the-consciousness-of-those-whom-it-represents-is-no-representation-what-i-do-not-know-i-do-not-worry-about&catid=241%3A10-34-in-defence-of-representation&Itemid=490&lang=en>, accessed 31st August 2013.

Riot not to Work Collective, *We Want to Riot not Work!: the 1981 Brixton uprisings*, London Workers Group, London 1982.

Roberts, Warren, *Jacques-Louis David, Revolutionary Artist: art, politics and the French Revolution*, University of North Carolina Press, Chapel Hill 1989.

Rocard, Michel, *À l'Épreuve des Faits*, Éditions du Seuil, Paris 1986.

Ros, Martin, *Night Fire: the black Napoleon and the battle for Haiti*, Sarpedon, New York 1994.

Rosemont, Franklin, and Charles Radcliffe (editors), *Dancin' In the Streets: Anarchists, IWWs, Surrealists, Situationists & Provos in the 1960s as recorded in the pages of Rebel Worker and Heatwave*, Charles H Kerr, Chicago 2005.

Ross, Kristen, 'Lefebvre on the Situationists: an interview', *October*, Number 79, Winter 1997, pages 69–83.

Rostow, Walt, *Concept and Controversy: sixty years of taking ideas to market*, University of Texas Press, Austin 2003.

Rostow, Walt, *Essays on a Half-Century: ideas, policies and action*, Westview Press, Boulder 1988.

Rostow, Walt, *The Diffusion of Power 1957–1972: an essay in recent history*, Macmillan, New York 1972.

Rostow, Walt, *The Stages of Economic Growth: a non-communist manifesto*, Cambridge University Press, Cambridge 1960.

Rostow, Walt, *View from the Seventh Floor*, Harper & Row, New York 1964.

Rousseau, Jean-Jacques, *Émile: or on education*, Penguin, London 1991.

Rousseau, Jean-Jacques, *Letter to Monsieur d'Alembert on the Theatre [Politics and the Arts]*, Cornell University Press, Ithaca 1960.

Rousseau, Jean-Jacques, *The Government of Poland*, Hackett, Indianapolis IA 1985.

Rousseau, Jean-Jacques, *The Social Contract*, Penguin, London 1968.

Rozanov, Danila, 'Voina: artists at war', *Open Democracy*, 17th February 2011, <www.opendemocracy.net/od-russia/danila-rozanov/voina-artists-at-war>, accessed 31st August 2013.

R.S. [Roland Simon], 'The Present Moment', *SIC: international journal for communisation*, Number 1, November 2011, pages 94–144.

Rudé, George, *Hanoverian London*, Sutton, London 2003.

Rumney, Ralph, 'The *Vague* Interview: 4/5/89', *Vague*, Number 22, 1989/90, pages 27–41.

Sabin, Philip, *Simulating War: studying conflict through simulation games*, Continuum, London 2012.

Sanborn, Keith, 'Postcards from the Berezina' in Napoléon Bonaparte, *How to Make War*, Ediciones la Calvera, New York 1998, pages 73–139.

Sanders, John, *An Introduction to Wargaming*, Pelham Books, London 1975.

Sanguinetti, Gianfranco, *On Terrorism and the State: the theory and practice of terrorism divulged for the very first time*, B.M. Chronos, London 1982.

Sariego, William (designer), *Red Russia*, Avalanche Press, Birmingham 2008.

Savage, Jon, *England's Dreaming: Sex Pistols and punk rock*, Faber and Faber, London 1991.

Scanlon, Jennifer, 'Jo Freeman' in Jennifer Scanlon (editor), *Significant American Feminists: a biographical sourcebook*, Greenwood Press, Westport 1999, pages 104–110.

Scheiner, Anne-Marie, 'Dissolving the Magic Circle of Play: lessons from Situationist gaming', <www.opensorcery.net/Dissolving.pdf>, accessed 31st August 2013.

Schiffin, André (editor), *The Cold War and the University: towards an intellectual history of the postwar years*, New Press, New York 1997.

Schutz, Lindsley, and Thomas Shaw (designers), *Stalingrad*, Avalon Hill, Baltimore 1963.

Schutz, Lindsley, and Thomas Shaw (designers), *Waterloo*, Avalon Hill, Baltimore 1962.

Scott, Harriet Fast, 'Soviet Military Doctrine in the Nuclear Age, 1945–1985' in Willard Frank and Philip Gillette (editors), *Soviet Military Doctrine from Lenin to Gorbachev, 1915–1991*, pages 175–192.

Seale, Patrick, and Maureen McConville, *French Revolution 1968*, Penguin, London 1968.

Serge, Victor, *Memoirs of a Revolutionary 1901–1941*, Oxford University Press, Oxford 1963.

Sex Pistols, *God Save The Queen*, Virgin 1977.

Shaw, George Bernard, Sidney Webb, Graham Wallas, Oliver Clarke, Annie Besant and Hubert Bland, *Fabian Essays*, George Allen & Unwin, London 1889.

Sheehan, Neil, *A Bright Shining Lie: John Paul Vann and America in Vietnam*, Pimlico, London 1998.

Sheehan, Neil, Hedrick Smith, E.W. Kenworthy and Fox Butterfield, *The Pentagon Papers: the secret history of the Vietnam war*, Bantam Books, New York 1971.

Sherborne, Michael, *H.G. Wells: another kind of life*, Peter Owen, London 2010.

Short, Philip, *Mao: a life*, John Murray, London 2004.

Sibalis, Michael, 'The Napoleonic Police State' in Philip Dwyer (editor), *Napoleon and Europe*, Pearson, London 2001, pages 79–94.

Simmons, Bowen (designer), *Bonaparte at Marengo*, Simmons Games, Sunnyvale 2005.

Simmons, Bowen (designer), *Napoleon's Triumph*, Simmons Games, Sunnyvale 2007.

Situationist International, 'Contribution à une Définition Situationniste du Jeu', *Internationale Situationniste*, Number 1, June 1958, pages 9–10.

Situationist International, 'Détournement as Negation and Prelude' in Ken Knabb (editor), *Situationist International Anthology*, Bureau of Public Secrets, Berkeley 1981, pages 55–56.

Situationist International, 'Ideologies, Classes and the Domination of Nature' in Ken Knabb (editor), *Situationist International Anthology*, Bureau of Public Secrets, Berkeley 1981, pages 101–109.

Situationist International, 'Nos Buts et Nos Méthodes dans le Scandale de Strasbourg', *Internationale Situationniste*, Number 11, October 1967, pages 23–31.

Situationist International, 'The Adventure' in Ken Knabb (editor), *Situationist International Anthology*, Bureau of Public Secrets, Berkeley 1981, pages 60–61.

Situationist International, 'The Beginning of a New Era' in Ken Knabb (editor), *Situationist International Anthology*, Bureau of Public Secrets, Berkeley 1981, pages 225–256.

Situationist International, 'The Latest Exclusions' in Ken Knabb (editor), *Situationist International Anthology*, Bureau of Public Secrets, Berkeley 1981, pages 293–294.

Social Democratic Party, 'Basic Programme of the Social Democratic Party of Germany adopted by an extraordinary conference of the Social Democratic Party held at Bad Godesberg from 13–15 November 1959' in Susanne Miller and Heinrich Potthoff (editors), *A History of German Social Democracy from 1848 to the present*, St. Martin's Press, New York 1986, pages 274–287.

Sokal, Alan, and Jean Bricmont, *Fashionable Nonsense: post-modern intellectuals' abuse of science*, Picador, London 1998.

Small, Richard, 'The Training of an Intellectual, the Making of a Marxist' in Paul Buhle (editor), *C.L.R. James: his life and work*, Alison & Busby, London 1986, pages 49–60.

Smith, Chris, *Creative Britain*, Faber & Faber, London 1998.

Smith, Denis Mack, *Mussolini*, Granada, St Albans 1983.

Soboul, Albert, *Les Soldats de l'An II*, Club Français de Livre, Paris 1959.

Soboul, Albert, *Paysans, Sans-Culottes et Jacobins*, Librairie Clavreuil, Paris 1966.

Soboul, Albert, *The Sans-Culottes: the popular movement and revolutionary government 1793–1794*, Princeton University Press, Princeton 1980.

Sperber, Murray, 'Eisenstein's October', *Jump Cut*, Number 14, 1977, <www.ejumpcut.org/archive/onlinessays/JC14folder/October.html>, accessed 31st August 2013.

SPIR608 Political Simulations and Gaming, B.A. in Politics, University of Westminster, <en.wikiversity.org/wiki/SPIR608_Political_Simulations_and_Gaming>, accessed 31st August 2013.

Sprague, Jeb, 'Paramilitaries in Haiti', *Monthly Review*, Number 4, Volume 64, September 2012, pages 24–36.

Stallabrass, Julian, *High Art Lite: British Art in the 1990s*, Verso, London 1999.

Stallabrass, Julian, *Internet Art: the on-line clash of culture and commerce*, Tate, London 2003.

Stallabrass, Julian, *Contemporary Art: a very short introduction*, Oxford University Press, Oxford 2004.

Stalin, Joseph, 'Dialectical and Historical Materialism', *Problems of Leninism*, Foreign Languages Publishing House, Moscow 1954, pages 713–745.

Stalin, Joseph, *Marxism and Problems of Linguistics*, Foreign Languages Press, Beijing 1972.

Staudenmaier, William, 'Vietnam, Mao and Clausewitz', *Parameters: journal of the US Army War College*, Number 1, Volume 7, 1977, pages 79–89.

Stendhal [Marie-Henri Beyle], *A Life of Napoleon*, Open University, Milton Keynes 2004.

Stone, David, *Hammer and Rifle: the militarisation of the Soviet Union 1926–1933*, University Press of Kansas, Lawrence 2000.

Stonor Saunders, Frances, *Who Paid the Piper?: the CIA and the cultural Cold War*, Granta Books, London 1999.

Swain, Geoffrey, *Russia's Civil War*, Tempus, Stroud 2000.

Surrealist Group, 'Manifesto of the Surrealists Concerning *L'Age d'Or*' in Paul Hammond (editor), *The Shadow and Itself: Surrealist writings on cinema*, Polygon, London 1991, pages 195–203.

Taber, Robert, *The War of the Flea: guerrilla warfare theory and practice*, Paladin, London 1970.

Tanner, Peter, 'Games Without Commanders?', *Wargames Illustrated*, Number 213, June 2005, pages 36–38.

Tao Hanzhang, 'Commentary on Sun Tzu's *The Art of War*' in Sun Tzu, *The Art of War*, Wordsworth, Ware 1998, pages 61–130.

Temple, Julien (director), *The Great Rock 'n' Roll Swindle*, Virgin Films 1980.

The Centre of Attention, *Vive La République!: pagan images of the last Queen of the British Isles by her indigenous subjects*, <www.thecentreofattention.org/exhibitions/queen.html>, accessed 31st August 2013.

Théorie Communiste, 'Much Ado About Nothing', *End Notes*, Number 1, October 2008, pages 154–206.

Thomas, Paul, *Karl Marx and the Anarchists*, Routledge & Kegan Paul, London 1980.

Thompson, Paul, and Guy Lewis, *Revolution Betrayed?: a critique of Trotskyism*, Big Flame, Liverpool 1977.

Tiqqun, *This is Not a Program*, Semiotext(e), Los Angeles 2011.

Tolstoy, Vladimir, Irina Bibikova and Catherine Cooke, *Street Art of the Revolution: festivals and celebrations in Russia 1913–33*, Vendome Press, London 1990.

Tompsett, Fabian, 'Preface to the English Edition' in Asger Jorn, *Open*

Creation and Its Enemies, Unpopular Books, London 1994, pages 3–16.

Toussaint L'Ouverture, François-Dominique, *The Haitian Revolution*, Verso, London 2008.

TPTG [The Children of the Galley], 'The Rebellious Passage of a Proletarian Minority through a Brief Period of Time: the December rebellion and the post-rebellion developments as aspects of the crisis of capitalist relations in Greece' in Antonis Vradis, and Dimitris Dalakoglu (editors), *Revolt and Crisis in Greece: between a present yet to pass and a future still to come*, AK Press & Occupied London, Edinburgh 2011, pages 115–131.

Train, Brian (designer), *Algeria: the war of independence 1954–1962*, Fiery Dragon, Ontario 2007.

Train, Brian (designer), *Konarmiya: year of the Red tide*, Fiery Dragon, Ontario 2007.

Train, Brian (designer), *Red Guard!*, Schutze Games, Sydney 2002.

Tresham, Francis, and Mick Uhl (designers), *Civilization*, Gibson Games, Northampton 1980.

Triple Revolution Committee, 'The Triple Revolution' in Priscilla Long (editor), *The New Left: a collection of essays*, Extending Horizons Books, Boston 1969, pages 339–354.

Trocchi, Alexander, 'Invisible Insurrection of a Million Minds', *Invisible Insurrection of a Million Minds: a Trocchi Reader*, Polygon, Edinburgh 1991, pages 177–191.

Trotsky, Leon, *History of the Russian Revolution Volume 3: the triumph of the Soviets*, Sphere, London 1965.

Trotsky, Leon, 'Manifesto of the Communist International to the Workers of the World' in Bertil Hessel (editor), *Theses, Resolutions and*

Manifestos of the First Four Congresses of the Third International, Pluto Press, London 1983, pages 27–36.

Trotsky, Leon, *Military Writings*, Pathfinder, New York 1971.

Trotsky, Leon, *My Life: an attempt at an autobiography*, Penguin, London 1975.

Trotsky, Leon, *Revolution Betrayed: what is the Soviet Union and where is it going?*, New Park, London 1967.

Trotsky, Leon, *Terrorism and Communism*, New Park, London 1975.

Trotsky, Leon, *The New Course 1923*, New Park, London 1956.

Trotsky, Leon, 'The Paris Commune and Soviet Russia', *Leon Trotsky on the Paris Commune*, Pathfinder, New York 1970, pages 29–46.

Trotsky, Leon, *The Transitional Programme: the death agony of capitalism and the tasks of the 4th International*, New Park, London 1980.

Trotsky, Leon, 'Theses on the Conditions of Admission to the Communist International' in Bertil Hessel (editor), *Theses, Resolutions and Manifestos of the First Four Congresses of the Third International*, Pluto Press, London 1983, pages 92–97.

Tupitsyn, Margarita, *Rodchenko & Popova: defining Constructivism*, Tate Publishing, London 2009.

Tuters, Marc, 'The Locative Commons', *Futuresonic '04: mobile connections*, 28th April – 8th May 2004, Manchester, <www.futuresonic.com/futuresonic/pdf/Locative_Commons.pdf> accessed 31st August 2013.

Unamuno, Pablo Robertson de (director), *Invisible Forces at Furtherfield Gallery*, <vimeo.com/44856163>, accessed 31st August 2013.

Vachée, Jean-Baptiste, *Napoleon at Work*, Nonsuch, Stroud 2007.

Vague, Tom, *Vague: The West Eleven Days of My Life*, Number 24, London 1992/3.

Vague, Tom, *Anarchy in the UK: the Angry Brigade*, AK Press, Edinburgh 1997.

Vaneigem, Raoul, *A Cavalier History of Surrealism*, AK Press, Edinburgh 1999.

Vaneigem, Raoul, 'Basic Banalities' in Ken Knabb (editor), *Situationist International Anthology*, Bureau of Public Secrets, Berkeley 1981, pages 89–100.

Vaneigem, Raoul, 'Basic Banalities (II)' in Ken Knabb (editor), *Situationist International Anthology*, Bureau of Public Secrets, Berkeley 1981, pages 118–133.

Vaneigem, Raoul, *The Revolution of Everyday Life*, Practical Paradise, London 1975.

Vasiliev, Georgi and Sergei (directors), *Chapayev*, Len Films, Leningrad 1934.

Venturi, Franco, *Roots of Revolution: a history of the Populist and Socialist movements in 19th century Russia*, Phoenix, London 2001.

Vermorel, Fred, 'At The End, They Even Stole His Death', *GQ*, January 2011, pages 205–211.

Vermorel, Fred, and Judy Vermorel, *Sex Pistols*, Omnibus Press, London 1987.

Vernardakis, Christoforos, 'The Greek Left in the 2012 Elections: the return to the class vote', *Transform!: European journal for alternative thinking and political dialogue*, 11/2012, pages 128–134.

Viénet, René, *Enragés and Situationists in the Occupation Movement: France May '68*, Autonomedia, New York 1992.

Viénet, René, 'The Situationists and the New Forms of Action against Politics and Art' in Ken Knabb (editor), *Situationist International Anthology*, Bureau of Public Secrets, Berkeley 1981, pages 213–216.

Vradis, Antonis, and Dimitris Dalakoglu (editors), *Revolt and Crisis in Greece: between a present yet to pass and a future still to come*, AK Press & Occupied London, Edinburgh 2011.

Wallace, Martin (designer), *Liberté*, Valley Games, Alberta 2001.

Wakefield, Neville, *Post-Modernism: the twilight of the real*, Pluto, London 1990.

Warhol, Andy, *Popism: the Warhol Sixties*, Harcourt Brace Jovanovich, New York 1980.

Wark, McKenzie, *50 Years of Recuperation of the Situationist International*, Buell Center/Forum Project and Princeton Architectural Press, New York and Princeton 2008.

Wark, McKenzie, *The Beach Beneath the Street: the everyday life and glorious times of the Situationist International*, Verso, London 2011.

Wark, McKenzie, *The Spectacle of Disintegration: Situationist passages out of the 20th century*, Verso, London 2013.

Weber, Max, *From Max Weber: Essays in Sociology*, Routledge & Kegan Paul, London 1948.

Webster, Frank, *Theories of the Information Society*, Routledge, London 2002.

Webster, Paul, and Nicholas Powell, *Saint-Germain-des-Prés: French post-war culture from Sartre to Bardot*, Constable, London 1984.

Weiner, Myron (editor), *Modernisation: the dynamics of growth*, Basic Books, New York 1966.

Wells, H.G., *A Modern Utopia*, House of Stratus, Thirsk 2002.

Wells, H.G., *Little Wars: a game for boys from twelve years of age to one hundred and fifty and for that more intelligent sort of girls who like boys' games and books – with an appendix on Kriegspiel*, J.M. Dent, London 1931.

Wells, H.G., 'Russia in the Shadows', *The Open Conspiracy and Other Writings*, House of Stratus, Thirsk 2002, pages 331–413.

Wells, H.G., *The Shape of Things to Come*, Corgi, London 1967.

Wells, H.G., *The War of the Worlds*, William Heinemann, London 1898.

Weir, Jean, *The Angry Brigade 1967–1984: documents and chronology*, Elephant Editions, London 1985.

Widgery, David (editor), *The Left in Britain 1956–1968*, Penguin, London 1976.

Widgery, David, *Beating Time: riot 'n' race 'n' rock 'n' roll*, Chatto, London 1986.

Williams, Emmet and Ann Noel, *Mr Fluxus: a collective portrait of George Macunias 1931–1978*, Thames & Hudson, London 1997.

Williams, Gwyn, *Artisans and Sans-Culottes: popular movements in France and Britain during the French Revolution*, Libris, London 1989.

Williams, John, *Michael X: a life in black & white*, Century, London 2008.

Williams, Raymond, *The Politics of Modernism: against the new conformists*, Verso, London 1989.

Wilson, Anthony, *The Bomb and the Computer*, Barrie and Rockliff, London 1968.

Wilson, Tony, *24 Hour Party People: what sleeve notes never tell you*, Channel 4 Books, London 2002.

Winter, David, 'Welcome to Pong-Story', <www.pong-story.com/intro.htm>, accessed 31st August 2013.

Wise, David, 'A Hidden History of King Mob', <www.revoltagainst plenty.com/index.php/archive-local/93-a-hidden-history-of-king-mob.html>, accessed 31st August 2013.

Wright, Eric Olin, 'Class Struggle and Class Compromise in an Era of Stagnation and Crisis', *Transform!: European journal for alternative thinking and political dialogue*, 11/2012, pages 22–44.

Wright, Steve, *Storming Heaven: Class Composition and Struggle in Italian Autonomist Marxism*, Pluto, London 2002.

Wollen, Peter, 'Bitter Victory: the art and politics of the Situationist International' in Elisabeth Sussman (editor), *On the Passage of a Few People through a Rather Brief Moment in Time: the Situationist International 1957–1972*, MIT Press, Boston Mass, pages 20–61.

Woloch, Isser, *Napoleon and his Collaborators: the making of a dictatorship*, W.W. Norton, New York 2001.

Woodward, Gill, 'Interview with the Author and Ilze Black', 3rd July 2010.

Worcester, Kent, *C.L.R. James: a political biography*, State University of New York Press, Albany 1996.

Wright, Steve, *Home Sweet Home: Banksy's Bristol*, Tangent Books, Bristol 2007.

Xuyet, Ngo Van, '1945: the Saigon Commune', <libcom.org/history/articles/saigon-commune-1945>, accessed 31st August 2013.

Yalom, Marilyn, *Birth of the Chess Queen: a history*, Perennial, New York 2005.

Yes Men (directors), *The Yes Men*, United Artists 2003.

Young, John (designer), *Austerlitz: The Battle of Three Emperors, 2 December 1805*, SPI, New York 1972.

Young, Peter, and J.P. Lawford, *Charge!: or how to play wargames*, Morgan Grampian, London 1967.

Zamoyski, Adam, *1812: Napoleon's fatal march on Moscow*, Harper, London 2004.

Zeman, Z.A.B., *Prague Spring: a report on Czechoslovakia 1968*, Penguin, London 1969.

Ziemke, Earl, *The Red Army 1918–1941: from vanguard of world revolution to US ally*, Frank Cass, London 2004.

Zinoviev, Grigory, 'The Role of the Communist Party in Proletarian Revolution' in Bertil Hessel (editor), *Theses, Resolutions and Manifestos of the First Four Congresses of the Third International*, Pluto Press, London 1983, pages 68–75.

Žižek, Slavoj, *Revolution at the Gates: selected writings of Lenin from 1917*, Verso, London 2002.

Zucker, Kevin (designer), *The Sun of Austerlitz*, Operational Studies Group, Baltimore 2003.

5.0: INDEX

'On the eve of World War I in a self-organized commune in Spain, Yashmeen says: "Well, why not let them have their war? Why would any self-respecting Anarchist care about any of these governments with their miserable incestuous stew of kings and Caesars?"

"Self interest", said Ratty. "Anarchists would be the biggest losers, wouldn't they? Industrial corporations, armies, navies, governments, all would go on as before, if not more powerful. But in a general war among nations, every small victory Anarchism has struggled to win so far would simply turn to dust."'

Thomas Pynchon, *Against the Day*, page 938

Avalon Hill, generic wargame simulations, 118–20, 131; *Waterloo*, 162

avant-garde, 40–4, 46; capitalist, 55; democratised, 68, 85, 92–3; elitism of, 332; military origins of, 38; 1920s recuperated, 54–6, 60–2; 1950s European, 54; revolutionary politics disappearance, 55

Badiou, Alain, 141–42
Bailey, Bradley, 42n
Bailey, Jeremy, *Warmail*, 99
Bakunin, Mikhail, 250; 'invisible dictatorship', 167
Baltic Centre for Contemporary Art, Gateshead, 51, 106
Banks, Iain, 335n
Banksy, 65, 67, 100, 107, 329
Barbrook, Richard, 64n, 75n, 101–2n, 116n, 141n, 147n, 165n, 216, 217, 220n, 223, 276n, 278n, 318; *The Class of the New*, 37n
Barbus, first avant-garde art movement, 184–5, 202
Barcelona 1936, 219; nostalgia for, 328
Barker, John, 79n, 80
'barrack-room communism', 154
Bassford, Christopher, 267n, 269n
Bastille, 1789 fall of, 168, 186, 194, 196, 265
Baudelaire, Charles, 60
Baudrillard, Jean, 102, 156n, 169n, 170
Bauhaus, 40
Becker-Ho, Alice, 21, 36, 46–7, 51–2, 64, 104, 119, 161n, 258, 297n, 296n, 299, 300n, 304, 307, 310, 313, 310n, 316; game deployment, 50–1, 116–7
Beech, Amanda, 35
Bell, David, 174n, 179n
Berg, Aksel, 75n
Berger, Dan, 80n, 282n
Berger, Martin, 284n
Berghaus, Günter, 70n, 78n
Bernstein, Edouard, 243n, 250n
Bernstein, Michèle, 126–7, 130, 132–3, 207, 211n, 283
Bernstein, Sam, 166n, 170n, 234n
Besant, Annie, 294n
Bettleheim, Charles, 146n
Bey, Hakim, 101n

Biard, Roland, 156*n*, 214*n*

Biba, boutique, 80

Bibikova, Irina, 134–5*n*

Birmingham Centre for Contemporary Cultural Studies, 102–3

Black Jacobins, The, see James, C.L.R.

Black music, impact of, 71

Black Panther party, 282

Black, Ilze, 50, 67*n*, 71*n*, 72*n*, 79–81*n*, 83*n*, 97, 99, 115, 152, 154, 157–9, 201, 204*n*, 232*n*, 236*n*, 239*n*, 318*n*

Blackburn, Robin, 73*n*, 234*n*, 250*n*

Blackmer, Donald, 276*n*

Blair, Tony, 36–7

Blake, Lucy, 50

Blake, Peter, 69

Blake, William, 76, 83

Bland, Hubert, 294*n*

Blanqui, Louis-Auguste, 165–6*n*, 170*n*

Blast Theory, *Can You See Me Now?*, 99; *Uncle Roy All Around*, 99, 106

Blaug, Ricardo, 197*n*

Blazic, Lara, 205–7

Blinov, Alexei, 205–7

Boal, Augusto, 317

Bodlaender, Hans, 160*n*

'body counts', 279

bohemian neighbourhoods, 58–60, 79, 85, 105

Bologna, Sergio, 143*n*

Bolshevik Party, Russia, 21–3, 41; as Jacobins, 165, 325; elitist politics, 286; military discipline/virtue, 148–9, 151–2; military solutions, 153–4; 1917 coup d'état, 134, 148–9; organisational model, 115; power seizure, 124; Red Guards relegated, 147–8

Bolshevik sects: Red Bases fantasy, 73; worthy publications, 58, 69–70

Bolshevism: military glamour, 156; New Left coated revival, 65, 141–2, 144, 172; slogans of, 66

Bonaparte, Louis, 59

Bonaparte, Napoléon, 30–2, 122, 160, 162–4, 170, 300, 302, 312; Bonapartists, 23; concentration of forces, 309; 1800 crossing of the Alps, 177–80; cult of, 176; 'dictatorship of the bourgeoisie', 164;

downfall, 266; 1812 Russian campaign, 287; emperor, 175; hot pursuit expertise, 315–6; Jena cheers, 193–4; memoirs, 107; monopoly decision-making, 197; propagandists of, 201–2; 'Robespierre on horseback', 173; 'saviour of the nation' coup d'état, 174; skills of, 306; state power seizure, 196; warrior intellectual image, 179

Bonnot de la Bande, Jules, 144n

Bonorandi, Djahjah, 117

Boorman, Scott, 289n, 290n

Borg, Richard, 23, 321; *Commands & Colors: Napoleonics*, 23, 34–5, 234

Bornstein, Sam, 238n

Borsook, Paulina, 220n

Bourbon, Marie Antoinette, 187

Bourriaud, Nicholas, 105n

Bourrienne, Louis de, 175n, 177n,

Bourseiller, Christophe, 156n, 214n

Bovill, David, 235

Bracken, Len, 47, 157n, 214–5n, 258n

Branson, Richard, Virgin Music, 94

Brazil, 50, 106, 117

Breton, André, 41n, 42, 55

Bricmont, Jean, 102n

Bridger, Sam, 92n

Brigate Rosse, 282

Brinton, Maurice, 146n

Bristol, City Gallery, 100–1

Britain: 1997–2010 New Labour government, 36–7; Royal Navy power, 176

British General Staff, 261

Brotchie, Alastair, 42n

Brown, Howard, 196n

Brun, Carl, 186n

Brunswick, Duke of, 1806 Jena-Auerstädt humiliation, 31

Bürger, Peter, 39n, 41n, 45n

Buck-Morss, Susan, 135n, 149n, 195n, 242n

Budapest Workers Council 1956, 62, 127, 210–1, 213

Buhle, Paul, 243n

Bukharin, Nikolai, 151n, 285n

discipline of, 193; corrupted, 201; French Republic, 173, 185, 312; Haitian, 249–50; USA, 284

Claimants Union, 79

Clark, T. J., 43*n*, 70, 186*n*

Clarke, I.F., 261*n*

Clarke, Oliver, 294*n*

Clash, the, 87, 90, 96

class struggle, Absolute War, 301

Class Wargames, 33–5, 47, 65; boards and pieces, 108; *Communiqué #1*, 35*n*; *Communiqué #5*, 106, 129*n* 133*n*, 145*n*; *Communiqué #6*, 259*n*, 299*n*; *Communiqué #7*, 97; *Communiqué #8*, 295*n*; *Communiqué #9*, 248–9*n*, 257*n*; *Communiqué #10*, 248–9, 257*n*; film, 50–1, 97, 116, 204–5; interactive performances, 64, 334; performance importance, 314; Russian language film version, 204–5; 2007 training sessions, 47, 307, 313

Clausewitz, Carl von, 31*n*, 174*n*, 176*n*, 197, 231, 243, 257–8, 262–9, 272–4, 277–8, 281, 282–92, 296–9, 300–2, 305, 306*n*, 307–8, 309*n*, 310–1, 312*n*, 316, 319–20, 327–8, 330, 332–3; Bolshevik monopolising, 291; five strategic and tactical principles, 312, 328, 334; French translation of, 258; Lenin's appropriation of, 285; Mao's admiration for, 288; *On War*, 283, 285; strategy historicised, 332; theory training, 327

CND (Campaign for Nuclear Disarmament), 72

Cobb, Richard, 190*n*

Cockburn, Alexander 73*n*

Cohn-Bendit, Daniel, 48, 77*n*, 326, 330

Cohn-Bendit, Gabriel, 77*n*

Cold War: binary logic, 282; Absolute War strategy, 272; orthodoxies, 296; 'zero-sum' game, 277

Collin, Mathew, 93*n*

Commands & Colors: Napoleonics, see Fort Bedourete

Committee for the Maintenance of the Occupations, 78

Committee of Public Safety, 187, 190, 196

Commune des Arts, 186–8

communism, 'barrack-room', 154; cybernetic, 75, 78, 223; software, 102

Comninel, George, 167*n*

computer simulations, USA Vietnam, 279

concentration of forces, military strategy, 302, 308–11, 317, 320, 327

European insurrectionists, state manipulated, 290
European occupation movements, 255
Evans, Mike, 90*n*
Exquisite Corpse, 42

Fabian Society, 294
Facebook, 220–1, 324
Facing Reality, pamphlet, 245
Factory Records, 92
Fager, Anders, *Comrade Koba*, 333
Fanelli, Sara, 39*n*, 105*n*
Fanon, Frantz, 249
Farren, Mick, 71*n*
fashion, alternative, 86–7
Fazakerley, Gordon, 67, 96
Featherstone, Donald, 132
Festival of Reason, Notre Dame 1793, 189, 195, 202, 247
Fields, A. Belden, 156*n*
Figgis, Mike, 50*n*
Firebox, performances at, 333
Fisera, Vladimir, 77*n*
Flanagan, Mary, 42*n*, 44*n*
Fleapit, performances at, 333
Florida, Richard, 37*n*
Fluxus group, 43, 49, 64, 105; *Fluxboxes*, 44
Foner, Philip, 282*n*
Ford, Laura Oldfield, 232
Fordism, 61, 68, 72, 125, 169, 212; controlled consumption model, 62; ruling elite of, 63; Social Democrats practicing, 252
Forgács, Eva, 41*n*
Forrest, Alan, 192–3*n*
Fort Bedourete, 1802 battle of, 235, 237–8; *Commands & Colors: Napoleonics* re-mix, 23–5, 234–6, 230, 237, 240–1, 242, 247, 249, 257, 301, 308, 321–2, 325, 231, 253, 317
Foucault, Michel, 102, 144, 170, 215
Fountain, Nigel, 81*n*
Fox, Daniel, 186*n*
France: Catholic bourgeoisie, 54; higher education system, 73; peasantry, 169; Social Democrat and Communist parties, 60; Stalinist

Kriegsspiel, 258–9, 264, 267, 269–72, 277, 296, 300, 327; computerised, 280; impact of, 261; Japanese enthusiasm for, 270–1; rules of, 260–1; seductive predictions of, 262

Kronstadt sailors, elite troops, 22–3, 129–30, 138, 152, 305, 314, 316

Kronstadt Soviet, 157, 208*n*, 210, 212–13, 222; 1921 massacre of, 152, 218

Lacan, Jacques, 215

Lacouture, Jean, 154*n*, 166*n*

Laflin-Barker, Sue, 132*n*

Las Cases, Emmanuel de, 30*n*, 164*n*, 173*n*, 175*n*, 180*n*, 182*n*, 196*n*, 198–9*n*

Latham, John, 69

Lavalas movement, Haiti, 236

Lawford, J.P., 132*n*, 296*n*

Lazzarato, Maurizio, 143*n*, 221*n*

Leaving the 20th Century, *see* Gray, Chris

Lebel, Jean-Jacques, 78*n*

Lebovici, Gérard, 46, 258; 1984 murder of, 47

Leclerc, Charles, 24, 233, 321

Lee Boggs, Grace, 246*n*

Leeson, Bill, 259*n*

Lefebvre, George, 164*n*, 174*n*, 177*n*

Lefebvre, Henri, 59*n*, 60*n*, 61–2, 215

Left Bank, Paris, gentrification, 59

Left, the, mythologising by, 328; sects, 324

Lehman Brothers, 2008 bankruptcy of, 139

Leipzig, 1813 battle of, 305

Lenin, V.I., 114–15, 135, 138–9, 141–42, 144, 144–5, 151–2, 158–9, 167, 215, 243, 251, 298; authoritarian bureaucracy faith, 285; vanguard party, 128, 133, 138–9, 329

Leslie, Stuart, 272*n*

Lettrist International, 54, 59, 183, 202; *Potlatch*, 58; 1950 Notre Dame provocation, 57, 322; *The Coronation of Napoléon and Joséphine*, 183, 201

Levin, Thomas, 57*n*

Levitine, George, 184*n*, 187*n*

Lewis, Adrian, 275*n*, 277*n*, 290*n*

Malaparte, Curzio, 134*n*

Malevich, Kazimir, 56, 131

Maloney, Martin, 38*n*

Mao Zedong, 136; Clausewitz admiration, 288; *Go* player, 289; Maoist New Left, 214–5, 282, 278; three stage strategy, 288, 290

Marand-Fouquet, Catherine, 191*n*

Marat, Jean-Paul, 186*n*, 238, 326

Marcus, Greil, 57*n*, 59*n*, 95–6, 102–3, 105; *Lipstick Traces*, 95

Marcuson, Alan, 82*n*

Marengo campaign/battle 1800, 118, 122, 163, 172, 178, 197, 201, 301, 315; Bonaparte's role, 175–7; campaign, planning, 177, 303; official history censored, 180; re-enactment, 118, 120–1, 205–7, 293

Marinetti, Filippo, 183*n*

Markham, Robert, *Austerlitz*, 233*n*

Marx, Karl, 76, 139, 147*n*, 154, 164, 201*n*, 215, 246, 250, 252, 285; dialectical reasoning, 243; hopes of, 128

Mason, Paul, 220*n*

mass conscription, 266, 284; prophecies of, 192

Masséna, André, 122, 177

Mattick, Paul, 210*n*

Mauss, Marcel, 58*n*

Mawdsley, Evan, 128*n*, 138*n*, 148*n*, 155*n*

Maxim gun, 22

May '68, Paris, 48–9, 52, 76–8, 83, 95, 104, 107, 156–9, 166, 207, 211–3, 217–9, 296, 324, 327

McClendon, John, 244*n*

McConville, Maureen, 77*n*, 218*n*

McGinn, Bernard, 217*n*

McIver, Joel, 89*n*, 91*n*, 94*n*

McKay, George, 101*n*

McLaren, Malcolm, 86–92, 94–5, 96, 106, 217

McLaughlin, Mark, *War and Peace*, 118

McLellan, David, 243*n*

McLuhan, Marshall, 74*n*; neoliberal boosters, 220, 324–8

McNamara, Robert, 279*n*

McPherson, James, 45*n*

megalomania, political, 326

Melas, Michael von, 177–8, 180, 206

Melly, George, 67*n*, 71*n*, 84*n*

Nanterre University, 48, 61, 77, 78, 208
Napier, Charles, 258
Napoleonic myth, 199
Naquin, David, *Marengo*, 180*n*
Nash, Jörgen, 210*n*
Nashists, 210
nationalist iconography, Russian eclectic, 126
Naumann, Francis, 42*n*
Neale, Jonathan, 281*n*
Nechaev, Sergei, 167*n*
Nedelec, François, *Mai '68*, 161*n*
Negri, Toni, 141–2, 144; 221*n*; 'terrorist' framed, 143
Nelson, Harold, 146–7*n*
Nemours, Alfred Auguste, 235, 237, 238
Neo-Classicism: David invented, 185–6; Donkor's détournement, 232; Empire style recuperated, 202
neoliberal globalisation, 36, 50, 93, 101, 140, 143, 220, 223, 254, 324, 331; Debord anticipation of, 330; perpetual present of, 172
Net, the, 37, 74, 75*n*, 101–2, 140, 143, 212, 324; horizontal community politics, 215, 220–1; interactive capabilities, 216
Neumann, Franz, 139*n*
Neumann, John von, 273
Neville, Richard, 67*n*, 72*n*
New Left, 33, 68–70, 73, 76–8, 80–1, 156, 168, 214–8, 245–6, 282, 290–1, 324, 327; activists, 166; dominant orthodoxy within, 74; English pioneers of, 65, 72; 1980s recuperation, 254; after May '68, 253; Post-Modern recuperators, 141, 143–4, 170; USA, 67; vanguards, 158, 169–70, 213
New Wave, French cinema, 56
New York, 89; contemporary art market, 37; modernism, 43; Smolin gallery, 45
Newgate jail, 1780 burned down, 76
Nicholls, David, 235*n*, 246*n*
Nicholson-Smith, Don, 67, 68, 70
1968 & All That conference, London, 214, 216
Nkrumah, Kwame, 239
Noel, Ann, 43*n*
Nold, Christian, 235–6, 308, 317
Nolte, Ernst, 248*n*

Peers, Chris, 130–5, 137, 140–1, 144–5, 154, 156–7, 160, 324; *Reds versus Reds*, 21–2, 34–5, 65–9, 71, 73, 78–9, 81, 83, 105, 114, 165, 209, 213–4, 217, 222, 233, 240, 300, 305, 314, 316, 324–6, 328–9, 330–1, 332*n*, 333

Pelevin, Victor, 205

performances, interactive, 44

Perla, Peter, 258*n*, 260–2*n*, 270–1*n*

Pethybridge, Roger, 152–3*n*

Petrograd Soviet, 146, 244

Picot, Edward, 232

Pinkard, Terry, 182*n*, 194–5*n*, 197*n*

Plan 9, *Summer of Dissent* festival, 100

Plant, Sadie, 102–3, 105

Pol Pot, 156

politics: DIY, 331; militarisation, 136, 140, 148–53, 252–3; political theatre, 57

Pollock, Ethan, 103*n*

Pompidou, Georges, 48

Pop Art, 38, 44, 69, 105

Pop Situationism/Situationists, 98, 103–4, 106–8, 117, 137, 141, 213–4, 317, 322–3; recuperated, 105

Porta2030 wireless network, 99

Post-Modernism, 64, 104; 1980s boosters, 93

post-structuralism, 103–4, 142, 145, 246–7

Potlatch, October 1955 edition, 183

Pountain, Dick, 39*n*, 105*n*

Powell, David, *Austerlitz*, 229*n*; *Marengo*, 180*n*

Powell, Nicholas, 59*n*

Preobrazhensky, Eugeny, 153*n*

Priaulx, Allan, 77*n*, 218*n*

Prigent, Michel, 217*n*

Prisoners' Dilemma, 273

'prophet armed' image use, 136

Provo movement, Amsterdam, 72–3

provocations, 57, 65–6, 77, 79, 84, 88, 91, 94, 96, 101, 104–6, 141, 145, 163, 172, 189, 322–3

Prussian General Staff, 258–9, 260–1, 265, 300

psyching the opponent, 305–8, 317, 320, 327

psychogeography, 60, 64–6, 84, 91, 94, 96, 105–6, 303–4, 322–3;

digital technologies, 99
Pump House, London, 30–1, 33–5, 46–7, 116; history of, 36–7
punk movement, England, 86–90, 92–5, 102–3; assimilation of, 96; culture game, 91
Pussy Riot, 2012 *Punk Prayer* performance, 322
Putin, Vladimir, 126, 322; Voina provocations against, 160

Quarrie, Barrie, 162*n*
Quattrocchi, Angelo, 81*n*

Radcliffe, Charles, 68, 70, 71*n*, 73*n*, 83–4*n*
Radical Software Group, *Kriegspiel*, 47*n*
Raicer, Ted, *Reds!*, 158*n*
Rakhia, Yukko, 139*n*
Ramones, The, 89
RAND think-tank, US Air Force, 272–7, 280, 289–90, 327
Ransome, Arthur, 149–50*n*
Rapoport, Anatol, 273*n*, 277*n*
Rappolt, Mark, 323*n*
Rasmussen, Mikkel Bolt, 96*n*, 127*n*
Raspaud, Jean-Jacques, 54*n*
Raylab, London, 204–7, 219, 221, 305, 308, 311, 313, 316, 320
Rebel Worker, 68, 70, 73
recuperation, 56–7; English Situationism, 93; hippie radicals, 90; response to détournement, 62
Red Army, 135, 140, 148, 152–5, 201
Red Guards, 147–8, 192
Red Notes, 143*n*
Reds versus Reds, Cyberfest 2008, 129–35, 137, 140–1, 144–5, 154, 156–7, 160, 165, 209, 217, 257, 295, 305, 314, 316
Reed, John, 73, 134*n*, 148*n*
Reich, Wilhelm, 76
Reid, Jamie, 85–7, 89*n*, 100*n*, 105
Reisswitz, Georg von, 258, 260–1, 270, 277, 280
revolutions, militarised, 209
revolutionary conspiracy, Bolshevik style, 165
revolutionary festivals, 202; David directed, 188–9
revolutionary leadership, Situationist critique, 326

Bolshevik promises, 40; Bolshevik recuperation, 165; French recapitulation, 168; ideological dividing line, 81; libertarian dreams of, 126; militarised recuperation of, 138–9

Sibalis, Michael, 180*n*

Sideburns, 92

Simmons, Bowen, *Bonaparte at Marengo*, 180*n*; *Napoleon's Triumph*, 233*n*

Sinclair, Iain, 105

Situationism: Bolshevik recuperation, 145; contemporary groupies, 330; English, 65, 83–5, 88, 95–6; English recuperated, 93; founders, 56–7, 60; satirical remix style, 58; Strasbourg, 73, 77, 78, 83; tactics depoliticised, 105

Situationist International (SI), 33, 51, 62, 66, 70, 221; mimicking Bolsheviks, 63; Cosio d'Arroscia 1957 origin, 54, 67; dissolution of 1972, 157, 214–6, 329; English Section, 29, 71–2, 74, 322; English Section expelled, 76; Fifth Conference split, Stockholm 1962, 209, 211, 251–6, 252, 323; Scandinavian Section, 67, 96

Small, Richard, 238*n*

Smith, Chris, 37*n*

Smith, Hedrick, 280*n*

Smith, Patti, 89

Soboul, Albert, 169*n*, 186*n*, 190–3*n*, 201*n*

social control, Fordist methods, 53

Social Democrats, 21–3, 128, 147, 154, 219, 252–3, 284, 298; 1872 Anarchist split, 250; 1914 European capitulation, 285; Germany, 139; new generation of, 256

social media, McLuhanist boosters, 324

socialism: militarised version, 138–9, 142*n*, 145, 167, 285; triumph of militarised, 155

Socialisme ou Barbarie, 210, 245–6, 327

Socialist Realism, 55

Sokal, Alan, 102*n*

Sorbonne, May '68 liberated zone, 77

soviet democracy, recuperated, 140

spectacular domination, historical trajectory of, 204

Sperber, Murray, 126*n*, 135*n*

SPI, generic wargame simulations, 118–19, 131

Sprague, Jeb, 236*n*

St Bartholomew's Massacre 1572, 169

stacking, disallowed, 20

Staël, Germaine de, 173*n*

Stalin, Joseph, 125, 135, 155–6, 162, 165, 179, 244, 247*n*, 248–9,

325; as Bonaparte, 207; socio-linguistics philosophy, 103*n*, 144, 170; Trotskyist appropriation, 153

Voyer, Jean-Pierre, 54*n*

Waco massacre 1993, 49
Wakefield, Neville, 93*n*
Walker, Martin, 50*n*
Wallace, Martin, *Liberté*, 333
Wallas, Graham, 294*n*
war of manoeuvre Gramscian concept, 287, 312
war of position, Gramscian concept, 287
War of the Second Coalition, 1798–1802, 118, 123, 174, 176, 178
Wargames Research Group, 132
wargaming: adaptations, 301; Hapsburg and Ottoman figurines, 48; politicised, 64, 125; professional-hobbyist link, 296; *see also*, Horse-and-Musket
Warhol, Andy, Factory, 44
Wark, McKenzie, 59*n*, 63*n*, 104*n*, 107*n*, 206, 329*n*
'warrior intellectuals', 136, 39, 156, 252, 267, 283, 288, 320; US scientists as, 272, 276
Waterloo, 1815 battle of, 197, 199, 310
Watts uprising, 1965 Los Angeles, 62, 70, 83, 216
Weather Underground, 80, 282
Webb, Sidney, 294*n*
Weber, Max, 250*n*
Webster, Frank, 220*n*
Webster, Paul, 59*n*
Weider, Ben, 163*n*
Weir, Jean, 80*n*
Wellesley, Arthur, 306*n*
Wellington, Duke of, 306
Wells, H.G., 132, 146–7, 258*n*, 291, 292*n*; *Little Wars*, 25, 27, 34–5, 292–5, 311; *War of the Worlds*, 261*n*
Westwood, Vivienne, 86–7, 105
What is to be Done?, ICA exhibition, 114–5
Widgery, Dave, 72*n*, 94*n*
Williams, Emmett, 43*n*
Williams, Gwyn, 191*n*
Williams, John, 79*n*
Williams, Raymond, 39*n*, 41*n*
Wilson, Andrew, 260–1*n*, 270–1*n*, 277*n*, 279*n*

Minor Compositions

Squatting in Europe – Squatting Europe Kollective

Artpolitik: Social Anarchist Aesthetics in an Age of Fragmentation –
Neala Schleuning

The Undercommons – Fred Moten & Stefano Harney

nanopolitics handbook – nanopolitics group

Precarious Communism: Manifest Mutations, Manifesto Detourned –
Richard Gilman-Opalsky

Forthcoming:

Lives of the Orange Men – Major Waldemar Fydrich

Future Che – John Gruntfest & Richard Gilman-Opalsky

State in Time – Irwin

Islam & Anarchism – Mohamed Jean Veneuse

A Very Careful Strike – Precarias a la Deriva

Art, Production and Social Movement – Ed. Gavin Grindon

Hypothesis 891 – Colectivo Situaciones

Learn to Listen – Carlos Lenkersdorf

*A Short Philosophical Dictionary of Anarchism from Proudhon to
Deleuze* – Daniel Colson

As well as a multitude to come...

Richard Barbrook is Senior Lecturer in Politics at the University of Westminster, a trustee of Cybersalon and an active member of Class Wargames. He is the author of *Imaginary Futures: from thinking machines to the global village*; *The Class of the New*; and *Media Freedom: the contradictions of communications in the age of modernity*.